Imagining Brazil

Imagining Brazil

Edited by Jessé Souza
and Valter Sinder

LEXINGTON BOOKS

A division of
ROWMAN & LITTLEFIELD PUBLISHERS, INC.
Lanham • Boulder • New York • Toronto • Plymouth, UK

LEXINGTON BOOKS

A division of Rowman & Littlefield Publishers, Inc.
A wholly owned subsidiary of The Rowman & Littlefield Publishing Group, Inc.
4501 Forbes Boulevard, Suite 200
Lanham, MD 20706

Estover Road
Plymouth PL6 7PY
United Kingdom

British Library Cataloguing in Publication Information Available

The hardback edition of this book was previously cataloged by the Library of Congress as follows:

Imagining Brazil / Edited by Jessé Souza and Valter Sinder.
    p. cm.
    Includes bibliographical references and index.
    ISBN-13: 978-0-7391-1013-3 (cloth : alk. paper)
    ISBN-10: 0-7391-1013-6 (cloth : alk. paper)
    ISBN-13: 978-0-7391-1014-0 (pbk. : alk. paper)
    ISBN-10: 0-7391-1014-4 (pbk. : alk. paper)
    1. Brazil—Civilization—20th century. 2. Brazil—Politics and government—
20th century. I. Souza, Jessé. II. Sinder, Valter. III. Series.
    F2510.I497 2005
    981.06—dc22   2004028742

Printed in the United States of America

♾™ The paper used in this publication meets the minimum requirements of American
National Standard for Information Sciences—Permanence of Paper for Printed Library
Materials, ANSI/NISO Z39.48–1992

Contents

Part II   Literature and Culture

Introduction

Since the 1980s, structural transformations of world capitalism known by the general term "globalization" have become a challenge of great proportions for the peripheral societies. In the Brazilian case, a country that from 1930 to 1980 was transformed from one of the poorest societies on the planet into the eighth largest world economy thanks to an average annual increase of 7 percent during those 50 years of economic growth, the new context has meant economic stagnation and the aggravation of the serious social problems that had always characterized this society. For an entire new generation of young Brazilian intellectuals, the former "country of the future" is now rather a country with a past of exclusion and prejudice and with blatant violence each day more in evidence. This new reality asks to be understood according to new categories and questions.

Most of the authors gathered in this book are part of this more recent generation. Alongside them we have also selected some of the most important and recognized authors, Brazilian or otherwise, of what are already classic interpretations of Brazil. Our interest has been in providing a comprehensive and multifaceted picture to readers interested in Brazil, in such a way that the most diverse perspectives of academic interest would be represented. We have privileged diversity not only in relation to the authors, but also in relation to the manner in which the object of study is perceived. In this way, we have not only historians, political scientists, and sociologists, but also writers, literary critics, and scholars of culture, in an attempt to understand a complex society in all its richness and diversity.

The first part of the book, dedicated to the theme of the relationship between society and politics, begins with a chapter by Jessé Souza. In this, the author analyzes the process of Brazilian peripheral modernization, aiming to propose theoretical alternatives to the still-dominant paradigm, within and outside of the periphery, of the premodern vs. modern opposition upheld by the traditional theory of modernization. Theoretical contributions of Charles Taylor and Pierre Bourdieu are used to deconstruct the previous model and to reconstruct a new alternative approach that would privilege the focus in the opaque and impersonal forms of domination typical of modern institutions, such as market and State, while providing a way of perceiving the unthematized backdrop that allows to separate those enfranchised from those disenfranchised: citizens from under-citizens. The thesis is that this path would lead to an understanding of the singularity of class struggles in the periphery, especially the naturalization of inequality and the consequences of this in the peripheral context, without resorting to categories congenial to the old modernization Theory such as personalism, familism, and hybridism.

Leonardo Avritzer's chapter is an attempt to propose an alternative framework for the analysis of the process of formation of public space in Brazil. He proposes an approach to understand both nation-building in Brazil and the country's link to so-called Western modernity, through economic and administrative modernization. He analyzes the process of nation-building in Brazil in order to single out three characteristics—the formation of a strong private tradition, the lack of plural forms of association, and the presence of undifferentiated forms of mobilization. He argues that these three traditions were not wiped out during the process of modernization of the country. On the contrary, they led to a hybrid tradition between modern and non-modern, and public and nonpublic institutions.

Marcelo Neves's chapter follows the same path of the previous chapters that addressed the conditions of the practice of democracy and of citizenship in the peripheral context. His chapter addresses the problem of the lack of citizenship within the context of relations of under-integration and over-integration into the social systems, particularly the legal-political system. After delimiting the concept of citizenship and analyzing its symbolic-political uses (regarding constitutional declarations), the author examines how the exercise of these rights is put into practice in Brazil. According to the author, the dejuridification in the process of constitutional realization, which is related to the lack of autonomy and identity of the legal sphere, would be the origin of "under-citizenship" as well as of "over-citizenship."

The chapter from Thomas Skidmore is historical, focusing on Brazil's participation in the Paraguayan War (1864–1870). The war proved far more exhausting than expected, with Brazil, despite having an alliance with Argentina and Uruguay, shouldering almost all the combat against the stubborn Paraguayans. The consequences were profound for both Brazilian society and politics. In the chapter by Werneck Vianna, the pivotal point is the attempt to construct a link between scientific conceptions and their enormously effective influence on political world visions. In this sense, the text seeks to rebuild Max Weber's influence on Brazilian social thought regarding the national singularities of that reception and the important political consequences of the same, thereby constituting an innovative way of understanding contemporary Brazilian politics.

Antonio Sérgio Guimarães's concern has to do with the expression "racial democracy" and its dissemination, which he examines in this chapter, upholding the view that it was used in the 1950s by black activists, politicians, and intellectuals in order to design an ideal for interracial cohabitation and a political commitment to inclusiveness regarding black people in postwar Brazilian modernity—a commitment that was broken at the dawn of the military regime in 1964. The disclosure of the mythical character of that concept takes place amidst criticism over the fallacious dimension of political democracy, which in the 1980s becomes the main ideological weapon available for widening black people's share in Brazilian society.

Marcos Chor Maio's chapter, in its turn, examines the literature on the cycle of studies on Brazilian race relations written in the 1950s and supported by UNESCO, considering it to be a milestone that offered solid findings about the variety of such relations and the existence of racial prejudice and discrimination in Brazilian society. Some evaluations of these studies have asserted that the results of the UNESCO project frustrated expectations that Brazil could be used as a positive example for race relations and an instrument in the struggles against racism in the period following the Holocaust. This chapter takes a different stance in arguing that from the early stages of the organization of the project, Brazilian, French, and U.S. social scientists favored broadening the geographical scope under investigation because they were aware of several patterns of race relations and of racial prejudice in Brazil. Originally, a limited and idealized regional focus was to center on the state of Bahia, but soon the scope of investigation became almost national in including Rio de Janeiro, São Paulo, and Pernambuco.

The second part of the book, dedicated to the theme of the relationship between literature and culture, begins with a joint chapter by Valter Sinder and Paulo Jorge Ribeiro. In this chapter they chart how, after 1970, Brazilian cultural discourse was altered at its core. They attempt here to follow certain *traces* of those changes in the individual discourses of various activities, subjects, and critical attitudes of Brazilian society. There is no doubt that Brazilian society was profoundly altered from the 1970s on, but the ways in which those changes are perceived cannot—or should not—follow only interpretive canons of national meta-narratives, and consequently analyses developed mainly in Brazil. Heloisa Starling's chapter analyzes the form, as considered by several of the biggest names in Brazilian literature, of the category of the outsider and of the suburb as being the political peak of Brazilian social exclusion. In a country in which literature seems to have thematized subjects still not addressed by the social sciences, the reconstruction of this association is fundamental for a fruitful dialogue between these spheres of knowledge. João Trajano Sento-Sé's contribution, motivated by the celebrations of five hundred years after the "discovery," aims to investigate how Brazilian narrative is constituted. In Brazil, the concept of nation, entailing both its formation and historical trajectory, is understood as a privileged topic. This concept is also understood as something that has not been fulfilled, or rather fulfilled in an incomplete way, in the same way as this narrative has become typical of the canon of the Social Science in Brazil.

Dain Borges's chapter takes as presupposition that Brazil's best literary critics and social scientists have recently deciphered subversive social criticism in the turn-of-the-twentieth-century writer Machado de Assis. In its rereading, Machado's analytical moral critique of the deceptions inherent in the pursuit of success seems perfectly relevant to contemporary Brazil. In both his fiction and his ostensibly apolitical journalism (such as the two columns about abolition that are included here), historians have detected a shrewd analysis of slavery, domination, and patronage. Although the new interpreters have focused on the authenticity of Machado's reflections on Brazilian, and even Afro-Brazilian, identity, the Machado they are discovering has much to say about modernity and identities in other parts of the world.

Santuza Cambraia Naves's chapter analyzes styles of Brazilian popular music that arose in the 1960s, reading them in terms of continuity and discontinuity vis-à-vis bossa nova. The core argument is that, although the experiments in harmony of the bossa nova musicians influenced a number of songwriters of the following generation, the latter broke with the aesthetics of restraint pioneered by the former, which had been in keeping with various other cultural forms of the period such as concrete poetry and the architecture of Oscar Niemeyer. Popular musicians of the later generation, from protest music to *tropicália*, returned to the traditional Modernist view of Brazil as an in-exhaustible trove of cultural information, archaic and contemporary, regional and universal, and to Modernist aesthetics of excess.

Helena Bomeny's contribution is based on the idea that, in the Brazil of the Vargas era, the dilemma of intellectuals' participation in politics had one of its more memorable moments within the Capanema ministry, which concentrated a good portion of the examples that are always recalled to address the never peaceful relationship between intellectuals and politics. She asks how can we understand the assent of some, and the reclusion imposed on others? She argues that if it is no longer possible to speak of education and culture in Brazil without mentioning Gustavo Capanema—Minister of Education from 1934 to 1945—it is also impossible to remember that ministry without reference to the intellectuals that composed the so-called Capanema constellation. The memory of their participation in government has been recovered with an uneasy feeling because we must consider this period as part of the 1937–1945 Estado Novo (New State), a milestone of authoritarian rule in Brazil. How much did these intellectuals consent in the setting up of authoritarianism? How much of the political restrictions and curtailment of freedom did they accept? These are the questions discussed in her chapter.

In Brazil, literary art is a realm in which aesthetics—its "cosmopolitan component"—is inseparable from politics—its local component. This mixed, or "amphibious" nature of contemporary Brazilian literature can have the effect of alienating readers both domestically and abroad. For literary artists, fiction constitutes simultaneously the production and dissemination of knowledge. This dual project is only partially attained in Brazil, where book shows on television have in many instances replaced reading, and internationally, where foreign readers have tended to prefer texts produced for export by lesser Brazilian writers, who denounce social injustice through the use of shocking rhetoric. This representation addresses the difficulties that writers face in their "utopian" quest to explore the liberating aspects of art and politics in a country and in a region in which economic inequality, violence and social alienation are defining traits of the social order.

Jessé Souza and
Valter Sinder

1

SOCIETY AND POLITICS

1

The Singularity of the
Peripheral Social Inequality

Jessé Souza

The modernization theories that have accompanied the American effort at political reorganization of the "free world" since the Second World War have lost, for good reasons, the undisputed prestige that they enjoyed until the mid-1960s. Nevertheless, their basic presumption that perceives the relationship between the center and the periphery in the World System as an antinomic opposition between traditional and premodern countries and regions and modern countries and regions, continues to be alive in new and hybrid clothes. This is evidence that the surpassing of a theoretical paradigm, even when it is obviously inadequate and insufficient, cannot be "decreed." A theoretical transformation demands the explicit construction of an alternative paradigm that can explain the central issues of the old paradigm in a more convincing form, considering the failures and silences of the previous model.

This is the challenge that I would like to face in this chapter. I would like to try to demonstrate how the naturalization of social inequality and the consequent production of "under citizens" as a mass phenomenon in peripheral countries of recent modernization such as Brazil, can be more suitably perceived as a consequence, not of a supposed premodern and personalist inheritance, but precisely the contrary, as the result of the large-scale modernization process which has gradually been implanted in these societies as a result of the worldwide capitalist expansion. In this sense, my argument implies that the social inequality of peripheral societies such as Brazil and its naturalization in daily life is modern, given that it is linked to the effectiveness of modern values and institutions since their very successful importation "from the outside in." Thus, contrary to being "personalist" the process has been effective exactly because of the "impersonality" typical of modern values and institutions. This is what makes this process so opaque and difficult to perceive in daily life.

The importance of a change of paradigm in this field has more than just theoretical repercussions. The current chronic absence of opportunities for the future in peripheral countries such as Brazil is related to the obsolescence of the old political projects that were based on the traditional analyses criticized above. The tendency to believe in a "fetishism of the economy"—as if economic growth on its own could resolve problems such as exclusionary inequality and marginalization[1]—the habit of establishing regional cleavages between modern and traditional portions of a country, and even the populist crusade against corruption, are legitimated by this same stew of ideas. They serve as ideological cosmetics that hide the theoretical and political articulation of the specific class conflicts in the periphery. This is the thesis that I intend to defend in this chapter.

The theoretical difficulty in advancing constructive hypotheses in this field demands the articulation of two subsequent steps: 1) building the articulation between the value configuration subjacent to Western rationalism and its institutional anchoring, or that is, reconstituting a social-cultural version of the Marxist theme of "the spontaneous ideology of capitalism"; 2) to then reflect upon its application specifically in the context of "peripheral modernity." For the development of the first theme I would like to elaborate on an "insight" not completely developed by Max Weber in the realm of his comparative sociology of religions. I will combine this insight with concepts from two of the most promising critical approaches in sociology in the second half of the past century: the critical theory of recognition, whose principal exponent is Canadian philosopher Charles Taylor, and the sociology of Pierre Bourdieu.

As we know, Weber was primarily interested, in his monumental sociology of great world religions, in pursuing a comparative analysis of Western rationalism with the great Eastern religions in order to clarify why a new type of Society, that we call modern Western capitalism, arose only in the West and imposed structural transformations on all spheres of social life. Since the "revolution of consciousnesses" of aesthetic Protestanism was perceived as a particularly important moment in the explanation of this singular development in the West, neo-Weberian comparative sociology was marked by the search for "substitutes for the Protestant ethic" to identify both processes of modernization with chances of success, as well as those destined for failure.

One presumption implicit in this analytical strategy was the fact that it maintained not only the premises of "essentialist culturalism," that is a conception where culture is perceived as homogeneous, totalizing and undifferentiated, but also the stage notion of the sociological tradition of modernization to the degree in which it assumes that non-Western societies either repeat the steps of central Western societies through similitudes of the Protestant revolution—the case of Japan is the most eloquent in this context[2]—or they are condemned to premodernism. Only the repetition of the contingent process of Western "spontaneous modernization" could guarantee a passport to modern economic, political, and cultural relations. A good portion of culturalist and institutionalist sociology that is written both about Latin America as well as about Latin Americans, was and is still explicitly or implicitly marked by this presumption.

For Max Weber himself, nevertheless, it appears clear that the explanation of the "spontaneous rise" of Western rationalism in Europe and North America would differ fundamentally from the explanation of the ulterior development of the value and institutional structure of this rationalism as a consequence of the expansion of Western society for the entire planet. Fundamentally, this expansion would take place through the exportation to the periphery of the world system of the fundamental institutions of Western rationalism as "ready made artifacts" (fertigen Gebildes als Artefakt):[3] the capitalist market with its technical and material range and the centralized rational State with its monopoly on violence and disciplinary power.

The difficulty in discussing this theme is related to the necessarily naturalized conception that we have of social efficiency of the market and State. The generations that are born under the aegis of the disciplinary practices already consolidated in these institutions, the implicit opaque and contingent value hierarchy that runs through it in a non-transparent manner, assumes the naturalized form of a self-evident reality that needs no justification. To respond to the empiric imperatives of the State and the market comes to be as obvious as breathing or walking. We do not know any other way of being since early childhood. Since then we are all made and continually remodeled and perfected to attend these imperatives. It is this reality that allows and confers credibility to the scientific concepts that are unfamiliar with the contingent normative logic of these "subsystems." It assumes the form of any other natural limitation of existence, such as the laws of gravity, for example, against which we can do nothing.[4]

To advance in the direction of an alternative concept about the logic implicit to the operation of these institutions, therefore, it is necessary to reconstruct what I would like to call, with Karl Marx, "spontaneous ideology of capitalism." I call it "ideology" since I believe that both the market and the State are composed of value hierarchies that are implicit and opaque to the everyday consciousness, the naturalization of which—disguising them as "neutral" and "meritocratic"—is responsible for the legitimation of the social order that these institutions help to maintain. Access to this "spontaneous ideology" is essential for us to be able to perceive the importance of symbolic and cultural access to an understanding of the social production of inequality and under-citizenry, without appealing to the "culturalist essentialism" typical of the approaches that articulate personalism, familialism and patrimonialism, which disregard the articulation between values and their necessary institutional anchoring, the only link that can explain in what way values influence the effective behavior of agents.

For this desiderata, the contributions of the classics of sociology are precarious. Karl Marx, who invented the theme of "spontaneous ideology" as a specific mark of social domination under capitalism, left us "only" a description of the discontinuity between the production and circulation of commodities. This discontinuity causes the commodity of labor force to "appear" to the consciousness of those involved as if it is effectively sold for its fair value. In this way, the exploration of labor is not transparent. Marx lacks, however, an explicit articulation of the "value hierarchy" that is realized in the action of the market. The Weberian perspective also begins trapped in categories of "philosophy of consciousness," which forces him to find in the subject actor the source of all meaning and morality.[5] Thus, Weber is also incapable of perceiving, in its complete scope, the extension of the value, moral and symbolic horizon present in these institutional configurations exported from the center to the periphery as "ready made artifacts," according to his formulation.

It is precisely by clarifying this basic aspect of the explanation of the implicit value hierarchy that opaquely runs through the institutional effectiveness of the market and state that I would like to incorporate the reflections of Charles Taylor about the sources of the modern "self."[6] I am not interested here in Taylor's use of his investigations in the context of the debate about multiculturalism or about the debate between liberals and communitarians. I am interested in his comunitarianist starting point as a hermeneutic of social space based on his criticism of the "naturalism" that runs through both scientific practice as well as daily life. This perspective can be used to articulate precisely the value configuration implicit to Western rationalism that envisions, as we will see, a specific type of social hierarchy and also a singular notion of social recognition based on it. His criticism of the tendentially reified concept of the State and market as systemic magnitudes, as we see in Jürgen Habermas for example, appears to me correct and of decisive importance for a more suitable understanding of the process of expansion of Western rationalism from the center to the periphery, which takes place through the exportation of these institutions as ready artifacts in the Weberian sense of the term. The negation of the contingent symbolic and cultural character of these institutional materializations, that perceives them as realities guided according to criteria of formal effectiveness, would be equivalent to reduplicating, in a conceptual dimension, the effect of "naturalism" in daily life.

Essential to Taylor's scheme, and what carries it, in this case, far beyond the Weberian reflection, is that he is able to reconstruct the subjacent and opaque value hierarchy that is materialized in these two central institutions of the modern world, which unreflectedly and unconsciously command our daily dispositions and behavior. What makes the Taylorian reflection of interest to the social sciences, in my view, is that his reconstruction of the "history of ideas" is not an end of itself. Its strategy is to understand the genesis or archaeology of the concepts of good and of how they evolve and acquire social effectiveness. This point is crucial. Taylor is not interested in a mere history of ideas, but how and why they are able to take the hearts and minds of common people. For this reason his undertaking is sociologically relevant. Therefore, in the first place he is interested in the effectiveness of ideas—not their content. The content is only important to the degree that it explains the reasons for their collective acceptance.

Plato is a central figure in this context. He is the systematizer of the fundamental idea for the moral concept of the West, which is the idea that the Self is seen as threatened by desire (which is insatiable) and therefore must be subordinated and ruled by reason. Christianity adopted the Platonic perspective of the dominance of reason over the passions to the degree in which sanctity and the specfic "way to [Christian] salvation" is expressed in the terms of Platonic purity. Meanwhile, St. Augustine, by appropriating the Platonic tradition, engendered a radical novelty that would be essential to the specificity of the West: the notion of interiority. It was this link with the religiously motivated need that became the language of irresistible interiority. The link between the dominant ideas of the West and their effectiveness is perceived—in an obvious correspondence with Max Weber—as a process internal to Western religious rationalization. In this way, the ideally articulated concepts of good are linked to specific "ideal interests" based on the "religious" prize of salvation. This explains St. Augustine's paradigmatic place in the Taylorian scheme.

The process of interiorization initiated by Augustine was radicalized by Descartes. Since Descartes there has been a fundamental change in the terms and form in which virtue is conceived.[7] This change is radical given that it inverted the notion of virtue and of good that ruled until then. The former ethics of honor was reinterpreted in terms of the Cartesian ideal of rational control. Rationality was also no longer seen as substantive and came to be procedural. Rationality came to mean thinking according to certain canons. It is this new moral subject that Taylor calls the "Punctual Self." It would be Locke who systematized the new ideal of independence and self-responsibility, interpreted as something free of custom and local authority, transforming the "punctual self" at the basis of a systematic political theory.

The "self" is punctual given that it is unattached from particular contexts and therefore remodelable by means of methodic and disciplined action. For this new manner of seeing the subject developed a philosophy, a science, an administration, and organizational techniques destined to assure its control and discipline. The notion of the unattached self, by being rooted in social and institutional practices, is naturalized. These ideas, germinated for centuries, of calculating and instrumental reason and of will as self-responsibility, which, added up, lead to Taylor's central concept of the punctual self, were not able to dominate the practical life of people until the great revolution of the Protestant reformation. Here is another obvious point in common with Max Weber. For the two thinkers, the reformation was the midwife of both the cultural and moral singularity of the West. The Protestant revolution realized in practice, in the space of common sense and of daily life, the new notion of Western virtue. For this reason, for Taylor, to the notion of the punctual self must be added the idea of "affirmation of ordinary life" for an understanding of the moral configuration which dominates us today.

The theme of the affirmation of ordinary life is in opposition to the Platonic or Aristotelian concepts that exalted the contemplative life in opposition to the practical life. The revolution Taylor speaks of is that which redefined the social hierarchy to the point that the practical spheres of work and family, precisely those spheres in which everyone, without exception, participate, now come to define the place of the superior and most important activities. At the same time, there is a lack of respect for the earlier contemplative and Aristocratic activites. The sacralization of work, especially of manual and simple labor, of Lutheran origin and later generically Protestant, illustrates the historic transformation of large proportions for the entire redefinition of the social hierarchy that is our common thread in this text.

Taylor perceived that the social bases for a revolution of such consequences are due to the religious motivation of the reformative spirit. Upon rejecting the idea of the mediated sacred, Protestants also rejected the entire social hierarchy linked to it. This is the decisive point here. Since the gradations of greater or lower sacredness of certain functions is the basis of the (religious) hierarchy of traditional societies, to devalue the hierarchy based on this order is to withdraw the foundations of the social hierarchy as a whole, both in the religious sphere in the strict sense as well as in the other spheres under its influence. In this way, space was opened for a new and revolutionary (given its equalizing and egalitarian potential) notion of social hierarchy that came to be based on the Taylorian "punctual self," or that is a contingent and historically specific concept of the human being, presided by the notion of calculability, prospective reasoning, self-control, and productive labor as the implicit foundations both of its self-esteem as well as of its social recognition.

The social supports of this new concept of the world, for Taylor, are the bourgeois classes of England, the United States, and France. They were later disseminated by the subordinated classes of these countries and later in other countries with important and singular deviations.[8] The concept of labor within this context will not emphasize what is done but *how* labor is conducted (God loves adverbs). The social link suitable to interpersonal relations will be of the contractual type (and by extension constitutional liberal democracy the suitable type of government). In political language this new world vision will be consecrated under a form of subjective rights and in accord with the egalitarian tendency, universally defined. Taylor will call the set of ideas that are articulated in this context the principle of "dignity." Dignity will therefore designate the possibility of equality made effective, for example, in the potentially universal individual rights. Instead of premodern "honor," that presupposes distinction and privilege, dignity presupposes a universal recognition among equals.[9]

In this context, I am less interested in the Taylorian tension between a homogenizing disciplinary reason and an expressive singularizing reason, such as the existential and political conflict par excellence of late modernity,[10] and more in the repercussions of its discussion about the principles that regulate our attribution of respect and deference, or that is, the attribution of "social recognition" as a basis of the modern notion of legal and political citizenship. The location and explanation of these principles can help us to identify the operating mechanisms, in an opaque and implicit form, in the social distinction between distinct classes and social groups in certain societies. It can help us to identify the "symbolic operators" that allow each one of us in daily life to establish a hierarchy and classify people as more or less worthy of our appreciation or our disdain.

Thus, contrary to the hierarchizing criteria of Hindu civilization, for example, where the principle of ritual purity classified and declassified the distinct social castes,[11] *in the West, the implicit basis of social recognition came to be the sharing of a certain psychosocial structure.* It is this psychosocial structure that is the basis of the consolidation of rational-formal systems such as the market and the State, and later the principal product of the combined efficiency in these institutions. It is the generalization of these same preconditions that makes possible speaking of "citizenship" or that is, a set of rights and responsibilities in the context of the nation-state shared by all in a presumption of effective equality. Taylor's considerations about "dignity" as a basis for individual self-esteem and social recognition therefore relate to the

relationship between the sharing of a contingent emotional and moral economy and the possibility of social recognition for individuals and groups: *For
the rule of equality to be socially effective, the perception of equality in the
realm of daily life must be effectively internalized.*

Nevertheless, at the level of the abstraction of reflection developed by Taylor, it is not clear in what way this new hierarchy that comes to be implemented by the market and the States becomes effective as a basis for social
classification and of differential value between individuals and social classes.
Thus, to advance even one more step in our effort at concretization of analysis, I would like to use the studies of Pierre Bourdieu in order to suitably
conceptualize the basic issue that allows thinking of social recognition, objectively produced and institutionally implemented, as the very nucleus of the
condition that allows establishing *social distinctions based on opaque social
signs that are perceptible to everyone in a prereflexive manner.*

The union of the perspectives of Taylor and Bourdieu appears to me to be
interesting from various aspects. They appear to be complementary in the
sense that they develop aspects that overcome important deficiencies in each
other. It may be said that Taylor lacks a contemporary theory of class struggle. This is to the degree in which he speaks of the point of view of the North
American or European intellectual in the late twentieth century, when the central societies are supposedly pacified internally of the more virulent class conflicts, and entering a new phase of rearticulation of their political struggles.[12]
Bourdieu, however, presents a sophisticated analysis of the singularly opaque
and refracted form that the ideological domination, hiding its class character,
assumes in late modernity. I believe that Bourdieu's perspective allows us *to
go beyond a concept of recognition that assumes, at least tendentially, as effective reality the ideology of equality* prevalent in central Western societies.
As I hope to demonstrate, this starting point appears to me to be essential,
even if important modifications in its theoretical instrumental are needed,
also for an analysis of peripheral modernity.

At the same time, on the other hand, the genealogy of the implicit hierarchy that commands our daily life, developed superbly by Taylor, allows precisely clarifying the Achilles' heel of Bourdieu's entire argument. After all, by
concentrating solely on the instrumental factor in the dispute for relative
power between the classes in struggle for scarce resources, he does not perceive that this same struggle takes place in an intersubjectively-produced context, which maintains its contigence and with this the need for its critical
perfection, but removes, at the same time, the arbitrary fact of the mere imposition of power of the strongest. The theory of recognition can, in this
sense, explain the generative mechanism of the intersubjectively shared
"minimum normative consensus." It is this mechanism that contextualizes

and filters the relative chances of the legitimate monopoly over the distribution of scarce resources by the various social classes in dispute in a given society, a mechanism that is made secondary and not properly conceptualized by Bourdieu. Despite his unilateralness, however, Bourdieu's contribution to an understanding of the ideological form specific to late modernity, whether central or peripheral, appears to me to be essential.

Taylor, himself, in his text, "To follow a rule,"[13] offers an interesting view of the approximation between the two perspectives that I intend to conjugate here. Taylor, in reality, approximates Bourdieu and Wittgenstein considering a fundamental aspect of his own theory: the notion of "articulation." Taylor affirmed that "if Wittgenstein has helped us to break the philosophical thrall of intellectualism, Bourdieu has begun to explore how social science could be remade, once freed from its distorting grip."[14] Here the common enemy is the rationalist and intellectual trend, dominant in both philosophy and the social sciences. While the intellectualist tradition in these two fields of knowledge tends to perceive the understanding of a social rule, for example, as a process that is consumed at the level of representation and thinking, abstracting its corporal and contextual component, both Wittgenstein as well as Bourdieu emphasize the element of "practice." To obey a rule is in the first place a learned practice and not knowledge. The "practice" can be "articulated." That is, it can make explicit reasons and explanations for its "being this way and not any other" when challenged to do so, but, in most cases, this inarticulated background remains implicit, silently commanding our practical activity and encompassing much more than the borders of our conscious representations.

For Taylor, the fact that it is nonarticulated practice that commands our daily life establishes the need to articulate the hierarchy of hidden and opaque values that preside over our behavior. For this reason he names and reconstructs the sources of our notion of self. For Bourdieu, however, the same fact makes urgent a "psychoanalysis of social space." What for most of the sociological tradition is an "internalization of values" which tendentially evokes a more rationalist reading that emphasizes the most conscious and reflected aspect of normative and value-reproduction of society, for Bourdieu the emphasis is, to the contrary, on the pre-reflexive, automatic, emotive, spontaneous conditioning, or one that is "inscribed in the body" of our actions, dispositions, and choices.

In this context, the basic notion that I would like to use for my own purposes in the context of this selective appropriation is that of habitus. Habitus, contrary to the rationalist and intellectualizing tradition, allows emphasizing the entire set of cultural and institutional dispositions that are inscribed in the body and that are expressed in the body language of each one of us, transforming, in a matter of speaking, cultural and institutional value choices into flesh and bone. While for Marx the "spontaneous ideology" of capitalism was the fetishism of the merchandise that hid, under the mask of market equality, unequal production relations, for Bourdieu it would be the set of dispositions linked to a peculiar lifestyle that conforms to this habitus stratified by social classes, and that invisibly and subliminally legitimates the differential access to material and ideal scarce resources, the spontaneous ideology of late capitalism.

In his classic text about "Distinction"[15] Bourdieu explores the hypothesis, using as an empirical universe contemporary French society, that "taste" is the field par excellence of "social negation" by revealing it as an innate quality, and not one that is socially produced. The primary process of naturalized introjection of this legitimizing criteria of inequalities takes place from the cultural, familial, and educational inheritance on all their levels. What Bourdieu has in mind is the formation of a habitus of class, perceived as a nonintentional learning of dispositions, inclinations, and evaluative schemes that allows its possessor to perceive and classify, in a pre-reflexive dimension, opaque signs of cultural legitimacy. Since social distinction based on taste is not limited to the artifacts of cultural legitimacy, but includes all the dimensions of human life that imply some choice (such as clothing, food, forms of leisure, consumption options, etc.) taste functions as the prime sense of distincton, allowing the separation and joining of people and consequently, the forging of solidarities or constitution of group divisions in a universal (everything is taste!) and invisible form.

In the best pages of "Distinction," Bourdieu is able to demonstrate, with rich use of the interesting empiric material, that even our choices that are considered the most personal and recondite, from the preference for a car, composer, or writer to the choice of a sexual partner, are, in reality, fruits of the invisible threads that link interests of class or fractions of class, or even relative positions in each field of social practices such as the opposition between the recently arrived challengers and those already established by seniority. These invisible threads interlink and cement both affinities and sympathies, constituting the objectively defined solidarity networks or on the other hand, forge antipathies soldered by prejudice.

This beautiful idea of habitus operating as invisible threads that link people by solidarity and identification and that separate them by prejudice, which is equivalent to a notion of coordination of social actions perceived as unconscious and ciphered, nevertheless limits the richness of a fundamental idea for Taylor: the notion of "articulation" that allows thinking of a "transfer" between the reflected and the non-reflected. After all, if there is something that can be articulated it is because there is something that goes beyond pure unreflected habitus. For this reason, the absence of this dimension in Bourdieu's reflection means that the counterposition in relation to the "great illusion" of the social game is only reactively possible, without the questioning of rules as such. This reactive position stems from Bourdieu's concept, thought of in opposition to subjectivism,[16] which reduces social space to a space of conjunctural interactions, of which an entire esthetic and moral (the two terms must always go together) of class are countered objectively to a rival and contrary one, but never in relation to a shared level of common rules.[17]

This is the space where the contradictions of Bourdieu's analysis are more easily seen. The reasoning of the instrumental logic that reduces all social determinations to the category of power is seen here in all its fragility. At the limit it becomes incomprehensible that some social strategies and some "bluffs" work out and others do not. To get away from the absolute arbitrariness in this dimension of analysis it becomes necessary to request "something" beyond the simple "illusion" of the social game. As Axel Honneth points out, the competition between the various social groups only has meaning if we assume the existence of conflicting interpretations about a common field of rules that are recognized in a "trans-classist" manner.[18] It is because of the lack of this dimension that it is not clear why a given leading class would supposedly "choose" certain objectives and not others. In the same way it also does not explain why changes take place in the "command" of the social process, such as, for example, the substitution of a premodern aristocracy by the bourgeoisie at the dawn of modernity.

For both authors that I am discussing, modern society is unique precisely because it produces a configuration, formed by the illusions of immediate and daily meaning, that Taylor denominates "naturalism" and Bourdieu "doxa," which produce a "specific misunderstanding" by the actors of their own living conditions. For both, only a hermeneutic, genetic, and reconstructive perspective could reestablish the effective, even if opaque and non-transparent, preconditions of social life in a society of this type. Nevertheless, the concrete challenge here is to systematically articulate the unilateralities of each one of the perspectives studied in order to make them operational in the sense of allowing the perception of how morality and power connect in a peculiar way in the modern world and very particularly in the peripheral context.

Perhaps the factor that best expresses the deficiencies of Bourdieu's theory and exposes the necessity to link it to an objective theory of morality such as Taylor's is the radical contextualism of his analysis of the French working class. This analysis prevents perceiving collective processes of moral learning that go far beyond class barriers. This can be observed in Bourdieu's analysis about the French case, where the ultimate *patamar* of his analysis, as the negative fundament of all social distinction, is the situation of "necessity" of the working class. What reveals the contingent historic character and space-temporality context of this "necessity" is that it refers to the distinction of consumption habits within a dimension of social pacification typical of the Welfare State. What is seen as "necessity" in this context, compared to peripheral societies such as the Brazilian one, acquires a sense of historic and contingent consolidation of political struggles and multiple social and moral learning of effective and fundamental importance, which pass unperceived as such by Bourdieu.

Thus I would like to propose an internal subdivision of the category of habitus in such a way as to confer it a more detailed historic character that is nonexistent in Bourdieu's analysis, and to add, therefore a genetic and diachronic dimension to the theme of constitution of habitus. Thus, instead of speaking only of "habitus" generically, applying it to specific situations of class in a synchronic context, as Bourdieu does, I think it is richer and more interesting for my purposes to speak of a "plurality of habitus." If habitus represents the incorporation by subjects of evaluative schemes and dispositions of behavior based on a structural socioeconomic situation, then fundamental changes in the economic—social structure should consequently imply important qualitative changes in the type of habitus for all the social classes involved in some way in these changes.

This was certainly the case of the passage of traditional societies to modern societies in the West. The bourgeoisie, as the first ruling class in history that worked, soon broke with the dual morality typical of traditional societies that was based on the code of honor and constructed, at least to an appreciable and significant degree, a homogenization of a human type based on the generalization of its own emotional economy (the command of reason over the emotions, prospective calculation, self-responsibility, etc.) to the dominated classes. This process took place in all central Western societies in the most varied manners. In all the societies that were able to homogenize a transclassist human type, this was a desideratum sought in a conscious and decided form and not left to a supposed automatic action of economic progress. Thus, this gigantic historic homogenizing process that was later deepened by the social and political conquests of the initiative of the very working class—which certainly did not equalize all classes in all spheres of life, but certainly generalized and expanded fundamental dimensions of equality in civil, political and social dimensions as examined by Marshall in his celebrated text—can be perceived as a giant process of moral and political learning of profound consequences.

It is precisely this historic process of collective learning that is not adequately conceptualized by Bourdieu in his study of French society. It represents what I would like to call "primary habitus" in such a way as to call attention to the evaluative schemes and dispositions of behavior that are objectively internalized and "incorporated" in the Bourdieuian sense of the term, that allows the sharing of a notion of "dignity" in the Taylorian sense. It is this "dignity," effectively shared by all classes, which is able to homogenize the emotional economy of all its members to a significant degree, what appears to me to be the profound foundation of infra- and ultra-legal social recognition. It in turn allows social effectiveness of the rule of law and equality, and therefore, the modern notion of citizenship. It is this dimension of shared "dignity," in the nonlegal sense of "considering the other" and that Taylor calls attitudinal respect,[19] that must be disseminated in an effective form in society so that we can say that in this concrete society, we have the legal dimension of citizenship and equality guaranteed by law. It is worth repeating once again: *For there to be legal effectiveness of the rule of equality, the perception of equality in the realm of daily life must be effectively internalized.*

It is this dimension that therefore demands the effective transclassist value consensus as a condition for its existence, which is not perceived as such by Bourdieu. It is this absence that allows thinking of relations between the dominant and dominated classes as specular, reactive relations of a zero sum. The radical contextuality of his argument prevents perceiving the importance of historic conquests of this type of society, such as the French, what is made obvious by comparison with peripheral societies, such as Brazil's, where this consensus does not exist. Therefore by calling the generalization of the social, economic, and political preconditions of the useful subject "dignified" as citizen, in the Taylorian sense of intersubjectivity recognized as such, of "primary habitus" I do so to differentiate it analytically from two other also fundamental realities: "precarious habitus" and what I would like to call "secondary habitus."

The "precarious habitus" would be the limit below that of "primary habitus" or that is, it would be that type of personality and of dispositions of behavior that do not meet the objective demands for an individual or a social group to be considered productive and useful in a society of a modern and competitive type, and able to enjoy social recognition with all its dramatic, existential, and political consequences. For some authors, even affluent societies such as the German already present some segments of the poor and workers who live from social security precisely with these traces of a "precarious habitus,"[20] to the degree to which what we are calling the "primary habitus" tends to be redefined according to the new suitable levels of recent transformations of globalized society and of the new importance of knowledge. Nevertheless, as we will see, this definition only earns the status of a permanent mass phenomenon in peripheral societies such as Brazil.

What we are calling "secondary habitus" is related to the limit above of the "primary habitus" or that is, it is related to a source of social recognition and respect that *presupposes* in the strong sense of the term, the generalization of primary habitus to broad layers of the population of a given society. In this sense, the secondary habitus is already part of the social homogenization of the fundaments operatives in the determination of primary habitus and in turn institutes classificatory criteria of social distinction based on what Bourdieu calls "taste." But the precise conceptual determination of this triadic differentiation of the notion of habitus must be coupled to the Taylorian discussion of the moral sources institutionally anchored in the modern world, whether at the center or the periphery, for its proper problematization. Since the category of "primary habitus" is the most basic, to the degree in which it is from it that its lower and upper limits can be understood, we should explain its determination a bit. After all, people are not equally favored with the same social recognition by their "dignity as rational agent." This dimension is not as "shallow" as the simple political dimension of subjective "universable" and interchangeable rights suggest. The juridic dimension of legal protection is only one of the dimensions—although it is fundamental and very important—of this process of recognition.

If it is the useful, productive, and disciplined work that appears to be behind the "objective evaluation of relative value" of each one in this dimension, then the potential masking of inequalities behind the notion of "dignity" of the rational agent should be manifest more easily in this dimension. Reinhard Kreckel calls "ideology of performance"[21] the attempt to elaborate a single principle, beyond mere economic property, based on which is constituted the most important form of legitimation of inequality in the contemporary world. The idea subjacent to this argument is that it must have a "consensual background" (*Hintergrundkonsens*), of the differential value of human beings, in such a way that there can be—even if subliminally produced—a legitimation of inequality. Without this, the violent and unjust character of social inequality would manifest itself in a clear form to the naked eye.

To do so, the ideology of performance is based on the "meritocratic triad" that involves qualification, position, and salary. Of these, qualification, reflecting the extraordinary importance of knowledge in the development of capitalism, is the first and most important point that conditions the other two. The ideology of performance is an "ideology" to the degree in which it not only stimulates and rewards the capacity for objective performance, but legitimates permanent differential access to life chances and the appropriation of scarce goods.[22] Only the combination of the triad of ideology of performance makes the individual a complete and effective "signalizer" of the "complete citizen" (Vollbürger). The triad also becomes understandable because only through the category of "work" is it possible to assure identity, self-esteem, and social recognition. In this sense, differential performance at work must refer to an individual and can only be conquered by the individual. Only when these preconditions are given can the individual completely obtain personal and social identity. This explains why a housewife, for example, comes to have objectively "derived" social status, or that is, her importance and social recognition depend on belonging to a family or to a "husband." In this sense she becomes dependent on ascriptive criteria since in the meritocratic context of the "ideology of performance" she has no autonomous value.[23] The attribution of social respect to the social roles of producer and citizen come to be mediated by the real abstraction produced by the market and State to individuals thought of as "support for distinction" that establish their relative value. Kreckel's explanation about the preconditions for the objective recognition of roles of producer and citizen is important to the degree in which it is fundamental not only to refer to the world of the market and distribution of scarce goods as composed of values, as does Nancy Fraser, for example,[24] but is necessary to explain "what values" they are.

After all it will be the legitimating power that Kreckel calls "ideology of performance" that will determine for the social subjects and groups excluded, because of the absence of the minimal conditions for successful competition, in this dimension, objectively, its social nonrecognition and its absence of self-esteem. The "ideology of performance" would thus function as a type of sub-political legitimation encrusted in daily life, reflecting the effectiveness of functional principles anchored in opaque and nontransparent institutions such as the market and the State. It is nontransparent given that in the context of the daily consciousness it "appears" as if it were the effect of universal and neutral principals that are open to meritocratic competition. I think that this idea helps to concretely confer that which Taylor calls the "moral source" based on the notion of the "punctual self," although his ideological power and ability to produce distinction is not explicitly conceptualized by this author.

Based on the definition and the constitution of an ideology of performance as a legitimizing mechanism of the roles of producer and citizen, which are equivalent in the reconstruction that I am proposing, to the content of "primary habitus" it is possible to better understand their lower limit or, that is, "precarious habitus." Thus, if primary habitus implies a set of psychosocial predisposition reflected in the sphere of personality, the presence of the emotional economy and of cognitive preconditions for a performance suitable to attend the demands (variable in time and space) of the role of the producer, with direct reflection on the role of the citizen, under modern capitalist conditions, the absence of these preconditions, in some significant measure, implies the constitution of a habitus marked by precariousness.

In this sense, "precarious habitus" can refer both to the more traditional sectors of the working class of the developed and affluent countries such as Germany, as Uwe Bittlingmayer indicates in his study,[25] incapable of attending the new demands for continuous formation and flexibility of the so-called society of knowledge (*Wissensgesellschaft*), that now demands active accommodation to the new economic imperatives, as well as the secular rural and urban Brazilian "underclass." In these two cases, the formation of an entire segment of the unadapted, a marginal phenomenon in societies such as the German, and a phenomenon of masses in a peripheral society such as the Brazilian, is the result of the broadening of the definition that we are calling "primary habitus." In the German case the disparity between "primary habitus" and "precarious habitus" is caused by the growing demands for flexibility, which demands an emotional economy of a peculiar type.

In the Brazilian case, the abyss was created at the threshold of the nineteenth century, with the re-Europeanization of the country and its intensification since 1930 with the beginning of the process of modernization on a large scale. In this case, the dividing line came to be traced between the "Europeanized" sectors—or that is the sectors that were able to adapt to the new productive and social demands of a Europeanization that took place, also among us, by the importation as "ready made artifacts" in the Weberian sense, of European institutions and therefore, of an entire vision of the world subjacent to them—and the "precarious" and "non-Europeanized" sectors that tend, because of their abandonment, to a growing and permanent marginalization.

It is important to note that with the designation of "European" I am not referring to the concrete entity "Europe" or much less to a phenotype or physical type, but to the place and historic source of the culturally determined concept of the human being that will be crystallized in the empiric action of institutions such as the competitive market and the rational centralized State, which, from Europe, literally "dominated the world" in all of its nooks and crannies, including Latin America. The "European" and "Europeanness" once again to avoid misunderstanding, perceived as the empirical reference of a particular hierarchy of values that can—as in Rio de Janeiro, for example, in the nineteenth century, be personified by a "mulatto"—be transformed into a dividing line that separates citizen (primary habitus) from "under-citizen" (precarious habitus). It is the attribute of "Europeanness" in the precise sense that we are using this term here, that will divide into socially classifieds and declassifieds, individuals and even entire social classes, in exogenously modernized peripheral societies such as Brazil's.

Since the basic principle of the transclassist consensus is, as we see, the principle of performance and discipline (the moral source of Taylor's punctual self), it comes to be the generalized acceptance and internalization of this principle that causes the non-adaptation and the marginalization of these sectors to be perceived, both by society as well as by its victims, as a "personal weakness." It is also the universal centrality of the principle of performance, with its consequent pre-reflexive incorporation that causes the reaction of the unadapted to take place in a field of forces that is articulated precisely in relation to the theme of performance: positively by the recognition of untouchability of its intrinsic value, despite the very position of precariousness, and negatively, by the construction of a reactive wounded life style, that is, openly criminal or marginal.[26]

Meanwhile, the upper limit of primary habitus is related to the fact that the differential performance in the sphere of production must be associated to a particular "stylization of life" in order to produce social distinctions. In this sense, what we are calling "secondary habitus" would be precisely what Bourdieu had in mind with his study about the "subtle distinctions" that he analyzed in his "distinctions." It is in this dimension that "taste" comes to be a type of invisible currency, transforming both the pure economic capital as well as, and especially, cultural capital, "disguised as differential performance," based on the illusion of "innate talent" in a set of social signs of legitimate distinction based on the typical effects of the context of opacity in relation to their conditions of possibility.

But it is also necessary to add the objective dimension of morality, that in the final instance allows the entire process of fabrication of social distinctions which, as we saw, is ignored by Bourdieu. Thus the concept of secondary habitus[27] must also be linked, as we did with the concept of primary and precarious habitus, to the moral context, even if it is opaque and naturalized, to provide its effectiveness. If we perceive of the "ideology of performance" as a corollary for the "dignity of the rational being" of the Taylorian punctual self, the implicit and naturalized moral basis of the two other forms of habitus that we distinguish, I believe that secondary habitus can be understood in its specificity, above all, from the Taylorian notion of expressivity and authenticity.

The romantic ideal of expressivity and authenticity is interpreted by Taylor in "The Sources of the Self" as an alternative moral source to the "punctual self" and the principle of performance that commands it, to the degree in which it implies in the narrative reconstruction of a singular identity for which there are no preestablished models. Thus, if the "punctual self" is constituted by criteria that imply universalization and homogenization, in the same way as the categories of producer and citizen that concretely realize it, the "subject" of expressivism is marked by the search for singularity and originality, given that what should be "expressed" in "expressivism" is precisely the affective and sentimental horizon very special to each one. It is in this ideal—that is formed later as a reaction to the rationalizing and disciplinary demands of the institutionally anchored "punctual self"—that resides the danger of transforming itself into its counterpart in current conditions. The motto of the diagnostic of the epoch elaborated by Taylor in his "The Ethics of Authenticity" is precisely the growing threat of trivialization of this ideal, from its dialogical content of self-invention in favor of a self-referred perspective symbolized in what the author calls the "quick fix."[28]

The theme of "taste" as the basis for social distinction based on what we are calling secondary habitus, includes both the horizon of "substantive individualization," based on the ideal of original dialogical and narratively constituted identity, as the process of superficial individuation based on the "quick fix." Bourdieu does not perceive the difference between the two forms given that, for him, by force of his categorical choices, as we saw, the strategy of distinction is always utilitarian and instrumental. For my purposes, however, this difference is essential. After all, the recovery of the objectified dimension, elaborated by Taylor, is what explains, in the final analysis, the appeal and the social effectiveness even of the mass and *pastiche* version of this possibility for individuation.

The personfication of "taste" by Bordieu serves, above all, precisely as the definition of "distinct personality," a personality that appears as a result of innate qualities and as expression of harmony and beauty and reconciliation of reason and sensibility, the definition of the perfect and finished individual.[29] The struggles between the various factions of the dominant class take place precisely through the determination of the socially hegemonic version of what is a distinct and superior personality. The working class—which by definition does not participate in these struggles—is a mere negative of the idea of personality, nearly "non-persons" as Bourdieu's speculation about the reduction of workers to a pure physical force tends to see.[30] In this dimension of "secondary habitus" there does not appear to exist any difference in form between the modern societies of the center and the periphery. In this dimension of production of inequalities, contrary to what the "ideology of inequality of opportunities" proclaims in the advanced countries, the two types of society are at the same level.

The basic distinction between these two types of "modern" society appears to me to be located in the absence—in the peripheral societies—of a generalization of the "primary habitus" or that is, of the component responsible for the effective universalization of the category of useful producer and citizen in advanced societies. In all the societies that were able to "transclassistly" homogenize this fundamental quality, this was an objective sought as political, moral, and religious reform of great proportions and not left to the task of "economic progress." The "Great Awakening" of the eighteenth and nineteenth centuries in the United States was able to take to the frontier and to the slavocrat South the same moral seeds and religious fervor of the original thirteen colonies.[31] The English Poor Laws can also be understood as an authoritarian form of forcing those not adapted to the Industrial Revolution to the adoption of the psychosocial requisites of the new society that was created. Also in France, we have similar experience, as the classic book of Eugen Weber *Peasants into Frenchmen* exemplarily shows. The book's title already denotes the process of social transformation of homogenization that is the presumption of social effectiveness of the notion of citizenry.[32]

A concrete example can help to clarify what I have in mind when I seek to emphasize the importance of this factor to a suitable perception of the specificities of central and peripheral modernities. In this way, if I am correct, it would be the effective existence of a basic and transclassist consensus, represented by the generalization of the social preconditions that allows effective sharing in advanced societies of what I am calling primary habitus, that guarantees the social efficacy of Law. For example, if a drunk middle-class German or French driver kills a lower-class compatriot in an automobile accident, it is highly probable that the driver would be effectively punished under the law. However, if a drunk middle-class Brazilian hits a poor Brazilian, the chances are low that the law would be effectively applied in this case—very low. This does not mean that people are not interested in any way with what happened in the latter case. A police procedure would usually be opened and follow its bureaucratic course. But the result, in the large majority of cases, would be a simple acquittal or a punishment suitable for a minor infraction, as if a chicken or a dog has been hit.

It is that in the infra- and ultra-juridic dimension of social respect, a socially shared objective dimension, the value of the Brazil *non-Europeanized* poor— or that is one who does not share the emotional economy of the punctual self that is the contingent cultural creation of Europe and North America—is comparable to that of a domestic animal, which objectively characterizes his status as subhuman. In peripheral countries such as Brazil, there is an entire class of excluded and declassified people, given that they do not participate in the basic value context—what Taylor calls "dignity" of the rational agent. This is the condition needed to have a possibility for effective sharing, by all, of the idea of equality in this dimension that is essential for the constitution of a habitus, which by way of incorporating the plastic, adaptive, and disciplinary characteristics that are basic for the exercise of productive functions in the context of modern capitalism; we can call it "primary habitus."

Allow me to try to specify even more this central idea of my argument in this chapter. I speak of primary "habitus" given that it effectively concerns a habitus in the sense that this notion acquires in Bourdieu. It is the objectively shared evaluative schemes—even if they are opaque and nearly always non-reflected and unconscious—that guide our action and our effective behavior in the world. It is only this type of consensus—as if corporal, pre-reflexive, and naturalized—that can allow, beyond the legal dimension, a type of implicit accord that suggests, as in the example of the auto accident in Brazil, that some people and classes are above the law and others below it. It is as if there exists an invisible network that links the policeman that opens the investigation to the judge that decrees the final sentence, running through lawyers, witnesses, prosecutors, journalists, and others, who, through an implicit and never verbalized agreement, wind up acquitting the driver. What links all of these individual intentionalities in a subliminal manner and that leads to an implicit accord implicit among them is the objective and institutionally anchored reality of the nonhuman value of the victim. It is precisely the differential value between humans that is realized in an inarticulated form in all our institutional and social practices.

This is not a question of intentions. No Europeanized Brazilian of the middle class would confess, rationally, that he considers his compatriots of the low, non-Europeanized classes to be "sub-people." Many of the Europeanized middle class vote in leftist parties and participate in campaigns against hunger and similar movements. The dimension here is objective, subliminal, implicit, and non-transparent. It is also implicit in the sense that it does not need to be linguistically mediated or symbolically articulated. It implies, like the idea of habitus in Bourdieu, a complete vision of the world and a moral hierarchy that is based and is revealed as a social sign in an imperceptible form that apparently has little importance, like respectful inclination to show the unconscious social inferiority when meeting a superior (by the tone of voice more than by what is said, etc). What exists here are mute and subliminal social accords and consensus. But it is exactly for this reason that they are more effective. It is these accords that articulate—as if with invisible threads—solidarities and deep and invisible prejudices. It is this type of accord, to use the example of the crash victim, that would allow all those involved in the legal process—without any conscious agreement and even against the explicit expectations of many of these people—to declare their middle-class compatriot innocent.

Because of his radical contextualism that implies an ahistoric component, Bourdieu does not realize the existence of a transclassist component, that creates—in societies such as the French—an intersubjective and transclassist accord that effectively punishes one guilty for hitting a low-class French person. This is because this person is effectively in the sub-political and subliminal dimension, "one of the people" and "a full citizen" and not only physical and muscular strength or mere animal power. It is the effective existence of this component, nevertheless, that explains the fact that in French society, in a fundamental dimension, independently of belonging to class, all of them are citizens. This fact does not imply, on the other hand, that there are other dimensions of the question of inequality that are also manifest in a veiled and non-transparent form, as also demonstrated by Bourdieu in his analysis of French society. But the theme of taste, by separating people by links of sympathy and aversion, can and should be analytically distinct from the question of fundamental dignity of legal and social citizenship that I am associating here to what I call primary habitus.

The distinction by taste, so magnificently reconstructed by Bourdieu, presupposes in the French case a level of effective equality both in the realm of sharing of fundamental rights, as well as in the realm of the attitudinal respect of which Taylor speaks—in the sense that all are perceived as "useful" members even if they are unequal in other dimensions. In other words, the dimension that we are calling "primary habitus" is added to another dimension that also presupposes the existence of implicit evaluative schemes and shared unconsciouses. That is, a dimension that corresponds to a specific habitus in Bourdieu's sense, as exemplarily demonstrated by this author from his choices of taste, which we are denominating "secondary habitus."

These two dimensions obviously interpenetrate each other in various ways. Nevertheless, we can and should separate them analytically to the degree in which they obey the distinct logic of functioning. As Taylor would say, the moral sources are distinct in each case. In the case of primary habitus what is at stake is the effective dissemination of the notion of dignity of the rational agent which makes the agent productive and a full citizen. In advanced societies this dissemination is effective and the cases of precarious habitus are marginal phenomena. In peripheral societies such as Brazil's, precarious habitus—which implies the existence of invisible and objective networks that disqualify the precarious individuals and social groups as sub-producers and sub-citizens, and this, under the form of an unquestionable social evidence, both for the privileged as well as for the victims themselves of precariousness—is a mass phenomenon and justifies my thesis that what substantially differentiates these two types of societies is the social production of a "structural underclass" in peripheral societies.

This circumstance does not eliminate the fact that, in the two types of society, there is a struggle for distinction based on what I call secondary habitus, which has to do with the selective appropriation of scarce goods and resources and constitutes crystallized contexts and tendentially permanent contexts of inequality. But the effective consolidation, to a significant degree, of the social preconditions that allow the generalization of a primary habitus in the central societies, restricts sub-citizenry as a mass phenomenon to peripheral societies, marking their specificity as modern societies and calling attention to the specific class conflict of the periphery.

The effort of this multiple construction of habitus serves to go beyond subjectivist conceptions of reality that reduce them to face-to-face interactions. The auto accident described above, for example, would be "explained" by the personalist hybrid paradigm[33] based on the social capital found in the "personal relations" of the middle-class driver, who would wind up unpunished. This is a typical example of the subjectivist mistake of interpreting complex and dynamic peripheral societies, like the Brazilian, as if the structural social role were played by premodern principles such as social capital in personal relations. In this field, there is no difference between central or peripheral countries. Personal relations are important in the definition of individual careers and chances for social ascension, both in one case as in the other. In the two types of society, however, the economic and cultural capitals are structuring, which the social capital of personal relations is not.

If my analysis is correct, this interpretive scheme would allow explaining both the subjacent value and normative hierarchy, even if in a subliminal and non-transparent form, by the functioning of the market and the State, as the peculiar form through which these opaque signs acquire *social visibility* even if in a pre-reflexive mode. This type of approach would also allow discussing the specificity of peripheral societies such as the Brazilian, allowing to conceptualize both their singular inequalities as well as their complexity and undeniable dynamic elements, without appealing to culturalist essentialisms or personalist explanations—such as "hybrid" approaches, which are required to defend the existence of a premodern nucleus in these societies in order to conceptualize their social ills. The anachronism of this type of explanation, which never theoretically confronts the central issue of explaining in what way the "hybrid" principles are articulated, appears to me to be evident.[34]

Nevertheless, State and market are not the only fundamental realities of these modern societies whether central or peripheral. The public sphere is, as Habermas demonstrated,[35] a *third fundamental institution of modernity*, destined precisely to developing the reflexive criticism and the possibilities of collective learning. Nevertheless, as Habermas himself indicated, an effective public sphere presupposes, among other things, a rationalized "life world," or that is, in the context of the vocabulary that I am using in this text, an effective generalization of "primary habitus" in its virtualities of public and political behavior. This implies that in *our specific Brazilian case*, the public sphere would be as internally segmented as are the State and market. This aspect goes against certain excessively optimistic analyses about the virtues of this fundamental institution in peripheral societies.

Nevertheless, modern societies, once again, whether central or peripheral, also develop "social imaginaries" that are more or less explicit and reflected, beyond the subliminal effectiveness of the typical institutional apparatus that we are calling the "spontaneous ideology of capitalism." To an important degree, it is these imaginaries that allow the production of particular collective and individual identities to each specific cultural or national context.[36] In the case of the social imaginary peculiar to Brazilian society, this process only reaches its most definitive and long-lasting version with the consolidation of a nation-building experience based on the "corporative" and modernizing state of 1930. In this sense, the dimension of explicit ideology only corroborates and justifies the implicit dimension of "spontaneous ideology," constituting the specific conditions of a Brazilian "social imaginary." Gilberto Freyre, who, if certainly not the initiator, given that long before him this symbolic construction was already being constituted, was the great formulator of the "definitive version" of this explicit ideology that became "State doctrine" taught in schools and disseminated in the most diverse forms of state and private propaganda since 1930.

According to Freyre, the Brazilian singularity comes to be the propensity for cultural encounter, for the synthesis of differences, for unity in multiplicity. It is for this reason that Brazilians are unique and special in the world. They should, therefore, be proud and not ashamed of being "mestizo." Physical type functions as a reference of social equality and a peculiar type of "democracy" that is Brazilian alone. A major affinity with the "corporative" doctrine that became dominant as a substitution for the previous liberalism since 1930, is difficult to imagine. It is now part of Brazilian identity, both individual as well as collective. All Brazilians "like" to see ourselves in this form. The ideology acquires an emotional aspect that is insensitive to rational considerations. It casts anger and hate on those who question this truth that is so pleasant to native ears. The influence of this idea on the way that Brazil sees itself and is perceived is impressive.

Based on the influence of Freyre, this concept has a history of glory. By means of the concept of "plasticity" imported directly from Freyre, it comes to be central in Sérgio Buarque de Holanda's entire argument of the *cordial man*. This notion is central to Buarque's conception of personalism and patrimonialism, in which it represents the value and institutional singularity of Brazilian social formation. In this way, Buarque was transformed into the creator of the dominant self-interpretation of Brazilians in the twentieth century. For my interests here, it is worth reraising the idea of the *cordial man* which reproduces the essentialization and indifferentiation characteristic of the idea of hybridism and of cultural singularity such as a substantialized unity. The *cordial man* is defined as the Brazilian of all classes, a specific form of human being, who has a tendency that is both intersubjective, in the notion of personalism, as well as an institutional dimension, in the notion of patrimonialism.

For my purposes, however, what is essential is that this explicit ideology is articulated with the implicit component of the "spontaneous ideology" of the imported institutional and operative practices also in peripheral modernity, constructing an extraordinary context of obscuration of the causes of inequality and its naturalization in peripheral modernity. This has unfortunate consequences both for theoretical reflection and practical politics concerning the causes of inequality, especially for the victims of this process.[37] This appears to me to be the central point of the issue of *naturalization* of inequality, as abysmal as it is, in Brazil as well as in other peripheral societies.

NOTES

Translated by Jeffrey Hoff.

1. The fact that Brazil was the country with the largest economic growth in the world from 1930–1980, without the rates of inequality, marginalization and under-citizenship being radically altered, should be a more than evident indication of the mistake of this presumption. This, nevertheless, did not take place and does not take place today.

2. About this theme see the classic work of of Robert Bellah, *The Tokugawa Religion* (New York: Free Press, 1985), and the collection of Shmuel Eisenstadt, *The Protestant Ethic and Modernization: A Comparative View* (New York and London: Basic Books, 1968).

3. Max Weber, *Die Wirtschaftsethik der Weltreligionen, Hinduismus und Buddhidmus,* Studienausgabe (Tübingen: J. C. B. Mohr, 1998), 251

4. I do not admire that a critical theory such as the Habermasian, which admits this type of construction in its interior, perceives social conflicts, preferentially, only at the "front" between system and "life world" and no longer within the systemic realities. See the criticism of Johannes Berger: "Die Versprachlichung des Sakralen und die Entsprachlichung der Ökonomie" in *Kommunikatives Handelns: Beiträge zu Jürgen Habermas' "Theorie des kommunikativen handelns,"* ed. Hans Joas and Axel Honneth (Frankfurt: Suhrkamp, 1986).

5. The same occurs with the merely descriptive notion of "charisma." Since there is no presumption of inarticulated "collective meanings" which are responsible for leading, articulating, and providing their own direction, the connection of the leader with his followers becomes "mysterious" and comes to depend on the supposition of the existence, by part of the masses, on extra-quotidian or magical attributes of personality of the leader.

6. Charles Taylor, *Sources of the Self: The Making of the Modern Identity* (Cambridge: Harvard University Press, 1989).

7. Taylor, *Sources of the Self*, 159–176.

8. Taylor, *Sources of the Self*, 289–290.

9. Charles Taylor, "The Politics of Recognition," in *Multiculturalism*, ed. Amy Gutmann (Princeton, N.J.: Princeton University Press, 1994).

10. This aspect was developed in a polemical and stimulating manner, serving as the background for a grammar of contemporary political struggles, based on the poles of distribution and recognition in Nancy Fraser, *Justice Interruptus* (London: Routledge, 1997). For the problematic aspects between the individual and collective dimensions of the theme of recognition, see Seyla Benhabib, *Kulturelle Vielfalt und Demokratische Gleichheit*, (Frankfurt: Fischer, 1999), 39–46.

11. Weber, *Die Wirtschaftsethik der Weltreligionen, Hinduismus und Buddhidmus*, 1–97.

12. For a criticism of Taylor's and Fraser's positions, see Axel Honneth, "Recognition or Distribution?" *Theory, Culture and Society* 18, no. 2–3 (2001): 52–53.

13. Charles Taylor, "To Follow a Rule," in *Bourdieu: Critical Perspectives*, ed. Craig Calhoun, Edward LiPuma, and Moishe Postone, (Chicago: University of Chicago Press, 1993).

14. Taylor, "To Follow a Rule," 59.

15. Pierre Bourdieu, *Distinction: A Social Critique of the Judgment of Taste*, (Cambridge: Harvard University Press, 1984).

16. Pierre Bourdieu, *The Logic of Praxis* (Stanford, Calif.: Stanford University Press, 1990), 42–51.

17. Bourdieu, *Distinction*, 244.

18. Axel Honneth, *Die zerrissene Welt des Sozialen: Sozialphilosophische Aufsätze* (Frankfurt: Suhrkamp, 1990), 178–79.

19. Taylor, *Sources of the Self*, 15

20. Uwe Bittlingmayer, "Transformation der Notwendigkeit: prekarisierte habitusformen als Kehrseite der 'Wissensgesellschaft,'" in *Theorie als Kampf? Zur politischen Soziologie Pierre Bourdieus*, ed. Rolf Eickelpasch et al. (Opladen: Leske und Budrich, 2002), 225–54.

21. Reinhard Kreckel, *Politische Soziologie der sozialen Ungleichheit* (Frankfurt: Campus, 1992).

22. Kreckel, *Politische Soziologie der sozialen Ungleichheit*, 98.

23. Kreckel, *Politische Soziologie der sozialen Ungleichheit*, 100.

24. Fraser, *Justice Interruptus*.

25. Bittlingmayer, "Transformation der Notwendigkeit: prekarisierte habitusformen als Kehrseite der 'Wissensgesellschaft'," 233.

26. Florestan Fernandes, *A integração do negro na sociedade de classes* (São Paulo: Ed. Ática, 1978), 94.

27. Axel Honneth, in his interesting criticism of Bourdieu, tends to completely reject the concept of habitus, given the instrumental and utilitarian component that it inhabits. By doing so, however, Honneth runs the risk of "throwing out the baby with the bath water" to the degree in which what appears to be important is precisely to reconnect the concept of habitus with a moral instance that allows illuminating in the individual and collective dimensions, in addition to the instrumental aspect that is

non-renounceable, the process of moral learning. See Honneth, *Die zerrissene Welt des Sozialen*), 171.

28. Charles Taylor, *The Ethics of Authenticity* (Cambridge: Harvard University Press, 1991), 35.

29. Bourdieu, *Distinction*, 11.

30. Bourdieu, *Distinction*, 384.

31. Bellah, *The Tokugawa Religion*.

32. Eugen Weber, *Peasants into Frenchmen: The Modernization of Rural France* (Stanford, Calif: Stanford University Press, 1976).

33. In the version, for example, of Roberto DaMatta, see *Carnavais, malandros e heróis* (Rio de Janeiro: Zahar, 1978).

34. About this issue see my *A Modernização Seletiva: Uma Reinterpretação do Dilema Brasileiro* (Brasília: Ed.UnB, 2000), 183–204.

35. Jürgen Habermas, *Die Strukturwandel der Öffentlichkei* (Frankfurt: Suhrkamp, 1975).

36. Charles Taylor, *Modern Social Imaginaries* (Durham and London: Duke University Press, 2004).

37. It also explains the fact that the insurrectional potential of the lower class from the entire nineteenth century until today is reduced to local and passing rebellions, riots, and prepolitical violence in which the conscious articulation of its objectives never occurs.

BIBLIOGRAPHY

Bellah, Robert. *The Tokugawa Religion*. New York: Free Press, 1985.

Benhabib, Seyla. *Kulturelle Vielfalt und Demokratische Gleichheit*. Frankfurt: Fischer, 1999.

Berger, Johannes. "Die Versprachlichung des Sakralen und die Entsprachlichung der Ökonomie." In *Kommunikatives Handelns: Beiträge zu Jürgen Habermas' "Theorie des kommunikativen handelns,"* edited by Hans Joas and Axel Honneth. Frankfurt: Suhrkamp, 1986.

Bittlingmayer, Uwe. "Transformation der Notwendigkeit: prekarisierte habitusformen als Kehrseite der 'Wissensgesellschaft.'" In *Theorie als Kampf? Zur politischen Soziologie Pierre Bourdieus*, edited by Rolf Eickelpasch et al., 225–254. Opladen: Leske und Budrich, 2002.

Bourdieu, Pierre. *Distinction: A Social Critique of the Judgment of Taste*. Cambridge: Harvard University Press, 1984.

——. *The Logic of Praxis*. Stanford, Calif.: Stanford University Press, 1990.

DaMatta, Roberto. *Carnavais, malandros e heróis*. Rio de Janeiro: Zahar, 1978.

Eisenstadt, Shmuel. *The Protestant Ethic and Modernization: A Comparative View*. New York and London: Basic Books, 1968.

Fernandes, Florestan. *A integração do negro na sociedade de classes*. São Paulo: Ed. Ática, 1978.

Fraser, Nancy. *Justice Interruptus*. London: Routledge, 1997.

Habermas, Jürgen. *Die Strukturwandel der Öffentlichkei*. Frankfurt: Suhrkamp, 1975.

Honneth, Axel. *Die zerrissene Welt des Sozialen: Sozialphilosophische Aufsätze*. Frankfurt: Suhrkamp, 1990.

———. "Recognition or Distribution?" *Theory, Culture and Society* 18, no. 2–3 (2001).

Kreckel, Reinhard. *Politische Soziologie der sozialen Ungleichheit*. Frankfurt: Campus, 1992.

Souza, Jessé. *A Modernização Seletiva: Uma Reinterpretação do Dilema Brasileiro*. Brasília: Ed.UnB, 2000, 183–204.

Taylor, Charles. *Sources of the Self: The Making of the Modern Identity*. Cambridge: Harvard University Press, 1989.

———. *Modern social imaginaries*. Durham, N.C.: Duke University Press, 2004.

———. "To Follow a Rule." In *Bourdieu: Critical Perspectives*, edited by Craig Calhoun, Edward LiPuma, and Moishe Postone. Chicago: University of Chicago Press, 1993.

———. "The Politics of Recognition." In *Multiculturalism*, edited by Amy Gutmann. Princeton: Princeton University Press, 1994.

———. *The Ethics of Authenticity*. Cambridge: Harvard University Press, 1991.

Weber, Eugen. *Peasants into Frenchmen: The Modernization of Rural France*. Stanford, Calif.: Stanford University Press, 1976.

Weber, Max. *Die Wirtschaftsethik der Weltreligionen, Hinduismus und Buddhidmus, Studienausgabe*. Tübingen: J. C. B. Mohr, 1998.

2

Culture, Democracy, and the Formation of the Public Space in Brazil

Leonardo Avritzer

The formation of public spaces in societies in which there has been a late adoption of the modernity framework for state and society relations is a process that can assume different forms. In Brazil as well as in many Latin American countries there has been an analytical consensus of the late introduction of modern structures[1] and a strong disagreement on the consequences of such a fact for public life. Some authors would analyze the local tradition as being an antimodern tradition and, thus, essentially hierarchical and nonpublic whereas others will propose an approach according to which hybridism becomes the main result of the attempt to implement a public tradition.

Richard Morse has been the leading scholar in the first line of analysis. Proposing a broad argument for both Brazil and Latin America the author has argued that the ambiguity of Latin American institutions in relation to rights and democracy has to be searched in the specific reaction to liberalism, science, and individualism in the Iberian peninsula in the sixteenth century. For him "legal codifications such as the 1573 colonizing ordinances and the 1690 Laws of the Indies were essentially compilations which failed to work natural law principles and administrative decrees into a coherent whole."[2] The explanation the author offers for such a process is far from convincing: a unilateral and ideological process of rejection of both liberalism and individualism and a consensus around a neo-Thomist framework necessary to adapt the Hispanic American man to his local environment were the central elements of the process of national formation in Latin America. Morse's argument is far from convincing due to his attempt to transform a polemic on rights and justice which occurred in sixteenth century Spain[3] into an in-block rejection of modernity. Thus, he precludes in advance the attempt made in contemporary Latin America to retrieve the modern side of rights and constitutionalism and to build a democratic public space.

A second strain of analysis of the process of formation of Latin American societies is one based not on the rejection of liberal conceptions of individualism and rights but rather on the specificity of cultural structures which would become dominant in the region throughout its process of nation-building. This argument has its best and most sophisticated account in the work of the Mexican social theorist Nestor Garcia Canclini, who argues for the adoption of a framework on the hybridization between tradition and modernity for the understanding of Latin American societies. According to Canclini the central fact in the Latin American tradition is neither the existence of an alternative and parallel development to modernity nor the capacity of Latin American societies to reincorporate themselves into modernity, but rather their capacity to establish a new hybrid between modern and non-modern, public and nonpublic institutions. "The conflict between tradition and modernity does not appear as the crushing of the traditionalists by the modernizers, nor as the direct and constant resistance of the popular sectors determined to make their traditions useful. The interaction is more sinuous and subtle: popular movements also are interested in modernizing and the hegemonic sectors in maintaining the traditional—or part of it—as a historical referent and contemporary symbolic resource."[4]

In this chapter I will attempt to propose an alternative framework for the analysis of the process of formation of public space in Brazil, a framework according to which an initial detachment of Portugal and Brazil from modernity's framework led, indeed, to the construction of a privatist order in which there was no room for a public space. Yet, differently from both Morse and Canclini, I will propose an alternative framework in which cultural changes in the form of occupation of the public space lead to the possibility of overcoming hybridization. This chapter will have three parts. In its first part I will propose an approach to understanding both nation-building in Brazil and the country's link to the so-called Western modernity through economic and administrative modernization. I will analyze the process of nation-building in Brazil in order to single out three characteristics—the formation of a strong private tradition, the lack of plural forms of association, and the presence of undifferentiated forms of mobilization. I will argue that these three traditions were not wiped out through the process of modernization of the country. On the contrary they led to a hybrid tradition between modern and non-modern public and nonpublic institutions. In this chapter's second part I will analyze the attempt of modernization through introduction of modern economic structures. I will argue that Canclini's conception of hybridization is a closer empirical analysis of the phenomenon. Yet, differently from Canclini, I will argue that there is a recent trend of change in hybridization and the possibilities of formation of a democratic public space in contemporary Brazil. I will argue that there has been a change in the pattern of occupation of the public space from the late seventies on in Brazil, a change represented by both the emergence of new actors and by the introduction of practices at the public level. I will analyze voluntary associations in São Paulo and Belo Horizonte to show how new practices such as the search for organizational autonomy from the state and preference for participatory and democratic forms of decision making are predominating among members of associations. In this chapter's concluding remarks I will analyze the consequences of such changes for the constitution of a new pattern of public space.

MODERNITY AND THE ENCOUNTER
BETWEEN THE WEST AND LATIN AMERICA

Theories of the emergence of modernity and its expansion outside the Western core are typically based on the conflation between the cultural and the institutional dimensions.[5] They dissociate modernity from the emergence of Western rationalism, thereby conflating such processes as, on the one hand, differentiation, urbanization, increasing labor productivity, and the development of centralized political power and, on the other hand, the secularization of norms and values.[6] In this, they break with Max Weber's framework for the analysis of modernity, in which the emergence of modern structures of consciousness preceded the rationalization of economic structures. Max Weber differentiated between the two processes by pointing out the role of culture, in particular the rationalization of religious traditions, in the emergence of Western modernity.[7] For Weber,

> every attempt of explanation of the specificity of modernity must recognize the fundamental importance of the economic factor, above all take account of the economic conditions. But, at the same time the opposite correlation must not be left out of consideration. For though the development of economic rationalism is partly dependent on rational technique and law, it is at the same time determined by the ability and disposition of men to adopt types of practical conduct.[8]

It is well known that Weber pursued this analysis in order to reveal a contradiction between the evolution of economic and administrative rationalization, on the one hand, and their original cultural basis, on the other.[9] This contradiction lies at the root of his diagnosis of the iron cage—the pernicious and irreversible loss of the moral basis of rationalization. Yet, a second, equally important process can be deduced from the same phenomenon and is central for understanding the expansion of Western modernity and its encounter with non-Western traditions. This phenomenon is related to the fact that if Western modernity has its virtues—the possibility of morally and ethically legitimating economic and administrative rationalization—the expansion of Western modernity was carried out in some moments by the expansion of the modern market and the centralized administrative state and in others as the expansion of certain moral ideas. Latin America in its process of state formation came into contact with modernity in some cases through the expansion of an international market system,[10] in other cases through the constitution of empires,[11] and in other cases by the establishment of a process of internal dialogue with the moral structures of modernity. Yet, in all cases, there is a differentia specifica between the constitution and the expansion of the West. In each of these cases, the nature of the specific encounter would determine the constitution of different political structures.

The formation of Latin American societies and Brazil in particular followed a path of conflation between private and public. Privatism is linked to the very form of occupation of the country and nation-building. Portugal lacked both the resources and the population to colonize a country the size of Brazil. The solution envisioned by the crown to colonize the country was the privatization of the whole colonial enterprise. Between 1500 and 1549 a system of private initiatives through royal concessions called *Capitanias* was put in place. The King ceded an unusually large number of seigniorial rights to the captains, including "the right to enslave natives and sell them on the Lisbon market; to create towns and to nominate their magistrates."[12] Private concessions became the basis of the *capitania* system, which divided the country into twelve privately-held, hereditary tracks of land. The captains also held the right to "to condemn to death slaves, Indians, foot soldiers and free men" in criminal cases.[13] Thus, the first act of colonization in Brazil was a partial detachment from the separation between the state and the private already introduced by modernity. A differentiation proper to early modernity, the one between the household economy and the private, did not take place in Brazil either. Soon after they discovered Brazil, the Portuguese realized that, unlike Spanish America or India, there was no available wealth to be simply collected. Wealth would have to be generated through a system of large-scale agriculture. Again, the private solution prevailed as two successful *capitanias*, São Vicente and Pernambuco, introduced sugar plantations. The sugar plantation was an assemble of land, coerced labor, technical skills, capital, and patriarchal social relations gathered in order to produce sugar and to occupy the land.[14] The privatist landowner was the center of sugar plantation which became the major institution of colonization of Brazil until the early eighteenth century: he monopolized both economic and political functions, he was in charge of defending the territory against overseas and Indian invasions. The specific form of nation-building in Brazil generated a specific phenomenon which is the disproportionate size of the private sphere and the always open possibility of extending personal relations to the political realm. Franco[15] showed for postcolonial Brazil how the public activities of free man took place in the private space of the plantations. Such a historical phenomenon will have, as the Brazilian anthropologist Roberto DaMatta has pointed out, deep political consequences. It led to the establishment of what he calls a relational form of citizenship, a form in which personal relations between individuals allow the creation of a counterpoint to the universal precepts of equality and citizenship. For DaMatta, in the Brazilian social world what is expected in every situation of conflict or dispute is a ritual of acknowledgment which humanizes and personalizes formal situations, helping everyone involved to establish some sort of hierarchy. For him, the citizen is the universal and abstract category subjected to the law and it has to be contrasted with the familiar form of personalization of social relations.[16] In this sense, the subject of citizenship should be understood through this relational form of differentiation of social spheres:

> In Brazil, liberalism is a matter of the world of economics—metaphorically, the universe of the street—while the ideology and values of favor and patronage in general function in the universe represented by the metaphor of the home. Not only does each set of values carry a different weight, but they move in very different spheres.[17]

The introduction of institutions of a supposedly universalizing content has to be approached in relation to the specific culture in which they are inserted and analyzed in relation to the specific outcome generated by this combination. In the Latin American case the possibility to intertwine democratic institutions and particularistic cultural traditions created problems of deliberative inequality within the public space.

There is a second important element for the analytical approach of the process of formation of Latin American societies and Brazil which is the specific tradition of associationism developed in the region. Both in the pre- and the postcolonial periods there has been no tradition of plural and democratic forms of association. In the case of Brazil an associative tradition of a religious background has been the only form of association during the colonial period.[18] The most important characteristic of religious associations such as the *Misericordias* or the third order fraternities is the way they associated racial homogeneity with religious intolerance being unable to represent a form of social pluralization. The first plural forms of association to emerge in Latin America were the Masonic lodges which emerged in Peru in 1755, in Mexico in 1785,[19] and in Brazil in 1815.[20] Yet, even in this case, the evolution of the Masonic lodges was in the direction of their compatibilization with the Catholic religion and in the Brazilian case, even with the monarchy. In this sense, it is important to point out that a weak tradition of independent associations in Latin America emerged, at best, in the late nineteenth century already influenced by movement of mutual aid societies or by the socialist movement.[21] Thus, it is possible to point out the lack of collective forms of association or their late emergence as a second characteristic of the Latin American process of societal formation.

There is a third phenomenon which is important to have in mind to analyze the process of formation of public structures in Latin America, which is the development of an undifferentiated tradition of social mobilization organized around the idea of the purity of the popular. In the case of western Europe the cultural unification of the national state takes place in opposition to the existing popular cultures.[22] In the case of the Latin American countries a distinct process took place in virtue of its distinct temporality in relation to the European process of national unification and recovery of the popular culture. In Latin America both processes were simultaneous, leading to the association between national identity and popular culture. Such simultaneity led to two consequences central to the encounter between European modernity and the Latin American tradition: the first of these phenomena is that national elites did not reject popular culture. On the contrary, in most of the region countries, the popular culture was transformed into the main element of the national culture. Thus, popular culture in the region was not a leftover of a cultural form in extinction such as it was in most European countries in the nineteenth century[23] but was rather the result of a political articulation by the elites with the aim to preserve cultural and political autonomy in the moment of integration into the world economic system.[24] A second phenomenon is equally important to the understanding of the political status of the popular which is the fusion of the romantic notion of people—folk—with the Marxian conception of class generating the concept of popular classes.[25] In this latter form, the retrieval of the concept of people assimilated the romantic notion of purity (Herder) transforming the people into a unified and homogeneous entity which preceded the process of internationalization.[26] Such a conception hindered the extension of the concept of autonomy from the cultural to the political realm. Social movements appropriated the idea of the popular which led them not to immediately follow the logic of structural and social differentiation already taking place in countries such as Argentina, Brazil, and Mexico. On the contrary, the repertoire of collective action in Latin America will remain a nondifferentiated repertoire which led to the association of the ideas of class and people through the unlikely intertwinement of the Marxian and the romantic tradition. In this sense, it is possible to argue for a three-sided explanation for the difficulties in the construction of a public space in Latin America, an explanation in which there is a conjunction among 1) the transference of commercial and administrative elements from the West, elements unable per se to generate democracy; 2) such elements intertwined with a tradition of broad privatization and lack of associative tradition which prevailed during the process of national formation; 3) both elements where not easily overcome during the process of modernization due to the fact that the national elites opted for a culture struggle whose main element of opposition with the outside was the valorization of a popular and supposedly untainted culture which was not democratic. In this sense, three elements associate themselves in the process of formation of Latin American societies: an outside element, an element in the culture of the elites, and an element in the popular culture. Table 2.1 below summarizes the institutional and the cultural elements which created difficulties for the constitution of a democratic public sphere in Latin America.

Thus, the Latin American process of nation-building is a process in which a partial detachment of both Spain and Portugal from modernity associated with the particular conditions of the process of settling and colonization of the territory led to a nonpublic and nonpluralistic tradition.

MODERNIZATION, HYBRIDIZATION, AND THE FORMATION OF A PUBLIC SPACE IN BRAZIL

Modernization was the central project of twentieth-century Brazil. It assumed that the reproduction in countries outside the "Western core" of the economic, political, and social structures generated in these countries could be pursued through the introduction of economic modernization and industrialization.[27] Modernization theorists operated with a dualist framework whose assumption was a temporal process whose point of departure (t1) is a

Table 2.1

Cultural Element	Institutional Element	Hybrid Form
broad private sphere	separation between private and culture	penetration of the public by the private
homogeneous and non-plural forms of association	rights of association	non-plural sphere of association
homogeneous forms of collective mobilization	rights of communication	undifferentiated popular mobilizations

non-modern institutional structure and whose arrival point (t2) is the consolidation of modern institutions. Between (t1) and (t2) modernization takes place. Industrialization is the connecting process between the two temporalities. Yet, differently from the modernizers' assumption, the introduction of modern industrial structures in Latin America did not lead to democratic and public structures at the political and cultural levels but rather to the hybridization between modern and traditional economic, political, and cultural structures.

At the political level, modernization did not lead to the overcoming of the phenomena such as clientelism and its secondary manifestations: nepotism, rigging ballots, and disorganization of public services which were supposedly related to the characteristics of an agrarian economy.[28] Modernization did not lead to the overcoming of such characteristics due to the interest of the members of the political system to incorporate non-modern elements in order to strengthen their legitimacy or hegemony. Thus, non-modern practices within the Latin American and Brazilian political systems are not a leftover of previous political periods or social structures but rather a practice which can be articulated with modern forms of political behavior, as it is the case of the culture of the favor. "It is true that while European modernization is based on the autonomy of the person, the universality of the law, disinterested culture, objective remuneration and the work ethic, the favor practices personal dependency, the exception to the rule, interested culture and remuneration of personal services. . . . Referring to dependency as independence, caprice as utility, exception as universality, kinship as merit and privilege as equality" might seem incongruous to someone who believes that liberal ideology has a cognitive value but not for those who are constantly living moments of "loaning and borrowing."[29]

Thus, Latin American politics continued to be based in the culture of the favor after the introduction in the region of modern economic and administrative structures.[30] The political system incorporated elements such as hierarchy, nepotism, and particularism into a formally rational and democratic political system, thus, creating a political hybrid. In Latin American societies both the elites and the popular classes combine modern and traditional elements and the interpretation of such societies has to take that into consideration. The problem is how to construct a democratic society with a public space in such conditions or whether it is desirable as Garcia Canclini does to transform such an analysis in an arrival point in which it is not clear whether such a combination is a vice or a virtuous element or if it simply does not make sense to approach such a phenomenon through normative-laden concepts.

A more thorough analysis of the Latin American political hybrid shows that the hybridization between dependency and autonomy, universality and exceptionalism, and equality and privilege has strong antidemocratic consequences. In all these cases we are speaking of a set of practices which bind elites and masses and pose problems to the construction of democratic institutions. These practices influence the operation of the democratic institutions creating hindrances to their democratizing effects. Thus, the operation of democratic political institutions proper to the liberal democratic tradition is not capable of offsetting structures of power which have been partially overcome in the cultural tradition which has given birth to such institutions. It is not possible to reduce such a problem to the issue of assimilation of cultural standards because it generates an issue which is essential for a democratic theory, namely, how Latin American societies should position themselves normatively vis-a-vis the problem of how to create equal and nonhierarchical public space. In the next section of this chapter I will analyze the changes which occurred at the public level in the recent process of democratization in Brazil in order to point out new cultural potentials which might be used to construct a democratic public space.

THE FORMATION OF A DEMOCRATIC PUBLIC SPACE IN BRAZIL

Popular sectors in Latin America centered their political activities in the fifties and sixties in searching for a form of economic development independent from the international economic system. The central variable in this process was state control and the formation of a broad alliance for an autonomous process of economic development. At the political level populism complemented autonomous economic development, leading to a straight connection between political elites and disorganized masses, a process not challenged by democratic actors due to its instrumentality for the creation of an autonomous economic project. The lack of a societal perspective was one of the reasons authoritarianism could so easily seize political control. Once authoritarianism was in place no form of opposition was feasible because all known strategies of action were based on state control and an authoritarian state was not prone to such a strategy. It was during this period that both the democratic left, the liberals, and the social actors reevaluated the main elements of their forms of action.

The first important revision made by the democratic opposition during the process of liberalization was to shift politics from the realm of the state to the societal level. In the words of the Brazilian social scientist Francisco Weffort, if society did not exist it had to be invented, and, indeed it has been. The second important transformation which took place was the retrieval of the moral dimension of politics. Throughout the fifties and the sixties Latin

American politics involved the subordination of the moral dimension of politics to a substantive conception of political emancipation. Such a proposal was expressed by the opposition between formal and substantive democracy. The preclusion of a moral dimension of politics was thoroughly compatible with a nonnormative understanding of competitive politics. The overall consequence of the amoralization of politics was the impossibility to appeal to any generalizing dimension in the act of doing politics. The Latin American authoritarian regimes took advantage of such a fact when they broke with the remaining civil guarantees during the authoritarian period. Indeed, the only institutions which kept their commitment to moral values during the authoritarian period were the family[31] and the Church.[32] They were the center of the weak structures of social defense which existed in this period because their commitment to morality was pre-political. They were the founders of human rights movements. Thus, the second important revision made by the democratic opposition during the processes of liberalization was the acknowledgement of the need to introduce a moral dimension in order to reconstitute a pacified space for the exercise of politics.

The two above-mentioned structural changes in the understanding of political discourse led to changes in the form of conception of the idea of publicity. The role of expression of political ideas in public was deeply transformed, as well as the meaning of a public and democratic identity. Last but not least, social movements and voluntary associations became the standard form of organization and occupation of the public space. Allow me to develop each of these dimensions:

Expression: social actors in Brazil, in their search for the redefinition of their political roles, changed their conceptions on the aim of politics as the process of liberalization of the former authoritarian regime started to take place in Brazil in the mid-seventies. The first important sign of a transformation in social actors' self-understanding of the aims of their political actions was a change in the form of occupation of the public space. A different political language emerged at the public level—a language that would later play the role of constituting a common ground for the action of social movements and members of voluntary associations. Doimo[33] described the elements of a common language as the self-understanding of social actors as independent subjects, as proponents of grassroots forms of discussion and participation, and as claimants of human and social rights.[34] She showed how the transformation in social actors' self-understanding led to a change in the form of expression of social demands. Social actors occupied the public space by expressing to one another their aims. The number of publications on issues which were the concern of the population such as transportation, health care conditions, housing, ethnic issues, and human rights skyrocketed during the process of liberalization in Brazil as figure 2.1 below shows.

document

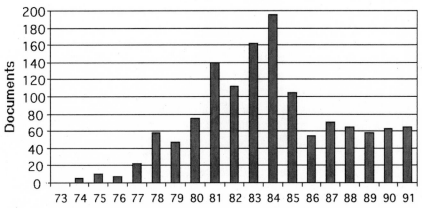

Figure 2.1. Number of Documents on Social Movements (1973–1991)
Source: Doimo, 1995

The increase in the number of documents and publications and in the forms of communication utilized by social actors shows two important issues: the first one is the effort of constitution of a common language different from the populist discourse which existed in the previous democratic period. In contrast to the language of the populist period, the language constructed by social actors was centered in the capacity of society to be the place for the plural organization of claims and demands. The second important issue is the transformation of the concept of occupant of the public space from a dispossessed mass to an autonomous actor capable of deciding his or her claims and the form of presenting them. State claims *in relation* to true were publicly disputed. State claims and policies in relation to the material conditions of the poor were publicly challenged and alternatives were presented. In all of these cases the source of this new form of making politics which will be adopted by social movements was the transformation in the forms of expression of claims at the public level.

Identity: Social actors in Brazil during the process of liberalization constructed a new collective identity. Such a collective identity involved the intertwinement of two processes—one formal and one substantive. The formal process was related to the challenging of the self-attributed popular identity. Throughout the process of liberalization social actors challenged the idea of homogeneous belonging to an undifferentiated popular sector and started to understand themselves as belonging to a pluralistic social space. Social actors reacted to the common process of external attribution of identity. In contrast to that they started a process of evaluation of the meaning of their primary and secondary ties. This has led to a different form of politicization of the social: one in which issues that have been contained at the private level started to be brought into public. There is an additional process connected to that which is the process of reinterpretation of the meaning of an identity constructed in public. Again, the element involved here is the challenging of a deterministic and teleological view of the public space centered on one single actor and one single conflict. In contrast to that, different actors occupied the Latin American public space in search for the acknowledgement of their particular pleas as citizens, a condition only formally equivalent to the plight of other actors.

> Popular mobilizations are no longer based on a model of a total society or on the crystallization in terms of the equivalence of a single conflict which divides the totality of the social into two camps, but on a plurality of concrete demands leading to a proliferation of political spaces.[35]

The new element which emerges during the process of liberalization in Brazil is the reevaluation by social actors of their form of action at the public level. Public identities in Brazil during the fifties and the sixties were based in three elements: they were rational in scope; teleological in their historical perspective, and functional in their understanding of the level in which an identity should be constructed. During the process of liberalization in Latin America all three elements which together formed a substantive conception of politics have been put at stake and substituted for a more plural and democratic identity. First of all, identities started to be related to the local level instead of the functional level. Second, political identities were oriented to the present instead of toward the future. And last but not least, rationality ceased to be identified with a project of homogenization of action and was linked to a conception of politics in which the plurality of social action would be a permanent feature of collective action. Social action was based on the capacity to raise issues such the material improvement of life conditions or the creation of forms of solidarity which might construct a tighter social network, or the search for a form of political autonomy which would put an end to the instrumentalization of material claims by political intermediaries. Improvement of poor neighborhoods, strengthening of the identity of the urban dweller, and the construction of the democratic citizen were all important elements in the construction of this new identity. The pluralization of actors and demands is the important issue to have in mind. Social actors claimed different social services or equipment, established different relations with political mediators, related in different ways to the cultural issue and adopted different models for the organization of their actions. Thus, the second element of the conception of public space constructed during the process of liberalization was the challenge of a homogeneous and teleological identity and its substitution by a plural and democratic one.

The Brazilian democratization produced an increase in the propensity for creation of voluntary and independent forms of association in the country. Boschi[36] showed that the number of voluntary associations created in Rio de Janeiro between 1978 and 1980 was higher than the number of associations created during the entire previous democratic period. Santos[37] showed a similar phenomenon for all categories of voluntary associations. Table 2.2 below shows the increase in the number of voluntary associations created in São Paulo, Rio de Janeiro, and Belo Horizonte during the process of democratization of Brazil (1974–1985).

It is worth calling attention to a series of phenomena: the total number of associations doubles between 1960 and 1970 and, in the case of Belo Horizonte, it triples between 1970 and 1980. The increase was lower in Rio de Janeiro than in Belo Horizonte and São Paulo due to the fact that Rio was the city, which for historical and political reasons, had the largest number of voluntary associations.[38] It is also important to have in mind that there has been not only a quantitative but also a qualitative increase in the form of association in Brazil. Some forms of voluntary associations which were not very strong before the mid-seventies increased in their number and influence: this is the case of neighborhood organizations: the number increased from 71 to 534 in the case of Belo Horizonte. The increases in São Paulo and Rio de Janeiro were also very impressive: among the total number of neighborhood associations existing in the two cities, 97.6 percent and 90.7 percent were created after 1970, respectively. Other types of associations were also completely new in all three cities: 92.5 percent of the associations of health professionals in São Paulo were created after 1970; 76.2 percent of the lawyers' associations in Rio de Janeiro were also created after 1970.[39] In the case of Belo Horizonte the totality of associations dealing with environmental, human rights, and ethnic issues (29 associations) were all created in this

Table 2.2: Number of Associations Created in the Major Brazilian Cities, 1940–1990

	Number of Voluntary Associations Created by Decade	Decade: 1941– 1950	Decade: 1951– 1960	Decade: 1961– 1970	Decade: 1971– 1980	Decade: 1981– 1990
São Paulo		288	464	996	1,871	2,553
Rio de Janeiro		188	743	1,093	1,233	2,498
Belo Horizonte		120	204	459	584	1,597

Source: Santos 1993/Avritzer 1998.

period. Thus, it is possible in the case of the three cities to speak about a very impressive process of change in the associative pattern, a process which involves the increase in the propensity to associate, the increase in the number of associations, the creation of associations dealing with the claim of material issues such as community improvement, and the emergence of associations dealing with post-material claims, such as environmental protection and human rights.

What are the main conceptions of these actors about their associations? How do they see their political participation? Why do they participate? How do they propose to internally organize their associations? How do they see their relation with the political system? It is to the response of this questions that I will now turn in order to approach the recent process of renewal within Brazilian society. A survey[40] of 311 members of associations in São Paulo and Belo Horizonte found voluntary associations distributed in the categories shown in table 2.3.

The first important element I decided to check in order to see how strong is the new associative culture emerging in Brazil, was to inquire into the nature of the work performed within associations and its relation with political mediators. I wanted to know what was the importance given by the members to the autonomy of their associations, an issue which has been discussed in Brazil since the beginning of the liberalization of the former authoritarian regime.[41] One of the central elements of the reevaluation made by the democratic opposition on the reasons why authoritarianism has succeeded in Brazil in 1964 was the weakness of the existing societal networks. Due to the prevailing political culture in the previous democratic period, the issue which appears as the central one to social actors was the creation of an autonomous form of inser-

Table 2.3: Types of Association of the Respondents in São Paulo and Belo Horizonte

	São Paulo	Belo Horizonte
Neighborhood assoc.	31.4 percent	15.7 percent
Professional	7.9 percent	16.4 percent
Education assoc.	15.7 percent	11.3 percent
Imp. of Health cond.	5.7 percent	3.8 percent
Environmental	3.6 percent	3.1 percent
Feminine	9.3 percent	3.1 percent
Human rights	3.6 percent	3.1 percent
Ethnic	3.6 percent	3.8 percent
Self-help associations	—	11.9 percent
Defense of specific causes	—	3.8 percent
Cultural assoc.	10.7 percent	6.9 percent
Academic assoc.	—	10.1 percent
Personal philosophies	—	3.8 percent
Entrepreneurial	8.6 percent	3.1 percent

tion into the economic world system.[42] Such a mistaken understanding of democratic politics led to an overall instrumentalization of politics, whose consequence was the perception that the center of democratic politics should be the integration into the state. During the process of reconstruction of an autonomous public space and an independent opposition in Brazil, the issue which emerged as central to social actors was the break with the corporatist tradition[43] of fusion between society and the state and the creation of an autonomous public space. Voluntary associations and new social movements[44] were part of this new space: human rights movements in the seventies; environmental movements and feminine movements in the eighties;[45] and urban social movements in the eighties and nineties[46] renovated the Brazilian public space. Members of voluntary associations kept this tradition intact by recurring to their own labor, by demanding a sharp separation between their associations and the political system. Asked about the predominant form of labor in their associations 73.6 percent of the respondents in Belo Horizonte and 56.6 percent in São Paulo defined their labor in their associations as voluntary. Asked about whether they belonged or not to a political party, 79 percent of the respondents in Belo Horizonte and 78 percent in São Paulo answered that they did not belong to any party. More important than that: asked if they would stop participating in their association in the case it would link itself to a political party, 67.3 percent of the respondents in Belo Horizonte and 49.3 percent in São Paulo said they would stop participating.

The answer to the above-posed questions points in the direction of analytical elements not approached so far by the literature on democratization: social movements which emerged at the public level during the process of democratization in Brazil did not simply vanish away, as some authors have claimed, or give space to the action of political parties. Voluntary associations were the form of institutionalization of the claims of social movement actors. Not only did their number increase, they also represented a place for the institutionalization of claims which were not institutionalized at the political level. The contact between associations and political parties is low, although they have a higher level of contact with public officials.

Members of voluntary associations were also asked about the reasons for their participation as well as their opinion about the prevailing practices within their associations (see table 2.4). Two important elements were involved in the response: the first element was a significative departure from what the literature maintained as a self-interested pattern of collective action.[47] Members of voluntary associations mentioned the improvement of their material condition as the third most important reason for participation in the case of São Paulo and the fourth most important reason for participation in the case of Belo Horizonte (each person was allowed to enumerate more

Table 2.4:   Motive for Participation in Voluntary Associations

	São Paulo	Belo Horizonte
To reach the material aim proposed by the association	17.1 percent	11.9 percent
To work for some form of social change	36.2 percent	37.1 percent
To join a collective environment	19.7 percent	30.8 percent
To strengthen the association internally	14.5 percent	30.2 percent

than one cause although they were enumerated in order of relevance). Even in the case of associations clearly related to material issues such as communitarian associations, the main reason for participation is not self-improvement of the material condition: in the case of Belo Horizonte only 16 percent of the respondents said that they joined their associations in order to reach the material aim of the association whereas 48 percent mentioned the work for some form of social change.

The second area in which very significative changes appeared was in relation to the practices internal to the associations. We focused on the conception of the members of voluntary associations about the internal practices of their associations in order to evaluate how internally democratic they were. Members of voluntary associations were asked which form of internal organization for their association they preferred. In all cases of associations in the two cities, respondents preferred more democratic than less democratic forms and straightly rejected *unipersonal* forms of leadership, as table 2.5 shows:

Table 2.5:   What is the Best Form of Organization of a Voluntary Association?

	São Paulo		Belo Horizonte	
	Yes	No	Yes	No
The highest deliberative level should be the board	30.6%	59.4%	36.5%	63.5%
The highest deliberative level should be the president	13.2%	86.8%	6.8%	93.2%
The highest deliberative level should be a members' assembly	73.05%	26.9%	84.9%	15.1%

It is possible to point out in all the cases in both cities a very strong preference for democratic forms of organization. Again, it shows that the forms of democratic organization introduced by social movements in the seventies and eighties did not vanish but were preserved as values and institutionalized at the civil level. Thus, it is possible to argue that members of civil associations in Brazil preserved and legally institutionalized the three main elements introduced by social movements during the previous decade: autonomy, organizational concerns, and democratic forms of participation. There has not only been a change in the patterns of association in Brazil but also a change which took place at the societal level vis-à-vis a tradition of making material claims through political mediators, establishing forms of fusion between state and society, and being favorable to unipersonal forms of political leadership. In all three cases, there has been a renewal of a democratic potential at the public level, the question being how this democratic potential can be utilized to broaden the existing democratic arrangements in the country.

MODERNITY AND THE FORMATION OF A DEMOCRATIC PUBLIC SPACE IN BRAZIL

The Brazilian itinerary in the twentieth century has moved around two poles: economic modernization and social modernity. The first process was based on the idea of an automatic process of transference of economic institutions from industrialized countries to Brazil. It was assumed that industrialization would generate the remaining modern structures proper to modernity, such as a modern state, a modern political system, as well as mechanism of accountability between state and society. However, the whole project floundered because its assumption of an opposition between formal and informal economy, traditional versus modern political system, private versus public relations proved itself empirically incorrect.[48] The result was a political hybrid which, as I have shown in section two of this chapter, contained strong anti-public elements such as the culture of the favor, a very broad concept of private, and the always open possibility of privatization of the public.

A second process has taken place in Brazil in the late twentieth century as a result of the reaction against authoritarianism. This process triggered social modernity, a process of reevaluation of a lack of a tradition of independent associations, of undifferentiated forms of mobilization and occupation of the public space. Social movements and members of voluntary associations struggled for organizational autonomy, for independence from political parties, and for a new pattern of action based on occupation of the public space and rejection of the fusion between state and society. They organized themselves democratically within their associations and demanded from the state acknowledgement of material and post-material claims. Which are the conditions for these new forms of action to lead to structural changes at the public level?

So far the central aspect of the recently created public culture has been a strong conflict between public and private practices. This struggle is caused by the fact that a hybrid political system which operated through the combination of formally rationalized rules and patrimonial forms of getting electoral support has managed to remain non-permeable to the new public culture. A permanent conflict between members of social movements and associations, the press, and a fairly modern public opinion, on the one hand, and traditional practices such as nepotism, clientelism, and political corruption has been the result of the attempt to apply rules of accountability to political actors who still operate according to a very different logic, is the central element of contemporary Brazil. Such a conflict already led to the impeachment of a president,[49] and to sharp crises between public opinion and the legislative as well as the judicial system. In all cases the conflict has been around the issue of political and administrative practices. The assimilation of a new public culture by political actors remains the noncontrollable element of the process of construction of a democratic public space in Brazil.

NOTES

1. Sérgio Buarque de Hollanda, *Raízes do Brasil* (Rio de Janeiro: Jose Olimpio, 1939); Oliveira Vianna, *Instituições Políticas Brasileiras* (Rio de Janeiro: Jose Olympio, 1951); Richard Morse, "The Heritage of Latin America," in *The Founding of New Societies*, ed. L. Hartz (New York: Harcourt, 1964) and Richard Morse, "Claims of Political Tradition," in *Politics and Social Change in Latin America: Still a Distinct Tradition*, ed. Howard Wiarda (Boulder, Colo.: Westview Press, 1989).

2. Morse, "Claims of Political Tradition," 96–97.

3. The other side of this polemic was represented by the work of Francisco Vitoria and the Salamanca school. Vitoria articulated his juridical thought around the idea of the *hominidad* of the Indians, that is to say, of the right of the Indians because they were men to be free and to have their sovereignty. Thus, instead of a unilateral rejection of rights and sovereignty that Morse argues has taken place in sixteenth-century Spain and Portugal was a reaction against a tradition of rights which already made its way into Iberian social thought rather than a parallel development involving a wholesale rejection of modernity. See L. Perena, *La Idea de Justicia en la Conquista de America*. (Madrid: Editorial Mapfre, 1992).

4. N. García Canclini, *Hybrid Cultures: Strategies for Entering and Leaving Modernity* (Minneapolis: University of Minnesota Press, 1995).

5. S. Eisenstadt and W. Schluchter, "Path to Early Modernities: a Comparative View" *Daedalus* 127, no. 3 (1998): 1–18.

6. J. Habermas, *The Philosophical Discourse of Modernity: Twelve Lectures* (Cambridge, Mass.: MIT Press, 1987).

7. M. Weber, *The Protestant Ethic and the Spirit of Capitalism* (New York: Scribner, 1930); W. Schluchter, *Rationalism, Religion, and Domination: a Weberian Perspective* (Berkeley: University of California Press, 1989.

8. *From Max Weber: Essays in Sociology*, ed. C. W. Mills, et al. (New York: Oxford University Press, 1958), 26.

9. Weber, *The Protestant Ethic*; Schluchter, *Rationalism, Religion, and Domination*; L. Avritzer, *A Moralidade da Democracia* (São Paulo: Perspectiva, 1996).

10. I. M. Wallerstein, *The Capitalist World-Economy: Essays* (Cambridge (Eng.) and New York: Cambridge University Press, 1979).

11. E. J. Hobsbawm, *The Age of Empire, 1875–1914* (London: Weidenfeld and Nicolson, 1987).

12. H. B. Johnson, "The Donatary Captaincy in Perspective," *Hyspanic American Historical Review* 52, no. 2 (1972).

13. J. C. Abreu and A. Brakel, *Chapters of Brazil's Colonial History, 1500–1800* (New York: Oxford University Press, 1997), 36.

14. S. Schwartz, "The Formation of Colonial Identity in Brazil," in: *Colonial Identity in the Atlantic World*, ed. N. Canny and A. Pagden. (Princeton, N.J.: Princeton University Press, 1987).

15. M. S. C. Franco, *Homens Livres na Ordem Escravocrata* (São Paulo: Atica, 1974).

16. R. DaMatta, *Carnivals, Rogues, and Heroes : an Interpretation of the Brazilian Dilemma* (Notre Dame, Ind.: University of Notre Dame Press, 1991), 68.

17. DaMatta, *Carnivals, rogues, and heroes*), 274.

18. L. Landim, "Para Além do Mercado e do Estado," *Cadernos do Iser.* (1993); C. R. Boxer, *The golden age of Brazil, 1695–1750: Growing Pains of a Colonial Society.* (Berkeley: University of California Press, Published in coöperation with the Sociedade de Estudos Históricos Dom Pedro Segundo, 1962), 319 and C. Boschi, *Os Leigos e o Poder* (São Paulo: Ática, 1986).

19. Xavier Francisco Guerra, *Mexico: del Antiguo Regimen a la Revolucion* (México: Fondo de Cultura, 1988).

20. Alexandre José de Mello Moraes, *Historia do Brasil Reino e do Brasil Império* (Belo Horizonte: Itatiaia, 1982).

21. June Hahner, *Poverty and Politics: The Urban Poor in Brazil (1870–1920)* (Austin: University of Texas Press, 1986); M. Conniff, "Voluntary Associations in Rio: 1870–1945," *Journal of InterAmerican Studies and World Affairs* 17, no. 1 (1975).

22. Peter Burke, *A Cultura Popular na Idade Media* (São Paulo: Companhia das Letras, 1978).

23. Burke, *A Cultura Popular na Idade Media*.

24. J. M. Barbero, *Dos Meios as Mediações* (Barcelona: Gilli, 1987).

25. F. C. Weffort, *O populismo na política brasileira* (Rio de Janeiro: Paz e Terra, 1978); Ernesto Laclau, "New Social Movements and the Plurality of the Social," in: *New Social Movements and the State*, ed. David Slater (Amsterdam: CEDLA: 1985)

26. Antonio Pasqualli, *Sociologia da Comunicação*. (Petrópolis: Vozes, 1961) and H. I. Schiller, *Mass Communications and American Empire*. (New York: A. M. Kelley, 1969).

27. Gino Germani, *Sociologia de la Modernizacion* (Buenos Aires: Paidos, 1969).

28. Victor Nunes Leal, *Coronelismo, Enxada e Voto*, 6th ed. (São Paulo: Alfa-Omega, 1946), 140.

29. Canclini, *Hybrid Cultures*, 48–49.

30. L. Roniger, *Hierarchy and Trust in Modern Mexico and Brazil* (New York: Praeger, 1990).

31. F. C. Weffort, "Why Democracy?" in *Democratizing Brazil*, ed. A. Stepan 327–50 (New York: Oxford University Press, 1989); Elizabeth Jelin, *Citizenship and Democratization* (Boulder, Colo.: Westview Press, 1996).

32. Thomas Bruneau, *The Church and Democratization in Brazil* (New York: Cambridge University Press, 1974).

33. Ana Maria Doimo, *A Vez e a Voz do Popular* (Rio de Janeiro: Relume Dumara, 1995).

34. Doimo, *A Vez e a Voz do Popular*, 124.

35. Laclau, "New Social Movements and the Plurality of the Social," 41.

36. Renato Boschi, *A Arte da Associação* (Rio de Janeiro Vértice, 1987).

37. Wanderley Guilherme dos Santos, *Razões da Desordem* (Rio de Janeiro: Rocco, 1993.)

38. There is very little data available on voluntary associations in Brazil before the twentieth century. The best source is Conniff (M. Conniff, "Voluntary Associations in Rio: 1870–1945.") He retrieved data from a census on voluntary associations made in Rio de Janeiro in the late nineteenth century. The data he presents is a good indication of two issues: that the propensity to associate was low but not nonexistent. He shows a significant number of associations in Rio at the turn of the century. Yet, it is clear from Conniff's data that most of these associations were religious brotherhoods corroborating the idea of a non-separation between private and public issues. (Conniff, "Voluntary Associations in Rio: 1870–1945"; Leonardo Avritzer, "Um Desenho Institucional para o Novo Associativismo," *Lua Nova* 39 (1997): 149–175).

39. Santos, *Razões da Desordem*.

40. The database from which the 311 respondents were selected was formed in the following way: in Brazil registration in a local notary is mandatory for voluntary associations and a summary of the association's constitution is required to be published in the city or state's official newspaper (Diário Official). In the case of Belo Horizonte, in which the empirical universe is smaller, all associations registered between 1940 and 1990 were searched in the state's official newspaper and formed a database from which were subtracted recreational and religious based organizations following Diamond's (L. Diamond, "Toward Democratic Consolidation," *Journal of Democracy* 5, no. 3 (1994): 4–17.) definition of civil associations. The research found 2964 voluntary associations, from which a stratified sample of 159 associations which preserved their internal proportional was made. In the case of São Paulo, due to the size of the universe, a procedure to reduce the number of associations in the database was devised. The list of associations was collected from the local notary for registry of

voluntary associations. He provided us with a list of the 1718 voluntary associations created between 1970 and 1990. Due to the size of the universe it has been decided to leave out four categories of associations already included in the sample in Belo Horizonte: self-help associations, associations with specific causes, and academic and personal philosophy associations. The Belo Horizonte sample is closest to the overall configuration of the universe; São Paulo's sample has a higher representation of associations which emerged after the 1970s. Among those who responded to the survey in Belo Horizonte and São Paulo, 50 percent were presidents of voluntary associations and 50 percent members of the board.

41. E. Sader, *Quando Novos Personagens Entram em Cena* (São Paulo: Brasiliense, 1989) and Avritzer, *A Moralidade da Democracia*.

42. F. H. Cardoso and E. Faletto, *Dependency and Development in Latin America.* (Berkeley: University of California Press, 1979).

43. Philippe Schmitter, *Interest Conflict and Political Change in Brazil* (Stanford, Calif.: Stanford University Press, 1971).

44. There is a huge discussion on whether there has ever been new social movements in Latin America. This discussion involved two misunderstandings: one on the nature of social movements in general and the other on the nature of Latin American social movements. The misunderstanding about social movements in general lies in the stress of post-material issues. If it is true that many new social movements, such as the peace and the environmental movements, put an overwhelming stress of post-materiality, it is, however, a mistake to reduce social movements to such a element. Many new social movements involved a clear material dimension as it has been the case of the feminist movement. See A. Melucci, *Challenging Codes: Collective Action in the Information Age* (Cambridge [England] and New York: Cambridge University Press, 1996). On the other hand, authors such as Foweraker or Azevedo and Prates reduced urban social movements to the claim of material negotiated good or political integration into the state. They missed the dimension of autonomy and the changes in the forms of participation.

45. S. Mainwaring and E. Viola, "New Social Movements, Political Culture and Democracy: Brazil and Argentina in the 80s," *Telos* 61 (1985): 17–52.

46. Boschi, *A Arte da Associação.*

47. Elisa Reis, "Desigualdade e Solidariedade," *Revista Brasileira de Ciências Sociais* 29 (1995): 35–49.

48. Canclini, *Hybrid cultures.*

49. Leonardo Avritzer, "The Conflict between civil and political society in Post-authoritarian Brazil," in *Corruption and Political Reform in Brazil*, ed. Rosenn and Downes. Miami: North South Center Press, 1998.

BIBLIOGRAPHY

Abreu, J. C., and A. Brakel. *Chapters of Brazil's Colonial History, 1500–1800.* New York: Oxford University Press, 1997.

Avritzer, Leonardo. *A Moralidade da Democracia.* São Paulo: Perspectiva, 1996.

——. "Um Desenho Institucional para o Novo Associativismo." *Lua Nova* 39 (1997): 149–175.

——. "The Conflict between civil and political society in Post-authoritarian Brazil." In *Corruption and Political Reform in Brazil,* edited by Rosenn and Downes. Miami: North South Center Press, 1998.

Barbero, J. M. *Dos Meios as Mediações.* Barcelona: Gilli, 1987.

Boschi, C. *Os Leigos e o Poder.* São Paulo: Ática, 1986.

Boschi, Renato. *A Arte da Associação.* Rio de Janeiro: Vértice, 1987.

Boxer, C. R. *The Golden Age of Brazil, 1695–1750: Growing Pains of a Colonial Society.* Berkeley: University of California Press, Published in coöperation with the Sociedade de Estudos Históricos Dom Pedro Segundo, 1962.

Bruneau, Thomas. *The Church and Democratization in Brazil.* New York: Cambridge University Press, 1974.

Burke, Peter. *A Cultura Popular na Idade Media.* São Paulo: Companhia das Letras, 1978.

Cardoso, F. H., and E. Faletto. *Dependency and Development in Latin America.* Berkeley: University of California Press, 1979.

Conniff, M. "Voluntary Associations in Rio: 1870–1945." *Journal of InterAmerican Studies and World Affairs* 17, no. 1 (1975).

DaMatta, R. *Carnivals, Rogues, and Heroes: an Interpretation of the Brazilian Dilemma.* Notre Dame, Ind.: University of Notre Dame Press, 1991.

Diamond, L. "Toward Democratic Consolidation." *Journal of Democracy* 5, no. 3 (1994): 4–17.

Doimo, Ana Maria. *A Vez e a Voz do Popular.* Rio de Janeiro: Relume Dumara, 1995.

Eisenstadt, S., and W. Schluchter. "Path to Early Modernities: a Comparative View." *Daedalus* 127, no. 3 (1998): 1–18.

Franco, M. S. C. *Homens Livres na Ordem Escravocrata.* São Paulo: Atica, 1974.

García Canclini, N. *Hybrid Cultures: Strategies for Entering and Leaving Modernity.* Minneapolis: University of Minnesota Press, 1995.

Germani, Gino. *Sociologia de la Modernizacion.* Buenos Aires: Paidos, 1969.

Guerra, Xavier Francisco. *Mexico: del Antiguo Regimen a la Revolucion.* México: Fondo de Cultura, 1988.

Habermas, J. *The Philosophical Discourse of Modernity: Twelve Lectures.* Cambridge, Mass.: MIT Press, 1987.

Hahner, June. *Poverty and Politics: the Urban Poor in Brazil (1870–1920).* Austin: University of Texas Press, 1986.

Hobsbawm, E. J. *The Age of Empire, 1875–1914.* London: Weidenfeld and Nicolson, 1987.

Hollanda, Sergio Buarque de. *Raízes do Brasil.* Rio de Janeiro: Jose Olimpio, 1939.

Jelin, Elizabeth. *Citizenship and Democratization.* Boulder, Colo.: Westview Press, 1996.

Johnson, H. B. "The Donatary Captaincy in Perspective." *Hyspanic American Historical Review* 52, no. 2 (1972).

Laclau, Ernesto. "New Social Movements and the Plurality of the Social." In *New Social Movements and the State*, edited by David Slater. (Amsterdam: CEDLA, 1985).

Landim, L. "Para Além do Mercado e do Estado." *Cadernos do Iser*, (1993).

Leal, Victor Nunes. *Coronelismo, Enxada e Voto*. 6th ed. São Paulo: Alfa-Omega, 1946.

Mainwaring, S., and E. Viola. "New Social Movements, Political Culture and Democracy: Brazil and Argentina in the 80s." *Telos* 61 (1985): 17–52.

Melo Moraes, Alexandre José de. *Historia do Brasil Reino e do Brasil Império*. Belo Horizonte: Itatiaia, 1982.

Melucci, A. *Challenging Codes: Collective Action in the Information Age*. Cambridge (England) and New York, Cambridge University Press, 1996.

Morse, Richard. "Claims of Political Tradition." In *Politics and Social Change in Latin America: Still a Distinct Tradition*, edited by Howard Wiarda. Boulder, Colo.: Westview Press, 1989.

———. "The Heritage of Latin America." In *The Founding of New Societies*, edited by L. Hartz. New York: Harcourt, 1964.

Pasqualli, Antonio. *Sociologia da Comunicação*. Petrópolis: Vozes, 1961.

Perena. *La Idea de Justicia en la Conquista de America*. Madrid: Editorial Mapfre, 1992.

Reis, E. "Desigualdade e Solidariedade: uma releitura do familismo a-moral de Banfield." *Revista Brasileira de Ciências Sociais* 10, no. 29 (1995).

Roniger, L. *Hierarchy and Trust in Modern Mexico and Brazil*. New York: Praeger, 1990.

Sader, E. *Quando Novos Personagens Entram em Cena*. São Paulo: Brasiliense, 1989.

Santos, Wanderley Guilherme dos. *Razões da Desordem*. Rio de Janeiro: Rocco, 1993.

Schiller, H. I. *Mass Communications and American empire*. New York: A. M. Kelley, 1969.

Schluchter, W. *Rationalism, Religion, and Domination: a Weberian Perspective*. Berkeley: University of California Press, 1989.

Schmitter, Philippe. *Interest Conflict and Political Change in Brazil*. Stanford, Calif.: Stanford University Press, 1971.

Schwartz, S. "The Formation of Colonial Identity in Brazil." In *Colonial Identity in the Atlantic World*, edited by N. Canny and A. Pagden. Princeton, N.J.: Princeton University Press, 1987.

Vianna, Oliveira. *Instituições Políticas Brasileiras*. Rio de Janeiro: Jose Olympio, 1951.

Wallerstein, I. M. *The Capitalist World-Economy: Essays*. Cambridge (Eng.) and New York: Cambridge University Press, 1979.

Weber, M. *The Protestant Ethic and the Spirit of Capitalism*. New York: Scribner, 1930.

———. *From Max Weber: Essays in Sociology*. Edited by C. W. Mills, et al. New York: Oxford University Press, 1958.

Weffort, F. C. *O populismo na política brasileira*. Rio de Janeiro: Paz e Terra, 1978.

———. "Why Democracy?" In *Democratizing Brazil*, edited by A. Stepan, 327–50. New York: Oxford University Press, 1989.

3

Between Under-Integration and Over-Integration: Not Taking Citizenship Seriously

Marcelo Neves

Citizenship (not in the technical-legal sense but as a legal-political institution of social inclusion) has been one of the most common themes of political rhetoric and of the discourse of the social sciences in Brazil with the end of military authoritarianism (1984–1985). The broadening of the debate does not imply, however, that there is agreement about the term's meaning. To the contrary, the more talk there is of citizenship, the more ambiguous the expression becomes.

Similarly, rhetoric about the citizens' rights intensifies and becomes more extensive as the structural and current conditions for its realization decrease. This is because citizenship, even when it is incorporated into the constitutional text through a broadening of the declaration of rights, is principally a term and issue of symbolic politics.

Firstly, I will semantically delineate the meaning of "citizenship" and its evolution. I will then discuss the construction and broadening of citizenship as a process of juridification, analyzing the question of the autonomy of the legal system as a condition for its realization. Finally, I will deal with the central theme of this chapter, the absence of citizenship, as a result of the relationships of under-integration and over-integration of individuals, especially in the legal-constitutional system, and will review some specific aspects of the problem.

FROM A NARROW TO A BROAD CONCEPT OF CITIZENSHIP

The notion of "citizens' rights," in the semantics of modern bourgeois revolutions, has a narrow meaning, pointing specifically to the right to participation in the state "will-formation." This is how the *droits de l'homme* are distinguished as individual pre-state rights, from the *droits du citoyen*, which would only become conceivable with the construction of the State as a political institution. Citizenship would remain restricted to "political rights."[1]

However, this strict semantic overcame liberal theoretical models, after having been adopted by Marx in "On the Jewish Question," in which he distinguishes *Menschenrechte* (human rights), defined as "the rights of a member of civil society, i.e., the rights of egoistic man," from political rights, which imply participation in the State as "a political community."[2] The *droits de l'homme* were seen critically as being a result of the "decomposition of man,"[3] while the *droits du citoyen* were seen as being politically integrative.

This concept, which limits citizenship to the right to political participation, has more recently been losing space in the language of the social sciences, and this is highlighted by the theoretical contribution of T. H. Marshall, which offers greater semantic scope. His perspective provides an evolving expansion of the concept to include civil, political, and social rights, the periods of formation of which had respectively covered the eighteenth, nineteenth, and twentieth centuries.[4] The equality inherent to citizenship will thus only be reached if it is also extended simultaneously to liberty (civil), participation (political), and (social) needs. It is in this broad sense that it came into "war" in the twentieth century with the capitalist class system, which was based on inequality.[5]

However, citizenship, oriented by the principle of equality, does not complete its evolutionary cycle in the three phases studied by Marshall. The title to the rights which were conquered and broadened in these phases, was, in the final analysis, individual. Classic political rights affirm the liberty of the individual to participate politically in the exercise of power, including associating and meeting with other individuals for this purpose. Even social rights, as *droits-créances* in contrast to *droits-libertés*,[6] refer to demands for state services for the benefit of the individual. In recent decades, citizenship has developed in the sense of conquering and broadening the rights related to collective and diffuse interests, the so-called third-generation rights.[7] It is true that with the rise of labor legislation there was also an emergence of collective rights, such as the right to strike, and also those that resulted from collective bargaining. Nevertheless, the most generalized demand for integration of collective rights into the reality of the States is something that has become apparent in only the past three decades.[8] The importance of rights related to collective and diffuse interests resides in the fact that they make possible concrete and efficient actions against the illegal and socially damaging practices of the large impersonal organizations, that are being increasingly strengthened in today's world. These actions would not have been possible during the individualist period of rights.

Finally, there arose the notion of reverse discrimination as the fifth phase of development in the content of citizenship. Dworkin, for example, based on a reconstructive analysis of U.S. Supreme Court jurisprudence, argued that positive discrimination of this type against those less favored can be perfectly in accord with the right—for Dworkin this is axiomatic—to equal consideration and respect.[9] This orientation has been adopted in the praxis of political groups, in courts' jurisprudence, and also in the realm of legislation. It aims at compensating negative social discrimination against ethnic and sexual minorities and the physically handicapped. Positive discriminations break with the universalistic concept of the rights of citizens, opening up this concept in a fragmented way to consider the particular differences and conditions of minority groups, without negating the principle of equality. This opening simply represents a pluralization of citizenship.[10]

CONQUEST AND BROADENING OF CITIZENSHIP AS A PROCESS OF JURIDIFICATION

The broadening of legal themes in the framework of the positivation of law[11] made juridification one of the critical problems of the modern state. Conceptualized "from the outside" as the expansion of law and "from within" as its increasing density or specialization,[12] the phenomenon of juridification was, in the realm of the intense debate in West Germany in the 1980s, classified into three basic types: juridification as increase and intensification of legislation, of bureaucratization, and of courts' adjudication or judicial review.[13] The juridifying effects on society were evaluated, on the one hand, negatively (alienation, bureaucratization, "colonization of the lifeworld"), and on the other, positively (insurance for liberty and status).[14] It is in relation to the positive aspect that it can be sustained that the conquest and broadening of citizenship implies a process of juridification of power relations.

The process of juridification developed in the modern state in four phases,[15] each having a specific meaning for the construction of citizenship.

In the first period, juridification led to rights of private persons considered as subjects to the sovereign's law, as it is linked to the concept of the "bourgeois state" of the absolutist period. To the degree in which these rights were not enforceable against the sovereign, but only against other subjects, they in fact still cannot be considered citizenship rights. The asymmetric relationship between the sovereign and the subjects, constituted by powers, privileges, and rights in the superior pole and by duties, obedience, and responsibilities in the inferior pole, was incompatible with the principle of equality which specified the notion of citizenship.

In the second phase, juridification led to the positivation of public rights of a liberal nature, corresponding to the bourgeois constitutional state. Private persons came to have rights that could be exercised against the "sovereign," who, in turn, was obliged to respect them in the legally preestablished sphere of action. Citizenship thus arose as an affirmation of the negative liberties, in the form of classic civil rights.

Later, with the rise of the democratic constitutional state, there was an emergence of public rights "in the form of general and equal suffrage and the recognition of the freedom to organize political associations and parties" ("juridification of the legitimation process").[16] In the language of Rawls, the principle of equal liberty came to be designated as the "principle of (equal) participation."[17] Liberty-autonomy gave space to liberty-participation.[18] Citizenship expanded affirming positive liberties, in the form of political rights.[19]

Finally, the problem of juridification in the context of the democratic welfare state was highlighted, bringing with it the positivation of social rights, compensatory intervention in the class structure and in the economy, public welfare policy, and the legal regulation of family and educational relationships.[20] It is to this phase that Habermas directs his criticism of juridification (*Verrechtlichung*), based upon the distinction between law as a medium and law as an institution. In the first case, "the law is combined with the media of money and power in such a way that it takes on the role of a steering medium itself," as in "most areas of economic, commercial, business, and administrative law."[21] By "legal institutions" Habermas means "legal norms that cannot be sufficiently legitimized through a positivistic reference to procedure."[22] To the degree in which "they belong to the legitimate orders of the lifeworld itself" (space of communicative action), "they need substantive justification."[23] In keeping with this analytical model, law as a medium would have a "constitutive power," while law as an institution "only a regulative function."[24] To the extent that law acts as a medium in the informally regulated spheres of the "lifeworld," as for example, in family and school law, juridification would have negative effects that are socially disintegrative. Instead, the internal colonization of the lifeworld is spoken of: "The thesis of internal colonization states that the subsystems of the economy and state become more and more complex as a consequence of capitalist growth, and penetrate ever deeper into the symbolic reproduction of the lifeworld."[25] The law as a medium, a systemic expression of purposive rationality, at the service of the economy and power, would invade the sphere of communicative action, based on understanding, and in this way would prejudice the construction of an intersubjective reason.[26]

But Habermas recognizes that juridification, also in the phase of the democratic welfare state, would have positive effects when the law as an institution would perform a regulative role in favor of the plexus of action of the life-world, orientated to reaching understanding, or would serve as a steering medium of the systems of action of the economy and of the state.[27] It is also undeniable that the social rights, as consequences of the interference of the legal system in the economic structure and in class relations, have a socially integrating function. Although it is fairly obvious, it is still indisputable that without social rights as *droits-créances*, the *droits-libertés* have no meaning. Thus, citizenship, as generalized integration in the social systems, based on law, broadens significantly with the conquest of social rights, even though, from the theoretical-critical point of view, they would be subject to a negative evaluation in light of the "loyalty of the masses" in the welfare state.[28]

In addition to the four phases referred to above, we can interpret the institution of the rights related to collective and diffuse interests and of reverse discrimination as a new moment in the process of juridification. Concerning the first group, positive law responds to the incapacity of the effective action of isolated individuals against the activity of large organizations. The class actions and those concerning the protection of diffuse interests allow more generalized and efficient access of individuals and groups to the benefits and advantages of the social system, thereby strengthening citizenship. Meanwhile, the reverse discrimination, in addition to legally assuring the integration of minorities in the social systems, institutionalizes the right to be different. By discriminating legally, they are guided by the egalitarian principle of citizenship.

AUTONOMY OF THE LEGAL SYSTEM AS A CONDITION FOR CITIZENSHIP

If, on one hand, the conquest and broadening of citizenship can be interpreted as a process of juridification, then, on the other, it is possible to conceive of the autonomy of the legal system as a condition for its undertaking.

The question of the autonomy of law has been handled in a more radical form by systems theory. In this perspective, positivity is defined as "self-determination" of law, or that is, operational autonomy of the legal system in relation to the determinations of its "environment."[29] The concept of "autopoiesis," which comes from biological theory,[30] is reconstructed[31] and it is affirmed that positive (modern) law reproduces primarily in accord with its own criteria and binary code (legal/illegal).[32] As in relation to other differentiated social systems, this does not concern autarchy, the absence of an environment.[33] Law is seen as "a normatively closed but cognitively open system."[34] At the same time in which positive law would factor self-reference through concepts, it would construct its hetero-reference through the assimilation of interests.[35] The self-referential closure, normative for the legal system, would not in itself constitute a finality of the system, but would rather be "a condition of possibility for openness."[36]

In this context, the legal system can assimilate, in accordance with its own criteria, the environmental factors, while not being directly influenced by them. The legal validity of the normative expectations is not determined immediately by economic interests, political criteria, ethical ideas, or even by scientific propositions;[37] it depends on the selective processes of conceptual filtering within the legal system.[38]

Divergences between Luhmann's theory of positivity and the discourse theory of law proposed by Habermas emerge particularly in reference to this point. For Luhmann, not only the suppression of the immediate determination of law through political interests and criteria of the powerful, but also the moral neutralization of the legal system are inherent in the positivity of law. Habermas recognizes that the boundaries between law and morality exist, insofar as he considers that the procedural rationality of moral discourses, which are not yet legally regulated, is incomplete, arguing that in these, disputes between parties cannot be decided from the perspective of a nonparticipant.[39] Although he does not deny the autonomy of the legal system, he ascribes to it an ethical or moral foundation:

> A legal system does not acquire autonomy on its own. It is autonomous only to the extent that the legal procedures institutionalized for legislation and for the administration of justice guarantee impartial judgment- and will-formation, and provide the channels through which a ethical procedural rationality gains entrance into law and politics. There can be no autonomous law without the realization of democracy.[40]

In this sense, Habermas maintains that positivity does not consist in doing away with problems of justification, but in displacing them.[41]

However, although there are differentiated theoretical concepts about the autonomy of the legal system, one of an ethical-procedural character, the other with a systemic-functional base, not only Habermas establishes a connection between the autonomy of law and democracy. For Luhmann, democracy in the political system is presupposed by the positivity of law.[42] Therefore, in both theories the autonomy of law can be seen as a pre-requisite for the realization of citizenship. In Habermas, this implies private autonomy in connection with public autonomy, or that is human rights and popular sovereignty reciprocally presupposed.[43] In Luhmann's model, citizenship can be read as a mechanism of inclusion of the entire population in the social systems, or that is, access to their benefits and advantages as well as dependence upon their rules and constraints.[44] Conceived in this way, it would be indistinguishably linked to the self-reference of the political and legal systems.[45]

Therefore, defining citizenship as public and private autonomy or as inclusion, presupposes autonomy of the legal system in relation to the concrete power of individuals and organizations, or that is, its conquest and expansion requires the untangling of law, power, and knowledge.[46] This does not mean that the legal "sphere" is not conditioned by economic and political factors, but only that citizenship is incompatible with obstructive and destructive interferences of political and economic particularisms in the reproduction of law. The political and economic influences in the legal system are subordinated to the criteria established by the legal system itself. This implies the generalization of law in the sense of including the entire population in its scope, meaning both access to its benefits and advantages as well as dependence upon its criteria. That is, citizenship presupposes not only equality of rights, but also of duties.[47] And this bipolarity is only possible if the legal system reproduces autonomously.

LEGAL-POLITICAL MOMENTS IN THE CONQUEST AND BROADENING OF CITIZENSHIP RIGHTS

The conquest of new citizenship rights and their broadening pass through three legal-political levels. First arises the semantics of human rights, which requires on the level of morality or of "values" the recognition and satisfaction of certain normative expectations that emerge in society and that are considered essential to social and system integration of individuals and groups. The semantics of human rights undeniably presupposes the development of moral consciousness, in order to build and broaden citizenship, as well as increased social complexity and differentiation.

Secondly, the semantics of human rights comes to be recognized by the State and incorporated into the constitutional system in the form of basic rights. This concerns, therefore, a response of the legal system to the demands for social and system integration, making them the content of constitutional norms. I do not think that the ethical-procedural and systemic-functional readings of basic rights definitively exclude each other: the first seeks to define them as the result of the opening of legal procedures to the evolution of moral consciousness to the postconventional level,[48] which implies a claim for consensus that is questionable under conditions of strong heterogeneity; the second interprets them as a response of positive law to the differentiation of society and the demand for inclusion of the various social systems.[49] Although the respective theoretical foundations would be antagonistic, the two readings are complementary, both understanding the emergence of human and basic rights as a conquest of modernity.

Evidently, the simple declaration of basic rights in the constitution does not mean there is a conquest and realization of citizenship. It is essential that the constitution have normative power,[50] that is, it must be integrated to the experience and action of citizens and public agents, in the form of reciprocal rights and duties. Citizenship demands, therefore, the concretization of constitutional norms referring to basic rights. Lacking such concretization, only the text remains, without its generalized normative meaning. Only when the constitution is a reflex of the public sphere,[51] does citizenship exist and develop as a political and legal institution of social inclusion. If the concretization of the constitution is obstructed by political, economic, and cultural factors, the autonomous reproduction of law does not take place. Therefore, references to citizenship found in the constitutional text remain the pretty façade of a construction totally in ruins.

NONEXISTENT CITIZENSHIP: RELATIONS OF UNDER-INTEGRATION AND OVER-INTEGRATION

With citizenship defined as egalitarian legal integration in society, it can be affirmed that it is absent when relations of under-integration and over-integration in the constitutional system are generalized, as is the case in peripheral countries, particularly in Brazil. In this case, inclusion is not established as simultaneous access to and dependence on positive law. Strictly speaking, however, it does not refer to allopatric relations between human groups in social space.[52]

Concerning the under-integrated, the concrete relationships in which they do not have access to the benefits of the legal system are generalized, although the under-integrated remain dependent on its coercive rules. Therefore, the under-citizens are not excluded. Although they lack the real conditions to exercise the constitutionally declared basic rights, they are not freed of the duties and responsibilities imposed by the coercive state apparatus, which radically submits them to its punitive structures. The basic rights do not play a relevant role on the horizon of their action and experience, even in the identification of the sense of respective constitutional norms. For the under-integrated, the constitutional clauses are relevant almost exclusively in their effective restrictions on liberties. This is also true for the legal system as a whole: the members of "the marginalized" lower classes (a large part of the population) are integrated into the system, as a rule, as debtors, those who are indicted, charged, defendants, condemned, and so on, not as those who have rights, who are creditors, or who take legal actions. But, in the constitutional field, the problem of under-integration takes on a special significance, to the extent that, in relation to the members of the popular classes, offenses against basic rights are practiced principally in areas of activity of repression by the state apparatus.[53]

The under-integration of the masses is inseparable from the over-integration of privileged groups, which, principally with the support of the state bureaucracy, develop their actions that block the reproduction of law. It is true that the over-citizens regularly utilize the democratic constitutional text—in principle, as long as this is favorable to their interests and/or to the protection of the "social order." Normally, therefore, to the degree in which the Constitution imposes limits to their sphere of political and economic action, it is placed aside. It therefore does not act as a horizon of legal-political action and experience of the powerful, but as an offer that, according to their contingent constellation of interests, can be used, misused, or left in disuse by them. This being the case, the guarantee of impunity is one of the strongest traces of over-citizenship.[54]

The so-called principle of non-identification of the Constitution,[55] which is closely linked to the principle of the unavailability (*Unverrfugbarkeit*) of law and of the impartiality of the constitutional state[56] is absent in the context of relations of under-integration and over-integration in the constitutional system.[57] To a certain degree, the constitution is only made concrete if interests of privileged groups are not compromised. Constitutionality against the interests of over-citizenship "is not advisable"; "it is not suitable to the environment." (No simplistic schematization should be deduced from this because legal conflicts between the over-citizens occur also at the constitutional level, conflicts that are rarely resolved according to the constitution. But if the status quo is threatened, they tend to resort to conciliatory formulas that "break" or "erode" the constitution.) Social reforms within the "constitutional order" are frequently characterized as subversive, insofar as they place on the agenda the abolition of privileges and or the occasional introduction of measures favorable to the under-citizens. Subjacent to the formal non-identification in the established constitutional text, the identity of the constitutional reality with the privileged classes and groups is found, in such a way that the institutionalization of basic rights is structurally disfigured. The normative actions and experiences of the under-citizen and the over-citizen implode the constitution, considered as a basic order of legal communication.[58] In these conditions, the constitution does not act as a mechanism of operational autonomy of law, and is deformed during its concretization process by virtue of the superimposition of special political and economic interests. This places us before the problem of dejuridification.

DEJURIDIFICATION AS NEGATION OF CITIZENSHIP

The debate concerning juridification and dejuridification in peripheral societies should be faced from a perspective different to that which has been developed in the countries of central modernity. From the standpoint of the distinction made by Blankenburg[59] between juridification in the plane of expectations (the establishment of "more" legal rules in the place of informal regulations) and juridification on the plane of action ("more" effective law), it could be formulated that in the countries of the periphery, juridification in the sense of increasing production of positive legal state norms would be opposed to dejuridification on the plane of the regulation of behavior. From this point of view, dejuridification would be considered only in the realm of "action" (effectiveness), although the dejuridifying tendencies also include, in the conditions of reproduction of peripheral societies, principally in the field of constitutional law, the "experience" of law (the normative expectations).[60] The supposed filtering of expectations through the drawing of a constitution by a constituent assembly is not followed, in any way, by a generalized orientation of normative expectations according to the constitutional text, that is, it is not accompanied by the congruent generalization of normative-constitutional expectations.[61]

In contrast to the notion of a dejuridifying constitutional reality, in the framework of legal pluralism, the objection can be made that other legal forms act in the place of positive law for the resolution of conflicts.[62] Concerning this restriction, it should be mentioned that the debate about juridification and dejuridification refers to positive law as a differentiated social system.[63] The "alternatives" to the unsatisfactory operation of positive law imply, in peripheral societies, both an "ethical-social" discourse[64] as well as the non-mediated interference of the code of power and of the economic code in the mechanisms for the solution of conflicts. The fact that in this social context many "social units" of a super-complex society have different codes of what is "legal/illegal"[65] does not lead, in any manner, to a topical legal rationality, as took place in the case of a postmodern law,[66] but primarily, to extreme legal insecurity the maintenance of which is related, contradictorily, to the conservation of privileges, and which is, therefore, detrimental above all to the socially "handicapped" (the "under-integrated"). This type of situation does not represent any pluralism as an alternative to legalism,[67] but diffuse reactions to a lack of legality.

The postmodern legal model—to which Sousa Santos adhered[68] to give support to his conception of legal pluralism—cannot be applied in these conditions. By denying the unity of law as an operationally differentiated communications chain, the postmodern legal theory sustains that the legal system is pluralistically instituted as a communications network, importing (de)constructive uncertainty and instability.[69] The problem of dejuridification implies, in the situation of peripheral countries, destructive insecurity in relation to the practice of conflict resolution and the orientation of normative expectations.

The notion of a postmodern constitutionalism refers to the opening of the constitution to the fragmentation of society, presupposing the inexistence of universalistic criteria of regulation of the public sphere. The constitution is thus presented as a mechanism to stimulate the "autonomy of the context"[70] or as a guide to "networks of relationships" between topical action systems, without imposingly interfering in the establishment of limits for their development and reproduction.[71] In the case of peripheral modernity, there cannot be a constitution that promotes the development of fragmentary and unstable contexts of its social environment, to the degree in which this, as a condition of its functioning and concretization, act destructively in relation to it. The problem is in the lack of realization of the constitution itself as a legal space of citizenship, or, as the postmodernists would say, citizenships.

THE LACK OF IDENTITY/AUTONOMY OF A SPHERE OF LEGALITY

I have already noted that if on one hand the conquering and broadening of citizenship can be interpreted as a process of juridification, on the other, it is possible to conceive of the autonomy of the legal system as a condition for its realization. *Contrario sensu*, dejuridification, as a negative condition of citizenship, implies a lack of autonomy of the legal system. Or that is, as long as the identity of the sphere(s) of legality is not built upon a generalized concretization of the constitution, there is no space for citizenship. In the plane of social theory, this is one of the specific problems of peripheral modernity, which can be characterized as "negative modernity," based upon both the systemic perspective as well as the model with moral- or ethical-procedural pretensions.

In accordance with systems theory, modern society would result from the social hyper-complexity linked to the functional differentiation of the spheres of action and experience. It would thus imply the disappearance of moral contents valid for all of the communication contexts, and the rise of operationally autonomous social systems, reproduced according to their own codes and criteria, while conditioned by their surrounding environment (autopoiesis).[72] In peripheral modernity, the social hypercomplexity and the dissolution of "moralism" which founded hierarchical differentiation, does not lead to the construction of social systems that, while they interpenetrate and even interfere with each other, are built autonomously on their respective topos. This places us before de-structured and destructuring complexity. Much more complicated social problems result from this than that which characterize the countries of "central modernity." The relationships between the "fields" of action assume self-destructive and hetero-destructive forms, with all the well-known consquences. Therefore, modernity is not built positively, by surpassing tradition through the rise of autonomous systems of action, but only negatively, as hyper-complexity that disintegrates traditional hierarchical moralism.

According to the moral- or ethical-procedural conception proposed by Habermas, modernity would be the result of the evolution of the moral consciousness in the sense that there was an overcoming of the preconventional and conventional structures with the advent of a postconventional moral.[73] This indicates a clear differentiation between system and "lifeworld,"[74] the latter as a horizon of "communicative action," oriented to reaching intersubjective understanding, the former as a space of intermediation of "purposive rational action" (instrumental and strategic action).[75] In this perspective modernity would demand, positively, the construction of a "public sphere," democratic topos discursively autonomous in relation to the systems steering media "power" and "money." Although indications of this "normative" claim can be identified in "central modernity," it does not appear to encounter a minimum basis in the social relations of "peripheral modernity." Here, modernity is built negatively as the disintegration of the conventional moral consciousness (and also of the preconventional), without resulting in the structuring of a postconventional or universalistic moral consciousness and certainly not in the autonomy of a "public sphere."

Even if we start from the fragmented conception of postmodernity, its construction in peripheral countries would have a negative meaning. The principal theories of postmodernity develop the notion of topical rationality in counterpoint to generalized systemic rationality and universalistic reason. This situation would involve interconnections of (de)constructive uncertainties between topical systems of communication.[76] In the case of peripheral (post)modernity, the interrelations between the fields of action tend, unpredictably, to be obstructive and destructive entanglements. This situation of social confusion of communication codes and criteria is characterized by difficulties in the construction of identity of the legal system, which stem directly from the lack of autonomy of the respective sphere of action.

Concerning moral- or ethical-procedural theory, I have already noted that the separation of the preconventional, primitive moral and the premodern conventional moral does not lead, in peripheral modernity, to the construction and development of postconventional moral consciousness. This is because the moral basis of law's unavailability and impartiality, in contrast to its systemic instrumentality,[77] does not find space in the intersubjective relations that deal with law. The trend is toward the political instrumentation of the law, whether by means of casuistic mutation of the normative structures, principally during authoritarian periods, or through the play of special interests that block the process of concretizing legal norms. In this context, private autonomy ("human rights") and public autonomy ("popular sovereignty"), although as a rule declared in the constitutional text, are rejected through the mechanisms of political destructuring of the process of concretizing the constitution.

In the same way, the Luhmannian model of autopoiesis is not applicable to the legal reality of peripheral modernity, especially in Brazil. The particularistic superimpositions of the political and economic codes over the legal issues make impossible the construction of the identity of the legal system. Instead of autopoiesis, there is the allopoiesis of law.[78] This means that a sphere of legality does not arise that, in accordance with its own criteria and in a congruently generalized form, is apt to recycle the influences that stem from its economic and political context, as well as from the so-called good relations. The entanglement of the legal code(s) with other social codes acts self-destructively and hetero-destructively. The problem does not reside, in principle, in the lack of cognitive openness (hetero-reference or adaptation), but in the insufficient operational closure (self-reference), which would be an obstacle to the construction of the legal system's own identity. If this identity can be seen on the plane of the structure of the normative texts, it is gradually destroyed during the process of concretizing legal norms.[79] This being the case, the congruent generalization of normative expectations is not built, in a broad measure, based on the constitutional and legal texts. This means that the very distinction between legal and illegal becomes socially blurred, whether by the lack of institutionalization or by the lack of identification of meaning of norms.[80] The most serious consequence is the destructive insecurity found in the relations of conflict of interest.

The last resort would be to affirm the autonomy/identity of pluralist legal spheres of action, in the postmodern perspective of law. Nevertheless, in this case, legal rationality is presupposed as the topical congruence of normative expectations and as the (de)constructive process of making compatible dissent between local systems of action. It is exactly the self-destructive incongruences of the normative expectations and the hetero-destructive incompatibilities of dissent between fields of action that impede the construction of identity of sphere(s) of legality in peripheral modernity.

In this context of a lack of congruently generalized rights, or, at least, topically congruent rights, the construction and broadening of citizenship is not possible. Citizenship means exactly the egalitarian legal integration in society, implying laws that neutralize the eventual economic and political inequalities. If this does not occur, the relationships of under-citizenship and over-citizenship destructive to the identity of the legal system prevail.

POLITICAL-SYMBOLIC FUNCTION OF THE CONSTITUTIONAL DECLARATION OF BASIC RIGHTS IN THE BRAZILIAN LEGAL EXPERIENCE

I noted above that for the conquest and broadening of citizenship, the adoption of the value or moral semantics of human rights in the constitutional text, in the form of basic rights, is not a sufficient factor. For citizenship to be achieved, it is essential that constitutional norms that refer to basic rights be made concrete.

In the Brazilian legal-political experience, the broadening of the constitutional regulations concerning basic rights did not have substantial relevance in the process of concretizing the constitution. This then being the case, "citizenship," built and broadened apparently within the constitutional texts covers up a reality of noncitizenship. Excluding, in a schematic fashion, the authoritarian periods, when citizenship was denied at the level of the constitutional charters and laws themselves (1937 and 1964), a growing expansion of basic rights is observed without verifying, in the realm of constitutional reality, a relevant response in the sense of the construction of citizenship. From the period when civil rights were restricted to free men and freed slaves in the "Imperial Charter" of 1824, to the broad recognition of civil, political, social, and collective rights in the constitutional text of 1988, there would have been an intense process of conquering and developing citizenship. But this evolution in the scenery of the constitutional stage does not have relevant significance in the legal-political praxis.[81]

The meaning of the constitutional declarations of citizenship rights can thus be questioned given that they have a very limited degree of legal effectiveness. The response appears to me to be found in their symbolic political importance. Paradoxically, the degree to which the normative-legal effectiveness of the constitutional declarations of rights is reduced, their symbolic function is strengthened. There is a type of hypertrophy of their political symbolic dimension in detriment to their normative-legal function.[82]

In this context, citizenship arises as a symbolic topos of constitutional discourse. From the perspective of the powerful, the constitutional declarations of citizenship rights perform the role of an alibi.[83] The State and the respective legislators or government administrators rhetorically present themselves as being identified with the values or principles of citizenship, while obstacles to their realization are attributed to "society." From the perspective of critics of the status quo, the declaration of citizenship rights serves as a symbolic reference to the discourse for the transformation of the real relations of power. By proposing and defending the constitutional text with a broader range of basic rights, they symbolically justify to the public their actions for the conquest of citizenship. From both perspectives, citizenship as a symbolic topos remains as discourse. The more it is discussed in the political sphere the more intense are the obstacles to its realization.

To a certain degree, the symbolic discourse of citizenship serves to hide the reality wherein structural problems of under-integration and over-integration within society, being situations of under-citizenship and over-citizenship, are inseparably linked to the positions and relations of the respective political agents. The symbolic alibi of the "citizen discourse" transfers the responsibility for the obstacles to citizenship to another and makes more difficult, in a certain way, the development of an effective self-criticism by individuals and groups of their positions in relationships of over-citizenship and under-citizenship. In this perspective, the symbolic and ideological topos "citizenship" can serve more to maintain the status quo than to improve the generalized and egalitarian legal integration in society, that is, it acts to impede the realization of citizenship.

CONCLUSION

In the realm of the social sciences and legal studies with sociological intentions that have recently been presented in Brazil, there is a tendency to counter the fragility of "civil society" and citizenship with a strong State, guided by legalism. Underlying this understanding of the problem is the mistaken idea that the state legal order, in the Brazilian case as well, self-reproduces consistently by means of generalized legality of the activities of government officials and representatives. To the contrary, it is exactly the minimum legal presumption of the construction of citizenship, legality as a generalization of the law in the sense of inclusion, which is absent. In the relations of power, the illegality of the practices of government officials and representatives, social groups and individuals is generalized, privileging above all over-citizenship to the detriment of the under-citizens.

It appears clear to me that, in this context of a lack of operational autonomy of the state legal order, it is not appropriate to speak of the strong State as a counterpoint to the construction of citizenship. The State is permanently blocked by concrete special economic and political interests, based both on the privileges of over-citizenship as well as on the pressures of under-citizenship.

The identity of a State sphere in counterpoint to the private particularistic interests is not built in a consistent form; this is because there is no constitutional and legal filtering of the interferences of the economy and power in State action. This being the case, the generalized codes "money" and "power" not only condition the law, but are destructively superimposed on it.

Therefore, the conquest and expansion of citizenship, in the Brazilian case, requires the construction of a public space of legality which, on one hand would promote the identity of the State before private interests and, on the other, would allow the egalitarian legal integration of the entire population in society.

NOTES

Translation by Jeffrey Hoff. The original version of this chapter was published in *Dados: Revista de Ciências Sociai* 37 (1994): 253–76. For this publication, the author added some notes and comments regarding more recent publications.

1. In this limited perspective, civil rights are not properly included in the realm of citizenship (political) rights, in the first place they constitute a form of state-organized preexisting human rights.
2. Karl Marx, "Zur Judenfrage," in *Werke*, ed. Karl Marx and Friedrich Engels, v. I, 15th ed. (Berlin: Dietz Verlag, 1988), 361 ff., esp. 362 and 364.
3. Marx, "Zur Judenfrage," 357.
4. T. H. Marshall, *Class, Citizenship, and Social Development* (Westport, Conn.: Greenwood Press, 1976), 71 ff.; also see Reinhard Bendix, *Nation-Building and Citizenship: Studies of our changing social order* (Garden City, N.Y.: Anchor, 1969), 92 ff. Although one can criticize the linear formulation found in Marshall's model of the moments of emergence of civil, political, and social rights, emphasizing the political struggle and the social movements in the conquest and broadening of citizenship. See Jürgen Habermas, *Faktizität und Geltung: Beiträge zur Diskurstheorie des Rechts und des demokratischen Rechtsstaats* (Frankfurt am Main: Suhrkamp, 1992), 103; Anthony Giddens, "Class division, class conflict and citizenship rights," in *Profiles and Critiques in Social Theory*, ed. Anthony Giddens (London: Macmillan, 1982), 171–73, 176; J. M. Barbalet, *Citizenship: Rights, Struggle and Class Inequality* (Milton Keynes: Open University Press, 1988); David Held, "Citizenship and Autonomy," in *Political Theory and the Modern State*, ed. David Held (Cambridge: Polity Press, 1989), 214–42; Danilo Zolo, "Democratic Citizenship in a Post-communist Era," in *Prospect for Democracy: North, South, East, West*, ed. David Held (Cambridge: Polity Press, 1993), 254–68. One cannot deny the importance of the trichotomic classification of the citizenship rights for a better understanding of the democratic constitutional state as a result of a process of juridification.
5. Marshall, *Class, Citizenship, and Social Development*, 84.

6. Luc Ferry and Alain Renaut, *Philosophie politique 3—Des droits de l'homme à l'idée républicaine*, 3rd ed. (Paris: Presses Universitaires de France, 1992), 26–32.

7. Celso Lafer, *A Reconstrução dos Direitos Humanos: Um Diálogo com o Pensamento de Hannah Arendt* (São Paulo: Companhia das Letras, 1988), 131 ff. With restrictions to the "normative inflation of the concept of citizenship," Zolo points to "the risk of diluting its historical and functional significance": (Zolo, "Democratic Citizenship in a Post-communist Era," 258–59). See also Norberto Bobbio, *The Age of Rights* (Cambridge: Polity Press, 1996), xi and xvi, note 9, referring to the "too vague and heterogeneous" character of the concept of a "third generation of rights."

8. Mauro Cappelletti, "Formaciones Sociales e Intereses de Grupo frente a la Justicia Civil," *Boletin Mexicano de Derecho Comparado* (New Series) XI, no. 31–32 (1978): 1–40; Mauro Cappelletti and Bryant Garth, "Access to Justice and the Welfare State: An Introduction," in *Access to Justice and the Welfare State*, ed. Mauro Cappelletti (Alphen aan den Rijn: Sijthoff; Bruxelles: Bruylant; Stuttgart: Klett-Cotta; Firenze: Le Monnier, 1981), 11–14.

9. Dworkin, Ronald, *Taking Rights Seriously*, (London: Duckworth, 1991), 223–39.

10. The reverse discriminations, which import the introduction of *competitive advantages* to socially discriminated minorities (Dworkin, *Taking Rights Seriously*, 224, specifically concerning the question of minority racial groups in the United States), are not confused with "social rights" in the classic sense as generic mechanisms of compensation for social inequalities. But it is undeniable that these rights are frequently entangled in concrete legal-political practice. For example, in the analysis of the recent difficulties of social rights, Frankenberg ("Why Care? The Trouble with Social Rights," *Cardozo Law Review* 17, no. 4–5 (March 1996): 1365–90, points to a close connection of these rights to those referring to collective and diffuse interests and to those of the discriminated minorities (specially Frankenberg, "Why Care?" 1389).

11. Niklas Luhmann, *Ausdifferenzierung des Rechts* (Frankfurt am Main: Suhrkamp, 1981), 129; Niklas Luhmann, *Legitimation durch Verfahren* (Frankfurt am Main: Suhrkamp, 1983), 144; Niklas Luhmann, *Rechtssoziologie*, 3rd ed. (Opladen: Westdeutscher Verlag, 1987), 211.

12. Rüdiger Voigt, "Verrechtlichung in Staat und Gesellschaft," in *Verrechtlichung: Analysen zu Funktion und Wirkung von Parlamentalisierung, Bürokratisierung und Justizialisierung sozialer, politischer und ökonomischer Prozesse*, ed. Rüdiger Voigt (Königstein: Athenäum, 1980), 16; Jürgen Habermas, *Theorie des Kommunikativen Handelns*, 2nd ed. v. II (Frankfurt am Main: Suhrkamp), 524; Raymund Werle, "Aspekte der Verrechtlichung," *Zeitschrift für Rechtssoziologie* 3 (Opladen: Westdeutscher Verlag, 1982): 4.

13. Voigt, "Verrechtlichung in Staat und Gesellschaft," 18–23. Werle, ("Aspekte der Verrechtlichung," 5) defends limiting the concept of juridification to the increase of laws and decrees in a certain period. In contrast to this position, see Voigt, "Gegentendenzen zur Verrechtlichung: Verrechtlichung und Entrechtlichung im Kontext der Diskussion um den Wohlfahrtsstaat," in *Gegentendenzen zur Verrechtlichung* (Jahrbuch für Rechtssoziologie und Rechtstheorie 9) ed. Rüdiger Voigt, 18 (Opladen: Westdeutscher Verlag, 1983), considering the "qualitative aspects" of juridification.

14. Voigt, "Verrechtlichung in Staat und Gesellschaft," 30.
15. Habermas, *Theorie des Kommunikativen Handelns*, v. II, 524 ff.; Marcelo Neves, *Verfassung und Positivität des Rechts in der peripheren Moderne: Eine theoretische Betrachtung und eine Interpretation des Falls Brasilien* (Berlin: Duncker & Humblot, 1992), 31 ff.; Marcelo Neves, "A Crise do Estado: Da Modernidade Central à Modernidade Periférica—Anotações a partir do Pensamento Filosófico e Sociológico Alemão," *Revista de Direito Alternativo* 3 (1994): 68 f.; Gunther Teubner, "Verrechtlichung—Begriffe Merkmale, Grenzen, Auswege," in *Verrechtlichung von Wirtschaft, Arbeit und sozialer Solidarität: Vergleichende Analysen*, ed. Friedrich Kübler (Baden-Baden: Nomos, 1984), 301 f.; Voigt, "Gegentendenzen zur Verrechtlichung," 21 f.
16. Habermas, *Theorie des Kommunikativen Handelns*, v. II, 529.
17. John Rawls, *A Theory of Justice*, (Oxford: Oxford University Press, 1990), 221.
18. Bernardette Pedrosa, "Estado de Direito e Segurança Nacional," in *Anais da VII Conferência Nacional da Ordem dos Advogados do Brasil* (Curitiba, PR, May 7–12, 1978), 193.
19. For the distinction between negative and positive liberties see Isaiah Berlin, "Two Concepts of Liberty," in *Four Essays on Liberty*, ed. Isaiah Berlin (London and New York: Oxford University Press, 1975); Alessandro Passerin d'Entrèves, *La Dottrina dello Stato: Elementi di Analisi e di Interpretazione* (Torino: Giappichelli Passerin d'Entrèves, 1962); C. B. Macpherson, "Berlin's Division of Liberty," in *Democratic Theory: Essays in Retrieval*, ed. C. B. Macpherson, Clarendon Press (Oxford: Oxford University Press, 1990); Charles Taylor, "What's wrong with negative liberty," in *Philosophical Papers*, ed. Charles Taylor, v. 2 (Cambridge: Cambridge University Press); Habermas, *Faktizität und Geltung*, 325 ff., who associates them, respectively, to the concepts of citizenship of the "republicans" and of the "liberals" (Habermas, *Faktizität und Geltung*, 327 f.).
20. Clearly, the liberal State did not do away with the regulation of family and educational relationships; nevertheless, the intensification and broadening of this regulation will later characterize the social State.
21. Habermas, *Theorie des Kommunikativen Handelns*, v. II, 536.
22. Habermas, *Theorie des Kommunikativen Handelns*, v. II, 536.
23. Habermas, *Theorie des Kommunikativen Handelns*, v. II, 536.
24. Habermas, *Theorie des Kommunikativen Handelns*, v. II, 537.
25. Habermas, *Theorie des Kommunikativen Handelns*, v. II, 539.
26. Later, in relation to the democratic constitutional state, Habermas diverged from the dichotomic concept which opposed "law as a medium" to "law as an institution," defining law as a "transformer" between system and lifeworld (Habermas, *Faktizität und Geltung*, 77 f., 108 and 217). Nevertheless, the problem of juridification as "colonization of the lifeworld" remains: it presents itself in the cases in which, in the relationship between law's instrumentality and unavailability (Habermas, *Faktizität und Geltung*, 583 ff.; Habermas, "Wie ist Legitimität durch Legalität möglich?"), the instrumentality prevails over the unavailability with destructive effects for the autonomous reproduction of law.

27. Habermas, *Faktizität und Geltung*, 536 ff. This being the case, Nahamowitz's criticism (Peter Nahamowitz, "Reflexives Recht: Das unmögliche Ideal eines post-interventionistischen Steuerungskonzepts," *Zeitschrift für Rechtssoziologie* 6 (1985): esp. 42) of Teubner and Willke, was justified, to the degree that, in an attempt to unite Habermas's discourse ethics to Luhmann's systems theory, Teubner and Willke came to neoliberal conclusions about Habermas's concept of juridification (Gunther Teubner and Helmut Willke, "Kontext und Autonomie: Gesellschaftliche Selbststeuerung durch reflexives Recht," *Zeitschrift für Rechtssoziologie* 6 (1984): 24 and 29; Gunther Teubner, "Reflexives Recht: Entwicklungsmodelle des Rechts in vergleichender Perspektive," in *Archiv für Rechts- und Sozialphilosophie* 68 (1982): 26 f. and 41–44, who later modified his position: Gunther Teubner, *Recht als autopoietisches System* (Frankfurt am Main: Suhrkamp, 1989), 81 f. and 85 f.

28. About the concept of "loyalty of the masses" in the welfare state, see Wolf-Dieter Narr and Clauss Offe eds., *Wohlfahrtsstaat und Massenloyalität* (Köln: Kippenheuer & Witsch, 1975). Following the line of Offe, Ulrich K. Preuß, "Perspektiven von Rechtsstaat und Demokratie," *Kritische Justiz* 22 (1982): 2, refers to the "domestication of the class struggle by means of the juridification of the labor struggle." The notion of the "loyalty of the masses" is closely linked to Bendix's conception (Bendix, *Nation-Building and Citizenship,* 89) that the struggle of the masses in western developed countries is guided more by a search for integration ("participation") in the system than by a demand for a "new social order" and can be characterized as an expression of "a conservative cast of mind." Critical in relation to the conception of the "loyalty of the masses," Niklas Luhmann, *Politische Theorie im Wohlfahrtsstaat* (München: Olzog, 1981), 10, emphasizes the constant change in the motivations of individuals in the welfare state.

29. Luhmann, *Ausdifferenzierung des Rechts*, 419 ff.; Niklas Luhmann, "Die Einheit des Rechtssystems," *Rechtstheorie* 14 (1983): 129–54; Niklas Luhmann, "Einige Probleme mit 'reflexivem Recht'," *Zeitschrift für Rechtssoziologie* 6 (1985): 1–18; Niklas Luhmann, "Positivität als Selbstbestimmtheit des Rechts," *Rechtstheorie* 19 (1988): 11–27; Niklas Luhmann, *Das Recht der Gesellschaft* (Frankfurt am Main: Suhrkamp, 1993), 38 ff.; Neves, *Verfassung und Positivität des Rechts in der peripheren Moderne,* 34. Meanwhile, Luhmann, *Das Recht der Gesellschaft,* 38 f., regards the concept of positivity to be unsatisfactory insofar as it can be reproached for "decisionism" or understood as a concept contrary to the concept of natural law, that is, it does not amount rigorously to the operative autonomy of law.

30. Humberto R. Maturana and Francisco Varela, *Autopoiesis and Cognition: The Realization of the Living* (Dordrecht: D. Reidel Publishing Company, 1980), 73 ff.; Humberto R. Maturana and Francisco Varela, *Der Baum der Erkenntnis*, 3rd ed. (Bern, München, and Wien: Scherz), esp. 55–60; Humberto R. Maturana, *Erkennen: Die Organisation und Verkörperung von Wirklichkeit. Ausgewählte Arbeiten zur biologischen Epistemologie* (Braunschweig and Wiesbaden: Vieweg, 1982), esp. 141 f., 157 ff., 279 f.

31. See primarily Niklas Luhmann, *Soziale Systeme: Grundriß einer allgemeinen Theorie* (Frankfurt am Main: Suhrkamp 1987); Hans Haferkamp and Michael Schmid, eds., *Sinn, Kommunikation und soziale Differenzierung: Beiträge zu Luhmanns Theorie*

sozialer Systeme (Frankfurt am Main: Suhrkamp, 1987); Dirk Baecker *et al.*, eds., *Theorie als Passion: Niklas Luhmann zum 60* (Geburtstag and Frankfurt am Main: Suhrkamp, 1987), esp. 394 ff.; Gunther Teubner and Alberto Febbrajo, eds., "State, Law, and Economy as Autopoietic Systems: Regulation and autonomy in a new perspective" *EYSL – European Yearbook in the Sociology of Law* 91/92 (Milano: Giuffrè, 1992). For a criticism of the reception of the concept of autopoiesis by the social sciences see Walter L. Bühl, "Grenzen der Autopoiesis," *Kölner Zeitschrift für Soziologie und Sozialpsychologie* 39 (1989), with special reference to the Luhmannian paradigm (Bühl, "Grenzen der Autopoiesis," 229 ff.); and for a comprehensive perspective on Luhmann's systems theory, Werner Krawietz and Michael Welker, eds., *Kritik der Theorie sozialer Systeme: Auseinandersetzungen mit Luhmanns Hauptwerk*, 2nd ed. (Frankfurt am Main: Suhrkamp, 1992). For a discourse-theoretical critical reading see Habermas, *Faktizität und Geltung*, 573 ff.; Jürgen Habermas, *Der philosophische Diskurs der Moderne: Zwölf Vorlesungen* (Frankfurt am Main: Suhrkamp, 1988), 426 ff.; Jürgen Habermas, *Nachmetaphysisches Denken: Philosophische Aufsätze* (Frankfurt am Main: Suhrkamp, 1988), 30 f.; Danilo Zolo, "Autopoiesis: un paradigma conservatore," *Micro Mega* 1 no.86 (1986) designates autopoiesis as an ideologically conservative paradigm. In another context, see Marcelo Neves, "Da Autopoiese à Alopoiese do Direito," *Anuário do Mestrado em Direito* 5 (1992).

32. Niklas Luhmann, "Die Codierung des Rechtssystems," *Rechtstheorie* 17 (1986); Luhmann, *Das Recht der Gesellschaft*, 165 ff.

33. Luhmann, *Legitimation durch Verfahren*, 69; Teubner, "Reflexives Recht," 20: "Autonomy of law refers to the circularity of its self-reproduction and not to its causal independence from the environment": Teubner, *Recht als autopoietisches System*, 47. Thus, it does not deal with (causal) isolation (Luhmann, 1995a: 15; Luhmann, *Die Gesellschaft der Gesellschaft,* 68; Luhmann, *Das Recht der Gesellschaft,* 43 f.

34. Luhmann. "Die Einheit des Rechtssystems," 139.

35. Luhmann, 1990a, 10; Luhmann, *Das Recht der Gesellschaft,* 393 ff.

36. Luhmann, *Soziale Systeme: Grundriß einer allgemeinen Theorie,* 606; cf. also Luhmann, *Das Recht der Gesellschaft,* 76; Luhmann, *Die Gesellschaft der Gesellschaft,* 68).

37. Luhmann, "Einige Probleme mit 'reflexivem Recht,'" 17; Niklas Luhmann, *Die Wissenschaft der Gesellschaft* (Frankfurt am Main: Suhrkamp, 1990), 593 f. and 663 f.

38. "External developments are neither, on one hand, ignored, nor, on the other, directly converted, according to the scheme 'stimulus-response,' into internal effects, but rather they would be filtered according to the criteria of selectivity within the structure of the law and adapted to the internal logic of normative development" (Teubner, "Reflexives Recht," 21). Cf. *supra* note 13.

39. Habermas, *Faktizität und Geltung*, 565.

40. Habermas, "Wie ist Legitimität durch Legalität möglich?" 16. Cf. also Habermas, *Faktizität und Geltung*, esp. 599, where the expressions "judgment" and "ethical" in each case would be replaced with the words "opinion" and "moral."

41. Habermas, *Theorie des Kommunikativen Handelns*, vol. II, 359.

42. Luhmann, *Ausdifferenzierung des Rechts*, 147.

43. Habermas, *Faktizität und Geltung*, 111 ff.

44. Luhmann, *Politische Theorie im Wohlfahrtsstaat*, 25 ff.

45. See Luhmann, *Politische Theorie im Wohlfahrtsstaat*, 26 ff., 35 and 118; Niklas Luhmann, *Gesellschaftsstruktur und Semantik: Studien zur Wissenssoziologie der modernen Gesellschaft*, vol. 1 (Frankfurt am Main: Suhrkamp, 1980), 31 f. and 168; Niklas Luhmann, *Gesellschaftsstruktur und Semantik: Studien zur Wissenssoziologie der modernen Gesellschaft*, vol. 2 (Frankfurt am Main: Suhrkamp, 1981), 239. In this period, he insisted that inclusion was a distinctive characteristic of modern society. Later Niklas Luhmann, *Die Gesellschaft der Gesellschaft* (Frankfurt am Main: Suhrkamp, 1997), 169 f. and 618–34; Niklas Luhmann, *Soziologische Aufklärung 6: Die Soziologie und der Mensch* (Opladen: Westdeutscher Verlag, 1995), 237–64; Luhmann (Niklas Luhmann, "Jenseits von Barbarei," in: *Gesellschaftsstruktur und Semantik: Studien zur Wissenssoziologie der modernen Gesellschaft*, v. 4, ed. Niklas Luhmann (Frankfurt am Main: Suhrkamp, 1995), 146 ff.; Luhmann (*Das Recht der Gesellschaft*, 582 ff.) changed his position concerning the difference between inclusion and exclusion, affirming that it functions as a Meta-Difference or Meta-Code which mediates the codes of all functional systems (Luhmann, *Die Gesellschaft der Gesellschaft*, 632; Luhmann, *Das Recht der Gesellschaft*, 583). But if this is the case, it seems to me to be difficult to continue to maintain that modern society is primarily founded on the principle of functional differentiation and that the difference "system/environment" is the principal one within society. To be consistent, the proposal that inclusion/exclusion functions as a *meta-code* which mediates all other codes requires admitting that society is primarily differentiated according to this *meta-difference*. It is in this sense that Stichweh (Rudolf Stichweh, "Inklusion/Exklusion, funktionale Differenzierung und die Theorie der Weltgesellschaft," in *Soziale Systeme: Zeitschrift für soziologische Theorie 3* [Opladen: Leske Budrich, 1997], 132) interprets the late work of Luhmann. However, concerning inclusion/exclusion *versus* the (functional orientated) difference system/environment, both deal rather with competing distinctions within the modern world society.

46. Claude Lefort. "Droits de l'homme et politique," in *L'Invention Démocratique: Les limites de la domination totalitaire*, ed. Claude Lefort (Paris: Fayard, 1981), 64.

47. Marshall, *Class, Citizenship, and Social Development*, 112 f.

48. Habermas, *Theorie des Kommunikativen Handelns*, vol. I, 353 ff.; Habermas, *Faktizität und Geltung*, esp. 138 ff.)

49. Niklas Luhmann, *Grundrechte als Institution: Ein Beitrag zur politischen Soziologie* (Berlin: Duncker & Humblot, 1965), esp. 23–25.

50. Konrad Hesse, "Die normative Kraft der Verfassung," in *Ausgewählte Schriften*, ed. P. Häberle and A. Hollerbach (Heidelberg: Müller, 1984).

51. Peter Häberle, *Die Verfassung des Pluralismus: Studien zur Verfassungstheorie der offenen Gesellschaft* (Königstein/Ts.: Athenäum, 1980), 87.

52. Neves, *Verfassung und Positivität des Rechts in der peripheren Moderne*, 94 ff. and 155.

53. In these circumstances, the normative notion of "inclusion sensible to difference" (Jürgen Habermas, *Die Einbeziehung des Anderen: Studien zur politischen Theorie* [Frankfurt am Main: Suhrkamp, 1996], 172–75) have no contextual reference.

54. It is clear that there are no people who are "absolutely" over-integrated or under-integrated in the highly complex modern world, because these positions are not based, as in premodern societies, on solid principles or norms but depend on concrete factual conditions of communication reproduction. However, there are individuals or groups who are generally found in the privileged pole of relationships of over-integration and under-integration. For this reason they can guide their expectations and conduct their actions counting on a great probability of impunity. For a study that supports my position in reference to Latin America in general see Gillermo O'Donnell, "Polyarchies and the (Un) Rule of Law in Latin America: A Partial Conclusion," in *The Un (Rule) of Law and the Underprivileged in Latin America*, eds. Juan E. Méndez, Gillermo O'Donnell, and Paulo Sérgio Pinheiro (Notre Dame, Ind.: University of Notre Dame Press, 1999), esp. 312 and 332, note 47.

55. Herbert Krüger, *Allgemeine Staatslehre*, 2nd ed. (Stuttgart, Berlin, Köln and Mainz: Kohlhammer Verlag, 1966), 178–85; Alexander Hollerbach, "Ideologie und Verfassung," in *Ideologie und Recht*, ed. Werner Maihofer (Frankfurt am Main: Klostermann, 1969), 52–57; Luhmann (*Das Recht der Gesellschaft*, 96) objects to this principle, arguing that non-identity of the Constitution implies an option for pluralist values. However, when one talks about the "principle of non-identification," one intends only to deny the exclusive link of the constitution to a totalitarian value or to a dominant social group, for which it would be simply a tool. It does not imply denying that the constitution makes no reference to any value at all.

56. Habermas, "Wie ist Legitimität durch Legalität möglich?"; Habermas, *Faktizität und Geltung*, 583 ff.

57. Neves, *Verfassung und Positivität des Rechts in der peripheren Moderne,* 53 ff. and 95 ff.

58. Note that I prefer the terms "under-citizen" and "over-citizen" to the expression "first, second and third class citizens" (Gilberto Velho, "Violência e Cidadania," *DADOS—Revista de Ciências Sociais* 23, no. 3 [Rio de Janeiro: IUPERJ/Campus, 1980], 362; Francisco Corrêa Weffort, "A cidadania dos trabalhadores," in *Direito, cidadania e participação*, eds. Bolivar Lamounier, Francisco C. Weffort and Maria Victoria Benevides (São Paulo: T. A. Queiroz, 1981), 141–144, which can lead to the mistaken idea that only the under-integrated lack citizenship. On the other hand, the conceptual distinction that I propose, although analogous, is sharply distinct from the anthropological concepts of super-citizen and sub-citizen to which DaMatta refers (Roberto DaMatta, *A Casa & a Rua*, 4th ed. [Rio de Janeiro: Guanabara Koogan, 1991], 100), associating the first to a space without rights related to the "street" and the second to a sphere of privileges ("rights without duties") that is domestic (the "universe of the home"). It appears to me an anthropological excess to link, in the Brazilian reality, the domestic space of the under-integrated (marginalized) to the notion of the privileges and not recognize that the "world of the street" can constitute a space of privileges of the over-integrated.

From a distinct perspective, based primarily on dependence (duties, responsibilities etc.) and not on access (rights, actions etc.) as two aspects of the concept of inclusion, Luhmann (*Das Recht der Gesellschaft*, 584 f.; Luhmann, *Die Gesellschaft der Gesellschaft,* 631 ff.; 1995a: 259 ff.) affirms that the "sector of exclusion"

(*Inklusionsbereich*) is highly integrated (because it is more dependent), while inclusion allows less integration. Nevertheless, as I formulate, under-integration and over-integration imply insufficient inclusion, whether because of a lack of access or of dependence, respectively. This is because both under-citizens as well as over-citizens lack citizenship.

59. Erhard Blankenburg, "Recht als gradualisiertes Konzept—Begriffsdimensionen der Diskussion um Verrechtlichung und Entrechtlichung," in *Alternative Rechtsformen und Alternativen zum Recht* (Jahrbuch für Rechtssoziologie und Rechtstheorie, Vol. 6), eds. Erhard Blankenburg, E. Klausa, and H. Rottleuthner (Opladen: Westdeutscher Verlag, 1980), 84.

60. Concerning the distinction between "action" and "experience," see Niklas Luhmann, "Erleben und Handeln," in *Soziologische Aufklärung 3: Soziales System, Gesellschaft, Organisation*, 2nd ed., ed. Niklas Luhmann (Opladen: Westdeutscher Verlag, 1991). Concerning the corresponding differentiation between the regulation of behavior and the assurance of the normative expectations as functions of law, see Luhmann, *Ausdifferenzierung des Rechts*, 73–91.

61. About the concept of law as "congruent generalization of normative expectations of behavior" see Luhmann, *Rechtssoziologie*, 94–106.

62. Boaventura de Sousa Santos "The Law of the Oppressed: The Construction and Reproduction of Legality in Pasargada," *Law & Society Review* 12 (Denver, Colo.: Law and Society Association, 1977); "Notas sobre a História Jurídico-Social de Pasárgada," in *Sociologia e Direito: Leituras Básicas de Sociologia Jurídica*, eds. Cláudio Souto and Joaquim Falcão (São Paulo: Pioneira, 1980); *O discurso e o poder: ensaio sobre a sociologia da retórica jurídica* (Porto Alegre: Fabris, 1988).

63. See Voigt, *Gegentendenzen zur Verrechtlichung*, 20; Habermas, *Theorie des Kommunikativen Handelns*, vol. II, 524, who uses, however, the expression "written law."

64. Sousa Santos, *O discurso e o poder*, 25.

65. Sousa Santos, "Notas sobre a História Jurídico-Social de Pasárgada," 116, used the expression "possessive privatization of the law."

66. Karl-Heinz Ladeur, "Perspektiven einer post-modernen Rechtstheorie: Zur Auseinandersetzung mit N. Luhmanns Konzept der 'Einheit des Rechtssystems,'" in *Rechtstheorie* 16 (1985).

67. See, in an opposite sense, Sousa Santos, "The Law of the Oppressed," 89 ff.; Sousa Santos, *O discurso e o poder*, 25.

68. Boaventura de Sousa Santos, "Law: A Map of Misreading. Toward a Postmodern Conception of Law," *Journal of Law and Society* 14 (1987): 279–302.

69. Karl-Heinz Ladeur, "Perspektiven einer post-modernen Rechtstheorie"; "Selbstorganisation sozialer Systeme und Prozeduralisierung des Rechts: Von der Schrankenziehung zur Steuerung von Beziehungsnetzen," in *Wachsende Staatsaufgaben—sinkende Steuerungsfähigkeit des Rechts*, ed. Dieter Grimm (Baden-Baden: Nomos, 1990); "Gesetzinterpretation, 'Richterrecht' und Konventionsbildung in kognitivistischer Perspektive—Handeln unter Ungewißheitsbedingungen und richterliches Entscheiden," *Archiv für Rechts—und Sozialphilosophie* 77 (1991); *Postmoderne Rechtstheorie* (Berlin: Duncker & Humblot, 1992).

70. Gunther Teubner and Helmut Willke, "Kontext und Autonomie: Gesellschaftliche Selbststeuerung durch reflexives Recht," *Zeitschrift für Rechtssoziologie* 6 (1984); Teubner, "Reflexives Recht"; Gunther Teubner, "Gesellschaftsordnung durch Gesetzgebungslärm? Autopoietische Geschlossenheit als Problem für die Rechtssetzung," in *Gesetzgebungstheorie und Rechtspolitik* eds. D. Grimm and W. Maihofer (Jahrbuch für Rechtssoziologie und Rechtstheorie 13) (Opladen: Westdeutscher Verlag, 1988); Teubner, *Recht als autopoietisches System*, 81 ff.

71. Ladeur, "Selbstorganisation sozialer Systeme und Prozeduralisierung des Rechts."

72. See references *supra* at note 12.

73. Jürgen Habermas, *Zur Rekonstruktion des Historischen Materialismus*, 3rd ed. (Frankfurt am Main: Suhrkamp, 1982), esp. 12 ff.; Jürgen Habermas, *Moralbewußtsein und Kommunikatives Handeln* (Frankfurt am Main: Suhrkamp, 1983), 127 ff.

74. Social evolution itself is defined by Habermas (*Theorie des Kommunikativen Handelns*, vol. II, 229 ff.) as a process of differentiation between system and lifeworld.

75. In this respect, see, in different phases of development of the "theory of communicative action," Habermas (Jürgen Habermas, *Technik und Wissenschaft als 'Ideologie'* [Frankfurt am Main: Suhrkamp, 1969], 62–65; Jürgen Habermas, *Legitimationsprobleme im Spätkapitalismus* [Frankfurt am Main: Suhrkamp, 1973], 9 ff.; Habermas, *Theorie des Kommunikativen Handelns*, vol. I, esp. 384; Habermas, *Theorie des Kommunikativen Handelns*, vol. II, 182 ff.; Luhmann, "Die Codierung des Rechtssystems"; Habermas, *Nachmetaphysisches Denken: Philosophische Aufsätze*, 68 ff). When I refer to the system as space of intermediation of purposive rational action, I do not neglect that in Habermas's model, the system plane and the sphere of action are clearly distinct, and the notion of systemic rationality has a figurative meaning: "Changes of state of a self-regulated system can be understood as quasi-actions, *as if* in them the capacity for action of a subject is revealed" (Habermas, *Zur Rekonstruktion des Historischen Materialismus*, 261). But it is undeniable that, in Habermas's work, the notion of system is closely linked to purposive rationality and, therefore, to the concepts of instrumental and strategic action (see, e.g., Habermas, *Technik und Wissenschaft als 'Ideologie'*, 63–65; *Zur Rekonstruktion des Historischen Materialismus*, 261; "Erläuterungen zum Begriff des kommunikativen Handelns (1982)," in *Vorstudien und Ergänzungen zur Theorie des Kommunikativen Handelns*, 2nd ed., ed. Jürgen Habermas [Frankfurt am Main: Suhrkamp 1986], 578 f.), while the concept of "lifeworld" is associated intimately to that of communicative action (see, e.g., Habermas, *Theorie des Kommunikativen Handelns*, vol. II, esp. 182; Habermas, "Erläuterungen zum Begriff des kommunikativen Handelns (1982)," esp. 593).

76. Ladeur, "Perspektiven einer post-modernen Rechtstheorie"; "Selbstorganisation sozialer Systeme und Prozeduralisierung des Rechts"; "Gesetzinterpretation, 'Richterrecht' und Konventionsbildung in kognitivistischer Perspektive"; *Postmoderne Rechtstheorie*.

77. Habermas, *Faktizität und Geltung*, 583 ff.; Habermas, "Wie ist Legitimität durch Legalität möglich?"

78. Neves, *Verfassung und Positivität des Rechts in der peripheren Moderne*, esp. 81 ff. and 182 ff.; Neves, "Da Autopoiese à Alopoiese do Direito"; Neves, "A Crise do Estado: Da Modernidade Central à Modernidade Periférica," 72 f.

79. The Kelsenian concept of self-production of law (Hans Kelsen, *Reine Rechtslehre*, 2nd ed. (Wien: Franz Deuticke, 1960), esp. 73, 228 and 283) remains in the hierarchical structural plane of normative-legal order. Therefore, contrary to what Ost proposes (François Ost, "Entre ordre et désordre: le jeu du droit. Discussion du paradigme autopoïétique appliqué au droit," *Archives de Philosophie du Droit* 31 [1986], 141–44), it is not appropriate to link it to the autopoietic paradigm, which refers primarily to the operational level and to the circularity of the reproduction of law. This is because the first can be abstractly transported to different States, while the second demands certain concrete social conditions.

80. The institutionalization and the identification of meaning, in addition to normatization, are defined by Luhmann (*Rechtssoziologie*, 94 ff.) as mechanisms of generalization of law.

81. Neves, *Verfassung und Positivität des Rechts in der peripheren Moderne*, esp. 110 ff.; Marcelo Neves, *A Constitucionalização Simbólica* (São Paulo: Acadêmica,1994), 153 ff.

82. Neves, *Verfassung und Positivität des Rechts in der peripheren Moderne*, 61–65 and 104–106; Neves, *A Constitucionalização Simbólica*.

83. Neves, *A Constitucionalização Simbólica*, 37–40 and 92–95

BIBLIOGRAPHY

Baecker, Dirk et al., eds. *Theorie als Passion: Niklas Luhmann zum 60*. Geburtstag and Frankfurt am Main: Suhrkamp, 1987.

Barbalet, J. M. *Citizenship: Rights, Struggle and Class Inequality*. Milton Keynes: Open University Press, 1988.

Bendix, Reinhard. *Nation-Building and Citizenship: Studies of our changing social order*. Garden City, N.Y.: Anchor, 1969 First published 1964.

Berlin, Isaiah. "Two Concepts of Liberty (1958)." In *Four Essays on Liberty*, edited by Isaiah Berlin, 118–172. London and New York: Oxford University Press, 1975.

Blankenburg, Erhard. "Recht als gradualisiertes Konzept—Begriffsdimensionen der Diskussion um Verrechtlichung und Entrechtlichung." In *Alternative Rechtsformen und Alternativen zum Recht* (Jahrbuch für Rechtssoziologie und Rechtstheorie, vol. 6), edited by Erhard Blankenburg, E. Klausa, and H. Rottleuthner, 83–98. Opladen: Westdeutscher Verlag, 1980.

Bobbio, Norberto. *The Age of Rights*. Cambridge: Polity Press, 1996.

Bühl, Walter L. "Grenzen der Autopoiesis." *Kölner Zeitschrift für Soziologie und Sozialpsychologie* 39 (1989): 225–253.

Cappelletti, Mauro. "Formaciones Sociales e Interesses de Grupo frente a la Justicia Civil" *Boletin Mexicano de Derecho Comparado* (New Series) XI no. 31–32 (1978): 1–40.

Cappelletti, Mauro and Bryant Garth. "Access to Justice and the Welfare State: An Introduction." In *Access to Justice and the Welfare State*, edited by Mauro Cappelletti, 1–24. Alphen aan den Rijn: Sijthoff; Bruxelles: Bruylant; Stuttgart: Klett-Cotta; Firenze: Le Monnier, 1981.

DaMatta, Roberto. *A Casa & a Rua*. 4th ed. Rio de Janeiro: Guanabara Koogan, 1991.

Dworkin, Ronald. *Taking Rights Seriously*. London: Duckworth, 1991 First published 1977.

Ferry, Luc, and Alain Renaut. *Philosophie politique 3—Des droits de l'homme à l'idée républicaine*. 3rd ed. Paris: Presses Universitaires de France, 1992.

Frankenberg, Günter "Why Care? The Trouble with Social Rights." *Cardozo Law Review* 17, no. 4–5 (March 1996): 1365–90.

Giddens, Anthony. "Class division, class conflict and citizenship rights." In *Profiles and Critiques in Social Theory*, edited by Anthony Giddens. London: Macmillan, 1982.

Häberle, Peter. *Die Verfassung des Pluralismus: Studien zur Verfassungstheorie der offenen Gesellschaft*. Königstein/Ts.: Athenäum, 1980.

Habermas, Jürgen. *Technik und Wissenschaft als 'Ideologie'*. Frankfurt am Main: Suhrkamp, 1969.

———. *Legitimationsprobleme im Spätkapitalismus*. Frankfurt am Main: Suhrkamp, 1973.

———. *Zur Rekonstruktion des Historischen Materialismus*. 3rd ed. Frankfurt am Main: Suhrkamp, 1982.

———. *Theorie des Kommunikativen Handelns*. Vol. I and II. 2nd ed. Frankfurt am Main: Suhrkamp, 1982.

———. *Moralbewußtsein und Kommunikatives Handeln*. Frankfurt am Main: Suhrkamp, 1983.

———. "Erläuterungen zum Begriff des kommunikativen Handelns (1982)." In *Vorstudien und Ergänzungen zur Theorie des Kommunikativen Handelns*, 2nd ed., edited by Jürgen Habermas, 571–606. Frankfurt am Main: Suhrkamp, 1986.

———. "Wie ist Legitimität durch Legalität möglich?" *Kritische Justiz* 20 (1987): 1–16.

———. *Nachmetaphysisches Denken: Philosophische Aufsätze*. Frankfurt am Main: Suhrkamp, 1988.

———. *Der philosophische Diskurs der Moderne: Zwölf Vorlesungen*. Frankfurt am Main: Suhrkamp, 1988.

———. *Faktizität und Geltung: Beiträge zur Diskurstheorie des Rechts und des demokratischen Rechtsstaats*. Frankfurt am Main: Suhrkamp, 1992.

———. *Die Einbeziehung des Anderen: Studien zur politischen Theorie*. Frankfurt am Main: Suhrkamp, 1996.

Haferkamp, Hans and Michael Schmid, eds. *Sinn, Kommunikation und soziale Differenzierung: Beiträge zu Luhmanns Theorie sozialer Systeme*. Frankfurt am Main: Suhrkamp, 1987.

Held, David. "Citizenship and Autonomy." In *Political Theory and the Modern State*, edited by David Held, 214–42. Cambridge: Polity Press, 1989.

Hesse, Konrad. "Die normative Kraft der Verfassung." In *Ausgewählte Schriften*, edited by P. Häberle and A. Hollerbach, 3–18. Heidelberg: Müller, 1984.

Hollerbach, Alexander. "Ideologie und Verfassung." In *Ideologie und Recht*, edited by Werner Maihofer, 37–61. Frankfurt am Main: Klostermann, 1969.

Kelsen, Hans. *Reine Rechtslehre*. 2nd ed. Wien: Franz Deuticke, 1960.

Krawietz, Werner, and Michael Welker, eds. *Kritik der Theorie sozialer Systeme: Auseinandersetzungen mit Luhmanns Hauptwerk*. 2nd ed. Frankfurt am Main: Suhrkamp, 1992.

Krüger, Herbert. *Allgemeine Staatslehre*. 2nd ed. Stuttgart, Berlin, Köln and Mainz: Kohlhammer Verlag, 1966.

Ladeur, Karl-Heinz. "Perspektiven einer post-modernen Rechtstheorie: Zur Auseinandersetzung mit N. Luhmanns Konzept der 'Einheit des Rechtssystems.'" *Rechtstheorie* 16 (1985): 383–427.

——. "Selbstorganisation sozialer Systeme und Prozeduralisierung des Rechts: Von der Schrankenziehung zur Steuerung von Beziehungsnetzen." In *Wachsende Staatsaufgaben—sinkende Steuerungsfähigkeit des Rechts*, edited by Dieter Grimm, 187–216. Baden-Baden: Nomos, 1990.

——. "Gesetzinterpretation, 'Richterrecht' und Konventionsbildung in kognitivistischer Perspektive—Handeln unter Ungewißheitsbedingungen und richterliches Entscheiden" *Archiv für Rechts—und Sozialphilosophie* 77 (1991): 176–194.

——. *Postmoderne Rechtstheorie*. Berlin: Duncker & Humblot, 1992.

Lafer, Celso. *A Reconstrução dos Direitos Humanos: Um Diálogo com o Pensamento de Hannah Arendt*. São Paulo: Companhia das Letras, 1988

Lefort, Claude. "Droits de l'homme et politique." In *L'Invention Démocratique: Les limites de la domination totalitaire*, edited by Claude Lefort, 45–83. Paris: Fayard, 1981.

Luhmann, Niklas. *Grundrechte als Institution: Ein Beitrag zur politischen Soziologie*. Berlin: Duncker & Humblot, 1965.

——. *Gesellschaftsstruktur und Semantik: Studien zur Wissenssoziologie der modernen Gesellschaft*, vol. 1. Frankfurt am Main: Suhrkamp, 1980.

——. *Ausdifferenzierung des Rechts*. Frankfurt am Main: Suhrkamp, 1981.

——. *Politische Theorie im Wohlfahrtsstaat*. München: Olzog, 1981.

——. *Gesellschaftsstruktur und Semantik: Studien zur Wissenssoziologie der modernen Gesellschaft*, vol 2. Frankfurt am Main: Suhrkamp, 1981.

——. *Legitimation durch Verfahren*. Frankfurt am Main: Suhrkamp, 1983.

——. "Die Einheit des Rechtssystems," *Rechtstheorie* 14 (1983): 129–54.

——. "Einige Probleme mit 'reflexivem Recht,'" *Zeitschrift für Rechtssoziologie* 6 (1985): 1–18.

——. "Die Codierung des Rechtssystems," *Rechtstheorie* 17 (1986): 171–203.

——. *Rechtssoziologie*. 3rd ed. Opladen: Westdeutscher Verlag, 1987.

——. *Soziale Systeme: Grundriß einer allgemeinen Theorie*. Frankfurt am Main: Suhrkamp, 1987.

——. "Positivität als Selbstbestimmtheit des Rechts," *Rechtstheorie* 19 (1988): 11–27.

——. "Interesse und Interessenjurisprudenz im Spannungsfeld von Gesetzgebung und Rechtsprechung," *Zeitschrift für Neuere Rechtsgeschichte* 12 (Wien: Manz, 1990): 1–13.

——. *Die Wissenschaft der Gesellschaft.* Frankfurt am Main: Suhrkamp, 1990.

——. "Erleben und Handeln." In *Soziologische Aufklärung 3: Soziales System, Gesellschaft, Organisation,* 2nd ed., edited by Niklas Luhmann, 67–80. Opladen: Westdeutscher Verlag, 1991.

——. *Das Recht der Gesellschaft.* Frankfurt am Main: Suhrkamp, 1993.

——. *Soziologische Aufklärung 6: Die Soziologie und der Mensch.* Opladen: Westdeutscher Verlag, 1995.

——. "Jenseits von Barbarei." In *Gesellschaftsstruktur und Semantik: Studien zur Wissenssoziologie der modernen Gesellschaft,* vol. 4, edited by Niklas Luhmann, 138–150. Frankfurt am Main: Suhrkamp, 1995.

——. *Die Gesellschaft der Gesellschaft,* vols. I and II. Frankfurt am Main: Suhrkamp, 1997.

Macpherson, C. B. "Berlin's Division of Liberty." In *Democratic Theory: Essays in Retrieval,* edited by C. B. Macpherson, 95–119. Oxford: Oxford University Press (Clarendon Press), 1990.

Marshall, T. H. *Class, Citizenship, and Social Development.* Westport, Conn.: Greenwood Press, 1976.

Marx, Karl. "Zur Judenfrage." In *Werke,* vol. I, 15th ed., edited by Karl Marx and Friedrich Engels, 347–377. Berlin: Dietz Verlag, 1988. (first published in *Deutsch-Französische Jahrbücher,* Paris, 1944).

Maturana, Humberto R. *Erkennen: Die Organisation und Verkörperung von Wirklichkeit. Ausgewählte Arbeiten zur biologischen Epistemologie.* Braunschweig and Wiesbaden: Vieweg, 1982.

Maturana, Humberto R. and Francisco J. Varela. *Autopoiesis and Cognition: The Realization of the Living.* Dordrecht: D. Reidel Publishing Company, 1980.

——. *Der Baum der Erkenntnis.* 3rd ed. Bern, München, and Wien: Scherz, 1987

Nahamowitz, Peter. "'Reflexives Recht': Das unmögliche Ideal eines post-interventionistischen Steuerungskonzepts," *Zeitschrift für Rechtssoziologie* 6 (1985): 29–44.

Narr, Wolf-Dieter, and Claus Öffe, eds. *Wohlfahrtsstaat und Massenloyalität.* Köln: Kippenheuer & Witsch, 1975.

Neves, Marcelo. *Verfassung und Positivität des Rechts in der peripheren Moderne: Eine theoretische Betrachtung und eine Interpretation des Falls Brasilien.* Berlin: Duncker & Humblot, 1992.

——. "Da Autopoiese à Alopoiese do Direito." *Anuário do Mestrado em Direito* 5 (1992): 273–98.

——. "A Crise do Estado: Da Modernidade Central à Modernidade Periférica— Anotações a partir do Pensamento Filosófico e Sociológico Alemão," *Revista de Direito Alternativo* 3 (1994): 64–78.

——. *A Constitucionalização Simbólica,* São Paulo: Acadêmica, 1994.

——. "Do Pluralismo Jurídico à Miscelânea Social: O Problema da Falta de Identidade da(s) Esfera(s) de Juridicidade na Modernidade Periférica e suas Implicações na América Latina," *Direito em Debate,* 5 (Ijuí: UNIJUÍ, 1995): 7–37.

O'Donnell, Gillermo. "Polyarchies and the (Un)Rule of Law in Latin America: A Partial Conclusion." In *The Un(Rule) of Law and the Underprivileged in Latin Amer-*

ica, edited by Juan E. Méndez, Gillermo O'Donnell, and Paulo Sérgio Pinheiro, 303–337. Notre Dame, Ind.: University of Notre Dame Press, 1999.

Ost, François. "Entre ordre et désordre: le jeu du droit. Discussion du paradigme autopoïétique appliqué au droit," *Archives de Philosophie du Droit*, 31 (1986): 133–62.

Passerin d'Entrèves, Alessandro. *La Dottrina dello Stato: Elementi di Analisi e di Interpretazione*. Torino: Giappichelli, 1962.

Pedrosa, Bernardette. "Estado de Direito e Segurança Nacional." In *Anais da VII Conferência Nacional da Ordem dos Advogados do Brasil*, 185–201. Curitiba, PR, May 7–12, 1978.

Preuß, Ulrich K. "Perspektiven von Rechtsstaat und Demokratie," *Kritische Justiz* 22 (1989): 1–12.

Rawls, John. *A Theory of Justice*. Oxford: Oxford University Press, 1990. (first published 1972).

Sousa Santos, Boaventura de. "The Law of the Oppressed: The Construction and Reproduction of Legality in Pasargada," *Law & Society Review* 12 (Denver, Colo.: Law and Society Association, 1977): 5–126.

———. "Notas sobre a História Jurídico-Social de Pasárgada." In *Sociologia e Direito: Leituras Básicas de Sociologia Jurídica*, edited by Cláudio Souto and Joaquim Falcão, 109–117. São Paulo: Pioneira, 1980.

———. "Law: A Map of Misreading. Toward a Postmodern Conception of Law." *Journal of Law and Society* 14 (1987): 279–302.

———. *O discurso e o poder; ensaio sobre a sociologia da retórica jurídica*. Porto Alegre: Fabris, 1988.

Stichweh, Rudolf. "Inklusion/Exklusion, funktionale Differenzierung und die Theorie der Weltgesellschaft." In *Soziale Systeme: Zeitschrift für soziologische Theorie 3* (Opladen: Leske + Budrich, 1997): 123–36.

Taylor, Charles. "What's wrong with negative liberty." In *Philosophical Papers*, vol. 2, edited by Charles Taylor, 211–29. Cambridge: Cambridge University Press, 1985.

Teubner, Gunther. "Reflexives Recht: Entwicklungsmodelle des Rechts in vergleichender Perspektive," *Archiv für Rechts—und Sozialphilosophie* 68 (1982): 13–59.

———. "Verrechtlichung—Begriffe Merkmale, Grenzen, Auswege." In *Verrechtlichung von Wirtschaft, Arbeit und sozialer Solidarität: Vergleichende Analysen*, edited by Friedrich Kübler, 289–344. Baden-Baden: Nomos, 1984.

———. "Gesellschaftsordnung durch Gesetzgebungslärm? Autopoietische Geschlossenheit als Problem für die Rechtssetzung." In *Gesetzgebungstheorie und Rechtspolitik* (Jahrbuch für Rechtssoziologie und Rechtstheorie 13), edited by D. Grimm and W. Maihofer, 45–64. Opladen: Westdeutscher Verlag, 1988.

———. *Recht als autopoietisches System*. Frankfurt am Main: Suhrkamp, 1989.

Teubner, Gunther, and Alberto Febbrajo, eds. "State, Law, and Economy as Autopoietic Systems: Regulation and autonomy in a new perspective" *EYSL—European Yearbook in the Sociology of Law* 91/92. Milano: Giuffrè, 1992.

Teubner, Gunther, and Helmut Willke. "Kontext und Autonomie: Gesellschaftliche Selbststeuerung durch reflexives Recht," *Zeitschrift für Rechtssoziologie* 6 (1984): 4–35.

Velho, Gilberto. "Violência e Cidadania," *DADOS—Revista de Ciências Sociais* 23, no. 3 (Rio de Janeiro: IUPERJ/Campus, 1980): 361–364.

Voigt, Rüdiger. "Verrechtlichung in Staat und Gesellschaft." In *Verrechtlichung: Analysen zu Funktion und Wirkung von Parlamentalisierung, Bürokratisierung und Justizialisierung sozialer, politischer und ökonomischer Prozesse*, edited by Rüdiger Voigt, 15–37. Königstein: Athenäum, 1980.

———. "Gegentendenzen zur Verrechtlichung: Verrechtlichung und Entrechtlichung im Kontext der Diskussion um den Wohlfahrtsstaat." In *Gegentendenzen zur Verrechtlichung* (Jahrbuch für Rechtssoziologie und Rechtstheorie 9), edited by Rüdiger Voigt, 17–41. Opladen: Westdeutscher Verlag, 1983

Weffort, Francisco Corrêa. "A cidadania dos trabalhadores." In *Direito, cidadania e participação*, edited by Bolivar Lamounier, Francisco C. Weffort, and Maria Victoria Benevides, 139–50. São Paulo: T. A. Queiroz, 1981.

Werle, Raymund. "Aspekte der Verrechtlichung." *Zeitschrift für Rechtssoziologie* 3 (1982): 2–13.

Zolo, Danilo. "Autopoiesis: un paradigma conservatore." *Micro Mega* 1 no. 86 (1986): 129–173.

———. "Democratic Citizenship in a Post-communist Era." In *Prospect for Democracy: North, South, East, West*, edited by David Held, 254–68. Cambridge: Polity Press, 1993.

4

The Paraguayan War: A Constitutional, Political, and Economic Turning Point for Brazil[1]

Thomas E. Skidmore

On November 12, 1864, the Paraguayan war-steamer *Tacuarí* set out to pursue the Brazilian steamer *Marquez de Olinda*, then heading upstream from Ascunción on the Paraná river. The faster *Tacuarí* soon overtook the Brazilian steamer and launched a shot across its bows, forcing it back to Ascunción. The Paraguayans then imprisoned the Brazilian crew and passengers, which included the governor-elect of the Brazilian province of Mato Grosso. This military operation was carried out on the direct orders of the Paraguayan dictator Francisco Solano Lopez, who subsequently had the ship's flag made into a rug for his presidential office.[2] It would not be the last of his defiant gestures toward his more powerful neighbor. A month later Paraguayan troops invaded Mato Grosso, overwhelming the Brazilian defenders.

The Paraguayans were not acting on whim. Their leader, Solano Lopez, believed that Brazil's intervention in Uruguay (including an invasion by Brazilian troops) in 1863–1864 had upset the power balance in the Plata basin and thereby threatened Paraguayan independence. By his bellicose reaction, however, Solano had triggered Brazil's greatest fear, which was that a hostile power might cut off the riverine access to its interior provinces, especially Mato Grosso. That fear became reality when the *Marquez de Olinda* was seized and its occupants ushered off to prison camp.

Why was Brazil subject to this attack on its flank? Why did Rio have to resort to such a roundabout route to communicate within its own kingdom? The answer is that overland transportation was very difficult and insecure. There were no proper roads, only uncertain paths that could defeat the best efforts of mule and wagon teams. Thus it was that the Empire could only achieve secure communication with its distant southwestern provinces by sending its steamers up the Plate and Paraná rivers.

The seizure of the *Marquez de Olinda* was only one in a long chain of power clashes that had occurred since the mid-1850s in the Plata basin. But it was enough to convince Brazil that war was becoming inevitable. From 1864 to 1870 the battle raged between the subsequently formed Triple Alliance (Argentina, Brazil, and Uruguay) and Paraguay.[3] What was at stake? Territory? Economic influence? National prestige? The mania of a few leaders? The answer is all the foregoing, but the interpretation of them depends on the nationality of the authors one reads. Perhaps on no other topic of South American history is opinion more divided (the War of the Pacific being a strong contender.)

One thing is certain, however. The war and the chain of events it set in motion proved a profound turning point for Brazil—a turning point symbolized by the fate of three powerful figures of the period, the Emperor Dom Pedro II; the Duke of Caxias, the leader of the Brazilian military forces; and Baron Mauá, a leading banker and industrialist with major financial interests in the Plata.

DOM PEDRO II AND THE END OF THE EMPIRE

In 1864 the Empire was at its zenith. Economically it had improved its foreign finances thanks to its near monopoly on the world coffee trade. Politically it had consolidated national unity, based on an elected legislature, and it had survived the manifold regionalist revolts of the 1830s and 40s. Socially the Empire had remained an agrarian society, dependent on slave labor (despite the end of the slave trade in 1850). Yet slavery had not yet aroused powerful opposition, unlike in the United States. In sum, Brazil was a vast haven of apparent stability in a continent where candillos and coups d'etat were commonplace.

But Brazil in 1864 could be viewed through another, less optimistic, lens. Its economy was tied to one agro-export, coffee. Economic diversification was minimal and industrial development almost nil. Electorally, the Empire rested on a narrow franchise with few prospects for democratization. Socially it clung to slavery in a world that had largely repudiated legal bondage. The Empire had its critics, but their voices were little heard. When the Paraguayans seized the *Marquez de Olinda*, few of the Brazilian elite, had they noticed it, would have thought conflict in the Plata could much affect their nation. The Emperor, for example, was optimistic. He thought the war would be "a nice electrical shock to our nationality."[4]

How did the war change the emperor's historical role?[5] If Solano Lopez turned out to the central figure in the Paraguayan War, Dom Pedro II was a close second. In 1864 the emperor had been on the throne for almost a quarter century. Starting his reign as a mere fifteen-year-old, Pedro had grown up to earn a reputation as a level-headed, discreet, sensible, and moderate monarch. Unlike his father, he had kept his extra-mural amorous life out of public view, thereby earning a reputation for Victorian rectitude.

One of the secrets of the Brazil empire's political stability over which Dom Pedro presided had been the skill with which the Conservative Party had dominated politics in the 1850s. This Conservative ascendancy had broken down in the early 1860s, however, as the Liberals rose in political influence.[6] The increasing acrimony of the resulting party competition complicated the role of Dom Pedro, who was supposed to act as the "moderating power" in the imperial constitutional system.

The war against Paraguay turned out to absorb the Emperor more than any other event in his long reign. In the course of the conflict, his moderate, discreet image faded. He became the implacable commander-in-chief, locked in combat to the death. For Dom Pedro, Solano Lopez was the bête noir, the evil influence who had to be extinguished.[7]

The Emperor's involvement in the war came early. In July 1865, when the Paraguayan invaders had reached the province of Rio Grande do Sul, Dom Pedro traveled to the battle front. He witnessed the Allied siege of Uruguayana, which resulted in a Paraguayan surrender. As the vanquished troops emerged, Dom Pedro insisted on humane treatment of the Paraguayan prisoners. After the battle the Emperor returned to Rio, determined to monitor every Brazilian effort in a war which was expected to be brief.

But no one in the Triple Alliance had counted on the Paraguayan will to resist. The Allies, which soon consisted primarily of the Brazilians (The Argentines and Uruguayans were largely in the process of withdrawing), pushed the Paraguayan troops off Brazilian soil and back onto their home ground, but the war was far from won. Although the Brazilians inflicted huge losses on the enemy, the Paraguayans fought a guerrilla-style war that confounded the inexperienced and ill-trained Brazilian troops.

The Brazilians were weakened by their lack of military preparedness. In fact, when the war began in 1864 Brazil had no national army. Instead, it depended on the National Guard, a type of militia which was closely tied to each locality or region where its units were located. When the Paraguyan War broke out, the imperial government appealed for volunteers. Although the initial response was heartening, enthusiasm soon waned. As the demand for combat troops grew, the Brazilian commanders urged the cabinet to act. They did so by authorizing the crown to purchase slaves for service in the army who would then be given their freedom after fighting in Paraguay. Later the offer was broadened to include any slave who agreed to join. Thus was felt one of the first long-term effects of the war. Under the pressure of foreign combat the first nail was pounded into the coffin of slavery.[8]

As the war dragged on, the United States offered in early 1867 to mediate a settlement. The Paraguayans, seeing no hope of victory, agreed. But Dom Pedro, in one of the most important decisions of his reign, refused. "Never," he proclaimed, adding that "We did not provoke the war and we will not propose the peace! If the sacrifice is enormous, the humiliation would be greater. Now we must keep on until the end!"[9] From that moment the Emperor became Brazil's greatest enthusiast for unconditional war. Dom Pedro was determined to see Solano Lopez captured, killed, or driven into exile. The Brazilian monarch had merely reinforced the image of Solano Lopez as the supreme symbol of Paraguay.

Dom Pedro's obsession led to a chain of events that proved fatal to his rule and, indeed, the empire itself. The initial link in the chain was the Brazilian army's inability to get their hands on Solano Lopez. Indeed, many of the officers considered the pursuit to be ignoble and pointless. That in turn frustrated the Emperor, who was determined to remove his archenemy from power. The second link in the chain was the growing war-weariness of the Brazilian public and its political leaders.

Dom Pedro's declaration of unconditional war against Solano Lopez forced the Emperor to break the unwritten rules of the imperial political system by summoning a Conservative cabinet despite the Liberal Party's majority in the lower house. Dom Pedro had been driven to take this step because the Liberal cabinet, headed by Zacharias de Góes e Vasconcellos, had failed to show wholehearted legislative support for the war. The Emperor had been pressured to act by the threatened resignation of the Duke of Caxias, the Allied Commander in Paraguay. Caxias was, not coincidentally, a prominent member of the Conservative Party (more on this below). Not surprisingly this act incensed the Liberals, who were already harboring a wing of dissidents who advocated the shrinking of imperial power. That dissident wing subsequently broke away altogether and founded the Republican Party in 1870. It was not by chance that the founding of that party coincided with the end of the war. It was those Republicans who produced the rationale for the overthrow of the Empire in 1889. The Emperor's obsession with Solano Lopez, finally satisfied when he was killed by Brazilian troops in 1870, had undermined Dom Pedro's own constitutional position.

What legacy did this create for Brazil? First, it dramatized the vulnerability of civilian power. The Emperor had relied once too often on his old friend Caxias, the father figure who had been his equestrian tutor and who had saved the monarchy in so many regional revolts. It was this same general-politician whose hospitality to the Liberals influenced Dom Pedro's 1868 decision to call for a Conservative cabinet. The Emperor became in 1889 the first—but was to be far from the last—representative of Brazilian civilian authority to be summarily expelled from power. Second, the fall of the Empire, so closely linked to Brazil's prolonged combat in the Plata, broke the last formal link with Portugal. The House of Braganza, which had surmounted so many challenges to its rule in the New World, finally succumbed to the Republican wave that had inundated all of America, save Cuba and Puerto Rico.[10]

THE DUKE OF CAXIAS AND THE RISE OF THE MILITARY IN BRAZILIAN POLITICS

The Duke of Caxias (who gained that title in 1868) is Brazil's greatest military hero.[11] He received his first title of Baron after having led the pro-monarchy forces in the defeat of the Balaiada revolt in the province of Maranhão from 1839 to 1841. Only a few years later he was called upon to confront a much more dangerous rebellion in Rio Grande do Sul. That conflict lasted ten years, from 1835 to 1845. During his command Caxias revealed an exceptional ability to achieve military victory, but also to negotiate a lasting peace afterward.

Caxias went on to enjoy a prominent political career in the Conservative party, twice serving as minister of war. Then came the final phase of Caxias's military glory. In late 1866 he was given command of the Brazilian forces in Paraguay, and soon thereafter the command of the entire Triple Alliance. He promptly demonstrated his familiar skills and led the troops in a series of decisive victories in 1867. In 1868 Caxias reacted angrily to criticism of his military leadership that was coming from Liberal party politicians back in Rio. He wrote a letter offering to resign as commander. The Emperor was deeply worried that Caxias's departure might cut short Brazil's crusade to capture or eliminate Solano Lopez.

Under pressure from Caxias, Dom Pedro decided to dismiss the Liberal cabinet and to summon a Conservative cabinet. The implications were multiple. First, the Emperor would be calling for a cabinet that lacked majority support in the lower house. Second, he was now favoring Caxias's own party. The result was the appearance of clear intervention by a military commander in civilian politics back home.

Caxias withdrew his threatened resignation and stayed on as commander until 1869, when he was succeeded by the Conde d'Eu, son-in-law of the Emperor. After the war Caxias returned to politics and was for three more years (1875–1878) the minister of war.

What was the legacy of Caxias's role in the Paraguayan War? On first
glance it was heroic. He was the legendary soldier who had once again
served the monarchy on the battlefield. But seen in a longer perspective, the
historical profile of Caxias takes a different shape. Brazil was to suffer
thereafter from a plague of general-politicians for whom the Duke was a
model. The Republic, for example, began in 1889 as a military coup. Its first
stewards were two generals, Deodoro Fonseca and Floriano Peixoto, whose
careers had been accelerated by their combat commands in the Paraguayan
War. 1889 was the beginning of a long series of military interventions in politics, lasting into the 1980s. The pattern of military presidents (1889–1894)
at the outset of the Republic gave way to civilian rule in 1894, but the military note was reintroduced by General Hermes da Fonseca in his successful
presidential campaign of 1910. His army handlers subsequently steered the
hapless general into a series of disastrous military interventions in state politics. The *tenente* revolts of the early 1920s brought a largely different,
younger generation of officers into politics. The Caxias of the Vargas era was
General Góes Monteiro. Like almost all modern Brazilian generals, and unlike Caxias, his combat had been limited to the barracks rooms and the Club
Militar. The coup of 1964 brought another parade of would-be Caxias
heirs—Castelo Branco, Costa e Silva, Médici, Geisel, Figueiredo. Once
again the generals believed that they alone knew which Brazilians could be
trusted. Finally, in 1985 the shadow of Caxias lifted with the return of civilian government.

BARON MAUÁ AND BRAZIL'S FAILURE
TO MODERNIZE THE ECONOMY

Baron Mauá was the prototype of the nineteenth-century entrepreneur who
saw how badly Brazil needed to modernize its infrastructure and begin industrialization.[12] He was responsible for the first gas lamp system built in
Brazil and the first steamship company that operated on the Amazon river. He
was also active in railroad construction and installing modern water systems
in Rio de Janeiro.

Mauá had also extended his operations far into Uruguay and Argentina. He
founded his own bank in 1854 and quickly became the principal creditor to the
Uruguayan government. This was to make him highly vulnerable when
the political storm hit Uruguay in the early 1860s. His bank suffered enormous
losses during the Paraguayan War, and in 1875 he was forced to declare a
moratorium on his bank's payments. Three years later he had to admit bankruptcy, and spent the rest of his years, until his death in 1889, struggling to pay

off his debts. The turning point in his career had been the losses caused by the Paraguayan War.

Mauá has often been seen as a visionary who overstepped his bounds, yet he had been Brazil's greatest hope for a vigorous effort to lift the country out of its eternal role as an agro-exporter. His demise and the lack of support he received in Brazil showed that Brazil's economic modernization was still decades away. If it had not been for the Paraguayan War and the great losses it brought to Mauá, the economic history of the last two decades of the empire might have been very different.[13]

CONCLUSION

The Paraguayan War was not only a disaster for Paraguay, it also had serious deleterious effects on Brazil. The Emperor became caught up in the self-righteous pursuit of a foreign demon. The Duke of Caxias set the pattern for military contempt toward the civilians. Mauá found himself deprived of the resources to continue his ambitious economic plans. In sum, Brazil was deprived of an opportunity to enter the twentieth century early.

Was the Paraguayan War as important a causal factor as I argue? Was Dom Pedro already on a fatal collision course with his political critics? Was Caxias's intervention in parliamentary politics in 1868 so unprecedented? Would Mauá's hubris have led him to financial ruin in any case?

At the least, their involvement in the war intensified the direction in which each man's career was heading. And by this bloody conflict over which no one had control, three prominent Brazilians were thrown into a historical maelstrom which none could have foreseen.

NOTES

Prepared for the Brazilian Studies Association (BRASA) meeting. Washington, D.C. November 13–15, 1997.

1. Indispensable editorial assistance was furnished by the director of the Urban Institute Press, Washington, D.C. Barbara Martinez patiently saw successive versions through the computer.

2. Solano Lopez has been the target of much heated rhetoric. The normally judicious C. H. Haring described him as "a ruthless dictator, vain, capricious, arrogant, absolutely without scruple, and at times ferociously cruel." *Empire in Brazil: A New World Experiment with Monarchy* (Cambridge, Mass.: W. W. Norton & Co. 1958), 82.

3. An interesting, albeit eccentric, account of the war is given in Gilbert Phelps's *Tragedy of Paraguay* (New York: Palgrave Macmillan, 1975). There is an enormous bibliography on the war, much of it concerned with military and diplomatic details. The interpretive orientation tends to depend on the nationality of the author. For a brief survey of this historiography, see the entry on the "War of the Triple Alliance" by Vera Blinn Reber in *Encyclopedia of Latin American History and Culture*, ed. Barbara A. Tenenbaum (New York: Charles Scribner's Sons, 1996), vol. 5, 443–6.

4. This phrase is attributed to Dom Pedro by C. H. Haring in his *Empire in Brazil*, 82.

5. The best biography of Dom Pedro is Heitor Lyra, *História de Dom Pedro II, 1825–1891*, rev. ed., 3 vols. (Belo Horizonte: Livraria Itatiaia Editora, 1977). Useful also is Pedro Calmon, *História de Dom Pedro II*, 5 vols. (Rio de Janeiro, 1975). The earlier one-volume biography, *Dom Pedro the Magnanimous: Second Emperor of Brazil*. (New York: Octagon Books, 1966) by Mary Wilhelmine Williams still has value for its citation of original sources. All three authors are highly favorable to the Emperor.

6. The post-1840 imperial political system lacks a reliable synthetic treatment. The most penetrating analysis is in the two works by José Murilo de Carvalho, *Teatro de Sombras: A Política Imperial* (São Paulo: Vértice 1988) and *A Construção da Ordem: A Elite Política Liberal* (Rio de Janeiro, 1980).

7. An eloquent rationale for Dom Pedro's obsession with Solano Lopez is given in the intriguing fictionalized memoirs by Jean Soublin, *D. Pedro II, O Defensor Perpétuo do Brasil: Memórias Imaginárias do Ultimo Imperador* (Rio de Janeiro, 1996), 210.

8. In his visit to the battlefront in 1865 Dom Pedro was disconcerted to find his troops the subject of ridicule by the Paraguayans, who dismissed the latter as racially inferior. Joaquim Nabuco thought this experience had been influential in convincing the Emperor to favor abolition. Wilma Peres Costa, *A Espada de Dâmocles: O Exercito, A Guerra do Paraguai e a Crise do Império* (São Paulo: Editora da UNICAMP, 1996), 183–4. Details on the slave participation in the war may be found in Ricardo Salles, *Guerra do Paraguai: Escravidão e Cidadania na Formação do Exercito* (São Paulo, 1990).

9. Williams, *Dom Pedro the Magnanimous*, 122.

10. One historian is unequivocal: "Figurativa e concretamente a Guerra da Tríplica Aliança transformou a força armada profissional em Espada de Dâmocles sobre a cabeça do Estado Imperial, papel que se reproduziria em outros contextos, a partir de outras determinações." Costa, *A Espada de Dâmocles*, 305.

11. The Duque de Caxias, whose given name was Luís Alves de Lima e Silva, lacks an uptodate scholarly biography. The existing literature is heavily colored by efforts to protect his reputation as "Patron of the Army."

12. Mauá, whose given name was Irireu Evangelista de Sousa, has been the subject of an excellent recent biography by Jorge Caldeira, *Mauá: Empresário do Império* (São Paulo: Companhia das Letras, 1995). Unfortunately the author chose to forego footnotes and thus the reader has no way to link the text to the sources. The same defect marks the earlier biography by Anyda Marchant, *Viscount Mauá and the Empire of Brazil* (Berkeley: University of California Press, 1965).

13. The question of whether Brazil might have found a way to grow faster and deeper in the nineteenth century is of course speculative. One economic historian argues that Brazilian government should have "invested earlier and on a larger scale in social overhead capital (as happened in the United States)" but also notes that "given the economic and political conditions . . . it would not be realistic to expect public-investment programs very different from what in fact existed." Nathaniel H. Leff, "Economic Development in Brazil, 1822–1913," in *How Latin America Fell Behind: Essays on the Economic Histories of Brazil and Mexico, 1800–1914*, ed. Stephen Haber (Stanford: Stanford University Press, 1997), 58–59. An analysis of Mauá's career has frequently been at the center of debate over the appropriateness of the Brazilian government's economic policies in the nineteenth century.

BIBLIOGRAPHY

Caldeira, Jorge. *Mauá: Empresário do Império*. São Paulo: Companhia das Letras, 1995.
Calmon, Pedro. *História de Dom Pedro II*, 5 vols. Rio de Janeiro: Livaria Itatiatia Editora, 1975.
Carvalho, José Murilo de. *A Construção da Ordem: A Elite Política Liberal*. Rio de Janeiro: Editora Campus, 1980.
——. *Teatro de Sombras: A Política Imperial*. São Paulo: Vértice, 1988.
Costa, Wilma Peres. *A Espada de Dâmocles: O Exercito, A Guerra do Paraguai e a Crise do Império*. São Paulo: Editora da UNICAMP, 1996.
Haring, C. H. *Empire in Brazil: A New World Experiment with* Monarchy. Cambridge, Mass.: W. W. Norton & Co., 1958.
Lyra, Heitor. *História de Dom Pedro II, 1825–1891*, rev. ed., 3 vols. Belo Horizonte, 1977.
Leff, Nathaniel H. "Economic Development in Brazil, 1822–1913." In *How Latin America Fell Behind: Essays on the Economic Histories of Brazil and Mexico, 1800–1914*, edited by Stephen Haber. Stanford: Stanford University Press, 1997.
Marchant, Anyda. *Viscount Mauá and the Empire of* Brazil. Berkeley: University of California Press, 1965.
Phelps, Gilbert. *Tragedy of Paraguay*. New York: Palgrave Macmillan, 1975.
Reber, Vera Blinn. "War of the Triple Alliance." In *Encyclopedia of Latin American History and Culture*, edited by Barbara A. Tenenbaum. New York: Charles Scribner's Sons, 1996. Vol. 5.
Salles, Ricardo. *Guerra do Paraguai: Escravidão e Cidadania na Formação do Exercito*. São Paulo: Paz e Terra, 1990.
Soublin, Jean. *D. Pedro II, O Defensor Perpétuo do Brasil: Memórias Imaginárias do Ultimo Imperador*. Rio de Janeiro, 1996.
Williams, Mary Wilhelmine. *Dom Pedro the Magnanimous: Second Emperor of Brazil*. New York: Octagon Books, 1966.

5

Max Weber and the Interpretation of Brazil

Luiz Werneck Vianna

Brazil is what it is, plus the interpretation produced about it since the creation of intellectual life here. This is because to interpret Brazil has been, before as now, less to evaluate and consider knowledge drawn from the facts than to make a projection of what we should become. In this sense, in our tradition, the act of interpreting, even though it does not dismiss the use of cognitive processes, has consisted above all in a normative exercise in which the use of scientific method is aimed more at attaining rhetorical force toward what is addressed than at properly establishing an explanation of its reality. To interpret, in this sense, is much more than to simply understand; it indicates a practice capable of directing inspiration to shape the raw material of our uncivil, asocial, chaotically fragmentary nature so that we can constitute ourselves as a nation. Modeling as a practice at the service of an utopia, like the racial utopia proposed by Silvio Romero, leading to the fusion of all ethnic groups, as a long-term process, in order to achieve the whitening of the Brazilian. Modeling lawless individuals, making them citizens within a context hostile to public life, within the lineage that goes from Visconde do Uruguai to Oliveira Vianna. Modeling that internalizes the aptitude to access the first world, as in the perspective of liberals such as Tavares Bastos and Roberto Campos.

In this sense, the ontology of the Brazilian can be found to have its presuppositions as much in the country of slavery and rural estates, and of the bourgeois revolution without revolution, as in the ideal level. So, as in Angel Rama's sensitive analysis of Latin America, signs would antecede reality, prefiguring them, even if the cost of this operation of pure volition supposed the artifice of disregarding the concrete reality of that to which it applies. The gap between signs and real things, which is the result of a recalcitrant hostility of reason toward a wretched and brutalizing contingency, the taking-root of depreciation, which became chronic among us Brazilians, of the expressivity of physique of the interests of common men, always in the name of a pledge of voluntaristic persecution of a future always mismatched and discontent with the state of things that rule in the real world.

As in the famous quotation of Euclides da Cunha, Brazil would be a creation of political theory. In this sense, to interpret Brazil should not necessarily follow the logic of understanding relationships that effectively exist between men, and between men and their natural environment, but should be to create Brazil, instrumentally manipulating institutions, people, and social values. Hence, the mark of Brazilian political idealism is not that which conceives itself as an ethics orientated toward transcendence, but is that which takes place in a world only accepted by it in the sense in which it suffers the intervention of national reason according to the interpretative canon of its elites.

Since the 1970s, when Brazilian social science regained the essayistic gender of the pioneers in the interpretation of Brazil, such as of Visconde do Uruguai, Tavares Bastos, Joaquim Nabuco, Euclides da Cunha, Silvio Romero, Alberto Torres Oliveira Vianna, Gilberto Freire, Caio Prado Jr., and Sérgio Buarque de Holanda among others, Weber, as Marx, has been one of the main theoretical references that has addressed the objective of explaining the singularity of our social formation. The institutionalization of the social sciences that occurred during these years did not implicate, in the context of Brazilian cultural production, a rupture with the essayistic gender of the extra-university intellectual elites of the Empire and of the first decades of the Republic, regaining with a new bibliography most of their themes, certainly as a reaction to another cycle of political authoritarianism initiated by the military coup of 1964. Also for this new production, which originated in the University or has its main public there, the act of interpreting the country appears as a moment precedent to acting upon it, at times motivating ideas of rupture, at times suggesting ways of continuity-discontinuity with its history.

A great part of the controversy, in the field of the concurrent interpretations that came to light in the 1970s, is articulated as different conceptions intrinsic to the systems of Marx and Weber, especially those in the axiological field, with obvious repercussions for the analysis of the behavior of the social actor and the conditioning effect exercised over him by social structures. These two classic authors, it is worth noting, are among the three most cited in Brazilian master's degree dissertations and doctorate theses in the social sciences (Melo, 1999), the other being Pierre Bourdieu. However, the quotation of these authors' work did not always consider what is effectively different between them. The loss in complexity in their original theoretical constructions is frequent in order to establish what were often idiosyncratic oppositions.

As for Marx, the appropriation of his work varied, as we know, due to the thematic options of its interpreters: the valorization of a subject such as political will as a recourse to overcoming a backwardness/modern disjunction, having motivated, principally outside of university circles, a reading that privileged his political texts, that contemplated the possibility of revolutionary leaps, originating a Marxism which has as a paradigm the Russian literature, while the preference for an analysis of the process of imposition of capitalism in Brazil leads to a closer approximation to the model of capital based on the English paradigm, and, in some important examples, to a vision that is closer to what is traditionally designated as being social-democracy.

"Our" Weber has been used by influential literature in the interpretation of Brazil mainly to explain the backwardness of Brazilian society, and it's because of this that the spreading of his influence has been limited to the sociology of modernization. Hence, the reference to this author, only from the perspective of backwardness, is associated with the diagnosis that claims the rupture as a necessary step toward the conclusion of processes of social change that lead to the modern, in our case with Iberian patrimonialism, the form of state of which is very close to Eastern despotism. But this rupture, obviously, bears no similarity to a Marxist or revolutionary concept of rupture, indicating, on the contrary, a path that could lead to the constitution of the public following the logic of the interests. So, a work that is radically inscribed in Western political culture, with its universalistic values, impasses, and promises of realization, is understood from an Eastern perspective and by the possible routes to its modernization. Consequently "our" Weber has much less influence on the inquiry into pathologies of modernity than on pathological forms of accessing the modern.

The Weber of today's hegemonic version, both in the social sciences and in public opinion regarding the interpretation of Brazil, has been that which indicates our backwardness as resultant of an original vice due to the specific type of colonization to which we were subjected, the so called Iberian patrimonialism inheritance, whose structures would have been even more reinforced with the transplanting, at the beginning of the nineteenth century, of the Portuguese state onto American soil. From this legacy, continually reiterated over time, would come the imprint of a certain form of state, which was harshly autonomous in its relation to civil society. This state, in stifling the world of private interests and inhibiting free enterprise, could have compromised the history of the institutions with organicistic conceptions about social life and could have led to an affirmation of bureaucratic rationality rather than to legal rationality. Still, according to this version, the absence of feudalism in Iberian experience, including in Brazil, could approximate the patrimonial form of our state to the Eastern political tradition, where clear frontiers to demarcate activities within the public and private spheres are not observed. Raimundo Faoro, in his classic book *Os Donos do Poder*, besides approaching the Iberianism of Eastern despotism, takes up the argument of Tavares Bastos and Sarmiento, two liberal Latin American authors of the nineteenth century. He points to the need, motivated by his case study, of proceeding to revise Weber's thesis that links the emergence of the capitalist spirit to a Calvinist ethics, in favor of the thesis that maintains that "only the countries stirred by feudalism" could be called to adopt the capitalist system, integrating the society and the state (Faoro, 1975, vol. 1:22).

We would not exactly be a Western case, since here the state, preceding interest groups, being more than autonomous in the view of civil society, would be committed to the realization of particular objectives of their rulers, while the public administration, seen as a good in itself, is converted into a patrimony to be exploited by them. Inscribed as in the political East—and it's important to remember here that Simon Schwartzman, in conceptualizing patrimonialism, a central concept in his influential book *Bases do Autoritarismo Brasileiro*, not only quotes the Marx of the Asiatic means of production but also Karl Wittfogel's classic about hydraulic societies of Eastern despotism (Schwartzman 1982:43)—we would have known a political system of cooptation superposed on that of representation, an estate-type society equally superposed over the structure of classes, the primacy of administrative law over civil law, a form of patrimonial-bureaucratic dominance and the individual as a being absolutely without initiative and without rights in regard of the state.

Such a version, hegemonic in the controversy about the explanation of Brazil, attempts to compare the physical dimension of interests to Brazilian metaphysics, historically centered in the idea of a communion between the state and the nation. The state, understood as being invested with a representation of society as a whole and with the role of the interpreter of its expectations, and above all, centred in the idea of the interest of the particular, must be shown to be compatible with the interest of the national community in order to have its legitimacy plainly recognized. Brazilian capitalism, derived from this metaphysics, will be, then, politically orientated, a pathological mode of access to the modern, implicating modernization without foregoing a rupture with the patrimonial past, which, furthermore, would continually reproduce itself because the elites would identify with this capitalism and hold political control of the process of social change. In restricting the free manifestation of interests and making difficult, with the practice of coopta-

tion, its aggregation in syndical and, mainly, political terms, the neopatrimonial state would favor the preservation of the chronic social inequalities in the
country.

Breaking free from this political orientation would mean, on one hand, a
political reform that would open up the state to the diversity of interests manifested by civil society, imposing the prevalence of the system of representation, and on the other, the emancipation of those interests from no matter what
type of tutored reasoning. The identification of an almost Asiatic character to
the Brazilian state as being an obstacle to liberty and the egalitarian patterns
of social partnership, is an argument that has as its point of departure its radical autonomy regarding civil society and what would be the dramatic separation between political goals and the sphere of private interests, leading,
then, to the suggestion that state reform should be driven to open up to this
sphere, fulfilling its democratic role in the administration and composition of
different and contradictory interests made socially explicit. Only the physics
of these interests can remove the old Brazilian metaphysical tradition, which
would be committed to the idea of a hierarchical and unequal society.

The rupture, then, as Tavares Bastos wrote in the nineteenth century,
should apply on the level of political institutionalization, especially in respect
of the form of the state, seeing that if you plainly concede complete liberty to
interests, they tend to produce a beneficial dynamic that could bring about
more social equality. Patrimonialism is a mark of the state, and not of society,
and from this interpretative perspective it cannot appear to be of an analytical dimension, particularly in its agrarian question: as the argument is specific
to the institutional, policy reform contains the germ of a possibility of a good
society. Weber's reading of the subject of patrimonialism, because it aims toward the paradigm of the classic East, in which the right of individual property is not recognized, a right which, since the Greeks, has originated with the
West, is thus prisoner of the perspective of the political institutions, crucially
the state, whence comes its emphasis on political reform and not on social reform. This explanatory axis deflects one of the major controversies of literature, opposing, on one hand, those that advocate, since Tavares Bastos until
the deputies of the constitutional assembly of 1891 and until followers today
of political reform as a prior basis for the modernization of the country, that
the legal country should change the actual country, and, on the other, those
that invert the meaning of this proposition.

According to the interpretation that privileges patrimonialism as a phenomenon according to the form of the state, what could be considered Eastern in politics would be dislocated by the affirmation of the interests. The
state of São Paulo, then, with the expansion of coffee exportation, would be
an outline of the West about which should be placed the institutional

architecture of representative democracy, and so the heavy burden of a parasitic state would be removed so as to give passageway to interests and to its free aggregation. In this sense, the saga of misfortune of Brazilian democracy is told from the point of view of the political overthrowing of São Paulo, which would have hindered the country to universalize its Western paradigm.

In this version, therefore, the so-called revolution of 1930 would have recovered the old Iberian thread of the precedence of the state over civil society, the Vargas era understood as a continuity to the cycle defined by the Pombal—Emperor Pedro II lineage, an imperial projection that at one time would express the same "main support of the structure" because they translate patrimonial reality into the centralized state order.[1] Except the interregnum of the hegemony of São Paulo between 1889 and 1930, or even the period of main political influence from this state between 1934 and 1937, the strength of tradition and the weight of the structures of the state induce a determination that "superior to anyone, steering and not passively molded" that leads the administrative team to dominate the political elite. And, thus, "in 1945, the dictator no longer feared the hegemony of São Paulo, only made possible on the basis of economic nondependent core groups, as was the case with the coffee economy," bringing its interests to the network of the state, the patrimonial place of the extraction of wealth and distribution of privileges, which then ties, also patrimonially, the São Paulo industrial park to its administration.[2]

The revolution of 1930 would therefore consist of a return to patrimonial roots, responding to the hidden movement of the structures, and not of an invention with which the controllers of the bourgeois order, ahead of the crisis of legitimacy of the Primeira República, would have extended the reach of the universalization of the state, imposing upon it greater autonomy regarding the sphere of interests, in this case the dominant class in São Paulo, in order to allow the incorporation of emergent actors in urban life, such as the military, entrepreneurs, laborers, and intellectuals, into the ordinate system. What was understood as the happy interregnum of 1889 to 1930, when the interests had met representation in policy and had shaped the state, in the institutional context of the Federalist Brazilian Constitution of 1891 and of the system of formally rational-legal dominance of which it derived, was, as is known, the republican moment in which the public sphere was appropriated by the private sphere and in which that system of dominance was in solidarity with the patrimonial order by way of the political system known in Brazil as *coronelismo*.

The interest, as an isolated instance, as already perceived in the classic lessons of English philosophical radicalism, in Hegel and Tocqueville, not to mention Marx, led to the particularism in the form of the state, and, in the backward conditions of Brazilian society, where the statute of personal dependence predominated, tended to match the oligarchic forms of command and the hierarchic type of sociability that prevailed in the country. The rule of the interest, during the *Primeira República*, then, does not confront traditional forms of dominance but subordinates them, changing the backwardness, such as in the exemplary demonstration of Victor Nunes Leal in his studies on *coronelismo*, into an advantage toward the modern that would be represented by the dominant economy in São Paulo under the direction of a patrician of landed origin, orientated by market values—São Paulo as Prussian-like state will be an invention of the Primeira República.

From the Eastern perspective (i.e., considering patrimonialism as a phenomenon of the state) this Weberian version of the interpretation of Brazil, more than identifying backwardness as being proper to the instance of the political phenomena, will tend to hide the patrimonial relations that constitute the fabric of sociability, losing sight of, in the controversial language of Brazilian social thinking, "the real country," especially the agrarian world and the relations of personal dependence that establish therein, and also losing sight of how its São Paulo paradigm, far from representing a line of opposition between backwardness and modernity, representation and cooptation, rational-legal order and patrimonialism, in truth, points toward an ambiguous composition of these polarities imprinting to a matrix of interest the mark of a private individualism diametrically opposed to the formation of civic culture.

The other point in the reception of Weber, from the perspective of political institutions to that of sociology, is centered in the agrarian question and in the patrimonialism of the societal base, and, mainly, from the East to the West, wherein the history and process of Brazilian development would be a result and integrated part of these, even though as a late and ambiguous case, as it combines the modern form of state of liberal architecture with the institute of slavery and patrimonial social organization. Weber, in this reading, is no longer used as a reference that contraposes itself to Marx in the question of state autonomy and of politics in general, taking from him the theoretical demarcation for the analysis of slave-based society and its estate-type organization, while in Marx one looks for concepts that can explain the country's inscription to the worldwide capitalist system and the transition to a "competitive social order" founded in a modern class structure.

From this we see, therefore, the heterogeneity in the Brazilian reading of Weber, that would be present as much in the interpreted version of those that identify quasi-Asian elements that would have presided over the formation of the national state, because of the transplant of the state patrimonialism from Portugal, as the root of our evils, as in that of those, like Florestan Fernandes, Maria Silvia de Carvalho Franco and José Murilo de Carvalho, to the extent in which they understand, in the words of the first, "the state . . . as the only entity that could be manipulated since the beginning . . . with views to its progressive adaptation to liberal political philosophy"[3] or, in those of the second, for whom the "administrative organisation of this period (the 1830s) was formally based on the bureaucratic principle of obedience to an abstractly defined public power, legitimated and expressed by legally decreed and rationally created norms,"[4] or, still, in those of the last, supporting that the imperial bureaucracy would not have constituted itself as an estate.[5] These analyses will provoke a shift of the inquiry into the cause of our backwardness to the open field of social relations, and the impact of their patrimonial nature on a state, in its original conception, of modern extraction.

According to this interpretation, whose axis is found in the characterization of the commitment that it established, after political independence, between the rational-legal and the patrimonial orders, between the liberalism of the political form and the inherited economic structures of the colony, between backwardness and modernity (the former understood as rational to capitalism), between representation and cooptation, the problem of rupture should not be referred to the state, but to the patrimonial pattern of social relations, and so "all the behaviour of the characters (comes) interlaced with the concession of graces, displaying the validity of the principle of personal control, a basis hardly propitious for the rational orientation of action."[6] From this perspective, the rupture would only be possible in the long-term as the result of molecular transformations in traditional relations, historically responsible for the contention over the affirmation of a class-based society in Brazil, characterizing the bourgeois revolution in the country as being dominated by a passive march, and, as such, better represented conceptually by the theme of transition, in this case, the transition from a slave-based order to a competitive social order.

The process of the differentiation of interests between colony and metropolis, whence appears the native spirit and adhesion to liberalism of the men who established independence, would have imported a particular form of internalization of liberal ideology in which yearnings for the "emancipation of the seigneurial estates from 'colonial guardianship'" would come to be expressed more than for "national emancipation."[7] However, after accomplishing independence, in the analysis of Florestan Fernandes, this movement inverts itself with the conversion of liberalism into a dynamic force of civil society born of independence, "a sphere in which it is affirmed and inside of which it fulfills its typical function of transcending and negating the existing order."[8] Transcendence and negation that, in the passage of colonial society to national society, would demand long-term historical processes, during the course of which would be produced, by the role of the ideology and of the lib-

eral institutions in the "hooded revolution" of independence, continual molecular transformations in which takes place, in the words of that author, the
burial of the past.[9] The intense mercantile blossoming that followed the rupture with the colonial pact, the nationalization of commercial export, altering
the economic functions of the rural landlord, as well as the social differentiation resultant of this, creating new qualified occupations and the incentive for
liberal professions, would have induced a "part of the global society" to de-
tach from "the pre-existing traditional structures" to begin to constitute its
"free sector," "the only sphere in which free competition could reach some
validity." Under this logic orrginates, despite "adverse socio-economic conditions (due to the persistence of slavery and patrimonialism), an area in
which the 'competitive system' can coexist and clash with the 'estate-type
system.'"[10]

The transition, therefore, of the slave-based order to the competitive social
order sets the pace of passive revolutions that, if understood in the Weberian
sense of types of domination and expressive modes of action that each of
them hold, involves a progressive process of realizing the modern in which,
by means of societal differentiation, basically, by the appearance and affirmation of new social roles whose execution are incompatible with the traditional order, the system of rational orientation of action tends to generalize itself, becoming, finally, hegemonic.

However, because of the passive nature of the path that makes dominance
viable, the system of rational orientation of action can coexist with patrimonial order, creating for the bourgeoisie the possibility to benefit from the modern as much as from backwardness: "(the bourgeoisie) commits equally to
everything that would be advantageous: and, for it, it was advantageous
to benefit from times of inequality and from the heterogeneity of Brazilian society, mobilizing the advantages that occurred as much due to *backwardness*
as to the *advancement of populations*."[11] Then, provided that the national
state is born "sufficiently modern," capable of "further modernization of its
economic, social and cultural functions," the effective matrix of the expansion of liberalism in the country,[12] since its origin, it has maintained the mark
of a familiarity with an order antithetical to its own, which, far from being im-
peditive to its affirmation, makes it possible, above all because it consists of
the economic basis from which it will be able to operate its form of inscription to worldwide capitalism.

São Paulo's trajectory, especially from the moment when coffee plantation
exportation came to be based on free labor, would be paradigmatic of how the
affirmation of the sphere of interests and the system of rational orientation of
homo oeconomicus would not have been enough for the imposition of competitive social order, importing, then, into a new scene, the reiteration of the

constituent ambiguity in Brazilian formation: on one side, the "accurate calculation" of *homo oeconomicus* of the capitalist culture of coffee and of the
emergent social types with the expansion of business and industrialization; on
the other, on the political plane, the preservation of the seigneurial style, the
extraction of consent and the practice of coercion by patrimonial methods and
forms. The competitive order, if it prevails in the economy, will not produce
vocational social agents for a rationalization of its world, distant "from a political philosophy . . . that can lead to capitalism as life style." As an isolated
instance, the interest and the social agents who better represent it, even in its
powerful São Paulo manifestation, remain confined to the horizon of the private sphere, "converting themselves to the liberalism of the traditional elites,
(becoming incorporated), in fact, to conservative circles and (passing) to
share forms of leadership and political dominance invariably conflicting or
inconsistent with the consolidation of competitive social order."[13] The modern interest, in its already specifically capitalist form, in abdicating a program
to radicalize liberalism, is born committed to practices that take advantage of
backwardness, such as, in the agrarian world, the production of surplus beginning with relations of personal dependence, and also associated with the
techniques of social control that disguise the existence of class structure and
hinder its free exploitation.

The failure of the economic elites of São Paulo, at the moment of transition to free labor and when the primacy of specifically capitalist relations
were secured, to effectuate "from above" the universalization of the competitive social order's agenda in the name of fulfilling the radical-liberal program to disseminate capitalism as life style, would have as a consequence a
construction "from beneath," the orientation of which would be aimed at de-
stroying the model of social heteronomy prevalent in Brazilian society, supposed by the patrimonial organization. Such a construction, for this reason,
should have as its starting point the affirmation of the interests of individuals
exposed to the statute of personal dependence or of precarious citizenship
from a social and political point of view. The "Gordian knot" to be cut in order to find a path toward competitive social order would not, then, be in the
state or in the interest in general, but in a certain type of interest that, to be
freely manifested, would be endowed with the ability to conform autonomous
identities, a new instance without which it would not be able to effectively
break with the legacy of patrimonial inheritance.

On this new path in the inquiry into the character of Brazilian patrimonialism, of which a change in focus from state to society results, the perception of
politics and of the state should have the agrarian monopoly as a starting point,
given that only there could be taken unawares, in the pure context of seigneurial domination, the thread of sociability that would involve individuals sub-

mitted to a situation of personal dependence, the condition in which to uncover the particular mode of articulation between the public and private dimensions and between the state and society, laying bare the internal connections in force in the modeling of the bourgeois order in the country, between the rational-legal and patrimonial planes. From this sociological perspective, which looks to analytically combine the micro- and the macro-foundations responsible for the formation of the state, new light is thrown on the dimension of interest that is no longer to be perceived as the place of innovation and of resistance to patrimonialism, but as the place of conservation of the status quo.

Maria Silvia de Carvalho Franco, in her classic book *Homens Livres na Ordem Escravocrata*, in using Weber's argument about the singularity of state bureaucratic organization in the modern West, proves empirically how, here, in conditions of scarcity of resources that could support state action, the process of public employee expropriation of the material means of administration would have only been formal to the extent in which, in reality, a good part of these means were financed with private resources. It was the poverty of the state agency and not its supposedly quasi-Eastern nature that would have given as an undesired result the fusion between public and private, thus allowing that the exercise of power derived from a public duty could be translated into a search of strictly singular ends.[14] Investigating the workings of the Municipal Chambers of *Paraíba* in the last century, the author expresses, in an exemplary fashion, the Weberian version that inscribes Brazilian patrimonialism as being societal in character and of agrarian roots:

> at the basis of the development of bureaucracy in public administration, is an essential character: the process of public employee expropriation of material means of administration, clearly separating official resources from the employees' private goods. In view of what was already exposed, it can be seen how this process of expropriation, in nineteenth-century Brazil, was stopped by the insuperable state of penury to which the public agencies were subjected. Although expenses were always restricted to the least necessary for the preservation of goods and for the continuity of state services, official resources were insufficient even for this minimum amount, compensating this lack with incursions into the pockets of the citizens and of the authorities. The result of this was that the public employee instead of becoming even more an executive who only managed the means of administration, it was preserved the situation in which he kept its property. This means, basically, that he could control them autonomously because *he possessed them*. His was the money with which public works were paid for; his, the slave whose work yielded; his, the house where public functions were carried out.[15]

Far removed, therefore, from the interpretation that characterizes the state as an instance radically independent of society, as in the literature that understands it as being patrimonial and responsible for backwardness, the version that identifies Brazilian patrimonialism as a societal phenomenon perceives it from an opposing perspective: the image of the Tutelary State would be just a simple appearance to disguise its actual nature as being Instrumental State. Although modern to the extent in which its administrative bureaucracy would be related to the principles of the rational-legal order, its actions would be "amended" in the plan of local life—in the "little kingdoms" of the landed gentry—being permanently "disavowed while autonomous and endowed with the ability to act according to its own objectives," private life drawing itself out within public life, "maintaining, also in this, personal dominance."[16]

The latecomer element would have its origin in civil society, from the structure of the forms of property and the prevalent work relations therein, and not in the state, imposing there a two-faced formula to ambiguously combine rational-legal dominance with traditional, and imposing to civil society an amorphism that would prevent it from knowing, during the transition to free labor, a capitalist structure of social classes, the personal power hindering to its object—the "poor, free men"—the perception of themselves as owner of rights and self-interests and to its subject—the dominant groups—the identification of their common economic objectives in order to act in unity.[17] In this way, in which the matrix of interest comes to produce social beings endowed with autonomy and defined social identity, it would be of importance, on one hand, to eradicate the preserved forms of societal patrimonialism within the process of the modernization of Brazilian society, and, on the other, to end the traditional ability of the private sphere to invade the public sphere, converting it into its own instrument.

The diagnosis formulated for this interpretation was singularized by the understanding that backwardness and modernity were not deemed, due to the form of unequal development of Brazilian capitalism, to be in agonistic contraposition, but to be in combination, leading to the accommodation of antithetic principles that would merge in a heteroclite manner in the state, as the above seeks to explain. With this background argument, the process of capitalist modernization, based on politically induced industrialization, as has been the way since 1930 and as had intensified in the two following decades, will be understood as a confirmation, in a specifically capitalist context, of an amalgam of principles and a system of order that would have presided over our formation, since it could reach a resolution without liberating the manifestation of class-structure and without dislocating the traditional elites from the interior of the state.

The *nacional-desenvolvimentismo* would have consisted of a new bourgeois praxis by means of which it would guarantee continuity to this old Brazilian solution, making compatible the ideals of economic modernization of the new elites with the preservation of the dominance of the traditional oligarchies, which would still keep a large part of the rural population under the statute of personal dependence. By definition, because it has multi-class support, the national-developmentary regime would consist of an innovation in the system of order, admitted by way of the syndical corporate structure and the grant of work protection legislation, the incorporation of workers of the urban formal market into the institutions and the ideology of the state, imposing on them, in exchange, a heteronomous situation, with what one hoped would reinforce its legitimacy and confer onto its project the simulacrum of a representation of the interests of the collective as a whole.[18]

It is about this conceptual foundation that the so-called theory of Populism, with a more veiled than explicit Weberian influence, also inspired in its beginnings by the work of the important Italian-Argentine sociologist Gino Germani,[19] will find its basis for the explanation of Brazil. This theory[20] would become, from the 1960s, particularly after the military coup of 1964, the common language of those who understood that Brazilian misery was due to the fact of Western rationality to be, here, submerged and conditioned to a private order of patrimonial style that would preserve the multi-class coalitions between the modern and the traditional elites and the unionism authorized by the corporate structure. This unionism, as a place of identification and aggregation of workers' interests, would be the privileged instance from which a rupture with the heteroclite form of state could be imposed, whose manifest function would consist of protecting, in the course of the modernization process, the conservation of tradition and the extra-economic modes of social control over the workforce, that is, not specifically capitalist.

Populism would result of the manipulation of the working masses, the majority of whom would originate from rural regions, mediated by the charismatic action of a leader, to be incorporated into the system of order by the double path of access to social rights and by the use of symbolic courses of integration, with what was found to take them to the abdication of autonomy as a class and to the loss of the distinction of their interests in favor of the interests of the coalition of elites that control the state. The charisma, in this case, would not behave as a enabling action to the enchantment of the world and as a fiat of the new, fulfilling its role in a process of conservation with controlled change and placing the interest, and not only of the workers, under the guardianship of the bureaucratic rationalization of the state. The request to charisma would be, then, a recourse of backwardness, and the interest of the worker should rebel against it, whose rationalization in the unions would reclaim the market as being the main direction—and not the state that would deny the construction of its autonomy—where the modern that would be intrinsically constitutive of it would find a free field in which to establish roots for the length of time of, and from "beneath," a new form of state.

As an interpretation of Brazil and as an ideology orientated toward action, the theory of Populism is born under the inspiration of the modern interest of industrial workers and of the necessity for their emancipation from the mechanisms of cooptation on the part of the state. In this sense, its paradigm is the market of São Paulo, and its strategic unity of analysis is the unionism of that state of the Federation. Centered in the problems of unionist and political representation of industrial workers, this theory relegates to abandonment the analytical vein of agrarian sociology and the movement of rural social actors, with what induces the perception of backwardness as a social region to be colonized by them. In this sense, many currents of leftist opinion, that in the 1970s had accepted the explanation of the theory of Populism, turned, anachronistically, toward the experience of the Labour Councils of Gramsci's youth in Turin, with the expectation to change society and the state from the factories. In this particular point, the theory of Populism came unexpectedly to reinforce the explanatory field of the Weberian version of patrimonialism of the state, to the extent to which, as such, it is limited to contrapose the coalition modern-backward, traditionally prevalent in the system of order, the social expression of the modern, without politics and without alliances to the "latecomer" classes of the subordinate sectors: the "laborer" who rises out of the theory of Populism doesn't have, by definition, the vocation to be allied to the peasant, being refractory, in general, to class alliances.

These Weberian versions of the interpretation of Brazil, although distant from each other, as has been demonstrated, do keep some affinities, most of all the São Paulo paradigm and the valorization of the matrix of interest as strategic to the country democratization. More substantively, the diagnosis of modernization operated within a neopatrimonial perspective, in accordance with the first version summarized here, and with the second version accomplished under the national-populist pact, both indicating the necessity of a historic rupture with tradition, present common elements, mainly in the indication of the state negative role in the formation of contemporary Brazilian society. The main difference, among many, that distinguishes them lies in the understanding of the strategic subject of interest, emancipationist in general for one, and in particular for the other, and only to the extent to which it is associated with the question of autonomy and class identity.

These versions were very well succeeded, although what was distinguishable between them was not always visible, especially at the end of the 1980s and the beginning of the 1990s. They were the ideal support of political forces that, after the promulgation of the 1988 Constitution, made themselves dominant in public opinion and in the organized segments of society, coming, later to assume the configuration of political parties in the PSDB (*Partido Social-ista Democratico Brasileiro*) and the PT (*Partido dos Trabalhadores*), not without reason born in the state of São Paulo,[21] the first, as well known, occupying the Presidency of the Republic, and the second the place of the biggest party of opposition in the country. However, neither the emancipation of political interests from those of the state has been virtuous to it, nor the disqualification of the Republic's idea in favor of that of the market, which has not been producing individuals endowed with rights and enjoying equal opportunities in life. On the other hand, the modern interest of industrial workers, despite the vigor demonstrated in the great social movements of the 1980s and the relative electoral force of the party to which these gave birth, turned its back on the republican theme and became prisoner of its particular interest, not assuming the capability of universalization, as was clear in the PT's political insulation in the presidential elections of 1989, 1994, and 1998, positioning that has recently been reviewed.

Under the domain of interest, almost two decades after the most democratic constitution that the country has ever known was promulgated, it can be ascertained, against the best opinions formulated by the dominant interpretations of Brazil, that the rational-legal order did not necessarily comply with justice, as well as from a sociologically "clean" class structure not automatically comes a political representation favoring the majority. They become power-ideas and meet with social actors who lead them to become concrete and, in this, prove that none are of arbitrary character, but that their intellectual and political success is very far from the foreseen practical results of their diagnoses: notwithstanding changes in the scenario, the malaise remains the same and the levels of exclusion and social fragmentation deepen. The modern, therefore, in any of the two versions, did not come to enchant the Brazilians' world but to rationalize their lives based on market values, increasing its dependence on it, as one could expect to be the case in a Weberian forecast.

At this time, in which all possibilities of a good society derived from promises made by the hegemonic interpretations of Brazil are run dry, we can sustain without a Republic interests live the logic of the market whether its interpreters want it or not. And without the Republic, which was the lost horizon of these interpretations—the first because it abandoned itself to the illusion that it is enough for the economy to autonomize itself to the servitude of politics and so reach the threshold of a good society, and the second because they believed they had reached the same objective but through the mobilization of the social—the question that persists is whether it is possible to construct a Republic from behaviors and projects that accredit the social and political actors to resolve the old dissociation between the public and private spheres, which accompanies the history of the country and of the dominant ideas in its political culture. Weber, with his intrinsic distance regarding Rousseau, does not seem to be the best authority for this problem. The Republic is a communitarian space, and, as far as the eye can see, irreducible to the globalization process that follows its inexorable course, in which interests also express values and a certain common history. The great challenge for a new interpretation of Brazil is in opening the field of investigations and possibilities so that the modern physics of "well understood" interests—i.e., endowed with the capacity of universalization to the extent to which they also comes to express public values—meets with Brazilian metaphysics,[22] putting it under its direction. This is not an objective that can be attained naturalistically, because it requires a reflexive intervention of society about itself (i.e., an interpretation), in order to select from its own history those subjects and reasons that may serve as guide.

NOTES

Previous versions of this text, which was radically altered in many parts, were published in *O Malandro e o Protestante*, ed. Jessé de Souza, (Brasília, UnB, 1999) and in *Novos Estudos Cebrap* 53 (March 1999). Translation by Derek Geoffrey Hart.

1. Raimundo Faoro, *Os Donos do Poder*, vol. 2 (Porto Alegre: Ed. Globo; São Paulo: EdUsp, 1975), 725.

2. Faoro, *Os Donos do Poder*, 725.

3. Florestan Fernandes, *A Revolução Burguesa no Brasil* (Rio de Janeiro: Zahar, 1975), 35.

4. Maria Silvia de Carvalho Franco, *Homens Livres na Ordem Escravocrata* (São Paulo: Instituto de Estudos Brasileiros-USP, 1969), 116.

5. José Murilo de Carvalho, *A Construção da Ordem* (Rio de Janeiro: Campus, 1980), 129.

6. Franco, *Homens Livres na Ordem Escravocrata*, 27.

7. Fernandes, *A Revolução Burguesa no Brasil,* 36.

8. Fernandes, *A Revolução Burguesa no Brasil,* 39.

9. Fernandes, *A Revolução Burguesa no Brasil,* 46.

10. Fernandes, *A Revolução Burguesa no Brasil,* 48.

11. Fernandes, *A Revolução Burguesa no Brasil,* 204 (emphasis in the original).

12. Fernandes, *A Revolução Burguesa no Brasil,* 38.

13. Fernandes, *A Revolução Burguesa no Brasil,* 146.

14. Franco, *Homens Livres na Ordem Escravocrata*, chapter III.

15. Franco, *Homens Livres na Ordem Escravocrata*, 126 (emphasis in the original).

16. Franco, *Homens Livres na Ordem Escravocrata,* 135, 138, and 230.

17. Franco, *Homens Livres na Ordem Escravocrata,* 231.

18. Florestan Fernandes, *A Sociologia numa Era de Revolução Social*, 2nd ed. (Rio de Janeiro: Zahar, 1976).
19. Particularly influential was Gino Germani, *Sociología de la Modernización*, (Buenos Aires: Paidós,1969).
20. For more information about this point, refer to *Sindicatos e Política* by Weffort, a work well received by Brazilian social scientists in the 1970s and 1980s (Francisco Weffort, *Sindicatos e Política*. (Livre-Docência thesis, USP, s/d).
21. Rubem Barbosa Filho, "FHC: Os Paulistas no Poder," in *FHC: Os Paulistas no Poder* (Niterói; RJ: Casa Jorge Editorial, 1995).
22. About Brazilian *metaphysics* and its relationship with the world of interests, see Luiz Werneck Vianna, *A Revolução Passiva: Iberismo e Americanismo no Brasil* (Rio de Janeiro: Revan, 1997) and Maria Alice Rezende de Carvalho, *O Quinto Século—André Rebouças e a Construção do Brasil* (Rio de Janeiro: Revan, 1998).

BIBLIOGRAPHY

Barbosa Filho, Rubem. "FHC: Os Paulistas no Poder." In *FHC: Os Paulistas no Poder*. Niterói; RJ: Casa Jorge Editorial, 1995.

Carvalho, José Murilo de. *A Construção da Ordem*. Rio de Janeiro: Campus, 1980.

Faoro, Raimundo. *Os Donos do Poder*. Porto Alegre: Ed. Globo; São Paulo: EdUsp, 1975.

Fernandes, Florestan. *A Revolução Burguesa no Brasil*. Rio de Janeiro: Zahar, 1975.

———. *A Sociologia numa Era de Revolução Social*. 2nd ed. Rio de Janeiro: Zahar, 1976.

Franco, Maria Silvia de Carvalho. *Homens Livres na Ordem Escravocrata*. São Paulo: Instituto de Estudos Brasileiros-USP, 1969.

Germani, Gino. *Sociologia de la Modernización*. Buenos Aires: Paidós, 1969.

Melo, Manoel Palacios Cunha. *Quem Explica o Brasil*. Juiz de Fora: Ed. UFJF, 1999.

Rezende de Carvalho, Maria Alice. *O Quinto Século—André Rebouças e a Construção do Brasil*. Rio de Janeiro: Revan, 1998.

Schwartzman, Simon. *Bases do Autoritarismo Brasileiro*. Rio de Janeiro: Campus, 1982.

Weffort, Francisco C. *Sindicatos e Política*. Livre-Docência thesis, USP, s/d.

Werneck Vianna, Luiz. *A Revolução Passiva: Iberismo e Americanismo no Brasil*. Rio de Janeiro: Revan, 1997.

6

Racial Democracy

Antonio Sérgio Alfredo Guimarães

> O mytho é o nada que é tudo
> O mesmo sol que abre os céus
> É um mytho brilhante e mudo . . . [1]
>
> —Fernando Pessoa

Scholars of race relations in Brazil are always intrigued with the origins and dissemination of the term "racial democracy." To start with, while it is attributed to Gilberto Freyre,[2] the expression is not found in his most important works and does not appear in the literature until rather late, in the 1940s. Why use a political metaphor to speak of social relations between blacks and whites? Why did the phrase express so perfectly a thought that concepts previously coined by social scientists—like Pierson's "multiracial class society"[3] or the United Nations Educational Scientific and Cultural Organization's (UNESCO) "harmonious race relations" (Maio 1997)—were incapable of expressing? These are some of the questions I try to answer in this chapter.

I did not read documents or newspapers of the time in a systematic way, but have concentrated on the newspaper articles and academic writings of some pioneer intellectuals in the study of "race relations" and tried, on that basis, to trace the chronology of the coining of the term "racial democracy."

The term seems to have been used first by Arthur Ramos[4] during a seminar in 1941.[5] Roger Bastide in an article published in the *Diário de S. Paulo* on 31 March 1944, in which he reports on a visit to Gilberto Freyre in Recife, uses also the same words, which seems to be already current among some intellectuals. Did Ramos invent the expression or hear it from Freyre? It is probably a free translation of Freyre's ideas on Brazilian democracy who used the expression "social democracy"[6] since the mid-1930s to refer to exactly the same thing.

As is well known, in his lectures at Indiana State University in the fall of 1944, he used another synonym, "ethnic democracy," to refer to Jesuit catechism: "but their excessively paternalistic and autocratic way of educating the indians sometimes developed in opposition to the first sketchy tendencies towards an ethnic and social democracy in Brazil."[7]

In the specialized literature, however, the expression makes its appearance a few years later. "Brazil is renowned in the world for its racial democracy," wrote Wagley in 1952, in his "Introduction" to the first volume of a series of studies on race relations in Brazil sponsored by UNESCO.[8] It appears that Arthur Ramos, Roger Bastide, and, later, Charles Wagley, introduced into the literature the expression that would later become not only celebrated, but the synthesis of the thought that characterized an entire era and a whole generation of social scientists. As we will see, Gilberto Freyre[9] is not entirely responsible, either for the ideas or their label; even if he inspired "racial democracy," he usually avoided calling it that and attributed to it a very specific meaning.

THE IDEA OF A RACIAL PARADISE

The idea that Brazil was a society without a "color line," without legal barriers to people of color rising to official posts or positions of wealth and prestige, was widespread in the world, especially the United States and Europe, well before the birth of sociology. That idea, in modern Brazil, gave rise to the mythical construction of a society without racial prejudice or discrimination. Slavery itself, whose survival weighed on the consciences of liberals like Nabuco, was understood by American, European, and Brazilian abolitionists as more human and bearable in Brazil precisely because of the absence of this color line.[10]

Célia Marinho de Azevedo[11] records the intervention of Frederick Douglass in a speech in 1858, in New York:

> Even in a Catholic country like Brazil—a country that we, in our pride, stigmatize as semi-barbarian—does not treat its people of color, free or slave, in the unjust, barbarous and scandalous way we treat them. . . . Democratic and Protestant America would do well to learn a lesson of justice and freedom from Catholic and despotic Brazil.[12]

Célia Azevedo also cites the opinion of Quentin, a Frenchman who in 1867 wrote that "the transition [to free labor] was particularly facilitated in Brazil by the fact that there is no race prejudice there."[13] Similarly, in the post-abolitionist period, Hellwig[14] collected a series of articles written by African-Americans between 1910 and 1940, reaffirming the generalized belief in a country without racial prejudice and discrimination, in which individual value and merit were not blocked by racial belonging or by color.

In the speech quoted above, Douglass traces a contrast between democracy and a sense of American injustice, on the one hand, and Brazilian justice and despotism, on the other, in dealings with men of color. But he does not go further. He does not use the word "democracy" to refer to social relations. Democracy had a purely political meaning and was related only to forms of government.

Historians do well to call this utopia the "myth of the racial paradise," because the expression "racial democracy" is not only more recent but involved in a more specific web of meanings.

In the 1930s, when the first black political movement in Brazil was organized—the Frente Negra Brasileira (Black Brazilian Front), this utopia was not questioned, at least not immediately. For example, in his "Message to American Blacks," Manoel Passos,[15] president of the União Nacional de Homens de Cor (National Union of Colored Men), preferred to emphasize the abandonment to which the black population was condemned, its lack of schooling and archaic customs, as responsible for the "degeneracy" of blacks. Even the "color prejudice" that blacks felt was partly attributed to the moral weakness of black population groups.[16]

This self-flagellation was only reverted with the democratization of the country in 1945, when new black organizations arose and were, in a way, included by the Second Republic. They were included in the sense that they operated freely, as well as influencing national life in cultural, ideological, and political terms. The Teatro Experimental do Negro (TEN), founded in 1945, is doubtless the most important of these organizations.

ANTECEDENTS: "SOCIAL AND ETHNIC DEMOCRACY" IN FREYRE

Gilberto Freyre was the first modern sociologist to return to the old utopia of the racial paradise, dear to the common sense of abolitionists, and clothed it in science. In 1936, in *Sobrados e Mucambos*, Freyre returned to the images of "aristocracy" and "democracy" to contrast the rigidity of patriarchal organization and the flexibility of relations between races:

Even what was most obstinately aristocratic in the patriarchal organization of the family, the economy and culture was affected by what was always most contagiously democratic, democratizing and even anarchic in the amalgamation of races and culture and, up to a point, regional types, resulting in a kind of dismemberment of the hardest, least pliable forms, because of an excessive shakiness or turmoil of their content.[17]

But the literary history of what became known as Brazilian "racial democracy" begins in the 1930s, more precisely in 1937, when Gilberto Freyre gives his lecture in Lisbon on "Aspects of the Influence of Race Mixture on Social and Cultural Relations between the Portuguese and Luso-descendants."[18] In this lecture, Freyre speaks of "social democracy" as of Luso-Brazilian civilization's most original and significant legacy to humanity.

> There is, with respect to this problem of growing importance for modern peoples—the problem of miscegenation, of Europeans' relations with black, brown, and yellow people—a distinctly, typically, characteristically Portuguese attitude, perhaps better described as Luso-Brazilian, Luso-Asian, Luso-African, which makes of us a psychological and cultural unit founded upon one of the most significant events, perhaps one could say upon one of the most significant human solutions of a biological and at the same time social nature, of our time: social democracy through race mixture.[19]

Imbued with the ideas of Iberian exceptionalism,[20] which he had imbibed from the pages of Unamuno and Ortega y Gasset, Freyre contrasts Luso-Brazilian social democracy with the merely political democracy of the English, in order to highlight the virtues of the former.

> By virtue of this cultural dynamism, which does not shut off European culture from other influences; by valuing in men, to the greatest extent possible, authentic qualities independent of color, social position, economic success; through equality—as much as possible—of social opportunities and of culture for men of different origins, regions molded by the Portuguese—molded by miscegenation—constitute today an anticipation of, or, more accurately, an approximation to, that social democracy from which currently more advanced peoples find themselves distant in their practice of that often inefficient, unjust, and anti-human political, merely political, democracy.[21]

However, the expression "ethnic democracy" coined by Gilberto Freyre emerged in the context of his activism against *integralismo*, the Brazilian fascist movement.

Continuous attacks against Freyre in Recife culminated, in September 1943, in a crushing *integralista* manifesto, signed by the Student Organization of the Law School of Recife, which tried to discredit him.[22] Mobilization of Left and democratic forces in defense of Gilberto Freyre was immediate. Among other things, he received an invitation from the Bahia Students' Union, seconded by other organizations there, to visit Salvador and receive a number of honors and awards. He accepted the invitation in November of that year and on November 26 he read his first lecture in Salvador at the Bahia

Medical School. In praise of Bahia and the Luso-Brazilian matrix of its culture, Freyre said:

Here [in Bahia] one finds, in an atmosphere that is sweeter than any other in Brazil, the results of ethnic democracy, inseparable from social democracy. And without social democracy, without ethnic democracy, without economic democracy, without socio-psychological democracy—the democracy whose types combine freely in new expressions, accepted, favored and stimulated by the organization of society and creation—what can mere political democracy be, if not a hoax?[23]

It is noteworthy that, beginning in 1937, Feryre no longer contrasts "democracy" with "aristocracy," as he did in *Mansions and Shanties*, but begins to emphasize the contrast between social democracy and political democracy. In his view, only the first seems immune to racism. And it is precisely racism, not only political totalitarianism, that Freyre vehemently condemns. While fascism was a peculiar weaving of totalitarianism into racism, Brazil and Portugal had found, in their tradition of race mixture, the antidote against such a danger. More than that, it was not only the tension between democracy and fascism, present in the European war, that helped define the "social" content of Brazilian democracy, but also the regional tension between a Luso-Brazilian matrix, consolidated in the north, and the various European influences still in gestation in the south. More than that: everything that was not genuinely Luso-Brazilian, mixed, synchretic, was seen as a danger for the young Brazilian democracy.[24] This is better expressed in the following excerpt:

In this sense the recent demonstration of civic energy in Bahia, its magnificent demonstration of a political spirit of concern not only with the narrow fate of the state of Baia, but with the vast Brazilian world that, in Rio Grande do Sul, is called Baia in the inclusive sense, will be seen as historic. It marks the beginning of a new period in the history of Brazilian culture. The old "Virginia of the Empire" rises with new imperial sense of its strength, its matriarchy and political and intellectual fecundity: the imperialism of democracy in parts of Brazil that are undecided between this tradition that is genuinely our own and the violently anti-Brazilian racism, Nazi-Jesuitical fascism under seductive disguises, including that of being "Hispanic."[25]

Elide Rugai Bastos[26] explains the exact sense of "social and ethnic democracy" in Freyre. Currently, at a time when the idea of democracy is intimately related to the idea of civil and individual rights of a universal nature, to speak of "ethnic" or "racial democracy" could lead us to associate these expressions to the rights to representation and authenticity of ethnic and racial minorities. Nothing is more unlike Freyre. Just as for the Spanish generation of 1898 or

1914, "in Gilberto Freyre, this [Iberian] character, responsible for social harmony, makes political democracy retreat into the background, giving way to
ethnic/social democracy. Moreover, he justifies the non-adoption in Brazil of
universal social and political measures, saying they would not be suitable to
a society marked by heterogeneity and a formation not typically western."[27]
     Freyre forged the idea of "social democracy" in the 1930s, against the ev-
ident absence of political democracy, either in Brazil or Portugal. In other
words, he sets himself the challenge of defining Luso-Brazilian participation
in the concert of democratic nations against the backdrop of the similarities
and sympathies of Vargas's and Salazar's autocratic regimes with fascism. He
relies on the fact that Luso-Brazilian culture is not only mixed but denies the
ethnic purity that is typical of the Italian fascist and German Nazi regimes.
From the "social" perspective, therefore, the Vargas and Salazar regimes were
democratic, given that they promoted the integration and social mobility of
people of different races and cultures. To use his words, it is a question of "social, essential, human democracy; political democracy concerns me little."[28]
     As for "racial democracy," Freyre only used the expression in 1962. At
the height of his polemic defense of Portuguese colonialism in Africa and
in the midst of the theoretical construction of what he was to call Luso-
Tropicalism, he decided to attack what he considered to be a foreign influence on black Brazilians, especially the concept of "negritude" coined by
Leopold Senghor, Aimé Césaire, Frantz Fanon, and others, and redrawn
by Guerreiro Ramos and Abdias do Nascimento.[29] In a speech at the Gabi-
nete Português de Leitura that year, Freyre said:

> My thanks go to those who participated by being present at the commemorations
> of Camões Day in Rio de Janeiro this year, and came to hear the words of some-
> one who, as a disciple of Camões' "varied color," is as opposed to the mystique
> of "negritude" as to "whiteness": two sectarian extremes that are contrary to the
> very Brazilian practice of racial democracy through *mestiçagem*: a practice that
> imposes special duties of solidarity with other mixed-race peoples. Especially
> those of the Portuguese Orient and Africa. Especially with those of black and
> *mestiço* Africans marked by the Portuguese presence.[30]

I will come back to Freyre later on, for now it is incumbent on me to detail
the use of the term by Roger Bastide.

ROGER BASTIDE'S ITINERARY OF DEMOCRACY

The history of the expression "racial democracy" begins a bit before the end
of the Second World War. Arthur Ramos[31] relates his intervention at a con-

ference in the United States in 1941 in the following terms: "I declared that we did not know what was really a democratic ambience since to speak of democracy we should distinguish different notions as, for example, political democracy, social democracy, racial democracy, religious democracy, etc."[32]

As we see Ramos repeats Freyre on the different meanings of democracy. But to understand better how Freyre's ideas gained international recognition we must turn now toward a French sociologist who worked extensively on Brazil's race relations during this period and survived by forty years Ramos, who died in 1949.

Roger Bastide took his first trip to the northeast of Brazil in 1944. His impressions from this trip, very much influenced by his reading of Freyre, helped him to form his first perception of race relations in Brazil. These impressions were to change only in the 1950s, when Bastide did research in the field with Florestan Fernandes on "blacks and whites in São Paulo," sponsored by UNESCO and the *Revista Anhembi*.

Bastide then contributed regularly to daily newspapers in São Paulo and other states, engaging in a fertile dialogue with local artists and intellectuals.[33] On March 17, 24, and 31, 1944, Bastide published a series of articles in the *Diário de S.Paulo* entitled "Itinerary of Democracy," a product of his visits to Georges Bernanos in Rio de Janeiro, Jorge Amado in Salvador, and Gilberto Freyre in Recife. Brazil was aligned with the United States, Great Britain, and Russia in the war against the Axis, while France continued to be occupied by German troops. The world was then divided between democracy and fascism.

In the first of the articles, Bastide explained that this had been "an ideological trip, through conversation, in which every great capital visited constituted a phase in the journey of democratic ideology."[34] The meeting with Bernanos in Rio de Janeiro was a pretext for Bastide to explore the universal idea of representative democracy. Bernanos, a militant Christian who had helped organize the French resistance from Rio by broadcasting over BBC London, had an eminently moral understanding of democracy, and extended it beyond the idea of civil rights in the direction of the ethics of political action. But here, the decisive point in this article is that Bastide includes Brazil in the list of democratic nations not because it obeyed a certain public ethics or even because it guaranteed the exercise of civil liberties, but because it engaged in a war against fascism in Europe and therefore shared a certain "concept of man's life and dignity."[35]

The second article, on meeting Jorge Amado in Salvador, focuses on something more specific: the constitution of the people and of popular culture, the subjects and esthetic form of Brazilian democracy. Bastide[36] opens the article with a quick reference to Jorge Amado's novel *Jubiabá*, "where he shows how, instead of using religion to compensate for their daily toils, little by little black people turned to trade unionism, which united them with their workmates in a community that went beyond race and provided another mentality, which is class." Bastide then argues that the people, for Amado, is not reducible to the proletariat, to an economic category, but expresses itself in celebration. "The people is made up of proletarians, no doubt, but is understood as the joy of the *festa*, as creator of esthetic values, as who maintains a certain culture, often the most delicious of all cultures." Jorge Amado, the communist who struggled for freedom, taught him the lesson that democracy is "the same as the birth of a culture."

In the third and last article of the series, on meeting Gilberto Freyre in Recife, Bastide reflected on the social order proper to Brazilian democracy, an order based on the absence of rigid distinctions between whites and blacks. This is the context in which, for the first time, the expression "racial democracy" appeared. Let us reconstitute the scene:

I returned to the city by streetcar. It was full of workers going home from the factory, who mixed their tired bodies with those of day-trippers returning from Dois Irmãos park: a population of *mestiços*, whites and blacks gathered fraternally, squeezed together, crammed onto each other in an enormous and friendly confusion of arms and legs. Close to me, a black man exhausted by the day's efforts let his sleepy head, covered in sweat, droop onto the shoulder of an office worker, a white man who carefully adjusted his shoulders to nest the head, as if to caress it. And this was the beautiful image of *social and racial democracy* that Recife offered me on my way back from the outskirts of the city at sunset.[37]

Brazilian democracy, as Bastide thought of it in 1944, was first of all "social and racial." But "social" had a very precise meaning that had nothing to do with Marshall's[38] social rights. It was the constitution of a social order in which "race" evolved into "class," but in which the "people" that resulted did not copy petit-bourgeois, European, and puritan cultural expressions, as in the United States, but built an original form of racially mixed, free, festive culture. The democracy to which Bastide refers, inspired in Freyre and Amado, cannot be reduced to civil rights and liberties, but achieves a higher region of esthetic and cultural freedom and miscegenated creativity and conviviality.

Most interesting, and indeed decisive, is that Bastide, unlike Freyre, calls this order "racial," even after recognizing the evolution from "race" to "class." This reference to social mixture and to the mixture of whites and blacks as "racial" shows the artificiality of the intended (academic) abolition of race, their evolution into "classes" and the academic rule of calling them "ethnic groups." In the language of newspapers and of politics, closer to common sense and "native" meanings, "racial democracy" and not "ethnic democracy" was to prevail.

THE FIRST MYTH: AGAINST RACIAL DEMOCRACY

The project on race relations in Brazil that UNESCO sponsored between 1952 and 1955 galvanized debate on these differences.[39] The discussion quickly polarized around the existence or not of "racial prejudice" in Brazil, as Bastide and Fernandes did not accept Wagley's conclusion, according to which Brazil, "throughout its enormous area of a half continent race prejudice and discrimination are subdued as compared to the situation in many countries. In Brazil three racial stocks—the American Indian, the Negro and the European Caucasoid—have mingled and mixed to form a society in which racial tensions and conflicts are specially mild, despite the great racial variability of the population."[40] On the contrary, Bastide and Fernandes referred to Charles Wagley's "racial democracy" not as something that could exist in fact, but as an ideal standard of behavior. Bastide wrote: "'We Brazilians,' a white man told us, 'are prejudiced about not being prejudiced. And that simple fact is enough to show how rooted racial prejudice is in our midst.' Many negative responses can be explained by this prejudice towards the absence of prejudice, by Brazil's faithfulness *to its ideal of racial democracy*."[41]

In other words, Bastide and Fernandes see no problem in reconciling the reality of "color prejudice" with the ideal of "racial democracy," and treating them, respectively, as a social practice and a norm that can contradict each other, coincide, and not necessarily be mutually exclusive. Actually, as we shall see, they were broadening Gilberto Freyre's notion of "social and ethnic democracy." For Bastide in the 1950s, "racial democracy" meant an ideal of equal rights and not just of cultural, artistic, and popular expression.

The position of Bastide and Fernandes had already been taken, in practice, by black intellectuals like Abdias do Nascimento and Guerreiro Ramos, who used the ideal of racial democracy to justify their political objectives of unmasking racial discrimination and removing the inhibitions of the "black mass." Thus, the debate over the existence of racial discrimination in Brazil did not yet question the consensus on "racial democracy," even as it polarized its significance.

In fact, the dissemination and political acceptance of the expression "racial democracy" may surprise today's activists: it was current in the black movement of the 1950s. One may recall, for example, that the newspaper *Quilombo*, edited by Abdias do Nascimento from 1948 to 1950, published a column precisely entitled "Racial Democracy," with articles signed by Brazilian and foreign intellectuals allied to the antiracist cause of the time: Gilberto Freyre, Arthur Ramos, Roger Bastide, Murilo Mendes, Estanislau Fischlowitz, Ralph Bunche.

The engagement of black militants with "racial democracy" is glaringly evident in Nascimento's inaugural speech to the First Congress of Brazilian Blacks in August of 1950:

We note how the widespread miscegenation, which was an imperative of our historical formation since the beginning of Brazil's colonization, is becoming, by the inspiration and imposition of recent advances in biology, anthropology and sociology, a well-defined doctrine of racial democracy, to serve as a lesson and model to other peoples with complex ethnic formations like our own.[42]

Freyre did not coin the expression, was even against it, since he spoke of its contradiction in terms (races are groups of descendents and therefore closed, unlike the democracy that Freyre preached). But he was also largely responsible for the scientific legitimization of the affirmation that in Brazil racial prejudice and discrimination did not exist and he maintained a certain distance from the discussion as long as the idea of "racial democracy" remained relatively accepted, whether as a trend or ideal standard of interracial relations in Brazil. In other words, as long as the antifascist struggle persisted and the antiracist struggle brought him close to the Left and progressive Brazilian writers. However, when the situation became polarized in Africa, with the wars of liberation, and in Brazil there was an ideological advance of "negritude" and of the movement for social reforms, Freyre praised "racial" or "ethnic democracy" as evidence of the excellence not only of Luso-Brazilian but Luso-tropical culture. Ironically, he treated "negritude" as a racial myth (or mystique):

Words that offend what is most democratic in Angola—its social democracy through that racial mixture that has been practiced by many Luso-Angolans, in the Brazilian manner—also offends Brazil; and it makes ridiculous—extremely ridiculous—the solidarity with Afroracists that certain diplomats, politicians and journalists in Brazil have today, some from the heights of their responsibility in a government of a largely mixed-race population like Brazil's. What affinity with these Afroracists, who are crudely hostile to the most precious democratic value that has been developed by people of Brazil—racial democracy—can Brazil have? Such diplomats, politicians and journalists, by proceeding in this way, are either being confused about Afroracism, dressed up as a democratic movement with a liberal cause, or they are confusing other Brazilians. We Brazilians cannot be, as Brazilians, anything other than a people that is antisegregationist par excellence: whether segregationism follows the mystique of "whiteness" or the myth of "negritude." Or even "yellowness."[43]

With later political events, especially the victory of conservative forces in 1964, Freyre's idea of a "racial democracy" fully realized on the level of culture and *mestiçagem*, indeed, of the national formation, prevailed.[44]

At a time of so many different kinds of democracy—political, economic, social, racial, ethnic, etc.—some had to be considered false, others genuine. In 1964, in the context of the breakdown of Brazilian democracy precisely in the name of preserving democratic values and ideals, the idea that "racial democracy" was not so much an ideal as a myth came to maturity; it was a racial myth, to use Freyre's words. The author of this expression was precisely someone who was in critical dialogue with Freyre's work and ideas from the beginning of his education: Florestan Fernandes.[45]

Using the same contrast between "aristocracy" and "democracy" and the same concept of "myth" used by Freyre, his dialogue with Freyre could not be more explicit:

Therefore, the historical-social circumstances noted here led to the emergence of the myth of "racial democracy" and its manipulation as an articulation of societal mechanisms of disguised defense of "aristocratic" attitudes, behavior and ideas of the "dominant race." For the opposite to occur, it would have to fall into the hands of blacks and mulattos; and they would have to enjoy equivalent social autonomy to exploit it in the opposite direction, with their own ends, as a factor of democratization of wealth, culture and power.[46]

The breakdown of the democratic pact that had been in force between 1945 and 1964 and that included blacks, both as an organized movement and as a founding element of the nation, seems to have decreed the death, too, of the "racial democracy" of those years. From then on, gradually, political militants and black activits were to refer to both relations between blacks and whites and the ideal standard of these relations as the "myth of racial democracy." The objective was clear: to oppose official ideology sponsored by the military and proclaimed by Luso-Tropicalism.

In 1968, Abdias do Nascimento, a few years away from his exile, already spoke of a "hoax": "Racial status, manipulated by whites, prevents blacks from becoming aware of the hoax that in Brazil is known as racial democracy, democracy of color."[47]

In 1968, too, in a statement made at an event organized by *Cadernos Brasileiros*,[48] the tensions between Abdias do Nascimento and the nationalist Left are clear and signal the end of "racial democracy" as a political commitment. The use of "negritude" in a multiculturalist sense and with ecumenical intentions appears here:

I understand that blacks and mulattos—men of color—need to have a racial counter-ideology and a counter-position on economic and social matters. Brazilians of color run up simultaneously against two changes: a) Brazil's socio-economic change; b) the change in relations of color and race. This is where Negritude comes in as a revolutionary concept and action. Affirming the values of black African culture in our civilization, Negritude affirms its ecumenical condition and its humanistic destiny. It confronts the reactionary element contained in the configuration of mere class struggle of its economic-social complex, because this simplification is a way of preventing or holding back the awareness of being cheated because of the color and poor class to which [the black person] belongs.

In 1977, on his return from exile, Abdias wrote and published, in Lagos, *The Racial Democracy in Brazil: myth or reality?* which was published in Brazil in 1978 as *O Genocídio do Negro Brasileiro*. In the preface, Florestan Fernandes wrote:

[Abdias] does not speak of a "Second Abolition" or locate black and mulatto segments of the Brazilian population as African stocks with peculiar cultural traditions and historical destinies. In sum, for the first time, the definition of democracy in a multiracial society emerges: either that society is democratic for all races and confers economic, social and cultural equality on all of them, or there is no such thing as a multiracial democratic society.[49]

THE SECOND MYTH: AGAINST IDENTITY POLITICS

As we already know, after 1970 black political movements in Brazil reappeared from the starting point of the re-elaboration of the black resistance tradition inscribed internationally in Du Bois's Pan-Africanism, Diop's Afrocentrism, Fanon's anti-colonialism and Abdias do Nascimento's Quilombismo. Throughout the 1980s, the "myth of racial democracy" would be systematically denounced as a dogma of "white supremacy" in Brazil.[50]

The discomfort of Brazilian academe in the face of the advance of the black movement focuses on several important points: first, a certain exaggeration on the part of activist discourse, which is evident in the use of terms like "genocide" to refer to the behavior of Brazilian society with regard to blacks, and the desire to make people believe that the oppression of blacks in Brazil is worse than in the U.S. or South African situation. In other words, the movement's propaganda to transform Brazil's image as a paradise to one of racial hell.[51] Secondly, the movement's intention to politicize Brazilian racial classification, redefining identities like *"preto," "pardo"* or *"moreno"* as *"negro,"* without success because the greater part of the population can at best assimilate this definition slowly.[52] Thirdly, an evident gap between the political discourse of activists and the electoral behavior of the masses, which are much more permeable to populist and labor-centered views than to the Afro-centric appeals of the MNU.[53]

From a theoretical perspective, the academic reaction began with the effort to reinterpret Brazil undertaken by DaMatta,[54] in terms of the dichotomy between "individual" and "person," borrowed from Louis Dumont,[55] culminating in the suggestion that race relations in Brazil are conducted according to a "fable of the three races."[56] Later, reacting to the analysis of Michael Hanchard,[57] who saw the public denouncement of racism in Brazilian society as the end of the myth of racial democracy, Peter Fry wrote, "That does not mean we must discard 'racial democracy' as false ideology. As a myth, in the sense in which anthropologists use the term, it is a powerful set of ideas and values that mean that Brazil is Brazil, to borrow an expression from Roberto DaMatta."[58]

Lilia Schwarcz[59] summarizes that position as follows:

> Thus, using Lévi-Strauss's terms, we could say that the myth is "extenuated but does not disappear" (1975). In other words, the myth continues to be useful even after its rational deconstruction, which means that even recognizing the existence of prejudice in Brazil, the idea of racial harmony is imposed on the facts and even on awareness of discrimination.

In other words, it seems that the denouncement of the "myth of racial democracy" by Florestan Fernandes in 1964, which backed up all of the black mobilization and protests in the decades that followed and explained the distance between discourse and the practice of prejudice, the discrimination and inequalities between whites and blacks in Brazil is finally exhausted as academic discourse, though it contines to survive with some effectiveness as political discourse.

In Brazilian academe, the "myth" begins now to be understood as a key to understanding the national formation, while the contraditions between discourse and practices of racial prejudice began to be studied under a more suitable (albeit highly value-charged) heading of "racism." In other words, the same terrain on which the black movement had placed it. DaMatta himself, who inspired a new round of studies[60] that seek to define the specificity of racism in Brazil, began to use the expression "racism Brazilian style"[61] to compete with the expression "cordial racism"[62] coined by the media. Thus, democracy is no longer used with an adjective to explain Brazilian specificity; racism is.

What continues to be at stake is the distance between discourses and practices of race relations in Brazil, as Florestan Fernandes and Roger Bastide said in the 1950s. However, for the social sciences, the myth cannot be reduced to value judgments, as Freyre and Fernandes did, and transposed directly into politics; the facts of inequalities between blacks and whites in Brazil remain, in spite of the way people are classified. Indeed, racial differences are imposed on individual and social awareness, against the scientific knowledge that denies races (are they like witches that continue to frighten people or the sun that, ignoring Copernicus, continues to "rise" and "set"?). New studies of racial inequalities in Brazil, carried out initially by sociologists and demographers, have gained a hold in more disciplines, like economics,[63] and are leaving the universities to find a home in government planning agencies, where they back up the demands of black protest.

CONCLUSION

Between 1930 and 1964, what political scientists call a "populist" or "nationalist command economy" pact was in force in Brazil. In this pact, Brazilian blacks were entirely integrated into the Brazilian nation in symbolic terms, through the adoption of a national mixed-race or syncretistic national culture and, in material terms, at least partially, through regulation of the labor market and urban social security, reverting the situation of exclusion and neglect sponsored by the First Republic. In this period, the organized black movement concentrated on the struggle against racial prejudice through an eminently universalistic social policy of integration of black people into modern society, with Brazilian "racial democracy" as an ideal to be achieved.

The military coup of 1964 that destroyed the populist pact also burst the bonds of black protest to the political system, bonds mainly of Left nationalism. Even at the beginning of the 1960s, Brazilian foreign policy began to suffer strains because of the position Brazil took on liberation movements in the Portuguese colonies in Africa. The Brazilian black movement, influenced by the francophone *négritude* movement, emphasized African roots; this generated a reaction from intellectuals like Gilberto Freyre[64] in his crusade for the values of racial mixture and Luso-Tropicalism. Discussion of the nature of "racial democracy" in Brazil—whether it was a cultural reality (as Freyre and the conservative establishment would have it) or a political ideal (as the progressives and black movement thought)—led to the radicalization of the two positions. The accusation that Brazilian "racial democracy" was nothing more than "mystification," "hoax," and "myth" became consensual in the movement, as political participation was increasingly restricted and excluded the Left and cultural dissidents. Starting in 1968, the main Brazilian black leaders went into exile. The impossibility of containing social demands of black Brazilians in the narrow parameters of the Freyrean idea of "social democracy" became entirely evident. The Brazilian nation, mixed-race and syncretistic, no longer needed to claim a "not typically Western" origin. On the contrary, social classes and groups made civil, individual, and universal rights the main objective of social struggles.

The reconstruction of democracy in Brazil, starting in 1978, and the renaissance of black "culture" and protest went hand-in-hand. Indeed, they took place in a world in which the idea of multiculturalism was dominant, an idea of tolerance and respect for cultural differences understood as full, authentic and non-syncretic, unlike the postwar nationalist ideal. In this environment, all of the work to rebuild a democratic racial pact, in the form of efforts to incorporate it symbolically and materially in the Brazilian State, were fated to be very limited in their success.

It would be a mistake to attribute the growth of "black consciousness" and the cultivation of racial identity in Brazil of the 1970s to foreign, especially U.S., influence. On the contrary, the black cultural renaissance occurred during these years under the protection of the authoritarian State and its foreign policy interests. Moreover, the turn of the Brazilian black movement toward negritude and African origins dates to the 1960s and was itself responsible for political tensions around the ideal of racial democracy. Similarly, the ideas and name of "racial democracy," far from being a hoax of white dominant classes, as some activists and sociologists like to affirm, were for a long time a form of social integration with which black militancy agreed.

In sum, at the beginning "racial democracy" was the way Arthur Ramos, Roger Bastide, and others translated the ideas expressed by Freyre in lectures in Lisbon in 1937, at the University of Bahia in 1943, and the University of Indiana in 1944. These ideas were by-products of Freyre's reflections on Luso-Brazilian "social democracy." In this "translation," Ramos, Freyre, Wagley, and others omitted the Iberian and restricted definition that Freyre usually attributed to the term; on the contrary, they broadened it, emphasized its universalism as a "Brazilian contribution to humanity" (also claimed by Freyre), appropriate to the antifascist and antiracist coalition of the time. Thus transposed to the field of western individualism, racial democracy gained political content far from the purely "social" nature that prevails in Freyre so that, in time, the expression gained the connotation of the ideal of equality of opportunity and respect for civil and political rights that it had in the 1950s. Later, in the mid-1960s, "racial democracy" reacquired the original Freyrean meaning of racial and ethnic-cultural mixture as such. It thus became, for black activists and intellectuals like Florestan Fernandes, the mark of racism in the Brazilian manner, a racial myth. Finally, for some contemporary intellectuals, the myth has recently become a key for interpreting Brazilian culture.

Racial democracy, now dead, continues to live on as myth and is now understood either as false ideology or as an ideal that orients the action of social agents, or as an interpretative keyword for culture. And as a myth it will continue, for a long time, to be a representation of relations between blacks and whites in Brazil, between the social races[65]—the colors—that compose the nation.

NOTES

1. Myth is a nothing that is everything / The very sun that opens the skies / Is a brilliant and silent myth . . .

2. See Jessé Souza, "Democracia racial e multiculturalismo: a ambivalente singularidade cultural brasileira," *Revista Estudos Afro-Asiáticos* 38, dezembro de 2000: "Gilberto was supposed to have been the inventor of the concept of 'racial democracy,' which acted as the main impediment to the construction of racial awareness by blacks." For an interpretation of the genesis of the idea (not the term) "racial democracy" in Gilberto Freyre, see Elide Rugai Bastos, *Entre Don Quixote e Alonso el Bueno. Gilberto Freyre e o pensamento hispânico*, texto digitado, 2001.

3. Donald Pierson, *Brancos e Pretos na Bahia: estudo de contacto racial* (São Paulo: Editora Nacional, 1942).

4. Ramos 1943 apud Campos (*Arthur Ramos: Luz e Sombra na Antropologia Brasileira. Uma versão da democracia racial no Brasil nas décadas de 1930 e 1940*, 165).

5. Maria José Campos. *Arthur Ramos: Luz e Sombra na Antropologia Brasileira. Uma versão da democracia racial no Brasil nas décadas de 1930 e 1940*. Dissertação de mestrado, apresentada ao Programa de Pós-Graduação em Antropologia Social da USP (São Paulo, FFLCC-USP, 2002).

6. Gilberto Freyre, *Sobrados e Mucambos* (Rio de Janeiro: Editora Nacional, 1936).

7. Gilberto Freyre, *Interpretação do Brasil* (Rio de Janeiro: José Olympio Editora, 1947), 78.

8. Charles Wagley, ed., *Race and Class in Rural Brazil* (New York: Columbia University Press), 1952.

9. Gilberto Freyre, *Casa Grande & Senzala: formação da família brasileira sob o regime da economia patriarcal* (Rio de Janeiro: Schimidt, 1933); Gilberto Freyre, *Sobrados e Mucambos.*

10. See Célia Maria Marinho de Azevedo ("Abolicionismo e memória das relações raciais," *Estudos Afro-Asiáticos* 26, 1994) on the opinion of Ruy Barbosa, Joaquim Nabuco, André Rebouças, and others about race relations in Brazil.

11. Célia Maria Marinho de Azevedo. "O abolicionismo transatlântico e a memória do paraíso racial brasileiro," *Estudos Afro-Asiáticos* 30 (1996).

12. *apud* Azevedo. "O abolicionismo transatlântico e a memória do paraíso racial brasileiro," 150.

13. *apud* Azevedo. "O abolicionismo transatlântico e a memória do paraíso racial brasileiro," 156.

14. David J. Hellwig, ed., *African-American Reflections on Brazil's Racial Paradise* (Philadelphia: Temple University Press, 1992).

15. Manoel Passos, "A Message to American Negroes," *Phylon*, Third Quarter (1942): 284–86.

16. Roger Bastide and Florestan Fernandes (*Relações Raciais entre Negros e Brancos em São Paulo* [São Paulo: UNESCO-ANHEMBI, 1955]) refer to this phenomenon as "black puritanism." Florestan Fernandes, *A Integração do Negro na Sociedade de Classes* (São Paulo: Cia. Editora Nacional, 1965) explores the particular logic of "color prejudice."

17. Freyre, *Sobrados e Mucambos,* 355.

18. Read in July 1937, in Lisbon, by Manuel Murias, this lecture was published for the first time in *Conferencias na Europa* (Rio de Janeiro: Ministério da Educação e Saúde, 1938) and later republished, in 1940, by José Olympio Editora as *O Mundo que o Português Criou.*

19. Gilberto Freyre, *Conferencias na Europa* (Rio de Janeiro: Ministério da Educação e Saúde, 1938), 14.

20. Bastos, *Entre Don Quixote e Alonso el Bueno.*

21. Freyre, *Conferencias na Europa,* 18.

22. Freyre described the atmosphere in which he lived in the 1940s in Recife, when responding to Bahian students that organized the events: "It's not a question of answering. The word 'answer' will only give prestige to the insignificant campaign against me in an intimidated Recife: there are threats of aggression because last year's imprisonment is made impossible by the reaction it provoked; anonymous letters; graffiti on my family's house walls with obscene words painted not by kids who want to be out in the street but by junior Shylocks in the service not only of indigenous Nazis but of Jesuits as foreign to bathwater as to Brazil and the Brazilian clergy." Gilberto Freyre, *Na Bahia em 1943* (Rio de Janeiro: Cia. Brasileira de Artes Gráficas, 1944), 80.

23. Freyre, *Na Bahia em 1943,* 30.

24. The lecture "A Culture in Danger: the Luso-Brazilian One," given by Freyre in 1940 at the Royal Portuguese Reading Room, illustrates these regional and nationalist tensions.

25. Gilberto Freyre, "Um engano de José Lins do Rego," *O Jornal,* Rio de Janeiro, 25 jan., 1944.

26. Bastos, *Entre Don Quixote e Alonso el Bueno.*

27. Bastos, *Entre Don Quixote e Alonso el Bueno,* 62.

28. Gilberto Freyre, *O mundo que o Português criou* (Rio de Janeiro: Livraria José Olympio Editora Freyre, 1940), 51.

29. Roger Bastide, "Variations sur la négritude." *Presence Africaine* 36 (1961).

30. Gilberto Freyre, *O Brasil em face das Áfricas negras e mestiças* (Rio de Janeiro: Federação das Associações Portuguesas, 1962).

31. Ramos 1943 apud Campos (*Arthur Ramos: Luz e Sombra na Antropologia Brasileira. Uma versão da democracia racial no Brasil nas décadas de 1930 e 1940,* 165).

32. Ramos 1943 apud Campos (*Arthur Ramos: Luz e Sombra na Antropologia Brasileira. Uma versão da democracia racial no Brasil nas décadas de 1930 e 1940,*

165). Campos, in her Master's thesis, recovers Arthur Ramos' historical importance to international dissemination of the idea of Brazil as a "racial democracy," Brazilians as a "mestizo people," and Brazilian culture as "syncretistic." Campos, however, does not understand the historical and dated nature of the expression "racial democracy," preferring to use it as a founding myth, of undetermined origin, in the Levi-Straussian manner.

33. Fernanda Áreas Peixoto, *Diálogos brasileiros. Uma análise da obra de Roger Bastide* (São Paulo: Edusp/Fapesp, 2000).

34. Roger Bastide, "Itinerário da democracia I—Encontro com Bernanos," *Diário de São Paulo*, sexta-feira, 17 de agosto de 1944.

35. Bastide, "Itinerário da democracia I—Encontro com Bernanos."

36. Roger Bastide, "Itinerário da democracia II—Encontro com Jorge Amado," *Diário de São Paulo*, sexta-feira, 24 de agosto de 1944.

37. Roger Bastide, "Itinerário da democracia III—Em Recife, com Gilberto Freyre," *Diário de São Paulo*, sexta-feira, 31 de agosto de 1944.

38. T. H. Marshall, "Cidadania e classe social" (The Marshall Lectures) in *Cidadania, Classe Social e Status* (Rio de Janeiro: Zahar, 1967).

39. For a detailed analysis of the UNESCO-sponsored studies in Brazil in the 1950s, see Marcos Chor Maio, *A História do Projeto Unesco. Estudos Raciais e Ciências Sociais no Brasil.* tese doutorado (Rio de Janeiro: IUPERJ, 1997).

40. Wagley, *Race and Class in Rural Brazil,* 7.

41. Bastide and Fernandes, *Relações Raciais entre Negros e Brancos em São Paulo,* 123, my emphasis.

42. 1950 *apud* Abdias Nascimento, *O Negro revoltado* (Rio de Janeiro: Edições GRD, 1968).

43. Freyre, *O Brasil em face das Áfricas negras e mestiças.*

44. On *mestiçagem,* see Kabengele Munanga, ed., *Estratégias e Políticas de Combate à Discriminação Racial* (São Paulo: Edusp, 1999).

45. In 1964, Fernandes defended a thesis written for the examination for the Sociology I Chair at the University of São Paulo, *A integração do negro na sociedade de classes*, published in Boletim No. 301, Sociologia I, No. 12, FFLCH - USP the same year. In 1964, too, Florestan gave a lecture in the Introductory Course on Black Theater on the myth of racial democracy.

46. Fernandes, *A Integração do Negro na Sociedade de Classes,* 205.

47. Nascimento, *O Negro revoltado,* 22.

48. Abdias Nascimento, "Depoimento," *Cadernos Brasileiros* 47 (1968): 23.

49. Nascimento, *O Negro revoltado,* 20.

50. An excellent example of the radicalization of political discourse and its influence on academic discourse can be found in the title of Twine's book (1998).

51. Livio Sansone, "De paraíso a inferno racial," Salvador, *A Tarde,* Caderno 3 (9 de novembro, 1996).

52. Marvin Harris et al. "Who are the whites? Imposed census categories and the racial demography of Brazil," *Social Forces* 72 (1993): 451–62; Yvonne Maggie, "Aqueles a quem foi negada a cor do dia: as catogorias de cor e raça na cultura brasileira," in *Raça, Ciência e Sociedade,* ed. Marcos C. Maio and Ricardo V. Santos (Rio de Janeiro: Ed. Fiocruz/Centro Cultural Banco do Brasil, 1996).

53. Souza 1971; Santos 1985; Guimarães 2001.
54. Roberto DaMatta, *Carnavais, malandros e heróis* (Rio de Janeiro: Ed. Guanabara, 1979).
55. Louis Dumont, "Caste, racisme et 'stratification,'" *Homo Hierarchicus* (Paris: Gallimard, 1966).
56. Roberto DaMatta, "Digressão: a fábula das três raças, ou o problema do racismo à brasileira," in *Relativizando, uma introdução à antropologia social* (Petrópolis: Ed. Vozes, 1981).
57. Michael Hanchard, "Cinderela negra? raça e esfera pública no Brasil," *Estudos Afro-Asiáticos* 30 (1996).
58. Peter Fry, "O que a Cinderela Negra tem a dizer sobre a política racial brasileira," *Revista USP* 28 (1995–1996): 134.
59. Lilia Schwarcz, "Questão Racial e Etnicidade," in *O que ler na Ciência Social Brasileira (1970–1995)*, ed. Sérgio Miceli. Antropologia v. II (São Paulo: ANPOCS, 1999), 309.
60. Antonio S. A. Guimarães, "Racismo e anti-racismo no Brasil," *Novos Estudos Cebrap* 43, novembro de 1995; Carlos Hasenbalg, "Entre o mito e os fatos: racismo e relações raciais no Brasil," in *Raça, Ciência e Sociedade*, ed. Marcos C. Maio and Ricardo V. Santos (Rio de Janeiro: Ed. Fiocruz, Centro Cultural Banco do Brasil, 1996).
61. João Baptista Borges Pereira, "Racismo à brasileira," in *Estratégias e Políticas de Combate à Discriminação Racial*, ed. Kabengele Munanga (São Paulo: Edusp, 1996); Roberto DaMatta, "Notas sobre o racismo à brasileira," in *Multiculturalismo e racismo: Uma comparação Brasil-Estados Unidos*, ed. Jessé Souza (Brasília: Ed. Paralelo 15, 1997).
62. *Folha de S.Paulo/Data Folha* (1995).
63. R. P. Barros, Henriques and R. Mendonça, "A estabilidade inaceitável: desigualdade e pobreza no Brasil," in, *Desigualdade e Pobreza no Brasil*, ed. Ricardo Henriques (Rio de Janeiro: IPEA, 2000); Sergei Soares, "O perfil da discriminação no mercado de trabalho—homens negros, mulheres brancas e mulheres negras," *Textos para Discussão* 769 (IPEA, 2000).
64. Gilberto Freyre, *Integração das raças autóctones e de culturas diferentes da européia na comunidade luso-tropical: aspectos gerais de um processo* (Lisboa: Congresso Internacional de História dos Descobrimentos Freyre, 1961); Freyre, *O Brasil em face das Áfricas negras e mestiças*.
65. Wagley, *Race and Class in Rural Brazil*.

BIBLIOGRAPHY

Agier, Michel. *Anthropologie du carnaval. La ville, la fête et l'Afrique à Bahia*. Paris: Éditions Parenthèses, 2000.
Azevedo, Célia Maria Marinho de. "Abolicionismo e memória das relações raciais," *Estudos Afro-Asiáticos* 26 (1994): 5–20.

————. "O abolicionismo transatlântico e a memória do paraíso racial brasileiro," *Estudos Afro-Asiáticos* 30 (1996).

Barros, R. P., Henriques and R. Mendonça. "A estabilidade inaceitável: desigualdade e pobreza no Brasil." In *Desigualdade e Pobreza no Brasil*, edited by Ricardo Henriques. Rio de Janeiro: IPEA, 2000.

Bastide, Roger. "Variations sur la négritude." *Presence Africaine* 36 (1961): 7–17.

————. "Itinerário da democracia I—Encontro com Bernanos," *Diário de São Paulo* (sexta-feira, 17 de agosto de 1944).

————. "Itinerário da democracia II—Encontro com Jorge Amado," *Diário de São Paulo* (sexta-feira, 24 de agosto de 1944).

————. "Itinerário da democracia III—Em Recife, com Gilberto Freyre," *Diário de São Paulo* (sexta-feira, 31 de agosto de 1944).

Bastide, Roger, and Florestan Fernandes. *Relações Raciais entre Negros e Brancos em São Paulo*. São Paulo: UNESCO-ANHEMBI, 1955.

Bastos, Elide Rugai. *Entre Don Quixote e Alonso el Bueno. Gilberto Freyre e o pensamento hispânico*, texto digitado, 2001.

Campos, Maria José. *Arthur Ramos: Luz e Sombra na Antropologia Brasileira. Uma versão da democracia racial no Brasil nas décadas de 1930 e 1940*. Dissertação de mestrado, apresentada ao Programa de Pós-Graduação em Antropologia Social da USP, São Paulo: FFLCC-USP, 2002.

DaMatta, Roberto. *Carnavais, malandros e heróis*. Rio de Janeiro: Ed. Guanabara, 1979.

————. "Digressão: a fábula das três raças, ou o problema do racismo à brasileira." In *Relativizando, uma introdução à antropologia social*. Petrópolis: Ed. Vozes, 1981.

————. "Notas sobre o racismo à brasileira." In *Multiculturalismo e racismo, Uma comparação Brasil-Estados Unidos*, edited by Jessé Souza, 69–76. Brasília: Ed. Paralelo 15, 1997.

Dumont, Louis. "Caste, racisme et 'stratification.'" In *Homo Hierarchicus*. Paris: Gallimard, 1966.

Fernandes, Florestan. *A Integração do Negro na Sociedade de Classes*. São Paulo: Cia. Editora Nacional, 1965.

Folha de São Paulo/DataFolha. 1995. *Racismo Cordial*. São Paulo: Ed.Ática.

Freyre, Gilberto. *Casa Grande & Senzala: formação da família brasileira sob o regime da economia patriarcal*. Rio de Janeiro: Schimidt, 1933.

————. *Sobrados e Mucambos*. Rio de Janeiro: Editora Nacional, 1936.

————. *Conferencias na Europa*. Rio de Janeiro: Ministério da Educação e Saúde, 1938.

————. *O mundo que o Português criou*. Rio de Janeiro: Livraria José Olympio Editora, 1940.

————. *Na Bahia em 1943*. Rio de Janeiro: Cia. Brasileira de Artes Gráficas, 1944.

————. "Um engano de José Lins do Rego," *O Jornal*, Rio de Janeiro, 25 Jan., 1944.

————. *Interpretação do Brasil*. Rio de Janeiro: José Olympio Editora, 1947.

————. *Integração das raças autóctones e de culturas diferentes da européia na comunidade luso-tropical: aspectos gerais de um processo*. Lisboa: Congresso Internacional de História dos Descobrimentos, 1961.

———. *O Brasil em face das Áfricas negras e mestiças*. Rio de Janeiro: Federação das Associações Portuguesas, 1962.

Fry, Peter. "O que a Cinderela Negra tem a dizer sobre a política racial brasileira." *Revista USP* 28 (1995–1996): 122–35.

Guimarães, Antonio S. A. "Racismo e anti-racismo no Brasil." *Novos Estudos Cebrap* 43 (novembro de 1995): 26–44.

———. "A questão racial na política brasileira (os últimos quinze anos), São Paulo, *Tempo Social* 13, no. 2 (novembro de 2001): 121–42.

Hanchard, Michael. "Cinderela negra? raça e esfera pública no Brasil." *Estudos Afro-Asiáticos* 30 (1996).

Harris, Marvin, et al. "Who are the Whites? Imposed census categories and the racial demography of Brazil." *Social Forces* 72 (1993): 451–62.

Hasenbalg, Carlos. "Entre o mito e os fatos: racismo e relações raciais no Brasil." In *Raça, Ciência e Sociedade,* edited by Marcos C. Maio and Ricardo V. Santos. Rio de Janeiro: Ed. Fiocruz/Centro Cultural Banco do Brasil, 1996.

Hellwig, David J., ed. *African-American Reflections on Brazil's Racial Paradise.* Philadelphia: Temple University Press, 1992.

Maggie, Yvonne. "Aqueles a quem foi negada a cor do dia: as catogorias de cor e raça na cultura brasileira." In *Raça, Ciência e Sociedade*, edited by Marcos C. Maio and Ricardo V. Santos. Rio de Janeiro: Ed. Fiocruz/Centro Cultural Banco do Brasil, 1996.

Maio, Marcos Chor. *A História do Projeto Unesco. Estudos Raciais e Ciências Sociais no Brasil*, Rio de Janeiro, IUPERJ, tese doutorado, 1997.

Marshall, T. H. "Cidadania e classe social" (The Marshall Lectures). In *Cidadania, Classe Social e Status*. Rio de Janeiro: Zahar, 1967.

Nascimento, Abdiasdo. "Inaugurando o Congresso do Negro," *Quilombo* 10 (junho–julho de 1950): 1.

———. *O Negro revoltado*. Rio de Janeiro: Edições GRD, 1968.

———. "Depoimento." *Cadernos Brasileiros* 47 (1968).

———. *O Genocídio do Negro Brasileiro*. Rio de Janeiro: Paz e Terra, 1978.

Passos, Manoel. "A Message to American Negroes." *Phylon*, Third Quarter (1942): 284–86.

Peixoto, Fernanda Áreas. *Diálogos brasileiros. Uma análise da obra de Roger Bastide*. São Paulo: Edusp; Fapesp, 2000.

Pereira, João Baptista Borges. "Racismo à brasileira." *Estratégias e Políticas de Combate à Discriminação Racial*, edited by Kabengele Munanga, 75–78. São Paulo, Ed. Edusp, 1996.

Pierson, Donald. *Brancos e Pretos na Bahia: estudo de contacto racial*. São Paulo, Editora Nacional, 1971 (1942).

Sansone, Livio. "De paraíso a inferno racial," Salvador, *A Tarde*, Caderno 3 (9 de novembro, 1996): 9.

Santos, Jocélio Teles. "O poder da cultura e a cultura no poder. A construção da disputa simbólica da herança cultural negra no Brasil," Tese de doutorado, Departamento de Antropologia da USP, 2000.

Santos, Joel Rufino dos. "O movimento negro e a crise brasileira," in *Política e Administração* 2 (July–September 1985): 287–307.

Schwarcz, Lilia. "Questão Racial e Etnicidade." In *O que ler na Ciência Social Brasileira (1970–1995)*. Antropologia v. II, edited by Sérgio Miceli, 267–326. São Paulo: ANPOCS, 1999.

Soares, Sergei. "O perfil da discriminação no mercado de trabalho—homens negros, mulheres brancas e mulheres negras." *Textos para Discussão* 769 (IPEA, 2000).

Souza, Amauri de."Raça e política no Brasil urbano." *Revista de Administração de Empresas* XI (out-dez, 1971).

Souza, Jessé. "Democracia racial e multiculturalismo: a ambivalente singularidade cultural brasileira." *Revista Estudos Afro-Asiáticos* 38 (dezembro de 2000): 135–55.

——. *A modernização seletiva*. Brasília: Ed.UNB, 2000.

Twine, France Winddance. *Racism in a Racial Democracy: The Maintenance of White Supremacy in Brazil*. New Brunswick, N.J.: Rutgers University Press, 1998.

Wagley, Charles, ed. *Race and Class in Rural Brazil*. New York: Columbia University Press, 1952.

7

From Bahia to Brazil: the UNESCO Race Relations Project

Marcos Chor Maio

Race and race relations became hallmarks in Brazilian social thought and, more specifically, in the process of creation and institutionalization of the Brazilian social sciences. I credit this to the intense concern of Brazilian intellectuals with issues such as the country's belated capitalist development, its social and racial inequalities, the need to build a national identity, and the urge to set the country's overall standards at a level consistent with modernity.

It is important to add that race and ethnic studies decisively influenced the formation of important members of the Brazilian intelligentsia. The case of sociologist Gilberto Freyre is exemplar. In his preface to the first edition of *Casa-Grande & Senzala* (1933), Freyre links his meeting in the early 1920s, with the anthropologist Franz Boas, the professor at Columbia University who most influenced him, to his own identity as a member of an intelligentsia concerned with the destiny of Brazil. He emphasizes that one of his major concerns was miscegenation. As he affirmed: "I do not believe that any Russian student among the romantics of the nineteenth century was more intensely preoccupied with the destiny of Russia than was I with that of Brazil at the time that I knew Boas. It was as if everything depended on me and on those of my generation, on how successful we were in solving age-old questions. And of all the problems Brazil was confronted with, there was none that caused me so much anxiety as that of miscegenation."[1]

In the same preface, Freyre states that Boas's intellectual orientation "first revealed to me the black and the mulatto for what they are—with the effects of environment or cultural experience separated from racial characteristics. I learned to regard the difference between *race* and *culture* as fundamental."[2]

Freyre considered that it was Boas who taught him to appropriately approach the "black and the mulatto," failing to mention the entire set of non-European races and mestizos in general. Thus, Freyre implicitly acknowledges that the presence of the blacks in Brazil was the major symbol of the race mixture which gave Brazilian society its unique composition. Therefore, his attempt to reevaluate this outcome is concentrated on the relations between whites and blacks, depicted in the polar wordings of the titles of his first books: "*Casa-grande*" and "*Senzala*" and "*Sobrados*" and "*Mucambos*" (1936).

Freyre illustrates how important the issue of national identity was for Brazilian intellectuals of the 1930s. He thought he had found the core of the Brazilian national character in the *casa-grande* (Big House), emphasizing African, Ameridian, and Portuguese contribution of the emergence of a specific culture.

However, after World War II there was a certain displacement of topics related to national identity in the debate about Brazil. The new focus fell upon social inequalities. With the growth of industrial capitalism, the 1940s and 1950s brought deep changes to Brazilian society. The population grew, middle classes expanded, the working classes gained importance, the bureaucratic apparatus of the state changed, social demands rose in cities and in rural areas. Although these changes occurred unequally in the vast Brazilian territory, even in the more advanced areas of the southeast they were strong enough to catch the eye of many intellectuals, and were explained by the precepts of "developmentalist ideologies." During the same period there was an expansion of Brazilian universities and, more specifically, of the output of social scientists.

In this context, in the early 1950s there was a cycle of studies sponsored by the United Nations Educational, Scientific, and Cultural Organization (UNESCO), which was decisive for the professionalization of Brazilian social sciences. Sociologists and anthropologists such as Thales de Azevedo, Florestan Fernandes, Roger Bastide, Charles Wagley, Luiz de Aguiar Costa Pinto, Oracy Nogueira, Marvin Harris, René Ribeiro, among others, conducted these studies. Where did the idea of this cycle of studies come from?

This chapter will focus on the relationship between race studies and the social sciences in Brazil, taking the "UNESCO race relations project" on Brazilian race relations as a point of departure. My hypothesis is that the "UNESCO project" amounted to the successful implementation of the agenda for the social sciences as proposed by the Brazilian anthropologist Arthur Ramos in the last years of the 1940s.

This agenda followed the pragmatic tradition of social sciences in Brazil, which was systematically concerned with placing Brazil within the circle of modern nations. It included a series of topics that ultimately sought to shed light upon obstacles to modernization of Brazilian society. However, in the years immediately following the Holocaust, the success of a particular enterprise, such as the UNESCO project in Brazil, demanded a transatlantic network of social scientists that would place it in the larger context of the scientific quest for a reasonable explanation for the persistence of racism after World War II and the possible ways of overcoming it. These social scientists who studied Brazil were aware of certain goals included in UNESCO's agenda—such as industrialization, access to education and science—that emerged through pressures exerted by developing countries. In this sense, the "UNESCO race relations project" was based on the belief in a positive Brazilian sociability concerning race matters and on the urge to bring certain social segments of Brazil, including blacks, into modernity. The final design of the "UNESCO project" was the result of a concerted action that turned a research project—whose primary intention had been to enhance Brazil's positive image in race matters as an example to the rest of the world—into a plan to analyze Brazilian problems, such as: social disparities, racial inequalities, and the Brazilian style of racism (*"racismo à brasileira"*).

In order to better sustain my argument, I will first present a brief description of the origins of the "UNESCO race relations project." I will then focus on how the research project was put together, and will also discuss its findings. Finally, I will consider the project's impacts.

ARTHUR RAMOS AND THE AGENDA OF THE SOCIAL SCIENCES

In mid-October of 1949, Arthur Ramos finished drafting a plan that predicted "research projects about race and race relations and the biological and social aspects of miscegenation. . . . Three different countries would be chosen as the experimental basis for the projects, in order to see if race relations and the process of race miscegenation unravel in a harmonious or non-harmonious manner, from the point of view of social tensions."[3] At the same time Ramos foresaw the development of sociological and anthropological studies in Brazil.[4] Attuned to the agency's concern with racial problems and with the difficulties experienced by developing countries, Ramos thought it necessary to give special attention to the "study of black and native groups, so that they could be integrated with the modern world."[5]

In June of 1950, the Fifth Session of General Conference of UNESCO approved the research project on race relations in Brazil, but Arthur Ramos, who had been responsible for the idea, had died eight months earlier. He had not defined the details of the study he had in mind. It is remarkable, however, that even without his input the final design and the results of several investigations carried the same concerns that could be found in Ramos's reflections about Brazil.

In one of his last articles,[6] Ramos insisted that Brazil was a "laboratory of civilization," an expression he took from the North American historian Rudiger Bilden.[7] However, Ramos observed that only recently had Brazilian social sciences initiated a process of professional qualification that would allow them to be ready to study this "laboratory."[8]

Ramos believed that the institutionalization of the Social Sciences would provide a unique opportunity for going beyond the "armchair, bookworm" phase of studies about indigenous and black peoples.[9] He thought that the appropriate path would be the investigation of the heritage of slavery and its implications for understanding the Brazilian race situation, with special attention to the sociological factors of caste and class, the stereotypes of opinions and attitudes which maintain racism.[10]

Ramos pointed out that any interpretation of race relations in Brazil would have to be preceded by a series of investigations. According to Ramos, there was no homogeneous Brazilian cultural perspective. There were many cultures that only then were beginning to be studied and understood. Therefore, the existence of a national identity should be based on historical or social criteria.[11] Thus, the Social Sciences agenda, as presented by Ramos, prevailed in the design of the "UNESCO race relations project" in Brazil. The scope of the research project in Brazil was defined between June and December of 1950.

THE ORIGINS OF "UNESCO RACE RELATIONS PROJECT"

In September of 1949, the fourth session of the General Conference of UNESCO approved an antiracist agenda, in response to a demand made by the United Nations (UN).[12] When the Universal Declaration on Human Rights was issued in December of 1948, it impelled UN agencies, such as the Economic and Social Council (ECOSOC), to establish policies aimed at protecting ethnic and racial minorities.[13]

UNESCO has been established following the catastrophic results of World War II. One of its major goals was to understand the international conflict and its most perverse consequence, the Holocaust. The issue of race was also kept in the forefront of public attention by the persistence of racism, especially in the United States and in South Africa, the emergence of the Cold War, and the disruption of colonialism in Africa and Asia. UNESCO, with its egalitarian and universalistic perspective, stimulated scientific inquiry into racism that would address motivations, effects, and possible ways of overcoming it.[14] To this end, UNESCO encouraged in the early 1950s a cycle of studies about

Brazilian race relations. Research was conducted in economically traditional regions such as the northeast as well as in industrialized areas of the southeast, to present to the world the details of an experience in race relations that at that time was deemed unique and successful.[15]

Brazil's positive image in racial matters played a major role in UNESCO's decision to sponsor a research program there. The final research design expressed the concern of UNESCO's Department of Social Sciences and invited researchers to fulfill the international agency's resolution of "organizing in Brazil a pilot investigation about contacts between race and ethnic groups, in order to determine the economic, social, political, cultural and psychological factors favorable or unfavorable to the existence of harmonious relations between race and ethnic groups."[16]

The strongest evidence of such concern was the change in the original focus of the investigation. At first, the state of Bahia was the only area of investigation designated.[17] But, during the planning of the UNESCO Project, Rio de Janeiro, São Paulo, and later Pernambuco were included.[18] This change in the research design resulted from three factors: previous knowledge about Brazil among UNESCO staff members, understandings among Brazilian and non-Brazilian social scientists active in Brazil, and an existing tradition of investigating race relations in the country.

THE CHOICE OF BRAZIL

The belief in Brazil as an exemplar in race relations dated back to the nineteenth century, when reports from travelers, scientists, journalists, and politicians from Europe and the United States registered surprise at the peaceful coexistence between whites, blacks, and natives.[19] This image of a "racial paradise," contrasted with the turbulent U.S. experience, but it contradicted the views prevailing among Brazilian elites. After the belated end of black slavery (1888) and the creation of a republican regime (1889), these elites considered the massive presence of blacks and widespread miscegenation to be obstacles to the country's modernization.[20]

In the first decades of the twentieth century, particularly from the 1920s to the 1940s, this pessimistic view of the contribution of the founding races of Brazilian society was dislodged by a more positive outlook. Relations between blacks and whites in Brazil came to be perceived instead an indicator of tolerance and harmony. This shift can be attributed to economic, social, and political transformations in the country and an ongoing debate over the formation of Brazilian national identity.[21] The controversial belief in a Brazilian racial democracy, which found its most refined interpretation in the work of sociologist

Gilberto Freyre,[22] became an ideological cornerstone of racial integration. This view was substantial enough to attract international attention. It was in the wake of Nazi genocide that Brazil's seemingly harmonious race and ethnic relations became famous enough to attract the attention of UNESCO.

UNESCO's antiracist agenda reflected a new international juncture with two major political components: the struggle against racism as a result of the rise of undeveloped countries, many recently born out of decolonization in Africa and Asia; and pressure by the USSR on the United States during the cold war, manifested in one dimension by the Soviet critique of racism in the United States, which the USSR tried to side with third world countries.[23] It is therefore plausible to suppose that the choice of Brazil as an object of study could advance the ideological battle between the United States and the West against communism.

In 1949, Arthur Ramos became the head of UNESCO's Department of Social Sciences. A physician and an anthropologist, Ramos completed studies in psychoanalysis, education, and public health in his short life (1903–1949), but he is remembered today for his research and reflections on Afro-Brazilians. His studies exhibit two well-defined phases. In the first, he proposed to reexamine the biological work of Raimundo Nina Rodrigues, a pioneer in the scientific study of Brazilians of African descent, substituting the ideas of the Italian and French schools of criminology and psychoanalysis. In the second phase, Ramos studied Afro-Brazilians and their lifestyles from a cultural perspective, under the influence of the theory of acculturation. Ramos's later writings represent an attempt to consider the issue of Afro-Brazilians as a structural problem rather than a matter of culture.[24]

During World War II, Ramos became an outspoken critic of racism. He published four manifestos and a series of articles attacking Nazism and promoting the possible contributions that the social sciences could make to racial understanding in the aftermath of the war.[25] During the 1930s and 1940s, he maintained close ties with social scientists in the United States.[26] In the early years, the social sciences at UNESCO were dominated by the U.S. academic world.[27] UNESCO later acknowledged Ramos and his intellectual engagement with racism.[28]

Ramos's appointment resulted from a political deal between two ranking UNESCO actors. The first was Brazilian chemist Paulo Estevão de Berredo Carneiro, who represented Brazil's positivist, antiracist, and integrationist tradition. He also represented Brazil in UNESCO and on its Executive Board. The second was the director of UNESCO, Mexican intellectual Jaime Torres Bodet. Carneiro helped create and implement UNESCO and define its early policies. He was in close contact with English biologist Julian Huxley, the first General Director of UNESCO, and particularly with Bodet. Carneiro supported Ramos's appointment,[29] and Torres Bodet agreed. Ramos was also approved by Otto Klineberg,[30] a social psychologist in the tradition of Franz Boas and acting head of the UNESCO Department of Social Sciences.[31]

Responding to the directive of fighting racism, approved in the Fourth session of the UNESCO General Conference, "Study and Dissemination of Scientific Facts Concerning Questions of Race," Arthur Ramos implemented Klineberg's proposal to hold an international meeting of experts, most of them social scientists, to debate the scientific standing of the concept of race.[32] Ramos displayed keen sensitivity in selecting notoriously antiracist scientists to debate racial questions. Of the eight scientists who participated in the meeting in Paris[33] in December 1949, three had some experience in teaching or conducting research in Brazil: Claude Lévi-Strauss, Franklin Frazier, and Luiz de Aguiar Costa Pinto. The two representatives of Europe, where Nazi genocide had taken place, were Jews (Morris Ginsberg, Lévi-Strauss). From the United States, where "Jim Crow laws" were still in effect, Ramos invited an African-American (Franklin Frazier) and an English Jew (Ashley Montagu) who lived in the United States and had fought racism openly during the war. This meeting in Paris went beyond debating the scientific standing of the concept of race to propose a worldwide comparative research agenda on racial prejudice and discrimination. Frazier, Ginsberg, Costa Pinto, and Mexican Anthropologist Juan Comas recommended Brazil as one country in which such research should be conducted.[34]

Between January and May 1950, UNESCO's Executive Board worked on conducting "a pilot research project about race contacts in a Latin American country."[35] In April of 1950, the Swiss-U.S. anthropologist Alfred Métraux, who was experienced in ethnological investigations of native and black groups both in South and Central America, became director of the recently created UNESCO Division for the Study of Race Problems.[36] Brazilian anthropologist Ruy Coelho, a former student of Roger Bastide at the Universidade de São Paulo, and of Melville Herskovits at Northwestern University, became Métraux's main assistant. The division thus became a pro-Brazil pressure group within the Department of Social Sciences.[37]

The resulting Statement on Race was made public in May of 1950, during UNESCO's fifth session of the General Conference in Florence, Italy. It was the first document issued by an intergovernmental agency to negate any deterministic association between physical characteristics, social behaviors, and moral attributes. When the *Statement on Race* was publicized by such conclusions as "race is less a biological fact than a social myth and as a myth it has in recent years taken a heavy toll in human lives and suffering,"[38] UNESCO's Conference approved the research project on race relations in Brazil. Thus the radical statement denying the scientific validity of the concept of race was followed by the selection of a country with a population considered the result of miscegenation and therefore definite proof that such miscegenation was universal, and a refutation of the concept of a world inhabited by distinct races.[39] The scope of the proposed research project in Brazil as to be defined between June and December of 1950.

FROM BAHIA TO BRAZIL

Initially, the "UNESCO Project" planned to focus only on the state of Bahia because of a tradition of studies of blacks in the city of Salvador, going back to the late nineteenth century. These studies underscored strong influences of African cultures.[40] Bahia thus seemed an appropriate backdrop for UNESCO's purposes. Salvador's large proportion of black residents had also attracted the attention of U.S. researchers and was viewed as a laboratory in terms of race interactions.[41] Another opportunity arose while the project's design was being defined. Less than two weeks after the 1950 Conference in Florence, U.S. anthropologist Charles Wagley contacted UNESCO. He had been working in Brazil since the late 1930s, studying native communities and participating in the Brazilian-U.S. alliance during World War II.[42]

Wagley was in Brazil at the time and wrote Métraux to brief him about the activities generated by the joint project conducted by Columbia University and the State of Bahia.[43] Wagley then offered to work with the UNESCO Project. His offer was well received by Métraux and Coelho, because it amounted to the inclusion of a research project "fully designed and in progress, . . . requiring only to be conducted in the direction that we wish."[44] The topic of race relations was an integral part of the community studies being conducted in the interior of Bahia. Wagley also suggested that investigations be made in the city of Salvador, under anthropologist Thales de Azevedo, who was connected with the project cosponsored by Columbia University and the state of Bahia. Coelho approved the study in the capital of Bahia, "because investigations in Salvador would give us an idea of the conditions prevailing in an urban center."[45]

In the meantime, four other social scientists proposed broadening the scope of the UNESCO Project. Otto Klineberg observed, "São Paulo and Salvador are so different, in so many ways, that the fact that they are both cities seems to me almost irrelevant in this case. I think it would be very important to study race relations under a number of different conditions, and I would urge strongly once again that the study be not restricted to the situation in and around Bahia."[46] Charles Wagley shared this opinion.[47]

Brazilian sociologist Luiz de Aguiar Costa Pinto, a participant in the UNESCO debates over the scientific status of the concept of race, also wrote

Métraux about the project. He expressed interest in forming an agreement between UNESCO and the Social Sciences Department of the Faculdade Nacional de Filosofia of the Universidade do Brasil to "conduct, in Rio de Janeiro, in accordance with UNESCO's plan, the investigations and analyses required to research racial tensions in a Brazilian metropolitan area, analyzing the Brazilian racial situation from the perspective of a society going through a strong process of industrialization."[48]

In September 1950, Métraux contacted French sociologist Roger Bastide, a professor of the Universidade de São Paulo since 1938. This important figure in the study of Afro-Brazilian culture had written a series of sociological texts on blacks in Brazil.[49] Bastide knew Métraux personally and they shared intellectual and professional interests, such as the study of blacks in the Guyanas.[50] Métraux wrote Bastide, "Naturally, it will be in Bahia that our main efforts will be made, but I wish to research other regions of Brazil and I will need your advice for this matter. When I visit Brazil, I will look you up and we will discuss the quite complex aspects of this research project."[51]

Bastide had just served as the French representative to the Primeiro Congresso do Negro Brasileiro in Rio de Janeiro in August 1950, under the sponsorship of the Teatro Experimental do Negro (TEN—Black Experimental Theater); this political-cultural organization was in its heyday in the late 1940s and early 1950s. According to leader Abdias Nascimento, the event was intended to bring scientists and intellectuals closer to the black movement and to help pull together academic work and political action aimed at producing alternatives for reducing social inequalities between whites and blacks.[52]

At that juncture, TEN identified with UNESCO's recent choice of Brazil as "a socio-anthropological laboratory." Alberto Guerreiro Ramos, a mulatto sociologist active in TEN, proposed that the Primeiro Congresso do Negro Brasileiro should try to pressure the Brazilian government to convince UNESCO to sponsor an international congress on race relations.[53] Guerreiro Ramos thought that in the aftermath of World War II, UNESCO had a significant role to play in "integrating race minorities in the several countries in which they are more or less discriminated against."[54] To this end, UNESCO would have to present "practical suggestions, avoiding academic or merely descriptive studies that lead to a false consciousness about [discrimination]."[55]

In terms of political action against racism, an international congress on race relations would have had more political impact, but TEN's suggestion did not include the idea of a pilot research project on the matter with academic characteristics, like that suggested by UNESCO's General Conference in Florence. In this end, Guerreiro Ramos's proposal had no impact on UNESCO. But at least two social scientists actively engaged with UNESCO in designing the research project in Brazil, Charles Wagley and Costa Pinto, also participated in the Congress sponsored by TEN. Another participant, Roger Bastide, was contacted by Métraux immediately after the congress.

Bastide, still influenced by the TEN Congress, argued in responding to Métraux that the project should not be limited to a research effort. He thought it important to give a practical direction to theoretical reflections in order to foster a cooperative attitude between white intellectuals and black associations. In this way, at least in the southern part of Brazil, certain "taboos" could be broken and emerging tensions could be relieved. Bastide told Métraux about his plans to create a research center dedicated to the black community of São Paulo that would pull blacks and whites together and seek to influence government actions.[56]

These first steps in the assembly of the UNESCO research project indicate a wide-open scenario constructed on the basis of knowledge previously gathered by the social scientists on the staff, amplified by contacts and suggestions offered by Brazilian and non-Brazilian researchers with experience in teaching or research in Brazil and the effects of the Primeiro Congresso do Negro Brasileiro on anthropologists and sociologists involved in the research project planned on race relations in Brazil (Wagley, Costa Pinto, and Bastide). This process became even more complex during the second half of 1950.

BRAZIL SEEN FROM THE OUTSIDE

Between June and September of 1950 the Division for the Study of Race Problems of UNESCO's Department of Social Sciences was corresponding with some of the researchers who might participate in the UNESCO Project (Costa Pinto, Bastide, Wagley). The division got in touch with Klineberg and Paulo Carneiro, chief of the Brazilian delegation at UNESCO, who played a decisive role in "the Brazilian option."[57] In addition, Giorgio Mortara, a demographer from the Instituto Brasileiro de Geografia e Estatística (IBGE, the Brazilian Census agency), was asked to provide information and analyses of the race composition of the Brazilian population.[58] In September, Métraux and Coelho, incorporating suggestions and criticism by Klineberg,[59] wrote the final version[60] of the document that would shape the decision on the scope of the research program.[61]

The introduction to this document briefly analyzed the historical evolution of research on Brazilian race relations. In these studies, according to the authors, race relations "were never considered problems *per se* in Brazil, but as part of general social problems."[62] The abolition of slavery and the adoption of the republican regime had apparently solved "the problem of the black," and therefore until the 1930s the literature had focused on Afro-Brazilian culture, especially in the works by anthropologists Nina Rodrigues and Arthur Ramos. Economic and political changes brought about by the Revolution of 1930 highlighted the efforts of intellectuals dedicated to the issue of national identity. The best example was *Casa-Grande & Senzala* by Gilberto Freyre, which the document cited as "the most important landmark of the period."[63]

The 1930s also saw the emergence of a new structure in higher learning, with the creation of programs in social sciences in Rio de Janeiro and especially in São Paulo. In the Escola Livre de Sociologia e Política (ELSP) in São Paulo, a specific concern emerged with systematic social research. The document mentions study of topics such as the relations between blacks and whites and the assimilation and acculturation of immigrants (German and Japanese). The contributions of Donald Pierson, Roger Bastide, and Emilio Willems were highlighted in the text. During this period, researchers such as Ruth Landes, Franklin Frazier, and Melville Herskovits were working in Bahia on several anthropological and sociological aspects of the black population.

Métraux and Coelho mentioned the scarcity of studies on patterns of race relations in Brazil. Donald Pierson's study of race relations in Bahia, *Negroes in Brazil* (1942), was considered as a point of departure. Yet Pierson's outlook raised some doubts about appropriate techniques to be adopted in an investigation aimed at detecting the existence of racial prejudice in the country. According to the two anthropologists, "It is doubtful, for example, if the use of questionnaires, dealing directly with racial attitudes, provides an adequate picture of the situation. It must be borne in mind that in Brazil, it is considered disgraceful to have racial prejudice; as a result, such prejudice, when it does exist, may assume covert and subtle forms not revealed by the questionnaire technique. It seems essential, therefore, to add other methods and techniques which will make it possible to arrive at a more complete understanding of the pattern of race relations in Brazil."[64]

Although Brazil was considered to be a country that displayed only a small degree of racial tensions, special attention was being given to particular and sometimes subtle forms in which racial prejudice could present itself. It was therefore considered desirable to use other methodological tools such as qualitative interviews, participant observation, the Rorschach test, observation of certain attitudes based on the scale of social distance developed by U.S. sociologist Emory Bogardus, and others methods.[65] Again it is evident in the original research design that the "Brazilian option" did not preclude devoting close attention to the specificity of racial prejudice in the country.

UNESCO anthropologists believed that Brazil was a positive point of departure in the sense that because "concepts such as harmony and 'good' and 'bad' race relations are perforce relative, a comparative point of view imposes itself. Comparisons will be drawn not only between Brazil and the United States, but also between other countries on which there is available informa- tion."[66] Métraux and Coelho concluded that the proposed studies should take into account the living standards of whites and nonwhites, including wages, occupations, and the broader influence of the race variable on levels of com- petition in the job market. Even the role of religion in the dynamics of social relations and the study of stereotypes and the types of personalities found in minority groups should be investigated.[67] Finally, they proposed: "The main responsibility for the social and cultural side of the research projects will be given to Dr. Charles Wagley and his team. . . . Additional field workers will be needed outside of Bahia."[68]

MÉTRAUX REDISCOVERS BRAZIL

Although already familiar with Brazil, Alfred Métraux considered a trip to the country necessary "to predict the nature of the problems that should be studied and, at the same time, gain better acquaintance with scientific institutions and personalities who may be in charge of the execution of this part of our pro- gram."[69] Métraux accordingly visited Brazil in November and December 1950. Even before his arrival, he began to recognize that Brazil was not Bahia. In a conversation with Paulo Carneiro in Paris, Métraux commented, "the race ques- tion in Brazil has quite different characteristics from region to region, and . . . it would be necessary to take into account different geographic zones if the planned investigations are to give us a valuable view of the country as a whole."[70] In his report of the trip, Métraux mentioned that the main participants in assembling the UNESCO project were Wagley, Costa Pinto, and Bastide.[71]

Métraux arrived in Bahia on 17 November 1950. He met with Anísio Teix- eira and Charles Wagley and confirmed that research would be conducted not only in rural communities, as in the project cosponsored by Columbia Uni- versity and the State of Bahia, but also in the city of Salvador. Thales de Azevedo would be in charge of investigating the upward social mobility of blacks and the tensions created by such mobility in the capital of Bahia.[72]

Métraux proceeded to Rio de Janeiro the following week. Meeting with Costa Pinto, he became convinced by arguments of the importance of study- ing race relations in the context of industrialization and conducting research in what was then the Federal District (the capital) of Brazil. Costa Pinto's in- terests also combined well with UNESCO's wider objectives, as the Florence meeting had decided in favor of a specific research program about the im- pacts of industrialization in underdeveloped areas.[73]

Métraux arrived in São Paulo on 8 December 1950. From the UNESCO perspective, the *Escola Livre de Sociologia e Política* (ELSP) and the *Faculdade de Filosofia, Ciências e Letras* (FFCL) of the Universidade de São Paulo were the highest-ranking social scientific institutions in Brazil. Even before "the Brazilian option" was proposed, Donald Pierson had been approached about participating in a research program in Brazil. In early February of 1950, the acting head of the Department of Social Sciences, sociologist Robert Angell, requested information on the ELSP. Pierson responded with a brief report on its courses of study, research, and faculty, offering to work jointly with UNESCO in the future. He closed his letter expressing interest in participating in research on race relations in Brazil.[74]

Initially, Donald Pierson and Roger Bastide were to be the social scientists in charge of research in São Paulo. But when Métraux arrived in São Paulo, he found Pierson already committed to a vast community study project in the valley of the São Francisco river, in the northeast of Brazil. Pierson suggested that the sociologist Oracy Nogueira, another professor at the Escola Livre de Sociologia e Política, take his place.

Roger Bastide agreed to chair a committee responsible for the project in São Paulo consisting of representatives from the FFCL (Mario Wagner Vieira da Cunha) and ELSP (Oracy Nogueira and Octavio da Costa Eduardo).[75] Adopting the same rationale as in the case of Rio de Janeiro, Métraux pronounced it important to investigate race relations in São Paulo, a state experiencing rapid process of industrialization and urbanization and showing clear signs of racial tensions.

Actually, São Paulo and Rio de Janeiro were both included in the UNESCO Project to serve as counterpoints to the experience of Bahia. In a certain sense, the decision to do research in São Paulo embodied the tensions between politics and science, between UNESCO's initial expectations about Brazilian experience and the UNESCO Project per se. These tensions surfaced in Métraux's official trip report: "the scientific spirit that must guide our investigation would be betrayed if we were to discard new problems and hold on to a harmonious—but antiquated—state of affairs. Investigating only Bahia would give us an incomplete picture of the race question in Brazil."[76] In Métraux's evaluation: "Contrary to my previous plans, Bahia will no longer be the focus of our project. We shall study race relations as they appear in four communities and concentrate on the problem of social mobility in the city of Salvador. On the other hand, we shall concentrate on the rapidly deteriorating racial situation of São Paulo. Dr. Costa Pinto will undertake a similar study, but on a lesser scale, in Rio de Janeiro. I expect to get, at the end of the year, a picture of the racial situation in Brazil which will be close to reality and cover both the bright and dark sides."[77]

The design of the UNESCO Project was finalized a year later, when Métraux visited the city of Recife, in the northeast. Contacts between the Instituto Joaquim Nabuco, created by sociologist Gilberto Freyre in 1949, and UNESCO started in the first half of 1951. Freyre was interested in setting up a calendar of activities to be developed in conjunction with the international agency. He wanted to strengthen his recently created research center and use it to debate race relations in Brazil with the critics of his own socio-anthropological approach.[78]

Freyre visited UNESCO headquarters in August of 1951 and requested that the Instituto Joaquim Nabuco be invited to be a partner in the research project about race relations in Brazil.[79] The suggestion was immediately accepted because of the prestige enjoyed by Freyre, the Brazilian who was originally invited to head the Department of Social Sciences of UNESCO, even before Arthur Ramos was asked.[80] René Ribeiro, former student of Melville Herskovits at Northwestern University and head of the anthropology section of the Instituto Joaquim Nabuco, was selected to conduct research on the influence of several religions (Catholicism, Protestantism, and African cults) on race relations in Recife.[81]

In the first half of 1951, five months after his visit to Brazil, Métraux wrote about his trip. He published an article in the UNESCO periodical *Courier* under the suggestive title: "Brazil: Land Of Harmony For All Races?" It provided a contrasting view of the Brazilian racial scenario.[82] Métraux opened with historical, anthropological, and sociological comments on Salvador. The "great Brazilian 'Negro Metropolis,'" had made a paradoxical impression on him. African culture was strong and visible, but he reported having seen only few "really 'black' Negroes." Métraux concluded that Bahia was a land of *mestizos* in which a "new race" was emerging. In his opinion, intense miscegenation would lead to a lack of concern with racial identity. What actually prevailed were problems of a social nature. Drawing on Gilberto Freyre, Donald Pierson, and Frank Tannenbaum, Métraux concluded that the Portuguese heritage had created a more humane model of slavery than that of Anglo-Saxon America, a model that allowed the upward mobility of mulattos and blacks.

Métraux nonetheless called attention to the risk of oversimplifying the Brazilian racial situation. Although he noted frequent interracial marriages, they usually involved persons of the same class, rarely occurring between individuals occupying extreme positions in the complex system of Brazilian color classification.[83] This example allowed Métraux to consider Brazil as "an example of a country where relations between the races are relatively harmonious" but without failing to note that it "would be an exaggeration . . . to claim that racial prejudice is unknown." He cited numerous stereotypes in relation to black people. And the higher one went up social ranks, the more evident instances of color prejudice. In large cities like São Paulo and Rio de Janeiro, Métraux noted "unmistakable racism" among workers, stimulated by competition in areas subject to industrialization. He attributed racism in the southeast to the history of slavery, which kept blacks in positions unfavorable for competing with whites. In this sense, the difficulties experienced by blacks were not attributable to their color but to their position in the social hierarchy. Their expectations therefore converged on education as a means of ascending the social ladder.

Métraux minimized the effects of racial discrimination in Brazil, given that the forces of tradition do not allow interethnic conflicts, and thus help "solve the dilemma in Brazil." Yet at the end of the article, he stated "the eagerness shown by the Brazilian sociologists working with UNESCO to explore all favorable and unfavorable aspects of the question alike show the feeling of confidence with which Brazilians everywhere regard the racial situation in their country."[84]

The 1951 article reflected Métraux's ambiguity and imprecision but also his optimism. He revealed in part the reasons that led to the definition of a broad research program inside the UNESCO Project, but also the tensions between race discrimination and the myth of racial democracy. His visit to Brazil in the closing months of 1950 catalyzed the research program. Indeed, Métraux was deeply empathetic toward Brazil. Although he did not have a deep understanding of the reality of Brazilian race relations, he was open enough to absorb the view that Bahia could not represent all of Brazil. And thus the Brazilian mosaic was recognized and accepted.

The research activities of the UNESCO project were concluded and their findings were assembled between 1951 and 1952. Several aspects influenced the choice and development of individual projects. The first was the influence of a tradition of race studies, especially on Bahia and São Paulo. Just as important were teaching and research centers, particularly in the city of São Paulo. Also, UNESCO began in 1950 to demonstrate an interest in processes of industrialization and their impacts on underdeveloped regions, hence the inclusion of areas from the southeast of Brazil in the project. Finally, intellectual prestige, personal relationships, past research experiences, and a transatlantic network of scholars determined the outline of the case studies. Bastide and Métraux had shared a series of projects and intellectual affinities. Wagley had worked in Brazil since the 1930s. Costa Pinto's participation grew out of his professional and personal relationship with Arthur Ramos. Freyre's international fame accounted for the late inclusion of Recife in the project.

The UNESCO project obviously benefited from investigating more than a single Brazilian region. Its findings revealed a diversified situation.

Enormous social distance separated whites and blacks, and little social mobility occurred among nonwhites. In the north and northeast, racial prejudice was deemed to be subtle, but existent nonetheless. Research in southeastern areas looked at race relations in Brazil's major centers of development, Rio de Janeiro and São Paulo, where economic and social changes were intense. There, blacks and mulattos had been forced to deal during the last years of slavery with large numbers of European immigrants, and racial tensions were deemed more visible. The project also found that racial classifications in Brazil combined phenotypic definitions with nonbiological attributes such as class, status, and education. Thus a complex system of racial classification was revealed.

THE IMPACTS OF UNESCO RACE RELATIONS PROJECT

What were the echoes of the UNESCO racial relations project? Since the late 1970s, the project has come under growing criticism. The sociologist Florestan Fernandes became the major target of the critics, based on his studies about whites and blacks in São Paulo, written in partnership with the French sociologist Roger Bastide. Two of Fernandes' hypotheses were hotly contested. The first was that racial prejudice was an inheritance of Brazil's slavery heritage and, as such, would tend to wither away with the emergence of a modern liberal society. Carlos Hasenbalg[85] argued that prejudice and discrimination changed after the abolition of slavery, taking up new functions and meanings in the context of a capitalist social structure. At the same time, he argued that racist manifestations by the dominant racial group were not survivals, but were related to material and symbolic benefits gained by whites in face of the competitive disqualification of blacks. Thus, Hasenbalg sustained, there is not a logic inherent to capitalist development that would cause incompatibility between racism and industrialization.

Fernandes' second hypothesis to be criticized was that the insertion of individuals in groups, strata, and classes, specially in groups defined by their participation in the economic process, determined their ways of thinking, their representations of the world, and their conduct in the world. Fernandes, his critics sustain, gave too much weight to the concept of social class, diminishing the importance of the value given to race in the daily dealings among individuals and groups. Carefully controlling his data to eliminate the effects of class, Hasenbalg was able to argue, against those who claim that discrimination affects the poor more than it does people of color, that race was significantly related to poverty. Subsequent research has confirmed his findings.

If, however, Hasenbalg had focused on work of the other sociologists involved in the UNESCO project, such as Luiz de Aguiar Costa Pinto and Oracy Nogueira, he would have found in their work more points of contact with his own analysis. In the case of Costa Pinto,[86] modernity and racism were not mutually exclusive. Much to the contrary, social changes caused by capitalism in Brazil, specially after the revolution of 1930, allowed social mobility and the emergence of a black working class and a black middle class. Because it came up the ranks in a competitive social order, this black middle class faces barriers, prejudice, and discrimination from the dominant classes, and this led to the emergence of a racialized Afro-Brazilian elite and an ideology of blackness.

Costa Pinto stood apart from his colleagues in the UNESCO project, like Florestan Fernandes, because he believed that social changes caused by industrialization do not necessarily put an end to prejudice and to racial discrimination. They may even make them more serious.

Hasenbalg would also find it difficult to criticize Oracy Nogueira in the same manner that he did with Florestan Fernandes. In his study of race relations in Itapetininga, a small town in the state of São Paulo, Nogueira correlated census data with social stratification and race, finding that whites were the majority of all social classes, while Afro-Brazilians were almost always confined to the poorest groups.[87]

However, Nogueira argued that the absence of a clear "color line" in Itapetininga, and the general belief that whites and blacks of the same social level must face the same barriers to social advancement, make it hard to perceive that very small numbers of black people belong to higher social strata, something that confirms the absence of change in the collective status of the black population.[88] Actually, the abolition of slavery, the new republican regime, incipient urbanization, and industrialization in a small city did not lead to qualitative change in the previous asymmetrical relations between whites, blacks, and mulattoes in general. In this sense, Nogueira sustained that nonwhites face specific barriers which reduce their chances of upward social mobility, when compared to the chances of whites.

To be sure of his hypothesis, Nogueira made a comparative analysis of the social trajectory of Afro-Brazilians and Italian and Arab immigrants and their descendants between the late nineteenth century and the 1940s. At first, immigrants living in Itapetininga were mostly poor, but after fifty years they managed to move upward in the social ladder, reaching the same status as the traditional families of Portuguese origin. The opposite happened to blacks, who experienced stagnation in their social status.

While the social improvement of the immigrants did not depend on marriages with members of traditional families, this was an almost mandatory requirement for the status maintenance or improvement of blacks. Thus, Nogueira challenged the common statement—popular even today—that prejudice and discrimination in Brazilian society is based on social inequality, not on racial inequality.

The findings of Luiz de Aguiar Costa Pinto and Oracy Nogueira revealed different perspectives inside the UNESCO race relations project. In general the findings had in common an optimistic perspective about the future of race relations in Brazil. They thought that social and race inequalities could be overcome through universalistic public policies.

When examining the ideology of racial democracy, Nogueira saw more than the blurring of the discrimination against the social mobility of blacks. He did not consider the Brazilian racial belief as a mere false ideology. Racism in the Brazilian manner was ambivalent, because phenotypic criteria were combined with other classification principles, such as class and social distance, and thus did not lead to antagonistic situations nor to deep racial hatred. The myth of racial democracy is for him a part of the "national ethos," but it is also a parameter for racist behavior, because public opinion is sensitive to aggressive and overt displays of racial prejudice or discrimination. Precisely for this reason, Nogueira believed that the Brazilian style of racism (*racismo à brasileira*) could be surpassed by education, by the adoption of rational techniques of enlightenment that would change beliefs and behaviors of both blacks and whites.

BETWEEN SCIENCE AND POLITICS

The sociologists and anthropologists engaged in the UNESCO studies clearly perceived the articulation between science and politics, so clearly expressed in UNESCO's decision to initiate the "Brazilian research project." Even more, they associated scientific work with commitment. In other words, the social sciences were seen as the best instrument to understand reality, and social research was a privileged form of political commitment to and intervention in needed social change. What follows is a more detailed exposition of this argument, based on the reflections of Florestan Fernandes, one of the sociologists who achieved highest visibility in Brazil after the "UNESCO Project."

When drafting the research project to be conducted in São Paulo, Fernandes stated that "the investigation must be planned on a scientific basis, but its origin and goal are correspondingly *extra-scientific*: it will be used by an institution, UNESCO, that contracted it with the intention of using its results in the social reeducation of adults and in its policy of bringing together the races."[89]

The "UNESCO Project" was conducted at a moment in which the social sciences were going through a transition in Brazil. Having gained a foothold in the academic world in the 1930s, the social sciences tried to consolidate their institutionalization through the expansion of the number of departments and institutes during the next decades. They were also experimenting with new theoretical-methodological models capable of yielding a more solid training for this new character, the social scientist.

This process advanced during the democratic period that started in 1945. In the 1950s, when the "UNESCO Project" was being conducted, the question of which pattern of social and economic development should prevail in the country became a mandatory matter of debate. This debate followed several paths, but all of them involved the issue of the role of social scientists in times of social change. Despite the fact that the "UNESCO Project" focused on the specific subject of race relations, it became a "pretext" for several analyses of the transition from archaic to modern society, that is, the analysis of social stratification, social mobility, the obstacles to social changes, the role of intellectuals in public life and the incorporation of certain social strata into the modern society under construction in Brazil.

Therefore, the mere publication of data concerning a particular experience in race matters was seen by most of the social scientists involved in the "UNESCO Project" as quite a limited goal. After all, the opportunity presented by the sponsorship of an internationally known institution should be used to decipher Brazilian reality under new parameters. Even more, all these social scientists believed, in different degrees, that Brazil was a "laboratory of civilization." To deal carefully with this matter, we should consider more closely the conviction of these researchers that Brazilian society was endowed with a certain uniqueness.

In December of 1959, Florestan Fernandes wrote the preface to the book *Cor e Mobilidade Social em Florianópolis* (*Color and Social Mobility in Florianópolis*), written by his students, the sociologists Fernando Henrique Cardoso, ex-president of Brazil, and Octávio Ianni. This book was the result of a project supported by Brazilian government agencies. The book made public the results of a research effort that amounted to an extension of the "UNESCO Project" to the southern part of the country, a region which until then had not been properly studied.[90] This was the clearest example of the influence of the "UNESCO Project" in the process of institutionalization of the social sciences in Brazil. This investigation was the first substantial result of the activities under the discipline of Sociology I of the Department of Social Sciences of the University of São Paulo, coordinated by Florestan Fernandes.

In his preface, Fernandes considered that the studies about race relations were a precise indicator of the maturation of the social sciences in Brazil. Besides the importance of theoretical and empirical concerns that were mobilizing Brazilian social scientists, the study of patterns of race relations revealed an interest in answering questions of an immediate nature and with a political content. In Fernandes' own words:

> Nobody ignores how much cultural heterogeneity affected, affects and will continue to affect the possibility for the development of "Western society" in Brazil. In this respect, the issues pertinent to this subject have the dimension of a *national problem*, and this gives past and current investigations about the subject an unmistakable practical interest.[91]

However, Fernandes observed with sadness that society in general was not paying attention to the significance of such research projects. He attributed this lack of attention to the generalized belief that Brazil lived under the aegis of a "racial democracy." Thus, "racial democracy" ideology is an obstacle to the emergence of a new type of mentality capable of channeling efforts in the direction of an industrial society, democratic both in political and in social terms.[92]

Social scientists, according to Fernandes, should discover the foundations of social structure and thus indicate the mechanisms by which racism is reproduced. In this manner, the "*obstacles* to social change" would be identified.[93] Fernandes is unequivocal about this matter:

> There is not an effective racial democracy [in Brazil], because the exchanges between individuals belonging to distinct "races" start and end in the realm of a conventional tolerance. This tolerance may obey the requirements of "good manners," of a debatable "Christian spirit" or of the necessity of "keeping each one in his proper place." However, it does not bring men together except on the basis of merely coexisting in the same social space. Where this manages to materialize, it is a restrictive coexistence, regulated by a code that defends inequality, disguising it above the principles of the democratic social order.[94]

However, in Fernandes' view, the development of Western civilization in Brazil—amounting to industrialization, democratization of wealth and power, and social improvement—should be aware of "our sociocultural heritage," so that it would be able to cultivate whatever is compatible "with the democratic conception of life and with the creation of democracy in Brazil." He affirmed that this was so because, in his own words, "a people that stimulates swift programs of cultural change, without caring about intelligent and constructive criteria, pays exorbitant prices for social progress."[95]

Fernandes stated, moreover, that "Western civilization is sufficiently rich and plastic to allow for ample differences between national cultural systems, organized on the basis of their basic ideal values"; on this basis it would be necessary to increase the consciousness of citizenship and the more effective practice of democracy without canceling what he called "the tolerance woven into race relations and a minimum of detachment, which characterizes the expression of individualism and the autonomy of each person, both in the 'cultivated man' and in what is called the '*coarse man.*'"[96]

Fernandes no doubt startles us when he considers "conventional tolerance in race relations" the factor that at once condemns and redeems Brazilian civilization. In the face of the sweeping process of economic development, urbanization, and social mobility that attained new heights during Juscelino Kubitschek's government in the second half of the 1950s, and on account of his conviction that race inequalities are a "national problem," Fernandes warns us about the possible perverse effects of the absence of sociocultural parameters regulating the expansion of capitalism in Brazil. This would be an obstacle to "social reform in the Brazilian manner." In this sense, Fernandes recognizes the positive aspects of the type of sociability extant in Brazil. Florestan Fernandes, in his apparent paradox, spelled out the "Brazilian dilemma."

More than forty years later, I consider Fernandes' reflections on this theme to be quite up-to-date, such as: globalization, which has been causing rising tensions between universalism versus particularism; the challenges posed by multiculturalism in Brazil; the discussions about racial public policies in Brazil (including proposals for affirmative action). In this perspective, the tradition of Brazilian social thought and specifically the UNESCO race relations project still have much more to say to us about these matters than we have been hearing.[97]

Research under the auspices of UNESCO in the 1950s brought a series of consequences worth noting. First, there was a reinforcement of the Brazilian sociological tradition of investigating relations between whites and blacks, a line of investigation that had gained prominence in the 1930s with the writings of Gilberto Freyre and Donald Pierson. Second, social sciences in Brazil, which were then being institutionalized, expanded their scope and have systematically studied the issue of race relations since the 1950s. Third, the project produced a vast documentation about the existence of prejudice and discrimination against Brazilian blacks. Focusing on these issues, the UNESCO project prompted new questions about Brazil and helped identify difficulties, deadlocks, and conflicts in a society going thorough a strong and swift process of urbanization and industrialization. Research findings did not deny the importance of the myth of racial democracy. What they did in fact was reveal the tensions between the myth and the Brazilian style of racism (*racismo à brasileira*), a tension which had already been discussed by the black and white intellectuals and activists in Brazil.

NOTES

This chapter was translated by José Augusto Drummond.

1. Gilberto Freyre, *Casa-Grande & Senzala* (Rio de Janeiro: Maia & Schmidt, 1933) xii.
2. Gilberto Freyre, *Casa-Grande & Senzala*, xii.
3. Arthur Ramos, "Sciences Sociales. Programme pour 1951. Plan de Travail, Paris, 1949" *Coleção Arthur Ramos, I: 36, 29, 13*, Seção de Manuscritos, Biblioteca Nacional, Rio de Janeiro, Brazil.
4. Letter from Arthur Ramos to Alceu Maynard de Araújo, October 27, 1949 *Coleção de Manuscritos, I: 35, 13, 19*, Seção de Manuscritos, Biblioteca Nacional, Rio de Janeiro, Brazil.
5. Letter from Arthur Ramos to Clemente Mariani, October 14, 1949. *Coleção Arthur Ramos, I: 35, 17, 248a*, Seção de Mansucritos, Biblioteca Nacional, Rio de Janeiro, Brazil.
6. Arthur Ramos, "Os grandes problemas da antropologia brasileira," *Sociologia* 10, no. 4 (1948): 213–26.
7. Rudiger Bilden, "Brazil, Laboratory of Civilization," *The Nation* 128 (January 16, 1929): 71–74.
8. Ramos, "Os grandes problemas da antropologia brasileira," 213.
9. Ramos, "Os grandes problemas da antropologia brasileira," 214–15.
10. Ramos, "Os grandes problemas da antropologia brasileira," 219.
11. Ramos, "Os grandes problemas da antropologia brasileira," 219.
12. The Fourth Session of the UNESCO General Conference (*Study and Dissemination of Scientific Facts Concerning Questions of Race*) approved three goals: "1) To study and collect scientific materials concerning questions of race; 2) to give wide diffusion to the scientific information collected; 3) To prepare an educational campaign based on this information," in Records of the General Conference of the United Nations Educational and Cultural Organization, Fourth Session, Resolutions. UNESCO Archives (Paris: UNESCO, 1949), 22.
13. United Nations, Economic and Social Council, Comission on Human Rights, Fifth session. The Prevention of Discrimination and the Protection of Minorities, May 9, 1949, 6 p., in *Race Questions & Protection of Minorities*. REG 323.1. Part I up to 30/VI/50 (BOX 145), UNESCO archives.
14. Marcos Chor Maio, "O Brasil no Concerto das Nações: a luta contra o racismo nos primórdios da UNESCO." *História, Ciências, Saúde—Manguinhos* 5, no. 2 (March–June, 1998): 17–18.
15. On the series of studies of UNESCO Race Relations Project, see: Charles Wagley, ed., *Race and Class in Rural Brazil* (Paris: UNESCO, 1952); Thales Azevedo, *Les Élites de Couleur Dans Une Ville Brésilienne* (Paris: UNESCO, 1953); Luiz de Aguiar Costa Pinto, *O Negro no Rio de Janeiro: Relações de Raças numa sociedade em mudança* (São Paulo: Companhia Editora Nacional, 1953); Roger Bastide and Florestan Fernades, *Relações Raciais entre Negros e Brancos em São Paulo* (São Paulo: Editora Anhembi, 1955); Oracy Nogueira, "Relações Raciais No Município de

Itapetininga," in *Relações Raciais entre Negros e Brancos em São Paulo*, ed. Roger Bastide and Florestan Fernandes (São Paulo: Editora Anhembi, 1955). On the history of UNESCO Race Relations Project, see Marcos Chor Maio: *A História do Projeto UNESCO: Estudos Raciais e Ciências Sociais no Brasil* (Rio de Janeiro, Tese de Doutoramento em Ciência Política, Instituto Universitário de Pesquisas do Rio de Janeiro [IUPERJ], 1997), chapters 1 and 2; "UNESCO Race Relations Project," in *AFRICANA, The Encyclopedia of the African and African American Experience*, ed. Kwame Anthony Appiah and Henry Louis Gates, Jr. (New York: Basic *Civitas* Books, 1999); "The UNESCO Project: Social Sciences and Race Studies in Brazil in 1950s," *Portuguese Literary & Cultural Studies* 4/5 (2000); "UNESCO and the Study of Race Relations in Brazil: Regional or National Issue?" *Latin American Research Review* 36, no. 2 (2001).

16. Records of The General Conference of The United Nations Educational, Scientific and Cultural Organization, Fifth Session, Florence, 1950, Resolutions. Paris, July, 1950, p. 40, UNESCO Archives.

17. Alfred Métraux, "UNESCO and the racial problem." *International Social Science Bulletin* II, no. 3 (1950): 389.

18. Pernambuco was included in the second semester of 1951. I will return to this matter later on.

19. David Hellwig, *African-American Reflections on Brazil's Racial Paradise* (Philadelphia: Temple University, 1992); Thomas E. Skidmore, *Black Into White: Race and Nationality in Brazilian Thought* (Durham, N.C.: Duke University Press, 1993); Célia Maria Marinho de Azevedo, "O abolicionismo transatlântico e a memória do paraíso racial brasileiro," in *Estudos Afro-Asiáticos* 30 (December, 1996).

20. Renato Ortiz, *Cultura Brasileira e Identidade Nacional* (São Paulo: Editora Brasiliense, 1985).

21. Lilia M. Schwarcz, *O Espetáculo das Raças* (São Paulo: Companhia das Letras, 1993).

22. Gilberto Freyre, *Casa-Grande & Senzala*.

23. Kenan Malik, *The meaning of race: race, history and culture in Western society*. New York: New York University Press, 1996, 15–16; Paul Gordon Lauren, *Power and prejudice: the politics and diplomacy of racial discrimination* (Boulder & London: Westview Press, 1988), 195–96.

24. Arthur Ramos, *O Negro Brasileiro*, 2nd ed. (São Paulo: Companhia Editora Nacional, 1940); Arthur Ramos, *A Aculturação Negra no Brasil* (São Paulo: Companhia Editora Nacional, 1942); Mariza Corrêa, *As Ilusões da Liberdade: A Escola Nina Rodrigues e a Antropologia no Brasil* (São Paulo: EDUSF, 1998), 277–305.

25. Arthur Ramos, *Guerra e Relações de Raça* (Rio de Janeiro: Departamento Editorial da União Nacional dos Estudantes, 1943); Arthur Ramos, *As Ciências Sociais e os Problemas de Após-Guerra* (Rio de Janeiro: Casa do Estudante do Brasil, 1944); Arthur Ramos, "Prefácio," in *As Raças da Humanidade* ed. R. Benedict and G. Weltfish (Rio de Janeiro: Horizontes, 1945).

26. Ramos, *O Negro Brasileiro*; Ramos, *A Aculturação Negra no Brasil*; Ramos, *Guerra e Relações de Raça*; Ramos, "Curriculum Vitae, 1903–1945," 1945a; Ramos, "Prefácio," in *As Raças da Humanidade*; Arthur Ramos, "Prefácio," in *Brancos e*

pretos na Bahia: estudo de contato racial, ed. Donald Pierson (São Paulo: Companhia Editora Nacional, 1945c).

27. Peter Lengyel, *International Social Science: The UNESCO Experience* (New Brunswick: Transaction Books, 1986), 11.

28. Marcos Chor Maio, "Costa Pinto e a crítica ao negro como espetáculo," in *O Negro no Rio de Janeiro: relações de raças numa sociedade em mudança*, ed. Luiz de Aguiar Costa Pinto. 2nd ed. (Rio de Janeiro: Editora UFRJ, 1998), 22–28; Marcos Chor Maio, "O diálogo entre Arthur Ramos e Costa Pinto: dos estudos afro-brasileiros à 'sociologização da Antropologia,'" in *Ideais de Modernidade e Sociologia no Brasil: ensaios sobre Luiz de Aguiar Costa Pinto*, ed. M. C. Maio and G. V. Bôas (Porto Alegre: Ed.UFRGS, 1999), 210–212; Verena Stolcke, "Brasil: una nácion vista a través del cristal de la 'raza'"*Revista de Cultura Brasilieña* 1 (March 1998), 51–66.

29. In a letter to Arthur Ramos, Paulo Carneiro praises Ramos's writings and then informs him that: "to head [the Department of Social Sciences] in which there are problems that are both urgent and serious, I have suggested your name to Dr. Torres Bodet, Director general of UNESCO. He requested me to ask to you privately, about your possibilities of accepting the position. . . . The Executive Board, in its June session, will make the decision about which candidate will be invited. However, the general director would like to include your name in the list as his preferred candidate" (May 12, 1949, apud. Azeredo, "Antropólogos e Pioneiros: A História da Sociedade Brasileira de Antropologia e Etnologia," 209–210). In response to Carneiro's letter, Ramos wrote that "I can only interpret the terms of your letter, so complimentary to my person and to my work, as dictated by your generosity. The same interpretation goes for your recommendation, made to Dr. Torres Bodet, of my name as a candidate to the direction of UNESCO's Department of Social Sciences." Letter from Arthur Ramos to Paulo Carneiro, May 14, 1949, 1 p., in Paulo Carneiro papers, DAD/COC/FIOCRUZ. On Paulo Estevão de Berredo Carneiro, see: Maio, *A História do Projeto UNESCO*, chapter 1, 44–46.

30. In a letter to Ramos, Klineberg stated that "I Know of the correspondence between you and Paulo Carneiro. May I add, entirely unofficially, that I hope things will work out!." Letter from Otto Klineberg to Arthur Ramos, May 31, 1949, 1p. in Coleção Arthur Ramos, I – 35, 22, 1577, Arthur Ramos, Seção de Manuscritos, Biblioteca Nacional, Rio de Janeiro, Brazil.

31. Otto Klineberg had lived in São Paulo between 1945 and 1947, when he helped to create the Department of Psychology of the Universidade de São Paulo. Since the 1920s he had worked on the interface of anthropology and social psychology, influenced by Franz Boas, his professor, and had been on the forefront of the battle against racism in the United States. He had participated in Gunnar Myrdal's research project that led to the influential book *An American Dilemma* (1944). He also had an important role in the organization of UNESCO's Department of Social Sciences and felt a great empathy for Brazil, as can be noted in several parts of the Portuguese-language book *Introdução à Psicologia Social* (1946). On Klineberg, see Klineberg, 1974.

32. In a letter to Mr. Terenzio (from UNESCO's Bureau of External Relations), Otto Klineberg (Acting Head of the Department of Social Sciences) informed that "plans are under way for the meeting of experts in the various sciences which deal

with race. This meeting is being planned for the end of July, and invitations are in the process of being sent out." Letter from Otto Klineberg to Mr. Terenzio, May 30, 1949, 1p., Race Questions & Protection of Minorities. REG 323.1. Part I up to 30/VI/50 (BOX REG 145). This meeting was postponed, probably on account of changes in the Social Sciences Department. When he chose the scientists who would participate in the drafting of the *Statement on Race*, Ramos probably accepted suggestions by UNESCO staff members, specially Otto Klineberg.

33. The following scientists attended this meeting in Paris: sociologists Franklin Frazier (United States), Morris Ginsberg (United Kingdom), and Luiz de Aguiar Costa Pinto (Brazil); anthropologists Ernest Beaghole (New Zealand), Juan Comas (Mexico), Ashley Montagu (United States), and Claude Lévi-Strauss (France); the philosopher, educator, and politician Humayan Kabir (India).

34. Brazil was cited at least five times during the meeting, by Frazier, Costa Pinto, Ginsberg, Montagu, and Comas. See "Meeting of Experts On Race Problems," UNESCO/SS/Conf. 1/SR1, p. 10; UNESCO/SS/Conf. 1/SR3, 6, 9; UNESCO/SS/Conf. 1/SR4, 3, 4, 9. UNESCO Archives.

35. The Programme of UNESCO Proposed By The Executive Board. Part II—Draft Resolutions For 1951. Paris, 1950, 40. UNESCO Archives.

36. Alfred Métraux, *Itinéraires 1: 1935–953* (Paris: Payot, 1978). In a letter to Jorge Kingston, Head of the Department of Social Sciences of the Faculdade Nacional de Filosofia, Universidade do Brasil, Ramos informs that the Division for the Study of Race Problems was conceived by Otto Klineberg and that it may be able to start operating in December of 1949. Letter from Arthur Ramos to Jorge Kingston, September 14, 1949, Coleção Arthur Ramos, I – 35,16,215a, Seção de Manuscritos, Biblioteca Nacional, Rio de Janeiro, Brazil. With the death of Arthur Ramos on October 31, 1949, it is presumed that the Division for the Study of Race Problems was created only in April of 1950.

37. In a letter to Heloisa Alberto Torres, director of Rio de Janeiro's Museu Nacional, Métraux stated that "the tiny divison that I occupy at UNESCO [Division for the Study of Race Problems] is entirely Brazilian. As I write, I hear only Portuguese spoken around me. My assistant is Ruy Galvão de Andrade Coelho, strongly recommended by [Melville] Herskovits. My Secretary, Miss Bloch, is almost Brazilian." Letter from Alfred Métraux to Heloisa Alberto Torres, October 10, 1950, 1p. Arquivo Histórico Heloísa Alberto Torres, Itaboraí, Rio de Janeiro, Brazil.

38. "UNESCO Launches Major World Campaign Against Racial Discrimination." Paris, UNESCO, July 19, 1950, p.1, in Statement on Race. REG file 323.12 A 102. Part I (Box REG 146). UNESCO Archives.

39. Maio, "O Brasil no Concerto das Nações: a luta contra o racismo nos primórdios da UNESCO," 403–5.

40. Raimundo Nina Rodrigues, *Os Africanos no Brasil.* (São Paulo: Companhia Editora Nacional, 1935); Ramos, *O Negro Brasileiro*; Ramos, *A Aculturação Negra no Brasil.*

41. Ruth Landes, *The City of Women* (Albuquerque: University of New Mexico Press, 1994); Franklin Frazier, "The Negro Family in Bahia, Brazil." *American Sociological Review* 7, no. 4 (1942); Donald Pierson, *Negroes in Brazil* (Chicago: University

of Chicago Press, 1942); Melville Herskovits, "The Negro in Bahia, Brazil: A Problem in Method" *American Sociological Review* VIII (1943).

42. Charles Wagley, *Uma Comunidade Amazônica* (São Paulo: Companhia Editora Nacional, 1957).

43. Letter from Charles Wagley to Alfred Métraux, June 6, 1950, 1, in Race Questions & Protection of Minorities. REG 323.1. Part I up to 30/VI/50 (BOX REG 145), UNESCO Archives. The Columbia University—State of Bahia Project had been conceived by Anísio Teixeira, the Education and Health secretary of the state government. Its goal was to develop knowledge about three rural communities next to Salvador, in order to direct the design of future public policies that would affect the modernization of those areas (Letter from Ruy Coelho to Charles Wagley, July 27, 1950, p.1, in Race Questions & Protection of Minorities. REG 323.1. Part II up to 31/VII/50 (BOX REG 145), UNESCO Archives).

44. Letter from Ruy Coelho to Charles Wagley.

45. Letter from Ruy Coelho to Charles Wagley, 2.

46. Klineberg, Otto. "Comments on memorandum regarding research on race relations in Brazil," August 1, 1950, 4, in Race Questions & Protection of Minorities. REG 323.1. Part II up to 31/VII/50 (BOX REG 145). UNESCO Archives.

47. Letter from Charles Wagley to Ruy Coelho, June 9, 1950, 2, in Race Questions & Protection of Minorities. REG 323.1. Part II up to 31/VII/50 (BOX REG 145), UNESCO Archives.

48. Letter from Costa Pinto to Alfred Métraux, July 31, 1950, 1, in Race Questions & Protection of Minorities. REG 323.1. Part II up to 31/VII/50 (BOX REG 145), UNESCO Archives.

49. Roger Bastide. *Estudos Afro-Brasileiros* (São Paulo: Editora Perspectiva, 1973).

50. Letter from Roger Bastide to Alfred Métraux, May 13, 1950, in Race Questions & Protection of Minorities. REG 323.1. Part I up to 30/VI/50 (BOX REG 145), UNESCO Archives.

51. Letter from Alfred Métraux to Roger Bastide, August 18, 1950, in Race Questions & Protection of Minorities. REG 323.1. Part II up to 31/VII/50 (BOX REG 145), UNESCO Archives.

52. Adbias Nascimento, *O Negro Revoltado*, 2nd ed. (Rio de Janeiro: Editora Nova Fronteira, 1982).

53. Alberto Guerreiro Ramos, "A UNESCO e as relações de raça," in *O Negro Revoltado* ed. A. Nascimento (Rio de Janeiro: Editora Nova Fronteira, 1982), 237-238.

54. Guerreiro Ramos, "A UNESCO e as relações de raça," 237.

55. Guerreiro Ramos, "A UNESCO e as relações de raça," 237. The strictly political content of Guerreiro Ramos's proposal was perhaps linked to the ebullient debate about racism in Brazil, particularly after the episode involving a North American actress, Katherine Durham, in São Paulo. She had been denied admittance in a hotel because she was Black. This episode of racial discrimination opened a series of congressional discussions about an antidiscrimination law, approved in 1951, the so-called Afonso Arinos law. On this episode, see: Quilombo, ano II, no. 10, 8 and 9,

June-July, 1950; Bastide and Fernandes (1955), 210–222. On Guerreiro Ramos's ideas on race relations in Brazil, see Maio, 1996.

56. Letter from Roger Bastide to Alfred Métraux, September 9, 1950, in Race Questions & Protection of Minorities. REG 323.1. Part II up to 31/VII/50 (BOX REG 145), UNESCO Archives.

57. Maio, *A História do Projeto UNESCO*, chapter 1, 50–54.

58. Letter from Giorgio Mortara to Robert Angell, August 1, 1950, 4 p., in Race Questions & Protection of Minorities. REG 323.1. Part II up to 31/VII/50 (BOX REG 145), UNESCO Archives.

59. Klineberg, Otto. "Comments on memorandum regarding Research on Race Relations in Brazil," 1–7. Race Questions & Protection of Minorities. REG 323.1. Part II up to 31/VII/50 (BOX REG 145), UNESCO archives.

60. The first draft of the document by Métraux and Coelho was not found in UNESCO Archives.

61. Alfred Métraux and Ruy Coelho, in "Suggestions for research on race relations in Brazil." Race Questions & Protection of Minorities. REG 323.1. Part II up to 31/VII/50 (BOX REG 145), UNESCO Archives.

62. Métraux and Coelho, "Suggestions for research on race relations in Brazil," 1.

63. Métraux and Coelho, "Suggestions for research on race relations in Brazil," 1.

64. Métraux and Coelho, "Suggestions for research on race relations in Brazil," 3.

65. Métraux and Coelho, "Suggestions for research on race relations in Brazil," 6–9.

66. Métraux and Coelho, "Suggestions for research on race relations in Brazil," 3–4.

67. Métraux and Coelho, "Suggestions for research on race relations in Brazil," 6–9.

68. Métraux and Coelho, "Suggestions for research on race relations in Brazil," 9.

69. Alfred Métraux, "Rapport au Directeur Général sur Mission au Brésil (16 Nov.–20 Déc. 1950)" in Race Questions & Protection of Minorities. REG 323.1. Part II up to 31/VII/50 UNESCO Archives (BOX REG 145), 1.

70. Métraux, "Rapport au Directeur Général sur Mission au Brésil," 1.

71. Métraux, "Rapport au Directeur Général sur Mission au Brésil," 1.

72. Métraux had access to the database about socioeconomic indicators collected for the Columbia University—State of Bahia project, under the direction of Thales de Azevedo, and visited the recently created Fundação para o Desenvolvimento da Ciência no Estado da Bahia, an institution dedicated to funding research, created by Anísio Teixeira. Besides this, Métraux visited two of the three rural communities under investigation: Azevedo, *Les Élites de Couleur Dans Une Ville Brésilienne*, 2–4.

73. T. Azevedo, *Les Élites de Couleur Dans Une Ville Brésilienne*, 4. On the participation of Costa Pinto in the "UNESCO Project," see Maio, "Costa Pinto e a crítica ao negro como espetáculo."

74. Letter from Donald Pierson to Robert Angell, February 15, 1950, in Race Questions & Protection of Minorities. REG 323.1. Part I up to 30/VI/50 (BOX 145), UNESCO Archives.

75. Métraux, Alfred. "Rapport au Directeur Général sur Mission au Brésil (16 Nov.–20 Déc. 1950)," 1, in Race Questions & Protection of Minorities. REG 323.1. Part II up to 31/VII/50 UNESCO Archives (BOX 145), 5. Although the committee was formed, it operated only for a short period of time. Nogueira, in a letter to Métraux,

reports having sent a copy of the project to Bastide, "president of the committee that was formed at that moment." (Letter from Oracy Nogueira to Alfred Métraux, December 22, 1950), in Statement on Race. REG file 323.12 A 102. Part I (Box REG 146), UNESCO Archives.

76. Métraux, Alfred. "Rapport au Directeur Général sur Mission au Brésil (16 nov.–20 déc. 1950)," 1, in Race Questions & Protection of Minorities. REG 323.1. Part II up to 31/VII/50 UNESCO Archives (BOX 145), 5.

77. Letter from Alfred Métraux to Melville Herskovits, January 29, 1951, p. 1, in Statement on Race. REG file 323.12 A 102. Part II UNESCO Archives (Box 147).

78. Marcos Chor Maio, "Tempo controverso: Gilberto Freyre e o projeto UNESCO," *Tempo Social* 11 no. 1 (1999): 115–18.

79. Métraux, Alfred. "Rapport sur mission au Brèsil," from October 10 to December 12, 1951 in Statement on Race. REG file 323.12 A 102. Part II UNESCO Archives. (Box 147), 1.

80. Hadley Cantril, professor of social psychology at Princeton University and co-ordinator of the UNESCO project entitled "Tensions Affecting International Understanding," immediately after a forum organized in Paris about "Tensions that Cause Wars" (in the Summer of 1948), had informally approached Freyre about the possibility of his acceptance of the chair position. Letter from Hadley Cantril to Gilberto Freyre, August 13, 1948, 1p. Arquivo Histórico da Fundação Gilberto Freyre (hereafter AHFGF). Cantril received Freyre's letter declining the informal invitation. Cantril thanked Freyre for his response, but he does not provide any details about the reasons presented by Freyre. Letter from Cantril to Freyre, December 9, 1948, 1 p., AHFGF. Freyre's letter to Cantril was not found.

81. Alfred Métraux, "Rapport sur mission au Brèsil," (October 29 to December 12, 1951), 2.

82. Alfred Métraux, "Brazil: Land of Harmony for All Races?" Courier (April 1951): 3.

83. Métraux, "Brazil: Land of Harmony for All Races?", 3.

84. Métraux, "Brazil: Land of Harmony for All Races?", 3.

85. Carlos Hasenbalg, *Discriminação e Desigualdades Raciais no Brasil* (Rio de Janeiro: Edições Graal, 1979).

86. Costa Pinto, *O Negro no Rio de Janeiro*.

87. Nogueira, "Relações Raciais No Município de Itapetininga," 479.

88. Nogueira, "Relações Raciais No Município de Itapetininga," 480.

89. Roger Bastide and Florestan Fernandes. "O Preconceito Racial em São Paulo (projeto de estudo)," in *Brancos e Negros em São Paulo*, ed. R. Bastide and F. Fernandes (São Paulo: Companhia Editora Nacional, 1959), 324.

90. Fernando Henrique Cardoso and Octávio Ianni, *Cor e Mobilidade Social em Florianópolis* (São Paulo: Companhia Editora Nacional, 1960), xxxix–xl.

91. Florestan Fernandes, "Prefácio," in *Cor e Mobilidade Social em Florianópolis* ed. Fernando Henrique Cardoso and Octávio Ianni, xi, author's emphasis.

92. Florestan Fernandes, "Prefácio," xi–xii.

93. Florestan Fernandes, "Prefácio," author's emphasis.

94. Florestan Fernandes, "Prefácio," xiv.
95. Florestan Fernandes, "Prefácio," xvi.
96. Florestan Fernandes, "Prefácio," xvi, author's emphasis.
97. Marcos Chor Maio, "O Projeto UNESCO: ciências sociais e o 'credo racial brasileiro,'" *Revista USP* 46 (2000).

BIBLIOGRAPHY

Azeredo, Paulor Roberto. Antropólogos e Pioneiros: A História da Sociedade Brasileira de Antropologia e Etnologia. São Paulo: Facudade de Filosofia, Letras e Ciências Humana, Universidade de São Paulo, 1986.

Azevedo, Célia Maria Marinho de. "O abolicionismo transatlântico e a memória do paraíso racial brasileiro." *Estudos Afro-Asiáticos* 30 (December 1996): 151–62.

Azevedo, Thales. *Les Élites de Couleur Dans Une Ville Brésilienne*. Paris: UNESCO, 1953.

Bastide, Roger, and Florestan Fernandes. *Relações Raciais entre Negros e Brancos em São Paulo*. São Paulo: Editora Anhembi, 1955.

———. "O Preconceito Racial em São Paulo (projeto de estudo)." In *Brancos e Negros em São Paulo*, edited by Roger Bastide and Florestan Fernandes. São Paulo: Companhia Editora Nacional, 1959.

Bastide, Roger. *Estudos Afro-Brasileiros*. São Paulo: Editora Perspectiva, 1973.

Bilden, Rudiger. "Brazil, Laboratory of Civilization." *The Nation* 128 (January 16, 1929): 71–74.

Cardoso, Fernando Henrique, and Octávio Ianni. *Cor e Mobilidade Social em Florianópolis*. São Paulo: Companhia Editora Nacional, 1960.

Corrêa, Mariza. *As Ilusões da Liberdade: A Escola Nina Rodrigues e a Antropologia no Brasil*. São Paulo, EDUSF, 1998.

Costa Pinto, Luiz de Aguiar. *O Negro no Rio de Janeiro: Relações de Raças numa sociedade em mudança*. São Paulo: Companhia Editora Nacional, 1953.

Fernandes, Florestan. "Prefácio." In Cor e Modilidad's Social em Florianópolis, Fernando Henrique Cardoso e Octávio Ianni. São Paulo: Companhia Editora Nacional, 1960.

Frazier, Franklin. "The Negro Family in Bahia, Brazil." *American Sociological Review* 7, no. 4 (1942): 465–78.

Freyre, Gilberto. *Casa-Grande & Senzala*. Rio de Janeiro: Maia & Schmidt, 1933.

Guerreiro Ramos, Alberto. "A UNESCO e as relações de raça." In *O Negro Revoltado*, edited by A. Nascimento. Rio de Janeiro: Editora Nova Fronteira, 1982.

Hasenbalg, Carlos. *Discriminação e Desigualdades Raciais no Brasil*. Rio de Janeiro: Edições Graal, 1979.

Herskovits, Melville. "The Negro in Bahia, Brazil: A Problem in Method." *American Sociological Review* 8 (1943): 394–402.

Hellwig, David. *African-American Reflections on Brazil's Racial Paradise*. Philadelphia: Temple University, 1992.

Klineberg, Otto. "Introdução à Antropologia Social." *Boletim* 75, Psicologia, no. 1. São Paulo: Faculdade de Filosofia, Ciências e Letras, 1946.

——. "Otto Klineberg." *History of Psychology in Autobiography*. Vol. 6. Englewood Cliffs, N.J.: Prentice-Hall, 1974.

Landes, Ruth. *The City of Women*. Albuquerque: University of New Mexico Press, 1994.

Lauren, Paul Gordon. *Power and Prejudice: The Politics and Diplomacy of Racial Discrimination*. Boulder and London: Westview Press, 1988.

Lengyel, Peter. *International Social Science: The UNESCO Experience*. New Brunswick: Transaction Books, 1986.

Maio, Marcos Chor. "UNESCO and the Study of Race Relations in Brazil: Regional or National Issue?" *Latin American Research Review* 36, no. 2 (2001): 118–36.

——. "The UNESCO Project: Social Sciences and Race Studies in Brazil in 1950s." *Portuguese Literary & Cultural Studies* 4/5 (2000): 51–53.

——. "O Projeto UNESCO: ciências sociais e o 'credo racial brasileiro.'" *Revista USP* 46 (2000): 115–28.

——. "Tempo controverso: Gilberto Freyre e o projeto UNESCO." *Tempo Social* 11, no. 1 (1999): 111–36.

——. "O diálogo entre Arthur Ramos e Costa Pinto: dos estudos afro-brasileiros à 'sociologização da Antropologia.'" In *Ideais de Modernidade e Sociologia no Brasil: ensaios sobre Luiz de Aguiar Costa Pinto,* edited by M. C. Maio e G. V. Bôas, 203–21. Porto Alegre: Ed.UFRGS, 1999.

——. "UNESCO Race Relations Project." In *Africana: The Encyclopedia of the African and African American Experience*, edited by Kwame Anthony Appiah and Henry Louis Gates Jr., 1918–1919. New York: Basic *Civitas* Books, 1999.

——. "Costa Pinto e a crítica ao negro como espetáculo." In *O Negro no Rio de Janeiro: relações de raças numa sociedade em mudança,* edited by Luiz de Aguiar Costa Pinto, 17–50. 2nd ed. Rio de Janeiro: Editora UFRJ, 1998.

——. "O Brasil no Concerto das Nações: a luta contra o racismo nos primórdios da UNESCO." *História, Ciências, Saúde—Manguinhos* 5, no. 2 (March–June 1998): 375–413.

——. *A História do Projeto UNESCO: Estudos Raciais e Ciências Sociais no Brasil.* Rio de Janeiro, Tese de Doutoramento em Ciência Política, Instituto Universitário de Pesquisas do Rio de Janeiro (IUPERJ), 1997.

——. "A Questão Racial no Pensamento de Guerreiro Ramos." In *Raça, Ciência e Sociedade*, edited by M. C. Maio and R. V. Santos, 179–93. Rio de Janeiro: Editora Fiocruz/Centro Cultural Banco do Brasil, 1996.

Malik, Kenan. *The Meaning of Race: Race, History and Culture in Western Society.* New York: New York University Press, 1996.

Métraux, Alfred. *Itinéraires 1: 1935–1953*. Paris: Payot, 1978.

——. "Rapport sur mission au Brèsil" (October 29 to December 12, 1951).

——. "UNESCO and the racial problem." *International Social Science Bulletin* 2, no. 3 (1950): 384–90.

——. "Brazil: Land of Harmony For all Races?" *Courier* (April 1951): 3.

Nascimento, Abdias. *O Negro Revoltado*. 2nd ed. Rio de Janeiro: Editora Nova Fronteira, 1982 [1968].

Nina Rodrigues, Raimundo. *Os Africanos no Brasil*. São Paulo: Companhia Editora Nacional, 1935.

Nogueira, Oracy. "Relações Raciais No Município de Itapetininga." In *Relações Raciais entre Negros e Brancos em São Paulo*, edited by Roger Bastide and Florestan Fernandes. São Paulo: Editora Anhembi, 1955.

Ortiz, Renato. *Cultura Brasileira e Identidade Nacional*. São Paulo: Editora Brasiliense, 1985.

Pierson, Donald. *Negroes in Brazil*. Chicago: University of Chicago Press, 1942.

Ramos, Arthur. *O Negro Brasileiro*. 2nd ed. São Paulo: Companhia Editora Nacional, 1940.

———. *A Aculturação Negra no Brasil*. São Paulo: Companhia Editora Nacional, 1942.

———. *Guerra e Relações de Raça*. Rio de Janeiro: Departamento Editorial da União Nacional dos Estudantes, 1943.

———. *As Ciências Sociais e os Problemas de Após-Guerra*. Rio de Janeiro: Casa do Estudante do Brasil, 1944.

———. *Curriculum Vitae: 1903–1945*. Rio de Janeiro, 1945a.

———. "Prefácio." In *As Raças da Humanidade*, edited by R. Benedict and G. Weltfish. Rio de Janeiro: Horizontes, 1945b.

———. "Prefácio." In *Brancos e pretos na Bahia: estudo de contato racial*, edited by Donald Pierson. São Paulo: Companhia Editora Nacional, 1945c.

———. "Os grandes problemas da antropologia brasileira" *Sociologia* 10, no. 4 (1948): 213–26.

Schwarcz, Lilia M. *O Espetáculo das Raças*. São Paulo: Companhia das Letras, 1993.

Skidmore, Thomas E. *Black Into White: Race and Nationality in Brazilian Thought*. Durham, N.C.: Duke University Press, 1993 [1974].

Stolcke, Verena. "Brasil: una nácion vista a través del cristal de la 'raza.'" *Revista de Cultura Brasilieña* 1 (March 1998): 51–66.

Wagley, Charles, ed. *Race and Class in Rural Brazil*. Paris: UNESCO, 1952.

———. *Uma Comunidade Amazônica*. São Paulo: Companhia Editora Nacional, 1957.

Wagley, Charles, Thales Azevedo, and Luiz de Aguiar Costa Pinto. *Uma Pesquisa Sobre a Vida Social no Estado da Bahia*. Salvador: Publicações do Museu do Estado, no. 11, 1950.

II

LITERATURE AND CULTURE

8

Brazilian Cultural Critique: Possible Scenarios of a Pending Debate

Valter Sinder and Paulo Jorge Ribeiro

A poet is not considered national just because in his verses he inserts many names of flowers or birds of the country, which would confer a nationality of vocabulary and nothing else. The local color is appreciated, but it requires touches of imagination, and let these be natural, not forced.

—Machado de Assis, *Instinto de Nacionalidade* (1858)

The emergence of the military-authoritarian state in 1964 suspended the constitutional civil guarantees and full political rights, clearly aiming at eliminating or freezing political opposition to the regime. In the cultural field however, the constitution of an eminently leftist culture was maintained. Roberto Schwarz perceives this as the determining factor in the "Brazilian cultural scenario between 1964 and 1969" because "the cultural presence of the left was not eliminated then and, furthermore, has been constantly growing since. Its production is dominant, and of remarkable quality in some fields. Despite the right-wing dictatorship, there is a relative cultural hegemony of the left in the country" (1978).[1]

This situation is substantially altered from the 1970s. The institution of the AI-5 in 1968 opens a new phase of the military-authoritarian regime inaugurated in 1964. In this new phase, crackdown reaches beyond the political-institutional perspective, and the security apparatus started to be less tolerant with any manifestation contrary to the political status quo. Literary, theater, and cinema censorships are intensified, which led criticism to the regime to become increasingly allegorical and *dissimulated*.

Paradoxically, during the '70s new dominant perspectives enabled possible new constructions *of* and *in* the Brazilian cultural scenario, starting to change the hues of a specific interpretive monopoly of Brazil. Another type of critique starts to arise—even if with multiple faces, origins, scenarios, and discourses—based on the perception of a certain heteroglossia of both the Brazilian society and its traditional critique. The new forms are still a minority in the Brazilian cultural scenario, and a large portion of the cultural and even scholarly establishment sees them as *reactionary* and *alien*,[2] but we can try to understand why they are systematically disqualified by part of the cultural vanguard of today. These *others* (that the Brazilian cultural and intellectual *hegemonic fields* generically call *postmodern*) represent cleavages in the classic and one-dimensional interpretations of Brazil—and right in the dominant cultural and academic positions.

In this chapter we intend to map how, by 1970, the Brazilian cultural discourse was altered at its core. We attempt here, as Derrida[3] suggests, to follow certain *traces* of those changes in the individual discourses of some activities, subjects, and critical attitudes of Brazilian society, because there is no doubt that Brazilian society was profoundly altered from the 1970s on, but the ways of perceiving those changes cannot—or should not—follow only interpretive canons of national meta-narratives and consequently analyses developed mainly in Brazil.

We aim here at an interpretation, rather than a synthesis, since many other works of varying and representative intent, range, and results have already mapped these changes.[4] What we do intend is to raise some questions, rearrange them in a perspective where theory and the *world of life* are not blatantly dissociated. Not that we naively force the world we study and the real world to coincide. Contrary to other studies, it is the discourses produced in Brazilian cultural studies that will be mapped here.[5]

We share Scott Lash's viewpoint, from which one perceives that today "there is a growing shift of the object of human sciences from the social to the cultural," which, according to Lash, is marked by "the recent explosion of cultural studies."[6] We will attempt to track, through diverse angles and scenarios, some issues found in the post-1970 Brazilian critique, highlighting the rupture in the *Brazilian paradigm* that many critics perceive in this period.

NEW SCENARIOS, NEW DISCOURSES: BRAZILIAN CULTURAL CRITIQUE FROM 1970 ON

At the turn of the 1970s, changes were painfully perceived in the scenarios, images, and discourses of Brazil, because they were not limited to the content of scholarly programs and curricula of the various subjects, but started to affect the *face of Brazil* itself, where the (new) agendas of civil society were then being redefined and the relationships between public and private universes were once again in debate. The end of the authoritarian-military period not only caused a rupture with the existing institutional regime, but also profoundly altered the way of thinking of the country.

Before continuing to analyze the proposed issue, a brief digression to address periodization seems appropriate. Precisely when and under which circumstances was the authoritarian regime inaugurated, and when did re-democratization start in Brazil—as regards the problems raised by human sciences? Should we start with the 1964 coup and follow events up to the 1979 amnesty or, perhaps, up to the election of Tancredo Neves by the Congress in 1985? Would it be possible to establish a more precise cutoff regarding the moment of passage from an authoritarian regime to the democratization operated within the field of human sciences (not in Brazil alone, obviously). If we dedicate some effort to articulating some significant prior issues, perhaps the generic question could be answered with a relatively precise date (even if always debatable, of course). Hence, we present hereunder some suggestions proposed by Silviano Santiago in a paper offered during the LASA (Latin American Studies Association) meeting in April 1997 with his reflections about cultural and literary critiques at the end of the twentieth century ("Crítica cultural, crítica literária: desafios de fin de siglo").[7]

Let us pose some derived questions.

> When could we say that Brazilian culture and the human sciences donned the (somber) attire of resistance to the dictatorship and at which time could we affirm they changed into the clear dress of democratization? When did the leftist coalition, having succeeded in resisting repression and torture, give way to significant internal differences? When did "Brazilian art [culture and human sciences] stop being markedly literary and sociological to become mainly cultural and anthropological"? When were the walls of critical reflection—which in modernity separated erudite from popular—toppled? When did the (spontaneous, precarious) language of interviews (in the printed press and TV) with artists and intellectuals replace the collective, dogmatic statements of professional politicians, becoming the means of communication with the new public?

The answers to the above questions restrict the historic moment under analysis to a period starting around 1968 and extending up to the mid-1980's. In other words, following Silviano Santiago's suggestions, we are defining the passage from the authoritarian regime to democracy as the moment when the battle waged by the left against authoritarianism stops being the hegemonic question in the Brazilian cultural and artistic scenario, as well as in human sciences, opening space for new problems and reflections inspired by democratization in Brazil.

The set of transformations verified in Brazilian society caused, in the words of Pereira,[8] a radical dissonance between pre-1960 and post-1970 Brazil because during the '60s

the "big issues" were discussed and in a tone that matched their "scale." In the '70s it was different. We were closer to something we could perhaps define as a process of "politization of daily life"—preferably issues that interfere in the day-to-day lives of people are raised and addressed.

However, in addition to the direct effects of the drastic internal politics that generated the above-mentioned scenario of redemocratization[9] Brazil was also affected by worldwide theoretical and political inflexions. The specter that haunted both the United States and Europe—postmodernism as a possible cultural critique—seems to have dramatically and definitively invaded our issues. Already a part of the curriculum since the early 1970s, it was in the next decade that it became a key issue that had to be addressed because of the new issues and matrixes of initiatives it started to raise in scholarly practices and political references.

The changes in the perception of Brazil are felt as a loss of the Brazilian *aura* not only in the day-to-day of a certain political militancy and activity but in the Benjaminean conception of works of art themselves. The very forms of acquiring intelligibility of the country—as both urban living space and cognitive *locus*—also start to shift in this period, changes conceived—at least analytically—in a limited gestation process. In addition to all these transformations at all levels, Brazil and its *brazilianity* start to display a new face.

By the end of the 1970s, the changes that Brazilian art and culture were undergoing can be illustrated by the controversy—mainly generated by filmmaker Cacá Diegues—called "ideological patrolling" at the time (in an interview with Póla Vartuck, the filmmaker attempted to preserve the democratic space of "the freedom of artistic creation, against all the intellectuals that, in the name of partisan ideologies, tried to impose a kind of censorship"). This and other similar statements had a jolting effect at the time because they disoriented—pointing to cracks—the left-wing coalition formed in the '50s and consolidated in the resistance to the authoritarian regime during the '60s and '70s.

The episode of the "ideological patrols" closes not only the sad period of repression, but the happy days of the leftist coalition as well. And yet, from this paradigmatic episode, it became apparent that both the unity of the left around a consensual and hegemonic project for Brazil and the possibility of perceiving Brazilian social problems with the objective of composing a unity of mind could no longer be viewed in a single dimension, without taking into account the plurality of the possible worlds then joining the cultural arenas[10] that were being created in Brazil.

At this moment, which many characterize by the absence of credibility of the great paradigms that until then legitimized the rules of science, multiple reassessments were made—deconstructions and new readings of Brazil and its interpreters. A good example is Ricardo Benzaquén de Araújo's book on Gilberto Freyre's work during the 1930s.[11] A PhD in anthropology dissertation in the early 1990s, this book reassessed part of Freyre's work based on the orality of his prose (i.e., from the repetition, the incompleteness, the imprecision found in Freyre's work, one of the characteristics mentioned by the critics in analyzing the author). Benzaquén considers that these characteristics, "which confer on his prose a rather appealing tone, much closer to that of a conversation,"[12] rather than indicating a possible incapacity of Freyre to reach a conclusion, or a lacking in scientificity, were an expression of his insertion in this type of narrative, where the incomplete is a part of its deepest "essence" (i.e., as in an essay).

> The emphasis on the "incomplete" and on imperfection should not lead us to suppose that the characteristic inconclusiveness of the essay is necessarily a praise of indefiniteness. Far from it, Freyre conveys the impression that he refuses a commitment with the idea of totality, i.e. with a concern with presenting a systematic and complete view of the issues addressed.[13]

By stressing that this aversion to totality is, in a way, linked to a vivid interest in capturing the essential, Benzaquén argues that this attitude enabled Freyre to depict Brazilian culture as the result of "uncountable conflicting antagonisms." Hence, Freyre's strategy regarding the issue of Brazilian cultural identity could be synthesized as an attempt to integrate region, race, and culture.

Aiming at reassessing some of these issues in a perspective of Social Sciences, which briefly touches the above-mentioned descriptions and their socio-institutional and analytical consequences, Maria Alice Resende de Carvalho[14] tried to analyze the perspectives in which these dilemmas were being debated. In order to do so, the author proposes that we acknowledge that in recent decades Brazilian social sciences alternated between two analytical strategies: the first privileged an analysis that could account for the authoritarian socio-institutional model dominant in Brazil since at least the foundation of the Republic; the other highlights the discontinuities of our process of social formation.

By privileging this second interpretive vector and highlighting its internal topic alteration, de Carvalho distinguishes this moment in her article perceiving that from the 1960s on the notion of city has replaced that of state in the

Brazilian analytical-interpretive tradition. This modification follows the core-shifting of the new standards of social life and both individual and collective perceptions (stressed by the growing and radical urbanization of the country during this period, aggregated with the socio-institutional transformations of all kinds, such as the unchecked growth of the large Brazilian cities and its multiple effects) and, consequently, as a locus of scholarly research.

During the 1970s, according to de Carvalho, the Brazilian critique starts to lose weight and certain sociological tropes that are sometimes excessively normalizing subside, now giving way to an anthropological analysis perspective that is more *comprehensive* than *explanatory*. This *trope* dominated the analyses of Brazilian society and had an explanatory strategy based on the issues involving the Brazilian authoritarian tradition. This discourse, produced hegemonically by the University of São Paulo canon, according to the author, was due to the fact that "throughout the '80s, the *opinion system* no longer shared a same semantic field and above all, no longer presented the same adherence to analytical prescriptions that continued to be produced at the university."[15]

Hence, these modifications were due to changes in intelligibility and the circulation of multiple demands and expectations from various points of society that occurred at an extremely fast pace. In an unquestionable and perceptive way they formulated the constitution of a world rather marked by social otherness and diverse forms of reception and action, which were increasingly dominating the social constitutions and the very social interpretations.

At the same time, one can observe (as Heloísa B. de Hollanda pointed out in 1981) "a certain uneasiness of the intellectuals regarding their scholarly practice," which way out was being designed by the "proliferation of recent studies—comprising an expressive range of reflection from university youth—from an anthropological perspective. The emerging sectors of intellectual production," she adds, "explicitly posed some restrictions to what they call 'orthodox aspects' of both classic and Marxist sociology."

This trend, built in response to a "need" to redefine the dominating categories in local cultural historiography, can and should be referenced to the external "needs" resulting from the theoretical shifts then verified in the field of western humanistic knowledge, which can be summarized as the gradual relinquishing of structuralist and Marxist formalisms that had dominated until then.

As Silviano Santiago poses the issue, "at the time of transition of the 20th Century to its 'end,' Sociology and the old scholar generation left the field and took their seats in the stands, giving way to Anthropology under the command of the emerging mappers of the cultural transformations then occurring in the country."

From then on, the range of university expectations is opened to fields and subjects of study other than those until then considered canonic. A good example is the case of the *Colleges of Belles-Lettres*, traditionally dedicated to the study of the culture of a minority, in this case the literati, which is expressed and dialogued via books, which then becomes aware of the culture of the majority.

This culturalist anthropological discourse is also marked by a revision of Brazilian interpretive tradition, more inclined to essayistic panels than to drive localized inference frames to ponder the Brazilian society. Outstanding in this tradition of the social sciences is Roberto DaMatta's pioneer *Carnavais, malandros e heróis*, first published in 1979. In this book DaMatta starts to rethink Brazil, trying to synchronically define through formulating rites of some of our identities our forms of cultural distinction and specificities: "In a word, this book aims at finding out what makes BRAZIL Brazil."[16] Rather appropriately, underlying DaMatta's work one can find attributes of the interpretivist-structuralist anthropology, inspired by a Rabelaisian Bakhtin, aesthetically carnivalesque.[17]

Treading a coexisting perspective linked to *stricto sensu* cultural studies, Silviano Santiago[18] observes the changes operated in the Brazilian literary and cultural statute. Also addressing the late '70s and early '80s, his work is a perfect complement to what DaMatta tried to achieve in *Carnavais*. Santiago indicates a clear modification in the *topos tropes* of this statute, since it stops being literary and sociological, taking up an anthropological and cultural form. This change, still according to Santiago, brings onto the stage new players who fight in favor of democratization *inside* the country, radically changing the critical projections expressed in the *upper* Brazilian modernism—in favor of erudite manifestations—now privileging production linked to pop and culture instead. Santiago sharply perceives that, among the main specificities of these new configurations, in this period.

This broad and open debate would occur in the field of art, no longer considered as the exclusive manifestation of the *belles lettres*, but as a multicultural phenomenon that was creating new and plural social identities. Both the false image of an integrated Brazilian nation imposed by the military through their control of the electronic media and the fraternal cohesion of the left, formed at the trenches, collapsed. Art relinquished the privileged stage of books and moved to the day-to-day of Life.[19]

Thus one attempts to dilute the conception of the work of art within a sacralizing conception found in Romanticism and still preserved in the Brazilian Modernism. This sacralizing perspective aimed at distinguishing the work of art by its universality and transcendence, hence denying the perception that the immanent cultural perspective could also have a degree of *originality* in which the singularity of the relationship template-copy would be altered.[20] It is clear that the discourses produced within this new *geography of ideas*[21] are crucially important for the self-acknowledgement of Brazilian society: the quest for an identity would also be fulfilled through new, much more pluralistic, discursive models—with all the ambiguities this concept had acquired in the Brazilian scenario. As Carlos Alberto Messeder Pereira rather appropriately puts it,

> Since the early '70s we live the increasingly explicit crisis of the "modern" paradigm designed around the '20s and '30s, which left as legacy a profile of Brazil that oriented us, with great legitimacy, throughout almost fifty years. This is the turn that the year of '68 represents from a cultural viewpoint. However, it is in the '80s that we will more radically experience the start of an "overcoming" of modernity in Brazil, both in the level of subjects of cultural production and of products or even theoretical formulations. The labels used in trying to identify this moment are most varied: "crisis of modernity," "post-modernity," "failure of utopias," and so on. In this sense, despite the development of the analyses, to me the critical reassessment of this "cultural/epistemological" is key.[22]

These changes operated inside the Brazilian discursive statute encompassed, in turn, not only their cultural and social configurations—in their multiple expressions—but also the very fictional narrative foundations of national literature, now marked by its urbanity and violence.[23] This change contains a recontextualization that cannot be discarded, which is vehemently described by Benedito Nunes:

> During the '70s, the grotesque realism would stand out. However, Brazilian authors would fail to don the cruel representations, as carnivalesque expressions, with the original comicality of this popular-based realism. Lost was the "regenerating force of laughter" to which Bakhtin refers and which the modernists were able to know and practice. The obscene is no longer the irreverent unclothing of social covers of the human body seen from below, genitally and sexually, and the free *fornicatio* gracefully executed by both Macunaíma and Serafim, but the exercise of violence and despair mirroring, as in Rubem Fonseca's *O Caso Morel* (1973), the image of a split man in search of his identity.[24]

The rupture of this literature vis-à-vis the previous one should be stressed, together with its critical and political specificity. In the words of Antonio Candido, now we

> are facing a literature of opposition. Opposition against the elegant writing; the ancient well-bred ideal of the country; opposition against the realist convention,

based on internal coherence and; its premise of a choice oriented by cultural convention; against narrative logic, i.e., the gradual concatenation of the parts by the technical dosage of the effects; finally against the social order, without the texts consequently manifesting a certain political position (which the author might have). Perhaps this is another trait of this recent literature: the implicit negative with no explicit affirmative of ideology.[25]

This perspective can be clearly illustrated by the short story "Intestino Grosso," which many believe to be a kind of crypto-interview of one of the most representative among the contemporary Brazilian writers, Rubem Fonseca. "Intestino Grosso," was published in *Feliz Ano Novo*, one of the books censored by the military regime, which caused one of the harshest reformulations of the issue of cultural policies in Brazil.[26] When asked about the coexistence or not of a Latin-American literature, the writer-character retorts curtly:

Don't make me laugh. There isn't even a Brazilian literature, with similar structure, style, and characterization, whatever. There are people writing in the same language, in Portuguese, which is already plenty and nothing more. I have nothing to do with Guimarães Rosa, *I am writing about people stacked in the cities while the technocrats sharpen the barbed wire.*[27]

In addition to the stylistic or gender disqualification of any literary identity in Brazilian literature—essentially contemporary—the scenario described by Fonseca stands out, a scenario that pervades his short-stories and novels: the large Brazilian megalopolis—and alongside, the great national utopias—leading to desolation, solitude, and a split of the individual that sees himself or herself disfigured in it, without a precise definition, or even an ontologically assured definition.[28] This derelict, unbelieving urban environment marked by violence and dissolution is not, however, the privilege of Rubem Fonseca's literature. An entire generation widely uses this scenario, formulating and building narratives that largely explore the city and its specters, composed, above all, by antisocial characters.[29]

The criticism against part of this literature is not irrelevant. The critics stress the lost aesthetic and moral referentials that literature—which these critics understand as the materialization of a High Culture—should represent. Trying to evade the constantly Adornean tone that pervades most of these discussions in Brazil and its cultural potentials, Silviano Santiago[30] comments that the Brazilian writer today – in sharp opposition to the nationalistic optimism of the literature of the '20s and the developmentist self-criticism of the '30s—is absolutely pessimistic as regards the hegemonic values of both the country and the West, and completely discarded the possibility of representing the Brazilian nation in a historic and global form, because it knows beforehand that the country's present is its fragmentation in multifaceted social groups, aggressively subjective, that are incapable of collectively and ideologically articulating themselves to form either what we call "brazilianity," or the even more complex "Brazilian globalization," as we call it.[31]

It is of the utmost importance to observe that this rereading of the Brazilian contemporary literature and culture and their consequences occurs simultaneously with a review of the Brazilian "literary and cultural past," where "this new history brings to the stage other modernities which then associate with and deconstruct the canonic modernities."[32] They are: the vanguard concretism and, primarily, a critical reassessment of modernism itself. Here, the new discursive forms proposed for a new discourse on national identity approach a new cultural critique linked with postmodernism: a criticism of centric and centripetal models, now in search of more pluralistic constructions and analyses of society, hence "making more complex the understanding of the relationship between Brazilian culture and modernity."[33]

As we can observe, there would be as many appropriations of these new cultural realities and even of cultural values—comprising here the very devices that articulate the city and its symbols, expressions, discourses, and images— as interpretive variables that could possibly be identified, thus creating a certain "uneasiness" regarding the self-identification of individuals and expressions that compose the perceptions and representations brought onto the stage. In other words, the discursive unit of social perceptions also conflicts with these new imaginative choices and criteria and their discursive repertoires.

Finally, we would like to highlight that in this brief characterization of this movement of passage from the authoritarian regime to democratization, we have tried to stress ruptures that seem important developments in the last twenty years. The slow relinquishing of structuralist and Marxist formalisms in favor of a linguistic pragmatism on one side, and the deconstruction on the other seem rather a unique Brazilian trend, a part of western humanistic knowledge.

NOTES

1. A first version of this chapter was published in "Pluralidad de discursos: Comunicación intercultural e interdisciplinaria em la postmodernidad y postcolonidad. Latinoamérica y la diversidade de discursos," in *Ibero-Amerikanisches-Forschungsseminar,* edited by Alfonso de Toro and Fernando de Toro (Leipzig: Institut für Romanistik der Univeristät, 2002).

2. It is interesting to note that these adjectives are the same used by Brazilian critique during the Vargas era to accuse Machado de Assis of composing an inauthentic national scenario, neither documental nor naturalistic. Cf. Mônica Pimenta Velloso, "A literatura como espelho da nação," *Estudos Históricos* 2 (1988). For a broad overview of the (canonic) Brazilian critique in its eternal confrontation against its *ancestral ghosts*, cf. João Freire Filho, *A elite ilustrada e o 'clamor anônima da barbárie': gosto popular e polêmicas culturas no Brasil moderno*. Tese de Doutorado. Rio de Janeiro, Departamento de Literatura Brasileira, Puc-Rio, 2001.

3. Jacques Derrida, *Gramatologia* (São Paulo: Perspectiva; EdUSP, 1973).

4. Some significant works containing rather vast and valuable bibliographical references can be found in the discussions around the various problems related with this chapter: in literature, cf. Renato Franco, *Itinerário político do romance pós-64: A Festa* (São Paulo: Ed. UNESP, 1998); Tânia Pellegrini, *A imagem e a letra* (São Paulo: Mercado das Letras/FAPESP, 1999); Nízia Villaça, *Paradoxos do pós-moderno: sujeito e ficção* (Rio de Janeiro: Ed. UFRJ, 1996); Flora Sussekind, *Tal Brasil, qual romance?* (Rio de Janeiro: Achiamé, 1984) ; Flora Sussekind, *Literatura e vida literária* (Rio de Janeiro: Jorge Zahar Editor, 1985); Armando Freitas Filho, Heloísa Buarque de Hollanda, and Marcus Augusto Gonçalves, *Anos 70: Literatura* (Rio de Janeiro: Europa, 1980); *Revista do Brasil*: Número especial dedicado à literatura brasileira na década de 80, 2, no. 5 (Rio de Janeiro: Governo do Estado do Rio de Janeiro; Secretaria de Ciência e Cultura; Prefeitura Municipal do Rio de Janeiro; Rioarte, 1986). In social sciences, an excellent survey was carried out by Mônica Velloso and Angélica Madeira, *Leituras brasileiras* (São Paulo: Civilização Brasileira, 1999). The work of Roberto Cardoso de Oliveira et al., *Pós-modernidade* (São Paulo: Ed. Unicamp, 1988), also comprises relevant works. In cultural critique, the debate between Schwartz and Santiago, which we will discuss later in this chapter, is a special reference. Schwartz's essay "As idéias fora do lugar," 1977, deserves being singled out because it announces contemporarily the author's debate against the "post-modern" critics of the time [sic], and from an extremely elaborate Marxist perspective. Also relevant are the critiques of Rouanet (Sérgio Paulo Rouanet, *As razões do Iluminismo* [São Paulo: Companhia das Letras, 1987]) and Moriconi (Ítalo Moriconi, *Situando o pós-moderno na teoria e na crítica brasileiras: politizando o saber, descentramento e desconstrução dos objetos num contexto de democratização* [Literary History Project: Datil, 1998]). The works about postmodernism in Brazil, according to scholarly matrixes, are in continuous expansion. Among others, see Luiz Costa Lima, "Pós-modernidade: contraponto tropical," in *Pensando nos trópicos* (Rio de Janeiro: Rocco, 1991); Jair Ferreira dos Santos, *O que é o pós-moderno?* (São Paulo: Brasiliense, 1986); Domício Proença Filho, *Pós-modernismo e literatura* (São Paulo: Ática, 1995); Therezinha de Jesus Barbieri, *Encenações do híbrido*. Tese de doutoramento apresentada ao Depto. de Letras da PUC-Rio, 1996; José Guilherme Merquior, *O fantasma romântico e outros ensaios* (Petrópolis: Vozes, 1980); and José Guilherme Merquior, "A aranha e a abelha: para uma crítica da ideologia pós-moderna," *Revista do Brasil*: Número especial dedicado à literatura brasileira na década de 80, 2, no. 5 (Rio de Janeiro: Governo do Estado do Rio de Janeiro; Secretaria de Ciência e Cultura; Prefeitura Municipal do Rio de Janeiro; Rioarte, 1986). Merquior is an author who exemplifies a political variant of

the discussion around postmodernism in Brazil; if in the first work he viewed positively the postmodern, considering that its "style" was already dominant in the western world since World War II, later Merquior categorically rejects it as an "ideology," since at that particular moment in Brazil, postmodernism had been taken up as critical instrument by groups opposing the military regime inaugurated in 1964, basically from the unorthodox left.

5. We attempt here to constitute a *"discursive-field"* approach to the Brazilian critique and the "transdiscursive positions" found in it. According to Mikhail Bakhtin, *Questões de literatura e de estética* (São Paulo: EdUSP, 1993), 99: *"To study the discourse by itself, ignoring its external orientation, is as absurd as studying psychological suffering outside the reality to which it is oriented and by which it is determined."* Emphasis by the author. Cf. Also Michel Foucault: "Sur l'archéologie des sciences. Réponse au Cercle d'épistémologie," in *Dits et écrits I* (Paris: Éditions Gallimard, 1994), "Réponse à une question," in *Dits et écrits I* (Paris: Éditions Gallimard, 1994) and "Qu'est-ce qu'un auteur?" in *Dits et écrits I* (Paris: Éditions Gallimard, 1994).

6. Scott Lash, "A reflexividade e seus duplos: estrutura, estética, comunidade," in *Modernização Reflexiva*, ed. Anthony Giddens, Ulrich Beck, Scott Lash (São Paulo: Ed. UNESP, 1995), 209–10.

7. Silviano Santiago, *Crítica cultural, crítica literária: desafios de fin de siglo*, 1997. LASA, Guadalajara, México. Datil in *Declíno da arte: Ascenção da cultura*, ed. Raul Antelo, Maria Lúcia de Barros Camargo, Ana Luiza Andrade and Tereza Virgínia de Almeida (Florianópolis: ABRALIC; Letras Contemporâneas, 1998).

8. Carlos Alberto Messeder Pereira, *Em busca do Brasil contemporâneo* (Rio de Janeiro: Ed. Notrya, 1993), 14.

9. For a broader a map of these issues, cf. Saúl Sosnowski and Jorge Schwartz, eds., *Brasil: o trânsito da memória* (São Paulo: EdUSP; University of Maryland, 1994).

10. The concept is taken from R. Morse's 1983 work, when he analyzed the specificities and positive aspects of Latin American culture in relation with Anglo-Saxon issues, in a pioneering essay against cultural diffusionism.

11. Cf. Ricardo Benzaquén de Araújo, *Guerra e Paz: Casa Grande e Senzala e a obra de Gilberto Freyre nos anos 30* (Rio de Janeiro: Editora 34, 1994).

12. Benzaquén de Araújo, *Guerra e Paz*, 185.

13. Benzaquén de Araújo, *Guerra e Paz*, 203.

14. Maria Alice Resende de Carvalho, "Violência no Rio: discursos semânticos e institucionais sobre os discursos sobre o mal." *Comunicação & Política*, ano I, v. I, n. 2, nova série, (Rio de Janeiro, dez/94–mar/95).

15. Carvalho, "Violência no Rio," 263.

16. Roberto DaMatta, *Carnavais, malandros e heróis: uma sociologia do dilema brasileiro* (Rio de Janeiro: Guanabara Koogan, 1990), 15.

17. Valter Sinder, "The nation borders and the construction of plural identities: Carnival, Rogues and Heroes or Roberto da Matta and the in-between place of Brazilian culture." *Portuguese Literary & Cultural Studies* 4. (Center for Portuguese Studies and Culture, New Bedford, Mass.: University of Massachusetts Dartmouth, 2000).

18. Santiago, *Crítica cultural, crítica literária: desafios de fin de siglo.*
19. Santiago, *Crítica cultural, crítica literária: desafios de fin de siglo*, 2.
20. Raul Antelo el al., eds., *Declíno da arte: Ascenção da cultura.* (Florianópolis: ABRALIC; Letras Contemporâneas, 1998). The collection organized by Antelo et al., maps this question in the perspective that art is not culturalized at the same pace as its objective becomes less transcendental.
21. According to F. Châtelet ("A questão da História da Filosofia hoje," in *Políticas da Filosofia*, ed. Dominique Grisoni [Lisboa: Moraes Editores, 1977], 41–42), a *geography of ideas* should be based on the formulation of "new discourses, in its genealogical, Foucaultean conception, in a confrontation that consists of a . . . double operation: decentralizing and distancing, a double operation that enables us a different view of the reality in which we are immersed and, at the same time, admits the possibility of importations that are decisive in the field of our contemporaneity."
22. Pereira, *Em busca do Brasil contemporâneo*, 10–11.
23. Cf. Renato Cordeiro Gomes, *Todas as cidades, a cidade* (Rio de Janeiro, Rocco, 1994); Renato Cordeiro Gomes, "O Histórico e o Urbano: Sob o Signo do Estorvo. Duas Vertentes da Narrativa Brasileira Contemporânea," *Revista Brasileira de Literatura Comparada* 3 (1996).
24. Benedito Nunes, "Reflexões sobre o moderno romance brasileiro," in *O livro dos seminários*, ed. Domício Proença Filho (São Paulo: LR Editores Ltda, 1982), 212.
25. Antonio Candido, "A nova narrativa," in *A educação pela noite e outros ensaios* (São Paulo: Ática, 1987), 212.
26. Cf. Deonísio da Silva, *Nos bastidores da censura: sexualidade, literatura e repressão pós-64* (São Paulo: Estação Liberdade, 1989).
27. Rubem Fonseca, "Feliz ano novo," in *Contos reunidos*, ed. Bóris Schanaiderman (São Paulo: Companhia das Letras, 1975). Emphasis by the authors. In one of his rare interviews, Rubem Fonseca ("Davi Neves e Rubem Fonseca falam de *Lúcia McCartney.*" *Filme Cultura*. Ano III, no. 17 (nov/dez, 1970): 27), categorically affirms this issue: "I am not as marginal as you [Davi Neves] are, but I am not connected to any type of previous literature. When critics speak of my books they even invent incredible things. Most Brazilian literature is regional, but I write about what I know: the city. Mine are urban values." For an analysis of the city in Brazilian literature and its redimensioning in contemporary literature, cf. Elisabeth Lowe, *The city in Brazilian literature* (London and Toronto: Fairleigh Dickinson University Press, 1982).
28. Cf. Paulo Jorge da Silva Ribeiro, *A perda da inôcencia. Etnografia e literatura como discursividades da crise do Rio de Janeiro contemporâneo.* Dissertação de mestrado apresentada ao Programa de Pós-Graduação em Ciências Sociais da Universidade do Estado do Rio de Janeiro, 1999.
29. It is precisely the relationship between such antisocial characters—which range from the social phobic to psychopaths, criminals, murderers, prostitutes, displaced people—and contemporary megalopolis that appear in writings such as *Vampiro* (1993), by Luciano Trigo, in Sérgio Sant'anna's works such as *Notas sobre Manfredo Rangel—repórter* (1991), *Senhorita Simpson* (1989), *O monstro* (1994), among others, in *Um taxi para Viena d'Áustria* (1991), by Antônio Torres, in Patrícia Mello's novels *Acqua toffana* (1994) and *O matador* (1995), in addition to the

recent *Elogio da mentira* (1998), in the most clearly postmodern narratives in our literature, such as João Gilberto Noll's, in the post-transitional novel by Luiz Eduardo Soares, *O experimento de Avelar* (1997), within the para-literary work by Rubem Fonseca himself and the recent narratives of the psychoanalyst and philosopher Alfredo Garcia-Rosa, to quote only a few of the relevant works and authors of Brazilian Literature. When asked about what amalgamates his intellectual preferences—psychoanalysis and philosophy—and his new mistress—detective-story literature—Garcia-Rosa, author of *Vento sudoeste (1999), O silêncio da chuva* (1998) and *Achados e perdidos* (1996) was incisive: a murder. Socrates, Oedipus and a crime itself, are the genesis not only of the traditions to which Garcia-Rosa subscribes, but can also be seen as a new negative ontology that crosses a significant portion of contemporary Brazilian literature.

30. Silviano Santiago, "Brasil, mostra a tua cara." *Idéias*, Jornal do Brasil, (20/4/1996).
31. Santiago, "Brasil, mostra a tua cara," 7.
32. Ítalo Moriconi, *Situando o pós-moderno na teoria e na crítica brasileiras*, 18–19.
33. Ítalo Moriconi, *Situando o pós-moderno na teoria e na crítica brasileiras*, 18–19.

BIBLIOGRAPHY

Antelo, Raul, Maria Lúcia de Barros Camargo, Ana Luiza Andrade, and Tereza Virgínia de Almeida, eds. *Declínio da arte: Ascenção da cultura*. Florianópolis: ABRALIC; Letras Contemporâneas, 1998.
Assis, Machado de. "Instinto de Nacionalidade." In *Obra Completa*, vol. 3. Rio de Janeiro: José Aguilar, 1959.
Bakhtin, Mikhail. *Questões de literatura e de estética*. São Paulo: EdUSP, 1993.
Barbieri, Therezinha de Jesus. *Encenações do híbrido*. Tese de doutoramento apresentada ao Depto. de Letras da PUC-Rio, 1996.
Benzaquén de Araújo, Ricardo. *Guerra e Paz: Casa Grande e Senzala e a obra de Gilberto Freyre nos anos 30*. Rio de Janeiro: Editora 34, 1994.
Candido, Antonio. "A nova narrativa." In *A educação pela noite e outros ensaios*. São Paulo: Ática, 1987.
Carvalho, Maria Alice Resende de. "Violência no Rio: discursos semânticos e institucionais sobre os discursos sobre o mal." *Comunicação & Política*, ano I, v. I, n. 2, nova série (dez/94–mar/95).
Châtelet, François. "A questão da História da Filosofia hoje." In *Políticas da Filosofia*, edited by Dominique Grisoni. Lisboa: Moraes Editores, 1977.
DaMatta, Roberto. *Carnavais, malandros e heróis: uma sociologia do dilema brasileiro*. Rio de Janeiro: Guanabara Koogan, 1990.
Derrida, Jacques. *Gramatologia*. São Paulo: Perspectiva; EdUSP, 1973.
Freitas Filho, Armando, Heloísa Buarque de Hollanda, and Marcus Augusto Gonçalves. *Anos 70: Literatura*. Rio de Janeiro, Europa, 1980.

Fonseca, Rubem. "Davi Neves e Rubem Fonseca falam de *Lúcia McCartney*." *Filme Cultura*, ano III, no. 17 (Nov.–Dec. 1970).

———. "Feliz ano novo." In *Contos reunidos*, edited by Bóris Schanaiderman. São Paulo: Companhia das Letras, 1994.

———. *Os prisioneiros*. Rio de Janeiro: Ed. Codecri, 1978.

———. *Lucia McCartney*. Rio de Janeiro: Olive Editor, 1973.

———. *O caso Morel*. São Paulo: Companhia das Letras, 1994.

———. *O cobrador*. São Paulo: Companhia das Letras, 1994.

———. *A grande arte*. São Paulo: Circuito do Livro, 1986.

———. *Bufo & Spalanzani*. Rio de Janeiro: Francisco Alves, 1985.

———. *Vastas emoções e pensamentos imperfeitos*. São Paulo: Circulo do Livro, 1990.

———. *Agosto*. São Paulo: Comanhia das Letras, 1993.

———. *O selvagem da ópera*. São Paulo: Companhia das Letras, 1994.

———. *Contos reunidos*. Edited by B. Schanaiderman. São Paulo: Companhia das Letras, 1994.

———. *Histórias de amor*. São Paulo: Companhia das Letras, 1997.

———. *E do meio do mundo prostituto só amores guardei ao meu charuto*. São Paulo: Companhia das Letras, 1997.

———. *Confraria das espadas*. São Paulo: Companhia das Letras, 1998.

Foucault, Michel. "Sur l'archéologie des sciences. Réponse au Cercle d'épistémologie." In *Dits et écrits* I. Paris: Éditions Gallimard, 1994.

———. "Réponse à une question." In *Dits et écrits* I. Paris: Éditions Gallimard, 1994.

———. "Qu'est-ce qu'un auteur?" In *Dits et écrits* I. Paris: Éditions Gallimard, 1994.

Franco, Renato. *Itinerário político do romance pós-64: A Festa*. São Paulo: Ed. UNESP, 1998.

Freire Filho, João. *A elite ilustrada e o 'clamor anônima da barbárie": gosto popular e polêmicas culturas no Brasil moderno*. Tese de Doutorado. Rio de Janeiro, Departamento de Literatura Brasileira, Puc-Rio, 2000.

Garcia-Rosa, Luiz Alfredo. *Vento sudoeste*. São Paulo: Companhia das Letras, 1999.

———. *Achados e perdidos*. São Paulo: Companhia das Letras, 1996.

———. *O silêncio da chuva*. São Paulo: Companhia das Letras, 1998.

Gomes, Renato Cordeiro. *Todas as cidades, a cidade*. Rio de Janeiro: Rocco, 1994.

———. "O Histórico e o Urbano: Sob o Signo do Estorvo. Duas Vertentes da Narrativa Brasileira Contemporânea." *Revista Brasileira de Literatura Comparada* 3 (1996): 121–30.

———. "Sob o signo do urubu: distopias urbanas." In *América: ficção e utopias*, edited by José Carlos S. B. Meiby and Maria Lúcia Aragão. São Paulo: EdUSP, 1998.

———. "O histórico e o urbano: sob o signo do estorvo duas vertentes da narrativa brasileira contemporânea." *Revista Brasileira de Literatura Comparada* 3 (1996).

Hollanda Heloisa Buarque de. "Bandeiras da imaginação antropológica." *Jornal do Brasil* (1981).

Lash, Scott. "A reflexividade e seus duplos: estrutura, estética, comunidade." In *Modernização Reflexiva*, edited by Anthony Giddens, Ulrich Beck, and Scott Lash. São Paulo: Ed.UNESP, 1995.

Lima, Luiz Costa. "Pós-modernidade: contraponto tropical." In *Pensando nos trópicos*. Rio de Janeiro: Rocco, 1991.

Lowe, Elisabeth. *The City in Brazilian Literature*. London and Toronto: Fairleigh Dickinson University Press, 1982.

Mello, Patrícia. *Elogio da Mentira*. São Paulo: Companhia das Letras, 1998.

———. *O Matador*. São Paulo: Companhia das Letras, 1995.

———. *Acqua Toffana*. São Paulo: Companhia das Letras, 1994.

Merquior, José Guilherme. "A aranha e a abelha: para uma crítica da ideologia pós-moderna." *Revista do Brasil* 2, no. 5: número especial dedicado à literatura brasileira na década de 80. Rio de Janeiro: Governo do Estado do Rio de Janeiro; Secretaria de Ciência e Cultura; Prefeitura Municipal do Rio de Janeiro; Rioarte, 1986.

———. *O fantasma romântico e outros ensaios*. Petrópolis: Vozes, 1980.

Moriconi, Ítalo. *Situando o pós-moderno na teoria e na crítica brasileiras: politizando o saber, descentramento e desconstrução dos objetos num contexto de democratização*. Literary History Project: Datil, 1998.

Morse, Richard. *"Peripheral" cities as cultural arenas (Russia, Austria, Latin America)*. Rio de Janeiro: IUPERJ, Série Estudos, no. 17, August, 1983.

Noll, João Gilbeto. *Rastros de verão*. Rio de Janeiro: Rocco, 1990.

———. *Bandoleiros*. Rio de Janeiro: Nova Fronteira, 1985.

Nunes, Benedito. "Reflexões sobre o moderno romance brasileiro." In *O livro dos seminários*, edited by Domício Proença Filho. São Paulo: LR Editores Ltda, 1982.

Oliveira, Roberto Cardoso de, et al. *Pós-modernidade*. São Paulo: Ed. Unicamp, 1988.

Pellegrini, Tânia. *A imagem e a letra*. São Paulo: Mercado das Letras/FAPESP, 1999.

Pereira, Carlos Alberto Messeder. *Em busca do Brasil contemporâneo*. Rio de Janeiro: Ed. Notrya, 1993.

Proença Filho, Domício. *Pós-modernismo e literatura*. São Paulo: Ática, 1995.

Revista do Brasil 2, no. 5: número especial dedicado à literatura brasileira na década de 80. Rio de Janeiro: Governo do Estado do Rio de Janeiro; Secretaria de Ciência e Cultura; Prefeitura Municipal do Rio de Janeiro; Rioarte, 1986.

Ribeiro, Paulo Jorge da Silva. *A perda da inôcencia. Etnografia e literatura como discursividades da crise do Rio de Janeiro contemporâneo*. Dissertação de mestrado apresentada ao Programa de Pós-Graduação em Ciências Sociais da Universidade do Estado do Rio de Janeiro, 1999.

Rouanet, Sérgio Paulo. *As razões do Iluminismo*. São Paulo: Companhia das Letras, 1987.

Sant'anna, Sérgio. *Notas sobre Manfredo Rangel – reporter*. Rio de Janeiro: Bertrand, 1991.

———. *Senhorita Simpson*. São Paulo: Companhia das Letras, 1989.

———. *O Monstro*. São Paulo: Companhia das Letras, 1994.

Santiago, Silviano. "Crítica cultural, crítica literária: desafios de fin de siglo. LASA, Guadalajara, México. Datil" (1997). In *Declíno da arte: Ascenção da cultura*, edited by Raul Antelo, Maria Lúcia de Barros Camargo, Ana Luiza Andrade, and Tereza Virgínia de Almeida. Florianópolis: ABRALIC; Letras Contemporâneas, 1998.

———. "Brasil, mostra a tua cara." *Idéias*, Jornal do Brasil (20/4/1996).

———. "Apesar de dependente, universal." In *Vale quanto pesa: Ensaios sobre questões político-culturais*. Rio de Janeiro: Paz e Terra, 1982.

Santos, Jair Ferreira dos. *O que é o pós-moderno?* São Paulo: Brasiliense, 1986.

Schwartz, Roberto. "Cultura e política, 1964–1969." In *O pai de família e outros estudos*. São Paulo: Paz & Terra, 1978.

———. "As idéias fora do lugar." In *Ao vencedor as batatas*. São Paulo: Livraria Duas Cidades, 1977.

Silva, Deonísio da. *Nos bastidores da censura: sexualidade, literatura e repressão pós-64*. São Paulo: Estação Liberdade, 1989.

Sinder, Valter. "The Nation Borders and the Construction of Plural Identities: Carnival, Rogues and Heroes or Roberto Da Matta and the In-Between Place of Brazilian Culture." *Portuguese Literary & Cultural Studies* 4. Center for Portuguese Studies and Culture. New Bedford, Mass.: University of Massachusetts Dartmouth, 2000.

Soares, Luiz Eduardo. *O experimento de Avelar*. Rio de Janeiro: Relume-Dumara, 1997.

Sosnowski, Saúl, and Jorge Schwartz, eds. *Brasil: o trânsito da memória*. São Paulo: EdUSP; University of Maryland, 1994.

Sussekind, Flora. *Literatura e vida literária*. Rio de Janeiro: Jorge Zahar Editor, 1985.

———. *Tal Brasil, qual romance?* Rio de Janeiro: Achiamé, 1984.

Torres, Antonio. *Um táxi para Viena d'Austria*. São Paulo: Companhia das Letras, 1991.

Trigo, Luciano. *Vampiro*. São Paulo: Iluminuras, 1993.

Velloso, Mônica Pimenta. "A literatura como espelho da nação." *Estudos Históricos* 2 (1998).

Velloso, Mônica, and Angélica Madeir,. *Leituras brasileiras*. São Paulo: Civilização Brasileira, 1999.

Villaça, Nízia. *Paradoxos do pós-moderno: sujeito e ficção*. Rio de Janeiro: Ed. UFRJ, 1996.

9

The Republic and the Suburb: Literary Imagination and Modernity in Brazil

Heloisa Maria Murgel Starling

In 1882—six years before Brazil became a Republic—Machado de Assis, in one of his few explicitly political satiric short stories, *A Sereníssima República*[1] (*Gentle Republic*), paints a strongly negative picture in order to evaluate the chances of expansion and consolidation of a republican and democratic national experiment. According to Machado, in a society consisting of spiders and politically instructed by men, the construction of the republican order has produced, as its main feature, a fossilized public power structure, a defective power system, the political actors' crystallization in the scene, and the absence of any significant project for the production of social wealth.

Above all, Machado de Assis insists, the political life of the spiders in *A Sereníssima República* has yielded, most importantly, great corruption. Even more than the misuse or the robbing of the common wealth, the corruption that figures in Machado's story means cultural degradation—in political relationships an ethical standard must be established, a measure of decency, a rule of justice in order to implement a republic, even in the case of a republic of spiders, doomed to an insipid existence in a hollow tree or in a corner of the garden of a shack in Rio de Janeiro.

Despite all this, that society was not ostensibly formed by groups of opportunist, voracious, cynical, egotistical, or dishonest spiders. Unlike Mandeville's[2] hedonic, vicious, deceitful bees, for instance, its members were particularly productive, practical, rather frugal, efficient, and very pragmatic spiders that were more fond of routine than of adventure. In political affairs, Machado explains, geometry was the only matter that set them apart without inflaming them: "Some understand that spiders should make their webs with straight threads, they constitute the rectilinear party;—others, on the contrary, think that spider webs ought to be made with curved threads,—they're the curvilinear party. There is still a third party, mixed and central, that holds the following postulate: spider webs should be woven with both straight and curved threads; it is the recti-curvilinear party; and, at last, a fourth political division, the anti-recti-curvilinear party, which makes a *tabula rasa* of all principles involved, and proposes the usage of some air-woven spider webs, transparent and light, in which there are no threads whatsoever."[3]

Therefore, the distinctive characteristic of this society's political behavior pattern was neither an unlimited egoism nor an attitude of apathy and social resignation among its members, who were willing to be taken where fate would lead them. On the contrary, the choice of an aristocratic republic model explicitly related to the eighteenth century Venetian experience aims to, as Machado says, "test the new society's political skills"—in addition to, of course, leading the spiders to adopt a common way of life that is "obsolete, lacking analogy to any other living government in its general features," which would certainly prevent it from "depreciative comparisons."[4]

Nevertheless, in addition to this, the spiders' reproduction of the Venetian model meant the assurance of solutions for the political problem represented by the citizens' ambition; such solutions aimed at protecting the republican experiment from the menace of internal corruption. In this case, the spiders in Machado de Assis's story seemed convinced that the adoption of an electoral system based on rotating offices was capable of stimulating the citizens' participation in public matters and, at the same time, preventing the power from being dangerously taken by an individual or a single faction. They just didn't take into account the corrosive effects of their ambition and conspiratorial assignments, and the fact that, at least in fiction, the spiders, like the Venetian noblemen, never content themselves with the goal of keeping what they already possess and, in their ambition to conquer new positions of power, they always end up putting the republican freedom at risk.[5]

Thus, in *A Sereníssima República*, the emergence of the corruption process is neither the result of the absence of intrinsically good institutions, nor of the effects of social inequalities on the establishment of political forms, or even of this society's low incidence of naturally virtuous citizens. In practice, it results from something else: men's—and spiders'—incapacity to generate a world of common meanings, that is, a place, a language, and a history that allow them to create the conditions to share a specific set of values and to decide, based on these values, which criteria to apply to their own insatiability.

In the vast pragmatic universe that surrounded the *Sereníssima República* conceived by Machado de Assis, where no utopia is presented as possible, the republican and democratic experiment is shown to be invariably deformed by the effect of corruption, especially by the deep disturbance introduced by Machado on the values that sustain and stabilize a political community. In fact, this effect accentuates, in the spiders' everyday political lives, the feeling of exploitation and of impotence with regard to the lack of confidence in others, that is, with regard to the perspective, experienced by almost everyone, that the others will probably not observe common rules. More than that, perhaps, the political corruption's effect increases the strength of the apparently irrefutable argument that it seems silly to obey the rules when one expects others to disobey them and that whoever happens to miss a chance of taking any kind of advantage or personal benefit in this society, even if it is by cheating at its rules, is necessarily seen as a fool.[6]

Machado de Assis's irony is a double one. Obviously, its aim is guided by the futility of the electoral alternatives of a political system, such as the Brazilian one at the end of the nineteenth century, in which participation is reduced and votes are twisted by the chances of manipulating the results—an argument suggested by the author in a note at the end of *Papéis Avulsos'* (*Loose Notes*)[7] first edition. This very irony also points to a republic's obstacles and precariousness, as the Brazilian one, that was restricted to more or less democratic mechanisms of representation and unable to offer its citizens effective conditions of active participation in the political spaces that constitute the basis of a public life.

To a certain extent, the picture Machado painted in this story questions the void that characterizes the intentions of establishing republicanism in Brazil. Furthermore, it suggests that this void determines in a definite way the conditions of strict pragmatism, the absence of a consistent public life project, the lack of republican conviction that for the next one hundred years will characterize the political history of the republic in Brazil.[8]

Nevertheless, the political community that constitutes the *Sereníssima República* is also a miniature of the Brazilian society, as Machado de Assis perceives it: a precarious society, under the constant menace of having to go "from a photograph to an epitaph,"[9] like his character Brás Cubas, from the perversity of the forms of domination engraved on the national reality throughout an agonizing nineteenth century to a presumption of modernity that enters untouched well into the twenty-first century. To be precise, this society's main feature, which moves embarrassingly through the centuries, is the complete uncertainty with regard to its due date, which results partly from the cynical and dismal expectation fueled by most of its inhabitants that corruption may become a regular and general behavior as in *A Sereníssima República*.

Being convinced that one lives in a society where one expects others to violate good behavior rules sooner or later not only reshapes social and political relationships of the eighteenth century, as Machado observes, but also instills a new behavior pattern as confirmed in his characters, characterized by an atmosphere of unfettered ambition, cynicism, competitiveness, jeer, scorn, indolence, and unscrupulous opportunism. To a great extent, this behavior pattern reflects the type of mechanisms and procedures that guide the modernization processes in the country, producing a peculiarly Brazilian phenomenon: the *paramodern* experience of a country immersed in the acknowledgement of the legitimacy of the values, the institutions, the principles, and the choices that form modernity's democratic repertoire and, at the same time, emerging from it, in the comparative sense of acquisition difficulties and of the internal development of these values, principles, choices, and institutions.[10]

The need to stimulate the Brazilian historical, social, and political imagination about this *paramodern* experience's constituent features has been at the core of Machado de Assis's literary reflection on the nation and apparently indicates the formation of a fictional matrix also aimed at, as much as toward, the Brazilian tradition of social and political thinking, exposing some of the secrets that form the peculiarity of our modern scene. This is, obviously, a unique matrix: it produces a particular type of imagination about Brazil and its inhabitants founded on the myth's heteronym, on the fictional impulse of applying still latent possibilities of a certain reality to the Brazilian everyday life, leading them to imagine that things could be different from what they really are.

To be precise, the capacity of making its potential forms visible, which is characteristic of the literary act, and the ability to act, to create new and more satisfactory ways of life in this very world, which is characteristic of politics, are interconnected. On the one hand, their existence is due to a common source—imagination. On the other hand, they share the peculiar task of inserting extrinsical criteria and references into human living space, producing the conditions for man to face his surrounding reality with awareness but no premeditation, but this does not mean that he yields to its weight. In a way, this ability to experience the world as reality and value allows the literary act, with its reorderings and inventions, to create radical doubts about the substance that makes up politics itself—the fatality of the action and of the decisions that determine it.

Due to this, an understanding of Brazil, constructed inside such a matrix never shows a translucent and crystal-clear image of the country. On the contrary, its reflection is always crooked or angled, in a double sense. In the sense of shape, it is "a type of cunningly warped net to gather from reality truths that are invisible to the naked eye, but that, when seen, force the reformulation of reality."[11] In the sense of memory, it produces a fantasy-oriented retrospective effort of imagination.[12] Every time this effort at remembering takes place, a story appears, that is to say, in a human being, the telling of what has happened is interrupted and "a compound narrative, an additional paragraph, is added to the world's resources"[13] — inside the fictional matrix, historic and literary borderlines still create the conditions for a retrospective effort of creative imagination, based on the work of memory, having Brazil as a horizon, images as an interpretation technique, and language as a mediation.

Therefore, coming from a very peculiar place where literature, politics, and history find their roots and are classified as "shades of a same color,"[14] the fictional matrix initiated by Machado de Assis's prose also reflects upon this concept of "modern" that is, in an unexpected point of view, almost like a Brazilian—or Latin-American—aberration and insists on showing retrograde and grotesque virtualities from the main historic projects of Brazil's insertion into the frames of western modernity. As Machado himself defines it, this matrix, constructed under the sign "of a Sterne-like or Xavier-de-Maistre-like free style" but undoubtedly with the addition of "a touch of pessimistic grumpiness,"[15] operates with the obstacles, the shallowness, the cruelty, the ridicule, the oppression brought about by a historically perverse variation of the concept of "modern"—a variation that, in the work of Machado de Assis, happens to the Brazilian society in the transition from Empire to Republic, in order to combine the political system's bureaucratic rigidness and the extreme mistreatment of the labor force with the Brazilian cultural matrices' traditional plasticity and to exhibit its modern tendencies.

For this very same reason, with the spectacular agility of Machado de Assis's prose, the narrator's bitter tone, his petulant rhetorical pirouettes, his moral ambiguity, his calm boldness, and his ironic intention give rise to a mechanism of corrosion that acts on the very structure of the narrative, having a double effect as consequence. In the first place, this effect empowers, through fiction, the sense of *mimesis* of the Brazilian society's intrinsic relationships of domination.[16] It should be said that the sense of faithful imitation of the national elite's characteristic shamelessness—this elite, with its "boasting vanity," its "luxurious wrapping," its incredible tendency to love others "for fifteen months and eleven hundred bucks, and nothing less,"[17]—ended up always distorting and bringing under its power everything that was brought onto the national scene by the "modern": scientific theories and philosophies, technological inventions, processes of democratization, political institutions, the Republic itself.

Secondly, however, this very peculiar *mimesis* effect also allows Machado de Assis's narrative prose to side with the illusions and the luck pertaining to a people that balances itself on another pole of eighteenth-century Brazilian society: Rio de Janeiro's poor people, which were neither slaves nor owners, with their anonymous and obscure lifestyle and whose lives were organized in order to serve the destiny of dependency and servility that the Brazilian patriarchal structure, frozen in the archaic pattern of labor relations and the violence of slavery, imposes on its subordinated layers. Machado seems to suggest that these people's lives lack purpose. It is an unproductive, one-sided life, which is fed by a routine of astounding passivity and by the constant usage of the survival tactics they have to employ during hard times and whenever social differences become more evident. Such tricks demand creative manipulation of—while, at the same time, maintaining and strengthening—the manorial domination rites associated with the people's own subordinate condition. A life that seems to recreate, at least in literature, the everyday life of a country that is able to enter the modern scene immersed in a paradoxical time, a time that passes in vain, leaving everything as it was because on its horizon lies nothing—or, more correctly, on its horizon lies the Brazilian social structure.[18]

Yet, also because of this same *mimesis* pretension of the relationships of domination, so peculiar to the fictional matrix initiated by Machado de Assis's prose, something that could have been the main event in Brazilian contemporary history—the slow progress of its processes of modernization—had its axis displaced, and our focus lands on a suburb. However, this kind of suburb is perhaps different from the one Dom Casmurro intends to analyze in his *História dos Subúrbios* (*History of the Suburbs*) in order to escape from the monotony of his declining years, before deciding to write about himself and tell the story of his jealousy and resentment.[19] But, in any case, a kind of suburb very close to the meaning in Walter Benjamin's definition: "suburbs are the cities' state of siege, the battlefield where the decisive combat between the town and the country, the modern and the traditional, erupts uninterruptedly."[20]

From this point of view, suburbs are an imaginary space that is counterposed to the modern city like an unfaithful mirror with no aesthetic or metaphysical qualities. As Jorge Luis Borges would write some years later in his first books of poetry,[21] Machado de Assis seems to extract from Rio de Janeiro's *eccentric neighborhoods*, a term he uses to refer to the neighborhoods of Gamboa, Copacabana, and Tijuca for instance, residues of a dreamed world tolling in its own way, on the outskirts, the temporal cadence of Benjaminian passages about Paris: the precise moment when something from the urban fabric is about to disappear, and this disappearance illuminates with a singular poetic lighting everything that condemned it, its other and its opposite.[22]

In Machado de Assis's view, suburbs constitute a peculiar kind of topography of the outskirts, always indecisively between the first urban houses and the very last rural area buildings, between the last decades of the nineteenth century and their survival in the twentieth century's early years, between the lost qualities of an evanescing culture and the corrosive, unfinished, tragic side of a ruin. Despite that, it was Euclides da Cunha, one of Machado de Assis's contemporaries, who added to this literary matrix the big news represented by the *sertão* (the backlands of the Brazilian Northeast) category. It is seen as another necessary fictional element in the composing of a topography of the outskirts, an element that was also caused by the representation of a threshold experience and particularly appropriate to enable the invention of the times and spaces of modernity that take place in a suburb called Brazil.

In this way, the presence of the category *sertão* in the composition of this suburb's topography, so peculiar to the fictional matrix founded by Machado de Assis, recovers, even if only partly, something about the debate on the routes of the Brazilian nation developed in Euclides da Cunha's *Os Sertões* (*Rebellion in the Backlands*)—something about the tragic chain of failures and incompletions led by the out-of-tune shock of the meeting of modernity's repertoire of values, principles, and choices and the implementation effort of the country's modernization projects; or something about the risks of barbarism emerging in Brazil's extremities in the name of the Republic and of establishing the evidence of its power.[23]

In fact, in Euclides da Cunha's argument, *sertão* is mainly an imagery of desolation that may appear in the small village of Canudos's dry, crooked, violent landscape as well as in the loneliness and abandonment brought about by the great watery mass on Alto Purus's Amazon borderline: a "sinister and desolate landscape" that always consumes itself before being completely formed; a land with no name or history, characterized by a dismal combination of geographic isolation, thinned-out population, wandering men, lost memory, and dispersed language.[24]

In describing Canudos, in northeastern Bahia of 1897, a world that seemed undone, beneath the notice of the republican nation's history and geography, Euclides da Cunha includes the elements that allow him to introduce in the *sertão* category the fiction pertaining to a land immersed in deep sadness, in the absence of values, in lines deviating from progress, in the irrationality of men, in the shock brought about by a vision of possible barbarism, a "soil that mixes up, and runs, and flees, and twitches, and falls down, and gets up."[25] However, in the Amazon's rubber plantations as well, *sertão* is understood as loneliness, isolation, and loss, the primitive force pertaining to a region that is still in transit between nature and culture, that is dominated by resistance to modernity and immersed in tradition: "History wouldn't reach that far out,"[26] Euclides da Cunha pondered, and this assertion translated into a representation of Brazil with a dimension of an abysmal void and also a conviction that the Republic itself, affected by this dangerous but appealing barbarism, was at risk of going backward in time and dissolving its political ability to act with impunity, savagery, and tragedy.

In Euclides da Cunha's opinion, "desert invokes desert,"[27] with this insinuating a hardly edifying history about the Brazilian Republic, its dream of modernity, and its modernization projects. In Machado de Assis, the *Seceníssima República*'s citizens lacked education about civil virtue, they lacked, perhaps in order to hold their vicious and arrogant peers back, the necessary knowledge and desire for freedom.[28] Euclides da Cunha tells the story of a compassionless Republic, characterized by the indifference between men and nature, between men and things, between civilizing illumination, the euphoria of technical progress and the fate of a people that "opens by means of carbine shots and machetes new trails toward their revolving itineraries, and revealing other unknown spots, where they would leave, as they had always left, in the form of tumble-down cottages or the destroyed aborigine's pitiful figure, the only products of these builders of ruins tumultuous struggles."[29]

In spite of this, it was only in the end of the decade of the 1930s that another writer, Graciliano Ramos, proclaimed the importance of projecting, beside a Republic filled with precarious ruins and inside the literary matrix initiated by Machado de Assis, a poetry of the shortage[30] as a counterpart to the prevalence of a model and hegemonic sense of the concept of modern currently adopted in the country. Such poetry of the shortage was able to include, in Brazil's public world, an awareness of Brazilian *outcasts'* political existence[31]—anonymous and insignificant, simple and obscure people, moving, in an unbalanced manner, through the nation's emptiness, at the mercy of a Republic that never vindicates them.

In fact, when Graciliano Ramos wrote *Barren Lives* (*Vidas Secas*), from May to October 1937, he faced a Republic without a desire for political and social incorporation of societal groups that, thus far, had been completely marginalized. In practice, the centralization and the authoritarianism that characterized the Brazilian political experience from 1930 on—and, particularly, after 1937's coup—had a double effect: on the one side, they grew further and further away from the notions that had led to the Revolution of 1930, in order to try to establish the Republic again and to impose the domination of the Union over the Federation, of corporations over citizens, and of the State over political community.[32]

On the other hand, the combination of centralization and authoritarianism after 1930 also turned into a national objective the pretension of modernity that has accompanied the Brazilian Republic since its implantation in 1889, generating a project based on the conviction that Brazilian archaism could be eliminated by a very authoritarian political form—the New State—that had the nation in tune with modernization. A whole generation of intellectuals somehow adapted to this displacement, intellectuals who were uneasy about the signs indicating Brazilian society's impenitent delay, who dreamed actively about transforming those signs into symbols of progress, but who ended up being impotent before a country they never entirely succeeded in deciphering.[33]

Nevertheless, the poetics of deprivation that Graciliano Ramos introduced into the literary matrix founded by Machado de Assis, mainly after the publication of *Vidas Secas*, seems to present a counterclaim to this ideal of modernization which, being authoritarian, radicalizes the perspective of the State as an exclusive agent of execution of the country's unification processes and the construction of the nation. Unquestionably, the absence of clear historical marks in a text like *Vidas Secas*, which is able to indicate with a rather unusual force the problems of political and social exclusion included in the assumptions of the construction of the national identity and in their mechanisms of integration,[34] recapitulates, somehow, the dreadful unproductivity of a time that drags itself forward. That is, a time that goes by in vain, as Machado de Assis suggests, moving back and forth infinitely and, in its trail, leaving everything exactly as it was.

In Machado de Assis's view, the time that feeds the processes of Brazilian modernization is unproductive because in its historical horizon lies the impressive passivity and the strong conformism that surrounds the country's social and political reality. In Graciliano Ramos's opinion, however, the time of modernization does not make advances because on this same historical horizon also lies a nation designed to shelter a people whom it does not recognize any more than does the Republic, as its own.

Thus, to Graciliano Ramos, the *sertão* could not simply be the desert in which Euclides da Cunha believes, that is, the primitive force of a region still in movement between nature and culture, dominated by the resistance against the modern and absorbed in tradition. In *Vidas Secas*, with its characters immersed in the enormous unproductivity of this time lacking meaning, *sertão* is a particular condition of exile—a condition of exile in the interior of one's own country.

Perhaps for this same reason, *Vidas Secas*'s characters—Fabiano, his wife, Miz Vitória, their two boys, and the female dog Baleia[35]—are always connected to a land that belittles them and denies them what they basically lack: hope for the end of the drought, a place geographically and socially stable, a patchwork of dreams, a chance of expressing their scanty desires. As Graciliano Ramos put it, in a letter written to his wife in May 1937, the absolute negative, the absurd deprivation generated by the *sertão*, this land in which any solid foundation yields paradoxically to the emptiness provoked by the limit of extreme fatigue, constitutes the elements capable of focusing the narrative mode that will orchestrate all the other images of the novel:

I wrote a short story about a female dog's death, something difficult, as you see: I tried to guess what occurs in a female dog's soul. I wonder if a dog really has a soul. I don't care. My pet dies wishing to wake up in a world full of guinea pigs. Exactly what we all wish. The difference is that I want them to appear before I fall asleep, and father Zé Leite intends for them to come to us in dreams, but deeply we are all like my Baleia and we hope for guinea pigs.[36]

Fabiano's eldest son precisely and effortlessly managed to interpret the reality of this painfully anomalous, unethical, and profoundly unfair *sertão* that winds its way slowly and heavily into the everyday lives of *Vidas Secas*'s characters—"hell," he insisted, conversing with his mother. About twenty years later, in 1956, during Juscelino Kubitschek's administration and, in the midst of what has perhaps been the most impressive modernization program in Brazil, the main character in *Grande Sertão: Veredas* (*The Devil to Pay in the Backlands*), written by João Guimarães Rosa, will return to the same definition made by the country boy in 1937, so that he, also, can try to understand the only social and geographical space he knew, the homeland where he was born: "we came from hell,"[37] the *jagunço*[38] Riobaldo Tatarana declared, with equal surprise and bitterness.

Nevertheless, during the 1930s, Graciliano Ramos could still imagine that the homeland was not only the *sertão* where one is born, but the Republic where one lives.[39] Probably for this reason, his characters also had, in the scope of their most intimate existence, the tenuous hope of arriving at the city, at this Republic where everyone can live freely and, therefore, where they would no longer experience the condition of their own exile:

They would go forward; they would come to an unknown land. Fabiano was happy; he believed in that land because he didn't know what it was like or where it was. Docilely he repeated Vitória's words—words which she murmured, because she had confidence in him. They trudged southward, enveloped in their dream. A big city, full of strong people. The boys at school, learning difficult but necessary things. The two of them old, ending their lives like a pair of useless dogs—like the dog they once had. But what were they going to do? They hung back, fearful. They were on their way to an unknown land, a land of city ways. They would become its prisoners. And to the city from the backland would come ever more and more of its sons, a never-ending stream of strong, strapping brutes like Fabiano, Vitória, and the two boys.[40]

In a way, there is a deliberate effort inside Graciliano Ramos's narrative to point out the paradoxical traces that are characteristic of a modernization project, which at times emphasize each citizen's hope to enjoy a daily life under a city's laws and with a lifestyle derived from them; while at other times the narrative indicates the certainty of the destruction of the modernization project. And it is only this precarious line between hope and damnation that nurtures Fabiano and his people's dreams.[41] On the contrary, in Guimarães Rosa, there is no doubt regarding the procedures and directions of this ambiguous concept of "modern." Such a concept is capable of producing a perverse mechanism from which the fortification of the cities disintegrated the *sertão* and its universe of incessant deformations without, however, substituting them for an expansion of the citizenship ideal.

In this sense and perhaps in a very specific way, *Grande Sertão: Veredas*'s narrative reconfigures the final movement proposed by *Vidas Secas*, to show the permanence of this new and absurd kind of exile capable of conforming the tragic destiny of a people who still today tries to strike a balance in the suburbs of the "modern," with no access to laws, to a minimal set of rights, to the Republic's political world:

> Suddenly those men could become a crowd, then a multitude of thousands and hundreds of thousands, emerging from the wilds, filling the roads and invading the towns. How could they know, even if they wanted to, that they had the power of being good, in keeping with a framework of rules and obedience? They would not believe themselves capable of it. They would want to gulp down all the good things they saw, looting and yelling. Ah, and they would drink, they would soon drink up every drop of rum in Januária. And they would seize the women, and fill the streets, and soon there would be no more streets, or children's clothing, or houses. The church bells would be set pealing, imploring God's help. Would it do any good? And where would the inhabitants find holes and caves to hide in—let God tell me that.[42]

When Guimarães Rosa published *Grande Sertão: Veredas* in May 1956, Juscelino Kubitschek, who had just assumed the presidency, still dreamed of inventing cities constantly aimed at the future, cities like Brasília, capable of representing an effort of national affirmation, a desire to integrate the interior into the center, Brazil into the world, tradition into the "modern." In order to consolidate Kubitschek's dream, 1956 also marked the release of the most ambitious modernization program ever presented to the country— the Targets Program—whose most characteristic content came from Kubitschek's inexorable belief in the almost magical formula of *developmentalism* as the main source of modernist norms—a formula he believed was able to produce, in Brazil and on the Latin American scene, an industrial, urban society with its roots in the utopia of an entirely modern city.[43]

In a way, *Grande Sertão: Veredas*'s narrative made a detailed record of the ruins, fragments, debris, and residue of all that which Brazil, being modernized by Kubitschek's *developmentalism,* was no longer able to exploit, and which the Republic had disregarded as unproductive, superfluous, useless: the compact mass of cowboys, muleteers, *jagunços,* diamond or gold prospectors, nomads, planters, whores, native Indians, elders, beggars, lunatics, invalids, cripples, idiots—a people who do not go anywhere; nobody demands their rights, as they are nobody. Just a crowd of paupers and the miserable who move around ceaselessly, leaving the *sertão* for the big cities, which symbolize, as they had in *Vidas Secas,* their last chance for escaping from a world of ridiculous hardship and deprivation. They are those who, at the end of *Grande Sertão: Veredas*'s narrative, discover the complete fruitlessness of this displacement.

Guimarães Rosa perhaps agreed to call them pariahs: somehow in this coming and going between an exiled collective identity in the suburbs of modernity and a lack of identity they have lost the qualities that could link them to the world of their equals and therefore found themselves reduced to an abstract barrenness of their human nature.[44] In the literary matrix founded by Machado de Assis, Guimarães Rosa might perhaps add that the Republic has lost its *plebeísta* (populist)[45] ideal; it has forgotten the humane and essentially political desire to extend the opportunity to enjoy citizenship to all its members.

For this reason, in the suburb, the *sertão,* as big as it may be, is that which one does not see: the archaic essence projected over a primitive society that lives far from the urban space and that which is apparently its opposite. It is any city and all other cities, the one that has lost its civic principles and the one that is already just the degradation of its public places, the city conceived to express modernization and the outskirts that have defined its appearance. Or as Guimarães Rosa himself argues: "*sertão* is the nowhere-land which can never be halved, but that each half territory remains larger than the original."[46]

In fact, *sertão* is doubled: neither one nor the other but what happens between them; it does not go anywhere; it always recovers itself in the middleground.[47] Not accidentally, right at the beginning of *Grande Sertão: Veredas*'s narrative, the *jagunço* Riobaldo Tatarana persuasively affirms: "the *sertão* describes itself: it is where the grazing lands have no fences; where you can keep going ten, fifteen leagues without coming upon a single house; where a criminal can safely hide out, beyond the reach of the authorities."[48] It is a world where everything is still to be done, and its opposite, the place of Fabiano and his people's exile, the land where the village of Canudos was massacred, the river where the Alto Purus's rubber-collector is ruined, the *Seréníssima República* in which a great opportunity was irreparably lost.

In this fiction-drenched Brazil, where the "sertão" is the Republic's only hope for political modernity, the literary matrix started by Machado de Assis seems to bring to the surface the landmarks for a narrative tradition belonging to the outskirts, apt to conform, whether by analogy, by shock, by displacement, by unfamiliarity, or by contrast, the fine trace that articulates certain themes and aspects of the republican thought to the fictional picture executed by its authors. From this movement, it germinates chiefly the encounter between Brazilian literary imagination and a nation whose political shape is invariably unstable and uncertain, where the Republic's normative ideals are still always in the making and modernity seems to emerge from the unresolved tension among the most modern, the most archaic and its remains. In the course of this encounter, its participants do whatever is possible: they turn the invisible into visible, they take history from the oblivion and from the occult, they recall and express what word states.

Any more than this, theirs is not to do.

NOTES

To Maria Alice Rezende de Carvalho, who knows the language of the suburbs.

1. J. M. Machado de Assis, "Sereníssima república," in *Papeis avulsos: obra completa* vol. 2, ed. J. M. Machado de Assis (Rio de Janeiro: Nova Aguilar, 1986).
2. B. de Mandeville, *The fable of the bees, or private vices, public benefits* (Oxford: Oxford University Press, 1924).
3. J. M. Machado de Assis, "Sereníssima república," 343.
4. J. M. Machado de Assis, "Sereníssima república," 342.
5. For an analysis of Venice, see Niccolò Machiavelli, "Discorsi sopra la prima deca di Tito Livio," in *Tutte le opere*, ed. Niccolò Machiavelli (Firenzi: Sansoni Editore, 1971), Libro I; Newton Bignotto, *Maquiavel republicano* (São Paulo: Loyola, 1991).
6. On civic virtue, see, among other titles: Robert D. Putnan, *Making democracy work: civic traditions in modern Italy* (Princeton, N.J.: Princeton University Press, 1993); Jeff W. Weintraub, *Freedom and community: the republican virtue tradition and the sociology of liberty* (Berkeley: University of California Press, 1992); Michael Walzer, *Spheres of justice (a defense of pluralism and equality)* (New York: Basic Books, 1983).
7. John Gledson, "A história do Brasil em *Papéis Avulsos* de Machado de Assis," in *A história contada*, ed. Sidney Chalhoub and Leonardo Pereira (Rio de Janeiro: Nova Fronteira, 1998). For the suggestion of analogy between Machado's fiction and the Brazilian political history see, for instance, John Gledson, *Machado de Assis: ficção e*

história (Rio de Janeiro: Paz e Terra, 1986); Berenice de O. Cavalcante, ed., "Literatura e história," *Tempo brasileiro* 81 (1985).

8. For the limits of the Brazilian Republican experience, see José Murilo de Carvalho, *Os bestializados: o Rio de Janeiro e a república que não foi* (São Paulo: Companhia das Letras, 1987); Renato Lessa, *A invenção republicana* (Rio de Janeiro: Topbooks, 1999); Maria Alice Rezende de Carvalho, ed., *República no Catete* (Rio de Janeiro: Museu da República, 2002).

9. J. M. Machado de Assis, "Memórias póstumas de Brás Cubas" in: *Obra completa* vol. 2, ed. J. M. Machado de Assis (Rio de Janeiro: Nova Aguilar, 1986).

10. On the selectivity of the country's modernization processes, see Sérgio B. de Hollanda, *Raízes do Brasil* (Rio de Janeiro: José Olympio, 1994); Jessé de Souza, ed., *O malandro e o protestante: a tese weberiana e a singularidade cultural brasileira* (Brasília: Ed. UnB, 1999); L. Avritzer and J. M. Domingues, ed., *Teoria social e modernidade no Brasil* (Belo Horizonte: Ed. UFMG, 2000); Wander M. Miranda, ed., *Narrativas da Modernidade* (Belo Horizonte: Autêntica, 1999).

11. Leyla Perrone-Moisés, "A criação do texto literário," in *Flores na escrivaninha*, ed. Leyla Perrone-Moisés (São Paulo: Companhia das Letras, 1990).

12. Charles Baudelaire, "O pintor da vida moderna," in *Obras completas,* ed. Charles Baudelaire (Rio de Janeiro: Nova Aguillar, 1996); Walter Benjamin, "A imagem de Proust," in *Obras escolhidas*, ed. Walter Benjamin, vol.1 (São Paulo: Brasiliense, 1987); Rainer Nagele, "The poetic ground laid bare (Benjamin reading Baudelaire)" in *Walter Benjamin: theoretical questions*, ed. David S. Ferris (Stanford, Calif.: Stanford University Press, 1996).

13. Hannah Arendt, "Sobre a humanidade em tempos sombrios; reflexões sobre Lessing," in *Homens em tempos sombrios*, ed. Hannah Arendt (São Paulo: Companhia das Letras, 1987), 28; E. Young-Bruehl, "Hannah Arendt storytelling," *Social research* 44 (1977); Seyla Benhabib, "Hannah Arendt and the redemptive power of narrative," in *Hannah Arendt: critical essays*, ed. L. P. Hinchman and S. K. Hinchman (Albany: State University of New York, 1994).

14. Walter Benjamin, "O narrador," in *Textos escolhidos*, ed. Walter Benjamin (São Paulo: Abril Cultural, 1980), 65; Olgária C. F. Matos, "O storyteller e o flâneur: Hannah Arendt e Walter Benjamin" in *Hannah Arendt: diálogos, reflexões e memórias*, ed. N. Bignotto (Belo Horizonte: Ed. UFMG, 2001).

15. Machado de Assis, "Memórias póstumas de Brás Cubas," 513.

16. Roberto Schwarz, *Um mestre na periferia do capitalismo: Machado de Assis* (São Paulo: Duas Cidades, 1990); Roberto Schwarz, *Ao vencedor as batatas* (São Paulo: Duas Cidades, 1992).

17. Machado de Assis, "Memórias póstumas de Brás Cubas."

18. Roberto Schwarz, *Um mestre na periferia do capitalismo: Machado de Assis*; Sidney Chalhoub, "Diálogos políticos em Machado de Assis," in *A história contada*, ed. Sidney Chalhoub and Leonardo Pereira (Rio de Janeiro: Nova Fronteira, 1998).

19. J. M. Machado de Assis, "Dom Casmurro" in *Obra completa* vol. 1, ed. (Rio de Janeiro: Nova Aguilar, 1986), 810 and 994.

20. Walter Benjamin, *Paris, capitale du XIX siècle; le livre des passages* (Paris: Éditions du Cerf, 1997).

21. Beatriz Sarlo, *Jorge Luís Borges: a writer on the edge* (Cambridge: Verso, 1993).

22. On the relationship between the suburbs and a threshold experience, see Olgária C. F. Matos, "Drama barroco: topografias do tempo," *História Oral* 1 (1998); Jacques Leenhardt, "Le passage comme forme d'expérience: Benjamin face a Aragon," in *Walter Benjamin et Paris*, ed. Heinz Wismann (Paris: Éditions du Cerf, 1986).

23. On Euclides da Cunha, see specifically: Francisco F. Hardman, "Brutalidade antiga: sobre história e ruína em Euclides," *Estudos Avançados* 26 (1996); Luiz Costa Lima, *Terra ignota: a construção de "Os Sertões"* (Rio de Janeiro: Civilização Brasileira, 1997); Nísia Trindade, *Um sertão chamado Brasil: intelectuais, sertanejos e imaginação social* (Rio de Janeiro: Revan, 1999).

24. Euclides da Cunha, "Os sertões," in *Obras completas*, ed. Euclides da Cunha (Rio de Janeiro: Nova Aguillar, 1995). See also Euclides da Cunha, "À margem da história," in *Obras completas*, ed. Euclides da Cunha (Rio de Janeiro: Nova Aguillar, 1995); Euclides da Cunha, *Um paraíso perdido: reunião dos ensaios amazônicos* (Petrópolis: Vozes; Brasília: Instituto Nacional do Livro, 1976).

25. Euclides da Cunha, "Antes dos versos," in *Obras completas*, ed. Euclides da Cunha (Rio de Janeiro: Nova Aguillar, 1995), 442–43.

26. Euclides da Cunha, "Os sertões," 537.

27. Euclides da Cunha, "Contrastes e confrontos," in *Obras completas*, vol. 2, ed. Euclides da Cunha (Rio de Janeiro: Nova Aguillar, 1995), 152–53.

28. Niccolò Machiavelli, "Discorsi sopra la prima deca di Tito Livio."

29. Euclides da Cunha, *Um paraíso perdido*, 146. For the compassion issue in the sense it is being used on this chapter, see Jean-Jacques Rousseau, *Discurso sobre a origem e os fundamentos da desigualdade entre os homens* (São Paulo: Abril Cultural, 1973).

30. Wander M. Miranda, "Vidas Secas Introdução crítica."

31. For the concept of pariah, see especially: Hannah Arendt, *La tradition cachée: le juif comme paria* (Paris: Éditions 10/18, 1987).

32. Luiz J. Werneck Vianna, *Liberalismo e sindicato no Brasil* (Belo Horizonte: Ed.UFMG, 2000); L. Lippi et al. *Estado novo: ideologia e poder* (Rio de Janeiro: Zahar, 1982).

33. Maria Alice R. de Carvalho, "Opinião e modernidade," *Presença* 13 (1989); Luiz Werneck Vianna, "O moderno na política brasileira" *Presença* 5 (1985).

34. Wander M. Miranda, "Vidas Secas Introdução crítica."

35. Graciliano Ramos, "Vidas Secas," in *Intérpretes do Brasil*, ed. S. Santiago *Intérpretes do Brasil* vol. II (Rio de Janeiro: Nova Aguilar, 2000)

36. Graciliano Ramos, *Cartas à Heloísa* (São Paulo: Secretaria Municipal de Cultura, 1992), 94.

37. João Guimarães Rosa, *Grande Sertão: Veredas* (Rio de Janeiro: Nova Fronteira, 1986), 383. For this tradition of hell determining the Brazilian literary culture see, for instance, Flávio Aguiar, "Visões do inferno ou o retorno da aura," in *O olhar*, ed. Adauto Novaes (São Paulo: Companhia das Letras, 1988); Alfredo Bosi, "Céu, inferno," in Alfredo Bosi, *Céu, inferno; ensaios de crítica literária e ideológica* (São Paulo: Ática, 1988).

38. In *Grande Sertão: Veredas*, *jagunço* is "a member of a lawless band of armed ruffians in the hire of rival politicos, who warred against each other and against the military at the turn of the century, in northeastern Brazil" in João Guimarães Rosa, *The Devil to Pay in the Backlands* (New York: Alfred A. Knopf, 1963), 494, originally published as *Grande Sertão: Veredas* (Rio de Janeiro: Livraria José Olympio, 1956).

39. For this distinction between homeland, nation, and republic, see Maurizio Viroli, *Per amore della patria: patriotismo e nazionalismo nella storia* (Milano: Laterza, 2001).

40. Graciliano Ramos, *Barren Lives*, trans. Ralph Edward Dimmick (Austin: University of Texas Press, 1965), 130–31.

41. On the construction of this paradox in Graciliano Ramos's narrative, see also: Miranda, "Vidas Secas Introdução crítica."

42. Rosa, *The Devil to Pay in the Backlands,* 319.

43. On this subject, see James Holston, *The modernist city: an antropological critique of Brasília* (Chicago: University of Chicago Press, 1989); Maria Victória de M. Benevides, *O governo Kubistchek: desenvolvimento econômico e estabilidade política* (Rio de Janeiro: Paz e Terra, 1979).

44. Arendt, *La tradition cachée.*

45. For a discussion of plebeianism see, for instance, Cícero Araujo, "República e democracia," *Lua Nova* 51 (2000).

46. João Guimarães Rosa. "No Urubuquaquá, no Pinhém," in João Guimarães Rosa, *Ficção completa* vol. 1 (Rio de Janeiro: Nova Aguilar, 1994), 697. For the relationship between republicanism and the city, see Newton Bignotto, "Três maneiras de se criar uma cidade" (mimeo).

47. Giles Deleuze, *Le pli. Leibniz et le baroque* (Paris: Minuit, 1988). See also Ettore Finazzi-Agrò, "A cidade e o deserto; (des) caminhos urbanos no Grande sertão," *Brasil Brazil* 11 (1998); Willi Bolle, "Grande sertão: cidades" *Revista USP* 24 (1994–1995).

48. Rosa, *The Devil to Pay in the Backlands*, 4.

BIBLIOGRAPHY

Araujo, Cícero. "República e democracia." *Lua Nova* 51 (2000).

Arendt, Hannah. *Homens em tempos sombrios.* São Paulo: Companhia das Letras, 1987.

——. *La tradition cachée: le juif comme paria.* Paris: Éditions 10/18, 1987.

Avritzer, L., and J. M. Domingues, eds. *Teoria social e modernidade no Brasil.* Belo Horizonte: Ed. UFMG, 2000.

Baudelaire, Charles. *Obras completas.* Rio de Janeiro: Nova Aguillar, 1996.

Benevides, Maria Victória de M. *O governo Kubistchek: desenvolvimento econômico e estabilidade política.* Rio de Janeiro: Paz e Terra, 1979.

Benjamin, Walter. *Obras escolhidas.* Vol. 1. São Paulo: Brasiliense, 1987.

——. *Paris, capitale du XIX siècle: le livre des passages.* Paris: Éditions du Cerf, 1997.

————. *Textos escolhidos*. São Paulo: Abril Cultural, 1980.

Bignotto, N., ed. *Hannah Arendt: diálogos, reflexões e memórias*. Belo Horizonte: Ed. UFMG, 2001.

————. *Maquiavel republicano*. São Paulo: Loyola, 1991.

————. *Três maneiras de se criar uma cidade*. s.n.t.

Bolle, Willi. "Grande sertão: cidades." *Revista USP* 24 (1994–1995).

Bosi, Alfredo. *Céu, inferno: ensaios de crítica literária e ideológica*. São Paulo: Ática, 1988.

Carvalho, José Murilo de. *Os bestializados: o Rio de Janeiro e a República que não foi*. São Paulo: Companhia das Letras, 1987.

Carvalho, Maria Alice R. de. "Opinião e modernidade." *Presença* 13 (1989).

————, ed. *República no Catete*. Rio de Janeiro: Museu da República, 2002.

Cavalcante, Berenice de O., ed. Literatura e história. *Tempo Brasileiro* 81 (1985).

Chalhoub, Sidney, and Leonardo Pereira, eds. *A história contada*. Rio de Janeiro: Nova Fronteira, 1998.

Cunha, Euclides da. *Obras completas*. Vols. 1 and 2. Rio de Janeiro: Nova Aguillar, 1995.

————. *Um paraíso perdido: reunião dos ensaios amazônicos*. Petrópolis: Vozes; Brasília: Instituto Nacional do Livro, 1976.

Deleuze, Giles. *Le pli. Leibniz et le baroque*. Paris: Minuit, 1988.

Ferris, David S., ed. *Walter Benjamin: theoretical questions*. Stanford, Calif.: Stanford University Press, 1996.

Finazzi-Agrò, Ettore. "A cidade e o deserto: (des) caminhos urbanos no Grande Sertão." *Brasil Brazil* 11 (1998).

Garbuglio, José Carlos, et al. *Graciliano Ramos*. São Paulo: Ática, 1987.

Gledson, John. *Machado de Assis: ficção e história*. Rio de Janeiro: Paz e Terra, 1986.

Hardman, Francisco F. "Brutalidade antiga: sobre história e ruína em Euclides." *Estudos Avançados* 26 (1996).

Hinchman, L. P., and S. K. Hinchman. *Hannah Arendt: Critical Essays*. Albany: State University of New York, 1994.

Hollanda, Sérgio B. de. *Raízes do Brasil*. Rio de Janeiro: José Olympio, 1994.

Holston, James. *The Modernist City: An Anthropological Critique of Brasília*. Chicago: University of Chicago Press, 1989.

Lessa, Renato. *A invenção republicana*. Rio de Janeiro: Topbooks, 1999.

Lima, Luiz Costa. *Terra ignota: a construção de "Os sertões."* Rio de Janeiro: Civilização Brasileira, 1997.

Lippi, L., et al. *Estado novo: ideologia e poder*. Rio de Janeiro: Zahar, 1982.

Machado de Assis, J. M. *Obra completa*. Vols. 1 and 2. Rio de Janeiro: Nova Aguilar, 1986.

Machiavelli, Niccolò. *Tutte le opere*. Libro I. Firenzi: Sansoni Editore, 1971.

Mandeville, B. de. *The fable of the bees, or private vices, public benefits*. Oxford: Oxford University Press, 1924.

Matos, Olgária C. F. "Drama barroco: topografias do tempo." *História Oral* 1 (1998).

Miranda, Wander M., ed. *Narrativas da modernidade*. Belo Horizonte: Autêntica, 1999.

Novaes, Adauto, ed. *O olhar*. São Paulo: Companhia das Letras, 1988.

Perrone-Moisés, Leyla. *Flores na escrivaninha*. São Paulo: Companhia das Letras, 1990.

Putnan, Robert D. *Making Democracy Work: Civic Traditions in Modern Italy*. Princeton, N.J.: Princeton University Press, 1993.

Ramos, Graciliano. *Cartas à Heloísa*. São Paulo: Secretaria Municipal de Cultura, 1992.

Rosa, João Guimarães. *Ficção completa*. Vol. 1. Rio de Janeiro: Nova Aguilar, 1994.

———. *Grande Sertão: Veredas*. Rio de Janeiro: Nova Fronteira, 1986.

Rousseau, Jean-Jacques. *Discurso sobre a origem e os fundamentos da desigualdade entre os homens*. São Paulo: Abril Cultural, 1973.

Santiago, S., ed. *Intérpretes do Brasil*. Vol. II. Rio de Janeiro: Nova Aguilar, 2000.

Sarlo, Beatriz. *Jorge Luís Borges: a writer on the edge*. Cambridge: Verso, 1993.

Schwarz, Roberto. *Ao vencedor as batatas*. São Paulo: Duas Cidades, 1992.

———. *Um mestre na periferia do capitalismo*: Machado de Assis. São Paulo: Duas Cidades, 1990.

Souza, Jessé de, ed. *O malandro e o protestante: a tese weberiana e a singularidade cultural brasileira*. Brasília: Editora UnB, 1999.

Trindade, Nísia. *Um sertão chamado Brasil: intelectuais, sertanejos e imaginação social*. Rio de Janeiro: Revan, 1999.

Viroli, Maurizio. *Per amore della patria: patriotismo e nazionalismo nella storia*. Milano: Laterza, 2001.

Walzer, Michael. *Spheres of Justice (A Defense of Pluralism and Equality)*. New York: Basic Books, 1983.

Weintraub, Jeff W. *Freedom and Community: The Republican Virtue Tradition and the Sociology of Liberty*. Berkeley: University of California Press, 1992.

Werneck Vianna, Luiz. *Liberalismo e sindicato no Brasil*. Belo Horizonte: Ed.UFMG, 2000.

———. "O moderno na política brasileira." *Presença* 5 (1985).

Wismann, Heinz, ed. *Walter Benjamin et Paris*. Paris: Éditions du Cerf, 1986.

Young-Bruehl, E. "Hannah Arendt Storytelling." *Social Research* 44 (1977).

10

Identity Is the Other

João Trajano Sento-Sé

It is through ritually activated memory that collective identities are reinforced and/or redefined.[1] Hence the central position occupied, since Halbwach at least, by studies on memory. In a similar way, it was from the moment this fact was acknowledged that the analysis of feasts and collective celebrations ceased to be the privileged subject of the study of primitive societies and started to draw the attention of political scientists, sociologists, and other researchers dedicated to matters concerning society. The milestones defined for collective celebrations related with the so-called broad-range communities usually refer to remarkable deeds, dramatic, almost agonistic moments when a new, morally positive order is established. It is true that such milestones typically incorporate a certain degree of randomness. However, once they effectively acquire the status of symbols capable of affirming a collective ethos, then they become points of reference that enable memory, in its unceasing work of event selection, to assert itself as a mechanism of construction of the socially shared reality.

Renan points out that collective memory is always selective. However paradoxical this may seem, it invariably involves choices, whether voluntary or not. Consequently, it implies forgetting. Once ritualized, it becomes a performance whose actors are also the audience, simultaneously performing and watching themselves. At such occasions, trivial things may be dressed in magnificent attire; infamous acts, if not altogether forgotten, acquire airs of noble deeds; and impressive actions, if not systematically transmitted to the new generations, may simply lose importance, and ultimately pass into oblivion. This is neither good nor bad, since most such statutes are provisional.

However, the random character of both celebrations and identity marks is seldom acknowledged. Typically, the calendar of civic festivities and patriotic celebrations is supported by a supposedly objective legitimacy that, in turn, also varies according to the beliefs and social convictions upheld by unquestioned authorities—be they shamans, astronomers, or historians.

At certain occasions, in contexts of political democracy, official ceremonies tend to be assigned a peculiar character. The motive of the celebration is also disputed, discussed over and over again, if not openly contested. The resulting debate does not necessarily disqualify the relevance of the historic and symbolic milestone under discussion, but reinforces the postulate that its importance results from the capacity (perhaps necessity) that societies have to set forth certain principles that reaffirm the social cohesion and the sense of belonging to the same political community.

Apparently, this was the case in the celebrations of the five hundredth anniversary of the discovery of Brazil. During at least two years, a full battery of events was prepared to commemorate the historical milestone from which Brazil officially exists. The celebrations were carefully planned, with the indispensable media coverage to mobilize the audience/protagonist and stir the expectancy required to ensure the grandiosity of the date. Historians, the modern guardians of collective memory, elaborately debated and questioned the validity of the accepted versions of the event, delving documents, correcting details, raising hypotheses. Many professors reorganized their curricula to emphasize studies on this particular period. Such messages were preferentially addressed to the coming generations. Books, new and old, took up the shelves in bookstores. As typically occurs whenever collective identities are asserted, there was a pervading claim to totality. As a result, groups that had not been properly contemplated brought up their own opposing versions—versions that had been forgotten because they were disquieting—and questioned the legitimacy of both the celebration and the ethos they commemorate. All this was appropriate: The preparation of the celebration is a part of the event itself, perhaps the most important one.

There were some peculiar characteristics in this celebration of the five hundredth anniversary of the discovery of Brazil. The round figure propelled it to unforeseen proportions. In turn, the size of the event itself seemed to commemorate the cultural, geographic, political and historical unity of a great nation, at a time when both its leaders and part of the local intelligentsia already considered the cause of national defense and sovereignty as an out-of-date banner, an aged concept. It is impossible not to be amazed by the odd fact that the object of the celebrations was so painfully experienced, if not daily anathemized: a sad fate.

For a number of years now, modernity, the obscure and forever unreachable object of desire of the Brazilian ruling class, has been firmly associated with principles inspired by the fall of the ideal of national sovereignty and the advent of a new order, ingenuously called post-national. In consolidating such diagnosis, some events concurred that are not entirely under our control: the policy of forming regional economic blocks, in a kind of reaction to the success of the European Community; the fiscal crisis of the Welfare State, which highlighted the limitations and the fragility of the State as the agent for promoting social justice; the information technology revolution with its unfathomable cultural, political, and economic developments. In the specific case of Brazil, one should add the downfall of the national/developmentalist model and its purported responsibility for two lost decades in social and economic development. This was the background against which the perhaps most painstakingly planned, prepared, and advertised national celebration took place, which should make us pause to ponder. Unquestionably, it was a civic festivity in which the foundations for the advent of a new nation were commemorated at a time when the driving notion itself was at least problematic.

And yet, it may well be that the problematic character of this driving notion—the Brazilian nation—might hold some valuable lessons itself. Perhaps it should be mentioned that this problematic character is not episodic. If we take the word of some of the men and women who have established themselves throughout history as the most outstanding interpreters of the Brazilian nation, it is precisely this problematic character that constitutes the most marked trait of our identity. At least in the restricted field of the social sciences this is so. In all the works comprised in the Canon of Brazilian social sciences, three aspects draw our attention: (1) all of them, without exception, rose to that position because they were dedicated to explain the reasons why Brazil became what it actually is; (2) a good number of times, such efforts resulted in conclusions in which the object of study could hardly be considered praiseworthy and, consequently, they focused on the probable causes of this fact; (3) in analyzing the Brazilian case, most such interpretations, whether from nationalist scholars or not, drew upon categories and notions largely used in European nationalist discourses.

The fact that we take these three as particular characteristics of the Canon of social sciences in Brazil might seem somewhat strange. In an attempt to overcome any doubts regarding this claim, I will discuss briefly each of these characteristics in the next section, hoping to clearly establish their appropriateness as a synthetic and necessarily provisional assessment of a significant parcel of the works comprised in the Brazilian Canon of social sciences. It is important to mention that we do not intend to analyze the entire body of works acclaimed in the field of social sciences in Brazil. This could never be done in the scope of a single chapter. I do not even intend to address the inherent complexity of the works selected. As this is an effort to present a synthesis, I leave aside some particular aspects that are of great importance within the works in question, or that could be relevant for the discussion of specific problems. The following is a cross-cut made in accordance with a particular subject of study: research into how was developed the narrative of Brazil in which the idea of a nation, its formation and historical evolution is taken as the main focus while this very same driving notion is seen as an objective either not reached, or only partly achieved, and in a distorted way.

BRAZILIAN CANON AND CIVILIZATION

In view of the above, a few opening lines should be dedicated to define the meaning of Canon I have adopted here. However, as this is not the core subject, I will not elaborate on the theme, which today is the subject of intense scholarly debate, especially in the United States, a debate that might be schematically explained as the opposition of two currents of thought more closely related than their respective advocates seem to consider. The first one defends the preservation of the so-called Western Canon, which comprises the body of works acknowledged as the classical works of Western History — itself a problematic category, at least — works that were raised to this position due to their aesthetic qualities and their "disturbing singularity".[2] The second current presents itself as a critical discourse against the traditionally accepted criteria used in defining the Canon and points out the political character of such selection. From this point of view, the body of works that constitutes the Western Canon is the expression of a racist, classicist, sexist, and puritan civilization, thus manifesting relationships of domination that have been developed throughout history. To the supposedly aesthetic perspective of the first, the political stance of the second is opposed.

Apparently, the fact that the Canon became a problem by itself stems from the definition of these two opposing currents: the established Canon is faced with a kind of counter-Canon. This discussion originated in the renewed activity of the so-called multiculturalism — a kind of academic epiphenomenon of the growth of political movements in defense of minority rights so common in America. And yet, both sides hold the Canon in a core position, preserving a kind of secularized aura around it. Neither seems to acknowledge, let alone ponder, that the Canon definition inevitably involves a certain degree of randomness. That, in order to be included in the Canon, a work depends as much — or even more — on the way it is received as on its supposed intrinsic qualities. That the inclusion of any works in the Canon is always subject to the unknown rules of chance. In another context, and addressing a different problem, Gabriel Tarde acknowledged that, in order to become truly social facts, and thus ensure their place in history avoiding oblivion and actual nonexistence, great deeds and inventions depend on the adherence of large social contingents and on their perpetuation through transmission to other generations, rather than on their own inherent qualities. In the discussions on the Canon, if we take this seldom-remembered insight on the mechanism through which certain habits prevail and specific values achieve social status, we will realize that there is certain haste and that excessive importance is being attributed to the current debate on the criteria that define the Canon.

In this chapter, Canon means a category that is not so selective, and perhaps less politically committed than the association with the ongoing debate might suggest. The use of this term does not mean an intention to delve its premise. This is a task better undertaken by someone with greater interest in it. Here, Canon is simply understood as the body of works recurrently read and discussed by scholars and researchers in the field of social sciences since it was first theoretically defined. Whatever the criteria may be, the three characteristics highlighted above can be extensively observed in the major works of Brazilian social sciences. It is worth recalling: the Canon consists almost entirely of works and authors dedicated to the analysis of themes related to Brazil and the specifics of its historical process; such analyses presented conclusions that were not very optimistic; many refer to the use of foreign notions and classic categories of nationalist discourses.

Let us take a list of works from any area within the field of social sciences in its broader sense. Historians might consider Antonil or Varnhagen as the origin of Brazilian historiography. "Purists" might move the starting line forward to Capistrano or, those more heterodox, to Manuel Bonfim. Those who are stricter will remember Eduardo Prado or, further along the line, Paulo Prado. From then on, the potentially endless list that includes Caio Prado Jr., Sérgio Buarque de Holanda, Nelson Werneck Sodré, and Florestan Fernandes is no exception to the rule. Names can be added if the list is prepared by sociologists or anthropologists (e.g. Euclides da Cunha, Gilberto Freyre, Alberto Torres, Oliveira Vianna). Mindful of the construction of the Brazilian State, political scientists would go as far back as José Bonifácio, perhaps even Frei Caneca. They would incorporate Uruguai, Joaquim Nabuco, and all positivist thinkers—orthodox or not. Whatever the selection, it is important to stress that all works included in the Canon are dedicated to the analysis of problems and dilemmas related to Brazil. Even interpreters who wrote about strictly theoretical questions, or about themes related with different contexts, are included in the Canon because of the narratives of Brazil they left us.

Unquestionably, this is a singularity. If we take the works of the so-called Holy Trinity of sociologic tradition—Marx, Weber, and Durkheim (even the most absent-minded freshman of any social-science college will know their names by heart)—we might note that all of them, with the probable exception of Durkheim (and a problematic exception at that), were devoted to, and became famous for, their analyses of themes not directly related to their nation of origin. If such a list parts from orthodoxy, the singularity of the Brazilian case becomes even more noticeable: Tocqueville, a French nobleman, is renowned both for his sharp criticism of the French Revolution and for his political analysis of America; Simmel's minimalism could define him as typically German, as French, English, or Italian. To continue along this line, or simultaneously broaden it, is to indulge in an unnecessary exercise to confirm the rule.

Obviously, a whole series of reasons could be developed to explain this singularity of Brazilian social sciences. It would start from acknowledging the position of Brazil at the outer edge of the Western cultural and scientific circuit (the assumption that ours might be considered a Western tradition is itself problematic), and would include the difficulty other centers have in accessing the Portuguese language, a difficulty that would lead Portuguese speakers and writers to address the "native audience." Even Richard Morse's unpleasant and misconstrued allegation that Brazilian theoretical production was poor because it followed too closely European and Anglo-Saxon Canons might be evoked by those whose psychoanalysis sessions were not sufficient to exorcize their chronic inferiority complexes.[3] Any of the above explanations, as well as many others, could plausibly justify this trend of the Brazilian sociological Canon (it is worth repeating that the term Canon is used here in the broadest possible sense). I will not discuss them here. The fact is that this is a recurring characteristic of the Brazilian production, which may be observed even in recent works, possible candidates to a future inclusion in the Canon.

The second and third singularities of Brazilian social sciences are closely articulated. Dissociation is an expounding device, rather than a substantive datum. The continuous effort of interpreting the Brazilian reality results in rather unpromising narratives of its historical process. We can state, with but a little margin for error, that the narratives of Brazil acclaimed in the Canon are based on lack and want, as if the great dilemma would invariably be "What do we lack to become modern?" Undoubtedly, this results from the fact that the interpreters, almost without exception, composed their narratives with one eye on Brazil and the other abroad. When turned to North America, they inquired what, in our colonization process, led to such a divergent result, to our detriment. When looking toward Europe, they delved the difficulties we faced to reach that stage of civilization. The idea of modernity has been both an obsession of the scholars who attempted to explain Brazil and a piece of cheap rhetoric used by members of the political elite who lacked imagination. The notions of lack, of want, of a step not taken have painfully pervaded a significant part of the narratives produced by the most qualified and renowned interpreters of Brazil. As a result, the aphorism "country of the future" led, through surprising ways, to the uncanny closeness of some of the most sophisticated spirits and the most shameless and sinister characters in our history.

We would not have to exert ourselves to verify that there is ample reason for the distressing conclusions: A visit to any pocket of poverty, selected among so many according to one's tastes and preferences, might simply provide us with more palpable and dramatic — perhaps aesthetic — outline to what we painlessly learn from the statistics. However, it is not always easy to understand the idealization of the *other*, the positive double against which Brazil almost invariably appears as a *pathos* of difficult cure. Such idealization might stem from the painful acknowledgement of the marginal position Brazil occupies in the international scenario, from Morse's unpleasant remark or from any other reason that might be advanced. What matters most, at least here, is that, since the fundamental notions on which the discourses of national affirmation were consolidated were borrowed, based on foreign experiences, they are, to say the least, the expression of a discourse-construction method in which the result is set in advance, from the moment the principles underlying its logic are defined. Phrasing it more directly: Whether or not they politically identified with nationalism, the authors of the various narratives of Brazil used the key notions of nationalistic discourses elaborated in Europe and in North America, and interpreted the Brazilian process in terms similar to those used in describing historic processes that had taken place in those foreign lands. Perhaps there was no other way. This remark should not be understood as the passing of a sentence, but rather as highlighting an aspect to help us approach the third trait of the Brazilian Canon mentioned above.

Concurrent with the process of market economy expansion, decadence of the great dynasties, decreasing power of the Catholic Church, and other changes that marked the dawn of a new era, the advent of the idea of a nation, in the modern sense of the word, is probably the most complex and multifaceted phenomenon that appeared in Europe since the start of the eighteenth century.[4] The major changes in the economic, cultural, political, and social spheres that occurred in a period marked precisely by the idea of rupture and disturbed by deep social tensions are linked to this phenomenon. Its complexity is evidenced by the fact that, even in Europe, the idea of nation affirmed itself in different ways, leading to equally diverse and often incompatible conceptions. Hence the difficulty we have in addressing the idea of a nation in the singular. Even leaving aside regional variations—by no means irrelevant—we can consider, a little schematically perhaps, the appearance of two significantly diverse models of nationalism: the French nationalism, of revolutionary and emancipatory inspiration, and the German nationalism conceived to recover the ancient *volk* traditions that were perceived as the depository of the true *ethos* of the German Empire.[5]

A second "national" distinction—more substantive and with greater analytical yield—between the two great lines along which the idea of a nation has been formed can be advanced. According to this second distinction, there would be an ethnic matrix for the construction of the idea of a nation to which only a republican political matrix could be opposed.[6] This distinction has been widely used in recent debates on the current validity of the idea of a nation as a principle of identity and political organization. According to it, the idea of a nation based on principles of ancestral belonging to an ethnic community, which inspired the Nazi nationalistic discourse and many of the bloodiest conflicts of the post–Cold War era, for instance, rests on mistaken assumptions and results in the most terrible and deplorable configurations the idea of a nation may support. This ethnic approach derives from the mistaken assumption that there is a supposedly pure race, historically averse to blending with other races. Furthermore, it posits a qualitative difference between ethnic groups, and consequently between nations. It also neglects the fact that it is an idea historically and socially developed, failing to acknowledge that, despite its effectiveness, nation is but a figment of man's creative imagination.[7] In other words, it presumes natural a phenomenon that derives its grandeur precisely from the fact that it is a social, cultural, and historical phenomenon. From this assumption stem some of the most terrifying characteristics of a certain kind of nationalism, such as xenophobia, totalitarianism and ethnic cleansing policies. Nazism is but the most abhorrent and deplorable historical example of the ominous consequences this type of error may lead to. It is not, however, the only one, nor even its inventor. It may blossom in many other fertile grounds within continental Europe.[8] It cannot be denied that this type of mistake, scientifically untenable and ethically intolerable, still has a reasonable power of persuasion in our days, invariably producing unbearable consequences.

Everything leads us to believe that most of the political rejection of nationalism and of the idea of a nation itself that gained strength in the second half of the twentieth century results from its ethnic matrix components. The same can be said of the repulsion felt by cosmopolitan artists and scholars that repel the supposedly xenophobic and parochial content they presume in any promotion of the idea of nation.

Turning to a second matrix of the idea of a nation may, however, lessen its negative character. According to this matrix, the idea of a nation is not only inseparable from, but also a condition of, the possibility of construction of the modern democratic State, an institutional apparatus of highly incorporating characteristics, based on a universal conception of justice that invests in each individual under its jurisdiction certain prerogatives that then become their inalienable rights. In other words, the idea of a nation would be one of the pillars on which stands one of the most artfully constructed and welcome characters of the modern world: the citizen. From this point of view, the prevalence of the idea of a nation as the founding principle underlying the condition of belonging to a national community and its institutionalized correlate, the national State, would be a basic condition for the maintenance and reproduction of Justice and the respect for both individual and collective rights. As it is based on the sacredness of certain secular moral principles, and because it is, at the same time, tributary and generator of a public *virtú*, this matrix is currently called republican.

While the origins of the ethnic matrix are rooted in the distant past, drawing on the songs of popular poets, the republican matrix stems from more recent phases of the history of civilization: Its founding moments are the modern revolutions; its poets are historians and philosophers. The republican-matrix idea of a nation combines a set of values that was analyzed, in a historical perspective, in the classic work of T. H. Marshall. From a series of events whose starting point can be found in the Glorious Revolution, still in the seventeenth century, followed by the War of Independence of the thirteen colonies and the French Revolution—the most spectacular and dramatic of them all—a new political, social, and economic order was founded, based on the universal declaration of the rights of man. The extension of civil rights, both political and social, to an increasingly larger set of individuals, now turned citizens, marks the process by which public virtue is transformed into a good to be universally shared. Belonging to a national community now means, in this perspective, the investment in such prerogatives, which are then legally guaranteed by the national State.

This last position is also seen with reservations and is subject to sharp criticism. Often, the universalization of prerogatives is denounced as mere formal rhetoric, lacking substantive content. Far from encompassing all who should be contemplated, it would mask a variety of relationships of domination. In a Marxist perspective, it would mask class domination. Currently, some say, it is the particularist expression of a specific political and academic tradition that pretends a universal tolerance that is not matched by its own political developments. Currently still, they would don universalizing colors that are in fact totalizing, hence incompatible with other traditions as respectable, defendable, and credible as itself. In this perspective, it would be dressing a policy of universal domination in cosmopolitan and plural attire.

Finally, according to both actual and virtual critics, the republican perspective would confound republicanism and democracy, which have been completely differentiated since their origins in Antiquity.

With varying emphasis, and via different paths, both founding matrixes of the idea of a nation—ethnic and republican—have points in common. Both— in diverse ways, I stress again—refer to virtuous historic processes and cast a number of paradigmatic heroes to play the role of mythical incarnations of the communities in question. Both consider the consolidation of a sound State as key, albeit diverging in relation to its size and roles. Finally, in both cases, a grandiose future appears as the promise of confirmation of rightness and re-iteration of the accepted values. Those are the overall characteristics of the discourses based on the idea of a nation that have set the tune for the modern civilizations. Peculiarly, they also work as notions seldom questioned in the theoretical analyses of those same civilizations.

Although the terms of the current debates are not the main subject of this discussion, it is important to mention a necessary exception regarding the terms applied in defining the first matrix: The key position of the ethnic reference in its definition banalizes it somewhat. It is true that the ethnic question has occupied a core position in a good part of the nationalist discourses identified there. Since it is a general definition, the stress should be in the trend to naturalize an abstract entity that, provisionally, could be called people. The belief in the material existence of this almost mythical entity is characteristic of the discourses that might be opposed to the republican perspective. The result of this substitution is the fact that, with the new term, the ethnic question will share its key position in the definition of the matrix with other core ideas such as custom, psychology, and tradition. The scope of the definition is thus expanded without losing its power vis-à-vis the republican matrix.

This is not the place to discuss the implications, unquestionably important, both epistemologically and politically, of each of the points regarding the two general ideas of nation. What is important is to stress that each of the postulates of what today is called republican nationalism are present both in the sociological and political analyses of the modern world and in their critique. They are as present today as were—around the late nineteenth century and early twentieth—the questions involved in the ethnic assumptions of the various forms of nationalism were present in the project of building a science of society. In both cases, the critical content was then present, and/or is present today. After all, as Brubaker appropriately states, nation is a political and social practice (i.e., it is not an idea that concerns theoreticians alone). It has an unquestionable materiality. The results of various experimentations on this ideal can be verified beyond the domestic field, within each of the national

States where it prevails. It develops further, with ominous consequences to some parties, in the relations between different civilizations and cultures (i.e., using the expression forged by diplomacy: in international relations).

It is therefore understandable that the notions involved in the idea of a nation were directly or indirectly involved in the sociological and political analyses in general. In this case, what is so singular in its acceptance and its use in the works that form the Brazilian Canon of social sciences? What distinguishes the Brazilian Canon of social sciences, as a Canon composed under the sign of the idea of a nation, from its European equivalents? The answer to this question leads, once again, to the two other differentiating characteristics that have been pointed out here. The local intellectual production included in the Brazilian Canon is singular because it not only focused on the hard effort of explaining Brazil, but also generally derived from this work rather unflattering diagnoses. The nation, subject to a thorough scrutiny, was typically approached as a problem and characterized by lack.

Various are the reasons pointed out as determining factors of Brazil's lacking, as many as the intellectual references used by the shrewdest and most skillful interpreters of the "national reality." This characteristic by no means reduces their skill and the importance of each one of them. In some cases, the diagnoses and theoretical references were not even the support for their most significant content. Nevertheless, this characteristic should not be neglected, especially considering how recurrently it appears.

It would be impossible to present a complete overall survey of its implications, a task that, if properly carried out, would require a number of volumes and a lifelong work. Hence, I would like to highlight two ideas that could exemplify the case in the short span of a chapter: the ideas of people and of revolution. This is a random choice. Many other notions could be used for this purpose. There are, however, good reasons for this choice.

By "people"—such a general notion today that, rather than analytical studies, it befits the political discourses aimed at unleashing strong emotions and establishing a feeling of empathy in the audience—one should understand approximately what we identify as society or, more recently still, in Brazil, what could be called civil society. The choice of this notion may be justified, despite the degree of randomness that invariably remains, because it is subject to a significant variety of approaches. The Brazilian "people," presented as a problem in defining the Brazilian nation, refers to arguments both inspired in racial doctrines and focused on questions related to the type of political organization, with the process of colonization or with the modes of custom law that took hold during the Brazilian historic process. In other words, the Brazilian people—its phenotype, its psychological traits, its culture, its indigence—was often seen as the paramount national problem.

The idea of revolution, on the other hand, is closely related to the process of building a bourgeois order, with the advent of a depersonalized and bureaucratic legal/political structure, with the consolidation of civic rights, both political and social, and, finally, with the formation of the idea of citizenship. In a way, it is more closely related to recent versions of the analyses of the idea of a nation and its present validity than with their "classic" versions. In Brazil, it was the favorite subject of Marxist intellectuals, albeit not the only one. Considered together, the notions of people and revolution present an interesting opportunity to explore two ends of the Canon: On one side, we observe the pathos of the Brazilian social formation, on the other, the pathos of its historic process and the construction of a bourgeois order by which Brazil ended up following paths that delayed its social, political, and economic development.

If we extract from some narratives of Brazil the meanings ascribed to the notions of people and revolution, we will have a kind of meta-narrative in which the dramatic character of its constitution is stressed. The relevance of this operation might be nil, but it may well clarify, and contribute to, the endless work of redefinition of the terms in which such narratives are composed, without detriment to their validity and importance. Above all, it may inspire new perspectives and alternative narratives of the problematizing of the Brazilian national identity.

BRAZILIAN PEOPLE AND NATION

Let us first look at the idea of people. In various ways and fields, it has been presented as a problem in defining the Brazilian nation. José Bonifácio already worried about the difficulty of forming a new nation in which a significant part of the population consisted of slaves. Moving into the Second Empire, we note that both the defenders of a centralized State, like Uruguai, and those who— inspired by the independence of the Thirteen Colonies—advocated federalism, like Tavares Bastos, argued their respective positions by focusing on the primitivism of the Brazilian people.

According to Uruguai, the concentration of power and the maintenance of a strong State were crucial to promote the Brazilian people, who needed the pedagogic action of the State to outgrow the minority status in which they found themselves. The marked upper hand of central power, contrasted Tavares Bastos, was precisely the biggest hurdle to be overcome if the Brazilian people—a people historically tied by bureaucracy and a centralized administration—were to achieve intellectual growth and develop initiative. Inspired by the example of North America, Tavares Bastos saw in federative decentralization the only possibility of unleashing a process through which the Brazilian people, driven by the new conditions, would seize the reins of its own destiny. Uruguai based his arguments on the French Restoration; Tavares Bastos in the North American federalism.

The extended duration of slavery—whose late suppression was not accompanied by any other measure of support to the newly-freed slaves, as Joaquim Nabuco, among others, advocated—and the multiracial profile of the Brazilian society were core issues in the inquiries as to our national character, in the labored formation of social thought in Brazil. The reasons for this are well known. The turn of the twentieth century is marked, in political terms, by efforts to consolidate the new republican order. From the viewpoint of more than a few high-profile intellectuals, this was the time when, finally released from the colonial legacy represented by the monarchy, the nation would materialize in an independent and autonomous way. In academic terms, it was a period during which racist theories were highly regarded both in Europe and the United States, and were lavishly used by local intellectuals.

The consequences of adopting racial theses in Brazil are well known: either the black race was anathemized while the native Indians were praised, or vice versa; racial interbreeding was either condemned as the true cause of the weakening of the race, or recommended as a way of "whitening" the population, a necessary condition for subsequent development.[9] According to Skidmore, the period between 1889 and 1914 was entirely dominated by theses according to which the low level of development of the Brazilian civilization was directly linked to the ethnic composition of its population.[10] Even in later periods we verify the persistence of some of these concepts. Their advocates, however, can hardly be found in the Canon: most lapsed into oblivion and the theses that inspired them have been disqualified; some are still remembered, like José Veríssimo, Sílvio Romero—as forerunners of the history of Brazilian literature—and Nina Rodrigues—as an ethnologist of some interest to the history of science in Brazil. Most likely, only one of the many works produced on the basis of racial assumptions may be considered as seminal: Euclides da Cunha's *Os Sertões*.[11]

Despite its unquestionably racist content, this is a permanent work. The barren and inhospitable Brazilian hinterland, its hostile topography, seldom found a narrator like Euclides da Cunha. It was to man, however, that he dedicated most of his attention. In several places he betrays a certain admiration for the capacity of the typical men and women of this barren hinterland to survive in such an unfavorable environment. He also acknowledges their remarkable capacity of using the hostile environment to successfully fight the various military expeditions sent against them, all with far greater firepower. The Canudos rebellion, however, is depicted by Euclides da Cunha as the result of the imbalance caused by racial mixing, giving rise to superstitious men and women who lacked in physical strength and reasoning capacity. Antônio Conselheiro, the rebel leader, is presented as the "reverse of a great man," capable of exercising a special influence on his followers precisely because he himself carries all the aberrations and superstitions that dominate the hinterland men and women.

Os Sertões is probably the first classic work of Brazilian social theory, a kind of proto-ethnographic analysis of the Brazilian countryside, of a part of our reality that until then had been ignored by the local intelligentsia, whose eyes were always turned to Europe or to North America: the expression of the dismal scenario that lay between the Brazilian nation and modernity. This diagnosis is not free from a high degree of internal tension: the author's hope of glimpsing in the hinterland men and women the foundations of a resplendent and powerful future nation is painfully opposed by the image of the dejected hinterland people of mixed origin, incompatible with the science-oriented and racist principles that inspired the author. Euclides da Cunha came close to seeing in the mixed hinterland men and women the early signs of a new race that would, in due time, assert itself amongst the most civilized ones. Besides being focused on the distant future, this belief, however, did not match the author's own theses.

The racist theses were not the only ones nurturing the belief that Brazil was a nation formed without a people deserving that name. This diagnosis is also present in one of the most beautiful and bitter essays on the theme: Paulo Prado's *Retrato do Brasil*. The titles of three of the four chapters into which the work is divided warn even the most distracted reader of their content: lust, greed, and sadness characterize the hybrid being that inhabits this "effulgent land." The maladies that afflict our people stem from our origin. From the coming together of a greedy and despotic, flawed-character colonizer and the indolence of the native people, coupled with their sensuality and that of the imported blacks, results a historical process marked by decadence. The result is not properly explained by any bias against racial mixing. At least this position is not explicitly stated in the work. We do not find even the slightest intention of presenting a general theory of the three races and their innate characteristics. In a vague and imprecise way, Paulo Prado refers the unfortunate result to a kind of sensual psyche, not used to discipline and rule, lazy, turned to pleasure and easy fortune, which was reinforced by interbreeding. Climate and the vastness of the land contribute to the reproduction and deepening of this psyche.

Much has already been written on the somewhat exaggerated incorporation of the impressions of foreign travelers in *Retrato do Brasil*. The highly impressionist character of Paulo Prado's descriptions was also stressed. In fact, his allusions to climate, to the character of the original peoples, and the forces of nature do not bear even the slightest trace of the scientific intent of Euclides da Cunha and the latter's methodic description. References to naturalists like Buckle, for instance, appear sporadically, with no conceptual commitments. It is possible to imagine that this was the author's true intention. The use of the word "retrato" (portrait) in the title may suggest several meanings.[12] It may well indicate the author's intention of capturing but a snapshot, an outline of what he saw as the reality that surrounded him.

According to Paulo Prado, the various peoples tend to have some particular characteristics. When they combine, they seem to produce a balance of inclinations in which virtues complement each other and defects are neutralized. Thus, in Spain, Paulo Prado contrasts the gaiety of the Andalusians with the somber nature of the Asturians. The happiness of the southern Chinese—"chins" in Paulo Prado words—is balanced by the earnestness of their northern neighbors. In Brazil, he concludes, all is sadness and desolation. Not surprisingly, some of the traits negatively highlighted in Paulo Prado's work can be found, with an inverted mark, in some trivial and conceited versions of the supposed Brazilian character (e.g. the purportedly exacerbated sensuality). Despite all this, even if it expresses bias and the uncritical assimilation of impressions of foreign travelers, irrespective of how untenable the consequences the author draws in his diagnosis—as untenable as the foundations of his own interpretation—the portrait of Brazil depicted by Paulo Prado is still acknowledged, with a melancholy worthy of the portrait it depicts, and remains as one of the bitterest narratives of Brazil and its misfortunes.

After the first jump in time that took us from 1902, the year *Os Sertões* was published, to 1928, when *Retrato do Brasil* appeared in print, it is time for a second jump, this time to 1936, the year in which *Raízes do Brasil* was first published. Even if we are presenting a Canon whose randomness is assumed as a principle, it seems appropriate to include a work that is above question, especially when this presentation involves leaps that leave works and authors of the greatest relevance unmentioned. After diagnoses inspired, first on racist doctrines, and then on the psychological characteristics of the people, it is worth bringing to the forefront an analysis that aims at identifying the maladies of the Brazilian society both in its social structure and its political counterpart. This is the case of the work that made Sérgio Buarque de Holanda an uncontested member of the Canon of Brazilian social sciences.

It might seem temerarious to dedicate only a few lines to such a widely read and acclaimed work, a work that is a key element in the education of researchers in the various fields of social sciences. It would be an exaggeration to imagine that all that could be said and written about *Raízes do Brasil* has already been said: it would certainly mean its death sentence. What matters here is to highlight the fact that, even from a viewpoint far apart from

Euclides da Cunha's biological determinism or Paulo Prado's proto-psychology, the diagnosis of the Brazilian people is not very favorable to the project of forming a prodigious and prosperous nation. In this case, no matter how repetitive this may seem, the basic notion is cordiality. This is the "finding" that synthesizes Sérgio Buarque de Holanda's diagnosis. It may well represent the key to his inclusion in the Canon of Brazilian social sciences, a Canon characterized by works that describe the particularities of the Brazilian people. Were we to be addressing politics, the State, or the economy, it would still be the key. Hence, it is possible to conclude that this is the reason why this category is so recurring in the discussions about *Raízes*—a truly seminal work. Rare are the categories that can synthesize so powerfully an analysis as sophisticated as this one.

Also written as an essay, *Raízes do Brasil* reviews the process of the colonization of Brazil, the Iberian legacy of our colonizers, and developments in the Brazilian social and political structure. From this viewpoint, the Brazilian social model is seen as the result of a peculiar superposition of the public and private spheres. More specifically, the logic of private relations contaminates the public space. As a consequence, Brazilians lack the civility mentioned by Elias,[13] the adjustment to certain imposed rules of conduct that characterize the interactions between citizens within the social space. In Brazil, the social space is an extension of the space of personal relations, and the State is an unfolding of the private sphere. Hence public sociability in Brazil is marked by a horror of interactions based on the impersonal character of law, its subsumption in practices based on emotions.

As a consequence, the cordiality of Brazilian men and women is a kind of superficial, "epidermal" interaction between individuals that works as a shield, protecting and preserving their privacy from the rules and sanctions of collective interaction. The result is a highly atomized society formed by islands of family networks and their associates. The precarious and episodic interactions do not foster a vigorous and autonomous public space, such as the one typically found in modern democratic societies.

Commentators have exhaustively noted the influence of Weber's work on Sérgio Buarque's analysis. Another and as significant influence is Tocqueville's reading of America, which, despite not being so commented on, pervades the entire book. The Brazilian historic process and above all its political developments appear as a kind of negative double of the American experience. The particularism and the familism, the self-sufficient economic units, the organization of both urban and rural spaces, and the concept of the State as an extension of family relations, all concur to the precariousness of the public space and the fragility of social links based on rules of civility. Using a term that, albeit foreign to Sérgio Buarque's work, is absolutely loyal to his narrative, it could be said that, according to him, in order to consolidate itself as a modern nation, Brazil lacks a strong and active civil society.

Combining Euclides da Cunha, Paulo Prado, and Sérgio Buarque de Holanda may seem somewhat odd, as each builds his respective narrative based on different theoretical assumptions, and reaches an equally diverse diagnosis. However, besides their common relevance in the Brazilian cultural and intellectual heritage, they also have in common the perception of a deficit that must be overcome to enable the Brazilian nation to be addressed as a sociological and political reality of the first order. Although this deficit is not restricted to its social constitution—and despite the fact that it is explored via different paths—all of them ascribe to society—its ethnic constitution in the case of Euclides da Cunha, the frailty of its disposition in Paulo Prado, and its historical constitution in Sérgio Buarque de Holanda—a significant portion of the reasons why the Brazilian nation is a problematic case. It is now time to discuss a second important notion inherent to the arguments surrounding the formation of European nations, a concept that takes up a sizable portion of some of the major narratives of Brazil—the idea of revolution.

REVOLUTION AND THE IDEA OF A BRAZILIAN NATION

There are various reasons to justify the selection of the idea of revolution in a chapter that, given its length, must be selective: the fact that this literature is more recent than the one dedicated to unravel the intertwining of the origins of the Brazilian people, located almost at the opposite end of the established Canon; the particularity that, in Brazil, it was the preferred subject of a certain current of social thinking linked to Marxist tradition; the recognition that this is possibly one of the most important notions of the modern era, its own symbolic milestone set in the French Revolution. These are but a few of the many reasons that could be listed here.

According to Hannah Arendt, revolutions, as well as wars, determined the face of the twentieth century. Itself a modern notion, after its original meaning—linked with the ideas of restoration and reform—had been superseded, revolution came to mean an originating, founding movement, unleashed by force and violence.[14] Hence, the idea of revolution refers to expectations of profound and radical changes, the passing from an intolerable and/or archaic situation to a new era: a liberation movement by which are established the favorable conditions that conduce to the reign of liberty. In short it invokes the idea of overcoming what is implicit in the perception that a certain situation should be superseded because it does not satisfy the ethical, political, and historical aspects of a new era. It comes very close, therefore, to the expectations created around the general diagnosis mentioned here of a lacking that characterizes the idea of a nation in Brazil. For no other reason, the idea of revolution is also present in the works of Sérgio Buarque de Holanda and Paulo Prado mentioned here, the subject of both the last chapter of _Raízes do Brasil_ and the postscript of _Retrato do Brasil_. In the former, the revolution is a slow and gradual continuous process, with no traces of the original violence discussed by Arendt—rather appropriate for a people that wishes to picture itself as affable, friendly, and tolerant. This process does not even have a symbolic milestone. Abolition, mentioned by Sérgio Buarque as the turning point between colonial agrarianism and a modern urban and industrial society, is a weak milestone lacking the radical and dramatic character of founding moments. It was chosen simply because there was no other more penetrating event. In Paulo Prado, revolution is more an existential imperative than a landmark, or a palpable historic possibility: it is the dramatic and agonistic convulsion necessary for the Brazilian people to break away from the lassitude, the dejectedness, the torrent of torpor and alienation in which it has been listlessly carried throughout most of its five-hundred-year history.

Anyway, at least in the works of Sérgio Buarque and Paulo Prado, the idea of revolution is a less central concept than it would be to those who theoretically and politically share the historic theory of Marx—probably its most profound and passionate interpreter. Let us take two of the most revered and quoted narrators of Brazil linked to this current of thought, Caio Prado Jr. and Florestan Fernandes. Once again, in the approach to the concept of Brazilian revolution, we find the singular nature of the Brazilian nation and its historic process under the label of insufficiency. It is never too much to repeat: the choice has a certain margin of randomness. It is not due to particular preferences, or to adherence to their theories. It has much more to do with the recurrence with which both are remembered as fundamental references in the literature on Brazil.

A good number of titles of the vast body of works of Caio Prado Jr. are quoted as references in the literature on Brazil. Amongst these I chose _A Revolução Brasileira_, not for the inherent qualities of the work in comparison to others by the same author, but because of its subject. Caio Prado Jr.'s approach to the Brazilian revolution has two implications that interest us at this moment. The first refers to the fact that the Brazilian revolution is understood as a long and slow process of changes in production relationships that would take Brazil from the dependence on the foreign market to a future predominance of the domestic market. It would take Brazil from the colonial status—remnants of which remain—to its consolidation as a structured and autonomous nation. This is the process that confers a singular nature to the

Brazilian case, so often brandished by Caio Prado Jr. against his left-wing opponents in debates (especially leaders and intellectuals of the Communist Party, as well as theorists advocating national-developmentism), whom he accused of importing exogenous theoretical models from alien historic experiences foreign to, and incompatible with, Brazilian reality. In the Brazilian revolution, there are none of the heroic and agonistic components Hannah Arendt and a considerable part of the revolution theorists—whether themselves revolutionary or not—speak of.

This aspect of Caio Prado Jr.'s approach apparently does not raise any problem in itself. In addition to being a theme that pervades practically all his works, including the most significant ones in the perspective of Brazilian historiography, it sustains a reasonably optimistic point of view with regard to the future virtuous unfolding of the process (i.e., it points to the creation of the conditions required for a successful conclusion, which, according to him, would not be too long in coming). To achieve this it would only be necessary for the process to be adequately understood and for the correct theory to inspire an effectively renovating program. This leads, however, to the second important aspect of the approach and, to understand it in the light of *A Revolução Brasileira*, it is necessary to refer to the historic moment when it was published.

A Revolução Brasileira was published in 1966, hence two years after the defeat of the 1945 democracy as a result of the military coup. The controversial nature of the work, despite the alleged optimism with regard to the future of revolution in Brazil, has a clear tone of accounts rendered, and reparation of blame. Curiously, there are no heroes of any kind in *A Revolução Brasileira*. The main targets of the accusations are the various left-wing groups that claimed to be revolutionary and which, based on incorrect diagnoses, imported literature inadequate for the case in question and ended up contributing to the ominous demise of the democratic regime. At the end of the book, one is left with the strange feeling that the supposedly revolutionary forces (especially the Communist Party and the national-developmentist currents) were the ones who precipitated the events that took place on April 1, 1964. The reading of this book indelibly imposes a negative mark on a period that was possibly the most intense as regards political debate and the organization of civil society in all five hundred years of Brazilian history. This anathemization is at the core of an interpretive current that has since gained strength in Brazil and which, due to the respectability of its author, will incontestably influence both the intellectual production and the future politics of the country.

The revolutionary forces, however, are not the only ones to appear in a negative light in the Brazilian revolution analyzed by its namesake book. The poorly organized and misinformed rural masses, the national bourgeoisie—whose revolutionary potential is dismissed as a myth created by the ignorance of its proponents—the workers and rural leaders—with their low sensitivity as regards the real needs of their followers—all, absolutely all the players called to the scene participated in the history of a failure. From then on, the history of the Brazilian revolution becomes the narrative of a defeat. One is left with the impression that, strictly speaking, there are no reactionary forces in Brazil because the efforts of the supposedly revolutionary currents themselves, with their obtuse vision, would suffice to keep the nation backward and dependent. Bearing all this in mind, it is surprising that the alleged optimism of the narrator is sustained, albeit more discreetly than it usually is purported to be. Despite this optimism, however, the Brazilian nation remains only a promise for the future.

The revolution focused on by Florestan Fernandes in *A Revolução Burguesa no Brasil* is the process by which the bourgeois order is instituted in Brazil. As stressed by Gabriel Cohn,[15] Florestan focuses on the appearance of a competitive and democratic society in Brazil, and on the limits imposed on its construction. Florestan delves into the conditions under which the Brazilian social system moves from a status order to a properly bourgeois and capitalist order. Here too, we can observe a concern for pointing out the singularities of the Brazilian-style transition.

Obviously, I do not intend in this work to summarize the extensive and thorough analysis presented in *A Revolução Burguesa no Brasil*. It is sufficient to stress the long process in passing from a colonial status to a national State, and from a strictly status-like and patrimonialist order to the bourgeois order. A process in which the interests, first of the big landowners and slave owners, and subsequently of the rural and/or commercial oligarchies, ended up absorbing the conditions created to implement a really competitive system, thus keeping the control of political and economic decision-making instruments at the top of the social pyramid. The conflicts and tensions generated as a result of the appearance of conditions for installing a competitive order have not been taken to the ultimate consequences by a bourgeoisie that evolved in the heart of the dominant class through a combination of the interests of both the landed aristocracy and the new capitalist class.

As a result of this revolution, a fragile bourgeoisie was formed in Brazil, incapable of affirming itself as the representatives of an effectively revolutionary conscience. The historic consequence of this process is that the economy is fragmented into tributaries of foreign interests and, in the labor area, the type of plundering and predatory interaction that prevailed during the slavery period is replicated in a new form. The development of autonomous and demanding labor classes and the consolidation of a civil society active in the transformation processes that led to the downfall of the colonial model were then suffocated by a succession of high-level stratagems that enabled the interests of the economic and political elites to be made compatible with the new conditions created by urban growth and the development of a capitalist economy.

Therefore, again in Florestan, despite a touch of optimism as regards the growth of organized workers' movements and the resulting increase in their capacity to make demands, the Brazilian historical experience appears as a succession of wasted opportunities to institute an autonomous, prosperous, and democratic national state, and to consolidate a competitive social order characterized by individual liberties.

Hence, far from the grandiose ideal, from the feats of virtuous heroes and ruptures aimed at promoting political, social, and civil rights and individual liberty, the revolution in Brazil is narrated by two of its most committed and discerning interpreters as something that fortunately did not come to pass. On the contrary, what we perceive in the Brazilian singularity is a contamination of the old by the new, the abdication, intended or not, by part of the players from virtuously fulfilling their historic destiny. In other words, perpetuation of the status quo, characterized by backwardness, predatory practices, and plundering. Also as a result of the Brazilian approach to revolution, the process of national consolidation is semantically construed as the reverse of more successful experiences that set the tone for the modern world and became the benchmarks of modernity. Obviously, it is only analytically that we can dissociate the narratives of the Brazilian people and the understanding of its historic process in the perspective of revolution. Both are deeply interrelated, one providing substance to the other. Not only are they based on the historic process itself, but on the very idea of nation that its intellectuals incrementally configured throughout history. The possible potential, located at the future, rather than the opening of plausible windows for a course correction is the consequence implied in the critique of its own creators.

CONCLUSION

Reflexes of successful experiences occurred in the main centers of "modern civilization" can be seen in all the narratives mentioned here, despite their authors repeatedly stating their intention to avoid uncritically transposing exogenous models to the Brazilian process. This can be translated as the values and labels of European culture, the industrious nature and intellectual vocation of the "pure" peoples, the democratic practices installed by the genuine revolutions that occurred on both sides of the Atlantic, or even as the intensity of public life in America, as described by Tocqueville. The stigma of lacking, deficiency, not to say failure, seems to hang over all the specific issues of each narrative, suggesting a kind of melancholic consensus. However, one should remember that all historic narratives are themselves historically rooted. This also holds true for sociological and political analyses. Faced with the persistence of iniquities and arbitrary attitudes so profound that they make situation portraits appear as variations on the same doleful theme, one is left with the impression that, immersed in their own contemporary scenarios, the narrators of Brazil (or part of them) delved the unfortunate past in search of the reasons for the dismal present.

In the face of this trend, doubt remains as to whether the despondency of the present does not contribute to cloud over possible virtues, promising aspects of this painfully experienced and melancholically narrated process that could lead to a knowledge that could contribute to different future narratives. It is possible that such narratives already exist, and that such an initiative does not necessarily have to start from scratch. If this is the case, what is called for is one of those almost archaeological efforts to redefine or—less radically— to expand the Canon. This could be a promising venture. A good start would be to make a less reverent reading of the existing Canon. This shows the importance of constructing meta-narratives of Brazil.

NOTES

The first version of this chapter was published in *Revista Internacional de Estudos Políticos* 2, no. 1 (2000). Translated by Paulo Garchet.

1. John Gillis, ed., *Commemorations: The Politics of National Identity* (Princeton, N.J.: Princeton University Press, 1996).
2. Harold Bloom, *O Cânone Ocidental* (Rio de Janeiro: Ed. Objetiva, 1995).
3. Richard Morse, *O Espelho de Próspero* (São Paulo: Cia. das Letras, 1988).
4. Eric Hobsbawn and Terence Ranger, *A invenção das tradições* (Rio de Janeiro: Ed. Paz e Terra, 1984).
5. Raou Girardet, *Nationalismes et nation* (Bruxelles: Editions Complexe, 1996).
6. Jürgen Habermas, *L'Integration Republicaine* (Paris: Fayard, 1998; Margareth Canovan, "Lasting Institutions: Arendtian Thoughts on Nations and Republics," *Graduate Faculty Philosophy Journal* 21, no. 2 (1999).
7. Benedict Anderson, *Imagined Communities* (London: Verso, 1983); Ernest Gellner, *Nações e Nacionalismos* (Lisboa: Gradiva, 1993).
8. Hannah Arendt, *Origens do Totalitarismo* (São Paulo: Cia. das Letras, 1989).
9. Thomas Skidmore, *Preto no Branco: Raça e Nacionalidade no Pensamento Brasileiro* (Rio de Janeiro: Paz e Terra, 1989).
10. Also according to Skidmore, the two exceptions were Manuel Bonfim and Alberto Torres who, in their efforts to interpret the reasons for the backward stage of Brazilian development, denounced the fallacy of the racial issue.

11. It is true that a name like Oliveira Vianna could be recalled. In this specific case, however, his works that are not directly inspired by racist theses are both more frequent and sufficient to ensure his place in the Canon, which is not the case of Euclides da Cunha. English translation 1944, *Rebellion in the Backlands*.

12. In the same way the subtitle of the work *Ensaio sobre a tristeza brasileira* seems to suggest its exploratory nature.

13. The closeness of the analysis by Sérgio to that of Elias is surprising, especially when in chapter V the first compares Brazilian society with Japanese civilization. However, it is important to note that there is no mention of Sérgio in the work of the German sociologist.

14. Hannah Arendt, *Da Revolução* (São Paulo: Ática, 1988).

15. Gabriel Cohn, "Padrões e Dilemas: o Pensamento de Florestan Fernandes," in *Inteligência Brasileira*, ed. Reginaldo Moraes, Ricardo Antunes, and Vera B. Ferrante (São Paulo: Ed. Brasiliense, 1986).

BIBLIOGRAPHY

Anderson, Benedict. *Imagined Communities*. London: Verso, 1983.

Arendt, Hannah. *Da Revolução*. São Paulo: Ática, 1988.

——. *Origens do Totalitarismo*. São Paulo: Cia. das Letras, 1989.

Brubaker, Rogers. *Nationalism Reframed: Nationhood and the Nation Question in the New Europe*. Cambridge: Cambridge University Press, 1996.

Bloom, Harold. *O Cânone Ocidental*. Rio de Janeiro: Ed. Objetiva, 1995.

Canovan, Margareth. "Lasting Institutions: Arendtian Thoughts on Nations and Republics." *Graduate Faculty Philosophy Journal* 21, no. 2 (1999).

Cohn, Gabriel. "Padrões e Dilemas: o Pensamento de Florestan Fernandes." In *Inteligência Brasileira*, edited by Reginaldo Moraes, Ricardo Antunes, and Vera B. Ferrante. São Paulo: Ed. Brasiliense, 1986.

Cunha, Euclydes da. *Os Sertões*. Rio de Janeiro: Francisco Alves, 1999.

Elias, Norbert. *O Processo civilizador*. Vols. I and II. Rio de Janeiro: Jorge Zahar Editor, 1990.

Fernandes, Florestan. *A Revolução Burguesa no Brasil*. Rio de Janeiro: Ed. Guanabara, 1987.

Gellner, Ernest. *Nações e Nacionalismos*. Lisboa: Gradiva, 1993.

Gillis, John, ed. *Commemorations: The Politics of National Identity*. Princeton, N.J.: Princeton University Press, 1996.

Girardet, Raou. *Nationalismes et nation*. Bruxelles: Editions Complexe, 1996.

Habermas, Jürgen. *L'Integration Republicaine*. Paris: Fayard, 1998.

Halbwach, Maurice. *On collective memory*. Chicago: University of Chicago Press, 1992.

Hobsbawn, Eric, and Terence Ranger. *A invenção das tradições*. Rio de Janeiro: Ed. Paz e Terra, 1984.

Hollanda, Sérgio Buarque. *Raízes do Brasil*. Rio de Janeiro, José Olympio, 1982.

Morse, Richard. *O Espelho de Próspero*. São Paulo: Cia. das Letras, 1988.

Prado, Caio Jr. *A Revolução Brasileira*. São Paulo: Ed. Brasiliense, 1987.
Prado, Paulo. *Retrato do Brasil*. São Paulo, Duprat-Mayença, 1929.
Renan, Ernest. "What is a Nation?" In *Nation and Narration*, edited by Homi Bhabha. London, Routledge, 1990.
Skidmore, Thomas. *Preto no Branco: Raça e Nacionalidade no Pensamento Brasileiro*. Rio de Janeiro, Paz e Terra, 1989.
Tarde, Gabriel. *As leis da imitação*. Porto: Rès, s/d.

11

The Relevance of Machado de Assis

Dain Borges

$\mathbf{A}$s Brazilian thinkers in the last twenty-five years confronted modernity, they found new relevance in the great psychological novelist of the late nineteenth century, Joaquim Maria Machado de Assis (1839–1908). Machado was roughly a contemporary of Mark Twain and Emile Zola, but his writing has never been weighed into the world literary canon; in the United States, he remains almost unknown.[1] And in a sense, Machado has been only recently revealed in Brazil. He matters to Brazilians more and differently now than he did during his lifetime. The rediscovery depended on readers finally recognizing hidden themes of social evil in his ambiguous writing, and it indicates the critical depth of contemporary Brazilian social thought. Critics such as Roberto Schwarz have used Machado to develop new insights into social power and the problems of liberal democracy in a divided polity. Others have simply benefited from Machado's exemplary engagement with the discontents of modernity, his skeptical *reasonableness* in opposition to the dogmatic *rationality* of the science and ideology of his times.[2]

Machado intrigues us today because of his exceptional rise from poverty and the maturity of his intellectual development as an autodidact. He was the son of a free Afro-Brazilian house painter and a Portuguese immigrant laundress. He got an incomplete primary education and was set to trade as a printer's boy. He broke into journalism, taught himself French and English, and by his thirties he had settled into a secure civil service job, married a Portuguese woman, and published stories, poems, and some unremarkable novels of courtship. Machado deliberately effaced details of his private life; he left no diaries, only bland letters, and a few oblique literary manifestos. Nothing we know of his life, except a rest cure for epilepsy or some other ailment, might explain why, around the age of forty, his writing suddenly rose to a new and strange level. He arrived at a new style of narrating and structuring novels and, between 1881 and his death in 1908, he published five brilliant novels, each of them a complex experiment with a different sort of narrator, all dealing with intrigues of courtship and adultery set in Rio de Janeiro. They display a range of reading and erudition and philosophical sophistication almost unthinkable in an autodidact.

Along with most details of his private life and thoughts, Machado deliberately hid most of his political opinions. Many biographers suspect that Brazil's sordid Paraguayan War of 1865–1870 changed him. Before the war, he was a partisan liberal political journalist. Afterward, he wrote weekly newspaper sketches, but his journalism became circumspect. He declined to engage in political and literary polemics, when that was the most common way to make and keep intellectual rank. He refused to speak out in favor of the abolition of slavery, when his best friends were abolitionist leaders. Instead, he rose in the civil service to the highest career rank in the Ministry of Agriculture and Public Works. It was an effective survival strategy. He weathered the republican revolution of 1889 relatively easily, while many of his friends suffered political persecution, censorship, and exile. In 1897, he became the founding president of the semiofficial Brazilian Academy of Letters, and he died in 1908 enjoying recognition as Brazil's leading writer. But his silence must have been more than a survival strategy—given the political critiques that critics have recently deciphered in his work, it must have been a deliberate subversive game.

Most of the revisionist criticism has been inspired by analysis of Machado's novels, but we can get some flavor of Machado's mature themes and style—his imagining of greater and lesser evils—by considering two short stories, "Rod of Justice" (1891) and "The Looking Glass" (1882).[3] In "Rod of Justice," Damião escapes from the seminary where his father has placed him. He hides in the house of Sinhá Rita, an independent widow and his uncle's mistress. Over the course of the day, he persuades her to help him by getting his uncle to talk to his father. And he also draws the attention of one of the slave girls whom Sinhá Rita is training to make lace. Toward evening, the girl has fallen behind in her work, and Sinhá Rita decides to whip her. She demands that Damião hand her the rod. And so the story ends: "Damião was pricked by an uneasy sense of guilt, but he wanted so much to get out of the seminary! He reached the settee, picked up the rod, and handed it to Sinhá Rita."[4] "Rod of Justice" explores the themes—paternalism and liberalism, emancipation and domination—that have preoccupied contemporary socio-political interpreters of Machado. "The Looking Glass: Rough Draft of a New Theory of the Human Soul," is another sort of story. Its narrator Jacobina tells how, in his youth, he had won a commission as second lieutenant in the National Guard. He is invited to visit his aunt, who shows off his new uniform, flatters him, and sets a large mirror in his bedroom. But when she is called away from the plantation, all the slaves treacherously run away overnight, leaving Jacobina alone in the farm house. The solitude is intolerable. A clock ticks the lines of a Longfellow poem: "never, forever; forever, never." After a few days, he glances in his mirror, and the outline of his body has blurred; he cannot see himself. Desperate, he hits on a solution: he puts his lieutenant's uniform back on, and his reflection reappears. Looking back, the mature Jacobina theorizes that we each possess an inner soul and an exterior soul. "It was me, the second lieutenant, who had found his exterior soul." "The Looking Glass" displays themes—identity and reality—present in many of the philosophical fables that Machado's friends found most delightful and sophisticated in his work, and that literary critics since then have read in new ways. Neither "Rod of Justice" nor "The Looking Glass" is entirely representative of his work, as neither develops an intrigue of courtship and adultery similar to those in his novels. However, both share one of his great themes, the end of innocence through the initiation of a young Brazilian into the deceptions and corruptions of adulthood.

Machado's contemporaries recognized his genius, but we have no evidence that any of them read him as he is read today. He was taken as an acid wit, a philosophizer, an ironist, who wrote parlor novels set in high society—quite cosmopolitan and perhaps not fully "Brazilian." Other Brazilian novelists—his elders and his contemporaries—seemed more obviously engaged with national problems, more daring in exploring modern social reality. Others catalogued the hills, forests, and waterfalls of the Brazilian landscape; others invented patriotic allegories of the encounter between Indian woman and Portuguese man; others attacked social problems like tenement buildings, or dissected unusual urban social types. Machado did not write much criticism, but in one of his critical essays, he distanced himself from the "scenic" patriotism of Romanticism, and in another he distanced himself from the deterministic psychology of Naturalism, saying in both essays that what a writer needs for verisimilitude is characters with depth and plausible motivation, characters worth studying because they cannot be reduced to their context.[5] In retrospect, Machado seems undogmatic and sensible. His contemporaries' social analysis is studded with psychiatric and sociological diagnoses that today seem absurd; Machado's own anti-psychiatry seems reasonable.

In the next generation, however, a few critics made the claim that he was not a parlor novelist, but the author of a great documentary panorama of the late empire, a sort of *Human Comedy* of Dom Pedro II's reign (1840–1889). In 1939, Astrojildo Pereira, founder of the Brazilian Communist party and a serious critic, argued emphatically that Machado was the "novelist of the Second Reign," and even a social novelist with an intuitive feel for the dialectic of history.[6] Since Pereira, many historians and social essayists have exploited Machado's thirty-volume collected works as a rich lumberyard of social observations. They have borrowed from his fiction and his newspaper columns alike to illustrate arguments about the technological modernization of Rio de Janeiro, or the oppressive practices of Belle Époque medicine and psychiatry.[7] And indeed, because Machado often wrote two or three columns a week on current topics, he commented on a wide range of the social transformation of Rio de Janeiro and the politics of Brazil, from 1860 to 1900.

By far the masterpiece of such "lumberyard" utilizations of Machado is the political theorist Raimundo Faoro's *Machado de Assis: A pirâmide e o trapézio* (The Pyramid and the Trapeze [1974]), which clips characters and situations from across Machado's complete works and reassembles them into a portrait gallery of types arrayed in social classes—a portrait that, not surprisingly, confirms Faoro's *Os donos do poder* (The Power Holders [1958]), a historical sociology arguing that, since colonial beginnings, Brazil's invertebrate society has been structured by a small state elite. In *Os donos do Poder*, an argument against Marxist theories of a ruling class, Faoro argues that a small patrimonial "estate" of bureaucrats and statesmen had created social classes, organizing Brazil and governing it, from colonial times through the twentieth century. *A pirâmide e o trapézio* is thus at times tendentious, but it is always a fascinating collage of snippets from Machado's work. By juxtaposing pieces of Machado's writing, Faoro makes interesting discoveries— for example, that Machado's portrayal of capitalists changes from stories set in the early nineteenth century to those set at the turn of the twentieth century. Arrayed in a continuum, these figures allow Faoro to reconstruct the metamorphosis of nineteenth-century slave owners into Brazil's early-twentieth-century "bourgeoisie" of bankers and speculators.[8]

The decisive new recognition of Machado, however, came from careful reading of the interactions among characters, and not from taking characters individually, as objective sketches of social types. Not a Brazilian, but the American critic Helen Caldwell, pointed out that when Bento, the narrator of *Dom Casmurro* (1900), accuses his wife Capitú of adultery, the crucial evidence lies in Bento's perceptions—for example, the meaning of a look in her eyes, or his observation that his son resembles his best friend Escobar. Caldwell detected just as many clues that Bento's perceptions are "misrecognitions", that he is "a Brazilian Othello." No Brazilian critic had more than hinted at catching the ambiguity, probably, as Roberto Schwarz has suggested, because Machado made Dom Casmurro a likeable, philosophical widower. While not necessarily agreeing that Capitú is "innocent" of adultery, virtually every reader since Caldwell has agreed that *Dom Casmurro* is much more interesting if we acknowledge the coexisting double meanings. Since Caldwell, advances in the interpretation of Machado have usually come through cautious, careful deciphering of hidden messages—usually running subversively counter to the surface story of his writing. These often require that the critic adopt the point of view of a subordinate or unsympathetic character, or pitilessly scrutinize the motivations of a "sympathetic" character.

The literary critic Roberto Schwarz has identified a central set of Machado's hidden critiques of Brazilian society, fictional conundrums about bondage and freedom that seem most relevant to the problems of Brazil as an extremely hierarchical class society today.[9] Schwarz developed his approach in the essay "Misplaced Ideas," part of *Ao vencedor as batatas* (1977).[10] In *Ao vencedor*, Schwarz argues that because Brazil was a slave society, masterless men had no place; they inevitably had to seek out the favor and patronage of slave-owning masters. This part of Schwarz's argument is not new. Machado's friend Joaquim Nabuco had made it emphatically in a great propaganda tract, *Abolitionism* (1883).[11] And it is only a modest extension of the arguments that the Universidade de São Paulo revisionist school of sociologists—Florestan Fernandes, Brazil's past president Fernando Henrique Cardoso, Octavio Ianni, and others—had been making since the 1950s about the deformation of capitalist rationality by slave property and slave production.[12] But Schwarz takes the argument further, generalizing the dilemma both to Brazilian society and to the particular nature of Brazilian literature. Liberal ideology, which assumes autonomous actors, was a "misplaced idea" in Brazil, even more unrealistic a description of social interactions than it was in Europe. Paradoxically, the poor fit between liberal theory and practice offered the best Brazilian novelists an opportunity similar to that of the Russian novelists: they could become skeptically distanced from the liberal self-justifications of a bourgeoisie. Schwarz thinks that Brazil's great nineteenth-century nation-building novelist José de Alencar was not quite able to take advantage of that opportunity; his novels incongruously mixed idealized scenes of romantic individualism with realistic scenes of Brazilian families' typical behavior.[13] The young Machado, perhaps because he had a conservative temperament, was able to exploit the opportunity. His early novels turn on young women using patronage ruthlessly to rise and marry well. Unlike Shakespeare's Romeo and Juliet, the aspiring lovers in Machado's early novels (and in Brazil) overcome obstacles to their marriage by ingratiating, wheedling, and manipulating patrons. Machado continually invented such situations of intricate favor-mongering. The story "Rod of Justice" lays it out more baldly than most of Machado's work, playing down the courtship plot and playing up both the melodrama of Damião's emancipation (from the seminary) and the mechanics of patronage.

Schwarz followed "Misplaced Ideas" with an argument about paternalism as domination in *Um mestre na periferia do capitalismo* (A Master on the Periphery of Capitalism, 1990), which tries to explain what Machado had accomplished, thematically and formally, by the step he took in 1881 from realistic but unremarkable early novels to his five extraordinary later novels. Schwarz argues that that step was the discovery of a form—a special narrative voice—that could manifest a content—a critique of the Brazilian upper class. In *Posthumous Memoirs of Brás Cubas* (1881), Machado created the narrative voice of self-serving Bras Cubas, whose strategic shifts and interruptions, shifts in tone in different circumstances, was a stylization of the social and political tactics of domination of the Brazilian upper class. Schwarz calls this voice "*volúvel*," fickle or volatile. Particularly in the episode of seduction and abandonment of the poor girl Eugênia, Brás employs insolent shifts in tone to subordinate and dismiss her. Schwarz dissects these as both a stylization and a literal exemplum of the tactics characteristic of Brazilian upper-class paternalism.[14] And finally, in *Duas meninas* (1997), Schwarz explored the tensions between emancipation and patriarchal domination in the childhood and adult relationships of the audacious Capitú and conservative Bento of *Dom Casmurro* (1899). For Schwartz, Machado is the novelist in whom today's Brazilian upper class can best reflect on its irrevocably reactionary legacy.

So far, the most fertile investigations of power and justice in Machado's novels have been analysis of upper-class paternalism and subaltern deference, very much following in the footsteps of Roberto Schwarz's readings. Sidney Chalhoub, for example, has suggested that Machado not only portrayed the characteristic viewpoint of manipulative paternalism, but also—even when the narrator is the patron—showed how dependents used the rhetoric of deference and loyalty to resist, manipulate, and wheedle their patrons.[15] This newly revealed, subversive Machado—Machado the critic of paternalism, clientelism, and patronage—has come to seem more relevant to contemporary intellectuals, perhaps because his satire of the self-interested manipulation inherent in the institutions and social relations of Rio de Janeiro during the empire speaks to a contemporary concern with justice and corruption. It may also speak to their sense of the breakdown of paternalism as a mode of social solidarity, as first the authoritarian governments of 1964 to 1985 and then a neoliberal democracy abandoned populist rhetoric and practice.

As it has become axiomatic that today's Brazil still lives out legacies of slave society, contemporary historians have benefited from reexamining Machado's analysis of slavery and abolition. During the 1880s, Machado was scandalously not an abolitionist propagandist, at a time when his leadership might have mobilized Brazil's free people of color.[16] Today, he is reread both as a moral critic of slavery and as a pseudonymous commentator on the abolitionist campaign.

It was never hard to see that Machado had a *moral* position against the cruelties of slavery. His fiction contained many unsensational portrayals of the cruelties of slavery, such as the scene in *Posthumous Memoirs* in which Brás Cubas encounters his boyhood slave page and whipping-boy, Prudêncio, now a free man and a slave owner himself, whipping a slave that he has purchased.

Brás reflects sardonically and pseudo-philosophically, that

> on the outside the episode I had witnessed was grim; but only on the outside. When I opened it up with the knife of rational analysis, I found a curious and profound kernel. It was Prudêncio's way of ridding himself of the blows he had received—passing them on to someone else. I, as a child, had sat on his back, had put a rein in his mouth, and had beaten him mercilessly; he had groaned and suffered. Now, however, that he was free and could move his arms and legs when and as he pleased [*era libre, dispunha de si mesmo*], now that he could work, relax, sleep, as he willed, unrestrained, now he rose and became top man: he bought a slave and paid to him, in full and with interest, the amount he had received from me. See how clever the rascal was![17]

But only now have Brazilian historians been able to make out what Machado meant in the series of columns he published under a pseudonym during the last months of the abolitionist campaign, under the heading "Bons Dias!" including two written when government action was imminent, that attack the generosity of abolition. The two crônicas written during the week of abolition, on May 11 and May 19, 1888, both comment on mass manumissions by planters in the face of imminent abolition. The first focuses on runaway slaves who had found employment on plantations as salaried workers, then mocks hopes that a virtuous republic might be established in the wake of abolition. The second comments on abolition through the fable—essentially a topical short story—of a master who celebrates "voluntarily" freeing his domestic slave, only to continue mistreating him. John Gledson, in an essay on the *Bons Dias!* crônicas, emphasizes that the crônicas show that Machado *had* commented on pressing political events, but that his contemporaries never guessed that it was Machado writing, and modern readers can decipher the political meanings only with the help of a critical annotated edition that explains obscure references.[18]

Raimundo Faoro offered an early and characteristically very shrewd reading of Machado's thesis in these two crônicas. According to Faoro, Machado was a persistent critic of abolition without a land distribution program. Certainly exaggerating, he says that, among those writing at the time, "only [Machado] insisted on the calamity that freedom might signify to the bondsman. The slave would be free, but he would be left without work and without bread, resorting to begging." Machado was suspicious of manumissions, interpreting their generosity as a tactic for getting rid of superfluous, old, and weak slaves. Faoro claims that the thesis of the second crônica, on the 19th of May, is that the freeing of a slave may simply hide the bad resort to get rid of a useless worker or domestic. Likewise, abolition leaves the freedman prey to starvation salaries.[19]

While Faoro identifies Machado's moral position, the historian Sidney Chalhoub has meticulously elaborated Machado's analysis of slavery and power in the crônicas. In *Visões da liberdade* (1990), Chalhoub makes the strongest claim of any contemporary social scientist to have "objectively" read Machado, discovered a subtly camouflaged thesis, and then tried to confirm or disconfirm it through further research. The second half of *Visões da liberdade* supposedly derives from a reading of the May crônicas based in new historical research into slavery, research that has arrived at conclusions probably only half-evident to Machado's generation. Chalhoub claims that Machado's sketches reflect on the changes in mentalities about slavery in Rio de Janeiro that had occurred between 1868 and 1888, even Machado's own change in attitude toward private manumissions. He argues that Machado intended to expose three motivations for abolition. First, the May 11th crônica points out that respect for private property in the form of slaves was no longer a sacred principle unifying the upper classes. Second, both crônicas illustrate the "bankruptcy of a particular strategy of domination" in which gratuitous manumission had often been used to turn ex-slaves into submissive free dependents after their freedom.[20] Chalhoub claims the humor in the May 19th crônica depends on Machado's readers easily recognizing that this style of deferential post-manumission relationship with former masters no longer existed. Third, despite the narrator-master's claim to be the one deciding everything, Machado lays emphasis on the slave's towering size ("you grew immensely"), which Chalhoub argues is a reference to slaves' growth in power between 1870 and 1888. The Greek etymology of the slave's name, "Pancrácio," could mean "all-powerful."[21] These three points, Chalhoub says, form "the Machadian vision of the historical process of abolition of slavery." The humor in the situation is that the master has no idea what is going on, or else is making himself ridiculous in keeping up appearances. The "perspicacity" of Machado has him have master tell Pancrácio that "you are free, you may go where you wish"; perspicacity, according to Chalhoub, because recent archival research had revealed that "*viver sobre si*," to live on one's own, was a common demand of slaves and freedmen in the city of Rio.[22]

Whether or not Chalhoub is guileless when he says that he began his research from hints dropped by Machado, rather than interpreting Machado after he had reached his own conclusions, he does plausibly extract theses from Machado's work that coincide with his own findings about the negotiated erosion of slavery between the 1871 Law of the Free Womb and 1888 Abolition. Part of the current appeal of Machado to Brazilian intellectuals is that his realist fictional situations and his journalistic essays seem to fit and to confirm new historical explanations of nineteenth-century institutions, explanations that point to long-term continuities of oppression in Brazil. That is to say, not only was Machado de Assis, like Roberto Schwarz, a Universidade de São Paulo revisionist, believing that clientelistic exchanges deriving ultimately from the logic of slavery vitiated liberal ideals, but he was also, like Sidney Chalhoub, a Universidade de Campinas revisionist, believing that abolition was a negotiated process timed by pressure from the slaves![23]

Although Machado did write often about slavery, and about the ramifications of oppressive powers throughout a slave society, he never wrote directly about race. This disappointed black radicals of his day, and it continues to disappoint those intellectuals who are trying to get Brazilian society to confront racial discrimination and the denial of black identity. A few characters are marked as "negros" or "Africans" in his work.[24] And he made occasional oblique references to skin color, particularly in the late novel *Counselor Aires's Memorial*. The narrator Aires, who seems more like a direct mask of Machado than any of his other narrators, rejoices at Abolition on May 13, 1888, and on May 18 writes in his diary of his sister's plan to auction her household effects:

> What do I know about auctioneers, or about auctions? When I die they can sell privately the little that I leave, at a discount or without one, and my skin along with the rest: it is not new, it is not handsome, it is not fine, but, still, it will be good for some crude drum or tambourine [*algum tambor ou pandeiro rústico*]. There is no need to call in an auctioneer.[25]

Presumably, this *could* be an allusion to Aires's origins in savage Africa and the savage slave trade, in drumming, flaying of corpses, and auctioning of human beings. And possibly, this could be an autobiographical statement of Machado's blackness. But it is quite oblique, considering that it is as close as Machado ever came to writing about his own racial origins. David Haberly has argued that the reference to skin is significant, that Machado conceived of and wrote of race, among other things, when he wrote of the difference between the inner self and an outer self. Thus Haberly proposes that all of Machado's work can be read as "a highly evasive and ambiguous journal of his passage from nonwhiteness to whiteness," and that the device of the "inner soul," and the "exterior soul" in "The Looking Glass" was Machado's way of speaking of the experience of becoming socially white in his role as a high civil servant and distinguished writer, playing a social masquerade.[26]

"The Looking Glass" can serve as a final touchstone of the many ways in which contemporaries—Brazilians and foreign Brazilianists—are rereading Machado de Assis. So far, the richest contemporary insights have come from analysis of Machado's long novels, crowded with "chess games," strategic interactions of dissimulation. José Luiz Passos has argued that Machado's great achievement as a world-class author is the development of new ways to convey the experience of testing and exploring human motives.[27] "The Looking Glass" has been a compelling fable, but it is superficially somewhat different in its emphasis on a single individual, and thus elicits different readings.

The British critic John Gledson has gone further than any Brazilian in asserting that Machado not only expressed firm political opinions in newspaper columns, but also inserted encoded political allegory into virtually all of his fiction. Apparently casual mentions of dates, public monuments, world events, and kings or politicians amount to a parallel narrative in the mature novels. Recently Gledson turned to *Papéis avulsos*, the collection of short stories in which "The Looking Glass" was published, and argued that every story mentions events that allow a reading of the characters' personal identity as an allegory for national identity. "The Looking Glass" obviously includes mention of Jacobina's commission in the rural National Guard, a largely ceremonial militia deeply implicated in county-level political bossism and election-rigging. The slaves' mass escape obviously refers the reader to the national question of the abolition of slavery. But less obviously, the aunt's great mirror had supposedly been acquired from a Portuguese noblewoman who arrived with the court's exile from Napoleon in 1808. Gledson claims that thus Machado sets up a reading of Jacobina's dilemma as Brazil's dilemma: unexpectedly faced with nationality and forced to define itself, the postcolonial empire could not discern any clear identity.[28]

Brazilians have been less inclined to read national themes into this story or into Machado's other "philosophical" fables. Rather, their readings have been psychological, both taking Machado seriously as psychological analyst of the pre-Freudian generation and seeing him as a critic of medical psychiatry, a precursor of R. D. Laing and Michel Foucault. Alfredo Bosi finds that "The Looking Glass" is the paradigm of Machado's stories of the mature period, most of which center on the confusion between mask and face, between dissimulating social roles and authentic self.[29] Antonio Candido reads the story as an allegory of division and the split self, in which the lost reflection is a version of the motif of the lost shadow.[30] Both these readings ring true to the logic of the story, but they don't quite convey its jarring swings in tone between the boy's horrified fear of going mad, and the cynical facetiousness with which the mature Jacobina theorizes and rationalizes his experience among a circle of idly philosophizing gentlemen:

> Every human being is born with two souls: one that looks from the inside out, another that looks from the outside in. . . . The exterior soul may be a spirit, an invisible aura, a man, many men, an object, an activity. There are cases for example, in which a simple shirt button is the whole exterior soul of a person—or it may be the polka, ombre, a book, a pair of shoes, a melody, a drum, and so forth. It's plain that the function of this second soul is, like that of the first, to infuse life. The two of them complete the man.[31]

"The Looking Glass," after all, is also a joke that the mature Jacobina plays on a pseudo-symposium of philosophizers, tantalizing their curiosity in order to silence them. Perhaps the allusions that Machado throws out profligately can, as they so often do, provide a coded key to another perspective on the characters. Despairing in the empty plantation house, watching for his aunt and relatives to return, Jacobina mouths the lines of Bluebeard's last bride from Perrault's fairy tale: "Sister Anne, sister Anne, don't you see anyone coming?" If the farmhouse is like Bluebeard's chateau (which also contained grand mirrors) and if his aunt's departure is thus like Bluebeard's test of his wives, then when his aunt says "I envy the girl who will be your wife," the overtones are ominous: Is she a doting aunt or a punishing monster? And if this plantation is like Bluebeard's chateau, what is the horrible locked secret that Jacobina might uncover? Machado wrote this story shortly after *Posthumous Memoirs of Brás Cubas*, which opens with a delirious encounter with Pandora. Possibly Jacobina's (and Machado's) joke is that the horror is looking into oneself—and realizing that the locked casket of fairy tales is perfectly vacant. The alternative to nothingness is to do what Jacobina did, to put on the silly uniform that is one's social, "exterior soul," and grow up.

This reading of "The Looking Glass" is supported by two later works in which Machado mockingly explored the situation of a man who attempts to seclude himself from society in order to philosophize without distraction. In "Só" (1885), Machado's weekend hermit Bonifácio is a confirmed bachelor. In solitude, he suffers only his own sterility, loss of love, and lack of ideas. As with the ticking clock of "The Looking Glass," time hangs heavily on Bonifácio during his weekend. The narrator assures us that he does not quite amount to Poe's sinister "Man of the Crowd," silent among the city throng, because he does seclude himself and he is "not capable of crimes."[32] In *Esau and Jacob* (1904), Counselor Aires attempts living away from social routines for a while, but is shortly overcome by the need to be among others.[33] Machado's argument about the soul of Brazilians seems to be that the alternative to an identity shaped by trivial social interactions is a vacuum. But is Machado speaking only about the soul of Brazilians, after all? One risk of the virtuoso analyses of Machado's critique of social institutions of the empire is that the brilliant reflections will wind up implying, as Roberto Schwarz does, that Machado's ultimate aim was to analyze the *Brazilian* upper class. Surely Machado was doing that. But just as surely, he was also aiming at many other things. Machado vehemently satirized modern Western philosophies that reduce human ends to a single transcendent goal—he even invented the philosophy Humanitism, a synthesis of all contemporary historicisms and Social Darwinisms of the 1880s. It is obvious that when he wrote, he entertained himself by weaving near-invisible literary allusions to European as well as Portuguese literature into the fabric of his narrative. He lived as a provincial, but he made his work engage perennial themes of world literature, French psychiatric theories of the 1880s, and the customs of Rio de Janeiro, the city where he was born, lived, and died. He was grappling with modernity, often rejecting the scientific resources of the nineteenth century in preference for the moralists of the seventeenth century, but in a way that speaks to us now. The contemporary Brazilian deciphering of Machado's imaginings of human motivation has revealed a Machado whose insights can speak to people and situations beyond Brazil.

NOTES

1. Daphne Patai, "Machado in English," in *Machado de Assis: Reflections on a Brazilian Master*, ed. Richard Graham (Austin: Institute of Latin American Studies and University of Texas Press, 1999); cf. Harold Bloom, *The Western Canon: The Books and School of the Ages* (New York: Harcourt Brace, 1994).

2. The distinction between skeptical and rationalizing traditions in modern thought in Stephen Toulmin, *Cosmopolis: The Hidden Agenda of Modernity* (Chicago: University of Chicago Press, 1990), esp. 198–201, might be helpful for deepening the reading of Machado proposed in Alfredo Bosi, *Machado de Assis: O enigma do olhar* (São Paulo: Atica, 1999); more characteristic is the reading by Kátia Muricy, *A razão cética: Machado de Assis e as questões de seu tempo* (São Paulo: Companhia das Letras, 1988), which takes the critique of rationality in Machado as a precursor of Foucauldian anti-psychiatry.

3. Machado de Assis, "Rod of Justice," 76–83, and "The Looking-Glass: Rough Draft of a New Theory of the Human Soul," 56–65, in *The Psychiatrist and Other Stories* (Berkeley and Los Angeles: University of California Press, 1963). Another Eng-

lish translation of "O espelho" is "The Mirror," trans. Wilson Loria, BRAZZIL, www.brazzil.com/shjul95a.htm, December 9, 2000.

4. Machado, "Rod of Justice," 83.

5. José Luiz Passos, "A sintaxe da vida: Ação e dissimulação em *Senhora* e *Iaiá Garcia*," *Espelho: Revista Machadiana* 3 (1977): 1–17.

6. Astrojildo Pereira, *Machado de Assis: Ensaios e apontamentos avulsos* (Rio de Janeiro: Livraria São José, n.d. [1959]), esp. "Romancista do Segundo Reinado," 11–42 (1939).

7. Nicolau Sevcenko, "A capital irradiante," in *História da Vida Privada no Brasil*, vol. 3, *República: Da Belle Époque à Era do Rádio*, ed. Nicolau Sevcenko (São Paulo: Companhia das Letras, 1998); Muricy, *Razão cética*.

8. Raimundo Faoro, *Machado de Assis: A pirâmide e o trapézio* (Rio de Janeiro: Globo, 1974); *Os donos do poder* (Rio de Janeiro: Globo, 1958).

9. Schwarz's method in reading Machado's fiction for structural homologies with patterns of social interaction clearly derives from the work of the sociologist and literary critic Antonio Candido, particularly the seminal 1970 essay in which Candido discerned "general rhythms" of social interaction in Manuel Antonio de Almeida's *Memoirs of a Militia Sergeant*: "The Dialectic of Malandroism," in *On Literature and Society*, trans. Howard Becker (Princeton, N.J.: Princeton University Press,1995), 79–103. See Schwarz, "Pressupostos, salvo engano, de 'Dialética da malandragem,'" in *Que horas são? Ensaios* (São Paulo: Companhia das Letras, 1987), 129–55, and Paulo Eduardo Arantes, *Sentimento da dialética na experiência intelectual brasileira: Dialética e dualidade segundo Antonio Candido e Roberto Schwarz* (Rio de Janeiro: Paz e Terra, 1992). Schwarz's arguments about the frustrations of liberalism in Brazil have affinities with the critiques developed by Fernando Henrique Cardoso, Emília Viotti da Costa, and others influenced by Florestan Fernandes's USP sociology. For a glimpse of that cohort around 1958, see Roberto Schwarz, "A Seminar on Marx: Reconsidering the Foundations of the Brazilian Left," *Hopscotch* 1, no. 1 (1999): 110–25.

10. Roberto Schwarz, "Misplaced Ideas," in *Misplaced Ideas: Essays on Brazilian Culture*, ed. John Gledson (London: Verso, 1992), Roberto Schwarz, *Ao vencedor as batatas: Forma literária e processo social no romance brasileiro* (São Paulo: Duas Cidades, 1977); *Um mestre na periferia do capitalismo: Machado de Assis* (São Paulo: Duas Cidades, 1990); *Duas meninas* (São Paulo: Companhia das Letras, 1997).

11. Joaquim Nabuco, *Abolitionism* (1883), trans. Robert Conrad (Urbana: University of Illinois Press, 1977).

12. Schwarz, "A Seminar on Marx"; Richard M. Morse, "Manchester Economics and São Paulo Sociology," in *Manchester and São Paulo: Problems of Rapid Urban Growth*, ed. John Wirth and Robert Jones (Stanford, Calif.: Stanford University Press, 1978), 7–34.

13. Passos, "A sintaxe."

14. Part of the argument has been published in English as Roberto Schwarz, "The Historical Meaning of Cruelty in Machado de Assis," *Modern Language Quarterly* 57, no. 2 (June 1996): 165–80.

15. Sidney Chalhoub, "Dependents Play Chess: Political Dialogues in Machado de Assis," in *Machado de Assis: Reflections on a Brazilian Master*, ed. Richard

Graham (Austin: Institute of Latin American Studies and University of Texas Press, 1999).

16. He left some hints that he considered political militancy incompatible with his position, by this time, as a mid-level civil servant handling issues having to do with slavery. Biographers have found evidence that within the ministry he pushed for enforcement of decisions freeing slaves imported from Africa after the 1831 law banning the slave trade.

17. Machado de Assis, *Epitaph of a Small Winner*, trans. William L. Grossman (New York: Noonday Press, 1952). (*Posthumous Memoirs of Brás Cubas*), ch. 68.

18. John Gledson, "Bons Dias!" in *Machado de Assis: Ficção e história* (Rio de Janeiro: Paz e Terra, 1986).

19. Faoro, *Machado de Assis*, 322, 325. "Somente ele insistiu na calamidade que a alforria poderia significar para o cativo. O escravo seria livre, mas ficaria sem trabalho e sem pão, entregue à medicância" (325). Faoro connects these crônicas to two manumission scenes in Machado's later novels: the discussion about freeing the slaves of the Baron of Santa-Pia in *Counselor Aires's Memorial* (1908) and Paulo's speech in *Esau and Jacob* (1904) saying that "now that the black is freed, it is the turn of the white [to be freed through a republican revolution]"; in light of the crônicas and other writings on abolition, Faoro interprets Paulo's speech as supreme irony on Machado's part. Faoro exaggerates in saying that Machado was the only such critic. Certain abolitionist leaders, such as André Rebouças, insisted on the need for land reform to accompany emancipation; see Maria Alice Rezende de Carvalho, *O quinto século: André Rebouças e a construção do Brasil* (Rio de Janeiro: IUPERJ and Editora Revan, 1998).

20. Sidney Chalhoub, *Visões da liberdade: Uma história das últimas décadas da escravidão na Corte* (São Paulo: Companhia das Letras, 1990), 99. Machado's novel, *Iaiá Garcia* (1878), turns partly on such a relationship, and Machado had commented on "charitable" acts of manumission in earlier crônicas; Manassés, "História de Quinze Dias," *Ilustração Brasileira*, July 15, 1877, in *Obras* vol. 3, 236–41; Machado de Assis, *Diário do Rio de Janeiro*, July 25, 1864, in *Obras*, vol. 2, 62–64.

21. Chalhoub, *Visões*, 82.

22. Chalhoub, *Visões*, 236, 238.

23. Jacob Gorender, *A escravidão reabilitada* (São Paulo: Atica, 1990) is a highly critical characterization of the UNICAMP revisionist historians of slavery.

24. To the best of my knowledge, no critic has systematically explored the possibility that characters whose color is unmarked might be read as brown or black. Given Machado's propensity to deliberately omit information, and let the reader trip over his own presumptions, we shouldn't exclude this possibility.

25. Machado de Assis, *Counselor Aires's Memorial*, 47 "May 18, 1888."

26. David Haberly, *Three Sad Races: Racial Identity and National Consciousness in Brazilian Literature* (Cambridge: Cambridge University Press, 1983), journal, 74; "The Looking Glass," 75, 80; skin, 97–98.

27. Passos, "Sintaxe."

28. John Gledson, "A história do Brasil nos *Papéis avulsos* de Machado de Assis," in *A História contada: Capítulos de história social da literatura no Brasil*, ed. Sidney

Chalhoub and Leonardo Affonso de M. Pereira (Rio de Janeiro: Nova Fronteira, 1998).

29. Bosi, *Machado*.

30. Antonio Candido, "An Outline of Machado de Assis," in *On Literature and Society*, trans. Howard Becker (Princeton, 1995), 104–18.

31. Machado, "The Looking Glass," 57.

32. Machado de Assis, "Só," *Obra completa*, vol. 2 (Rio de Janeiro: Nova Aguilar), 1044–50.

33. Machado de Assis, *Esau and Jacob*, trans. Elizabeth Lowe (Oxford: Oxford University Press, 2000), 71–74, chapters 31–32.

12

From Bossa Nova to Tropicália: Restraint and Excess in Popular Music

Santuza Cambraia Naves

In 1968, Augusto de Campos published in book form (*Balanço da bossa: antologia crítica da moderna música popular brasileira*) a number of articles written by himself and by such musicians as Júlio Medaglia and Gilberto Mendes, which had earlier come out in literary supplements of São Paulo newspapers. These articles analyzed, in addition to such other recent trends in music as Tropicália, the bossa nova style. Campos and the other authors championed an internationalist and modern stance in popular music, opposing the ideologues of a national art for the people and underscoring the importance of the innovative attitude adopted by the creators of bossa nova, foremost among them João Gilberto. They all attributed to Gilberto a position that valued restraint as opposed to the excessive emotionalism that had characterized the popular music of the '40s and '50s, and they also drew a parallel between Gilberto's art and other aesthetic manifestations of the '50s, such as Concrete poetry and the architecture of Oscar Niemeyer. According to these authors, by introducing an intimate musical register not unlike that of cool jazz, bossa nova was in harmony with the ideology of rationality, unadornedness and functionalism that marked other cultural experiences of the period. The authors, it should be added, emphasized bossa nova's break with earlier traditions of Brazilian popular music. Thus, like the Concrete poets, who had broken with the tradition of rhetorical, discursive, and subjectivistic poetry, bossa nova musicians, Gilberto in particular, were said to have adopted as a norm in their work the rejection of the melodramatic *sambas-canções* and boleros of the immediately preceding period, as well as all the singing style that went with these songs—the style, strongly reminiscent of opera singing, of Dalva de Oliveira and others.

This sort of interpretation, as developed by the Paulista poets and musicologists, eventually became canonical, an inescapable benchmark for all students of Brazilian popular music. But however profound and relevant these analyses may be, they have had the effect of giving exaggerated emphasis to the initial period of bossa nova, marked by a sort of musical experimentation along the lines established by Gilberto that was indeed congenial with the aesthetic goals of Concrete poetry. Some of the songs that started the new musical trend are veritable manifestos: Tom Jobim, with his partner Newton Mendonça, wrote two songs, "Desafinado" (1958) and "Samba de uma nota só" ("One-Note Samba," 1960), that introduced a kind of procedure in which words and music referred to each other, calling attention to what is new and subversive in bossa nova. Thus the stressed syllable of the word "*desafino*" ("I sing out of tune") is associated with a note that is entirely unexpected, given the harmonic conventions of pop songs of the time. Also, the lyrics of both songs are marked by a cool approach to the traditional love theme; in "Desafinado" the sentimental argument between lovers is in fact only a smokescreen for the discussion of an aesthetic issue.

It seems clear, then, that when the Concrete poets rhapsodize about "bossa nova" they are referring specifically to a music marked by intimacy, conciseness, rationality, and objectivity, all of which have to do with João Gilberto's aims. My intention is to contribute to this discussion with some additional data, emphasizing different aspects of what has come to be known as "the bossa nova style." To begin with, it should be said that not all members of the bossa nova movement felt the same urge as Gilberto to make a clean break with past styles in popular music, even if they unanimously acknowledged Gilberto's leadership, particularly the novel beat he introduced in guitar playing and his soft, unemotional singing voice, marked by perfect timing. The point is that bossa nova allows a number of different readings, if we take into account the statements of musicians who were members of the movement. Although they all see Gilberto as a leader, each of them adopts a different approach to the traditions of popular music. For instance, all bossa nova musicians admit that their re-creation of samba was influenced by American bebop and cool jazz. But some of them in particular stress the impact on their music of Mexican bolero, in particular Lucho Gatica. Discussing the influence of new trends in international popular music on his own work during his formative period, Roberto Menescal mentioned an album by Gatica, *Inolvidable*, in which only two instruments—guitar and bass—were used, in flagrant contrast with the big bands that traditionally backed bolero singers. According to Menescal, this example was important to him and other musicians of his generation, for it taught them to "listen to the guitar" as it engaged, singly, in a musical dialog with the bass.[1]

Another bossa nova pioneer, Carlos Lyra, mentions Mexican music, such as the boleros of Agustin Lara, as important to him and other members of his generation. Lyra cherishes the old *sambas-canções*, which he calls "Brazilian boleros," although he does make a distinction between those *sambas-canções* that were more "sophisticated" and those of a frankly melodramatic nature. According to him, Antônio Maria wrote songs of both kinds: "Ninguém me ama" is an example of exaggerated sentimentality, while "Ser ou não ser" and "Um cantinho e você" are much more refined songs. Lyra admits that his first interest in music was the *sambas-canções* sung by Dick Farney, and that his early efforts in songwriting were in this genre; he exemplifies with "Quando chegares" and even "Minha namorada," a sort of a transitional composition, half *samba-canção*, half bossa nova. According to Lyra, then, the new musical style came under a wide variety of influences: Mexican boleros, the Impressionism of Ravel and Debussy, the jazz songs of Gershwin, Cole Porter, Richard Rogers, Larry Hart, and many others. In addition to foreign influences, there were also various Brazilian rhythms, such as samba, *xaxado*, *valsa* (the traditional Brazilian waltz), and so on. Though João Gilberto is basically seen as a samba singer, Lyra concludes, there are other rhythms in bossa nova, ranging all the way from the waltz to the *baião*.[2]

In an earlier work, *O violão azul: modernismo e música popular*, (1998), I used the classification proposed by Wisnik[3] for the two fundamental modernist procedures: on the one hand, the constructivist rigor of Webern, which relies on the myth of the *engineer*, and, on the other, the resort to bricolage, characteristic of Stravinsky, Villa-Lobos, and other composers of the period. Analyzing Lévi-Strauss's *The Savage Mind*, Jacques Derrida[4] defines the "engineer" as "a subject who is the absolute source of his own discourse and builds 'every part of it.'" In *O violão azul* I argued that the myth of the engineer was not present in the experience of Brazilian modernism, for both the musicians and the poets in the movement tended to adopt the "anthropophagic" position advanced by Oswald de Andrade[5] in his manifesto, which makes them more like the *bricoleur* described by Lévi-Strauss: a kind of maker who defines himself by his incorporative way of proceeding, always resorting to instruments already available, in contrast with the engineer, who subordinates each specific task "to the acquisition of the raw materials and tools conceived and sought while the plan is being carried out."[6] The vivid images evoked by Lévi-Strauss, such as that of the *kaleidoscope* and of *collage*—successive visual patterns formed by the combination of a certain number of visual texts—helped me to think about the modernists' road to modernity without starting off from tabula rasa, attempting instead to create the "new type" by means of rearrangements that updated the various, though finite, repertoires of our cultural tradition.[7] My major concern was to underscore the fact that Brazilian musicians and poets shared a vision of Brazil as an inexhaustible universe of cultural information, ranging from the archaic to the contemporary, from the regional to the universal. Such a view of a bountiful cultural universe naturally led artists to the attempt to incorporate this cultural wealth into their works.

I see an affinity between João Gilberto's exclusive procedure, his creation of a concise and rational style by breaking with earlier musical forms, and that of the *engineer*, with his mythology that assumes the possibility of starting off from scratch, in a process where everything is created by the will (and the design) of a *demiurge*. Gilberto is supposed to have created bossa nova in the way of a demiurge, though there was no actual design behind the new trend, shared by a number of musicians. In other words, in the various accounts of the birth of bossa nova Gilberto is always portrayed as the "author" of a style: his unique guitar beat and way of singing. If it is quite clear that Gilberto captured the growing taste for small-combo jazz in his own time, it is undeniable that the new musical form that emerged is greatly indebted to his obsession with an entirely new rhythm and harmony, compatible with his own reading of modernity.[8] In this way Gilberto incorporated traditional repertoires, recreating with his own rhythm and harmony sambas written by other musicians by fusing them with jazz. But to do so he also broke with musical genres characterized by excess in all their manifestations, such as "operatic exhibitionism"[9] in musical arrangements relying on grandiose orchestral effects.

But I would like to return to my point: bossa nova style cannot be reduced to Gilberto's aesthetics; according to several musicians associated with bossa nova, it was much more diversified than that. A case in point here is Tom Jobim. Clearly, Jobim was influenced by Gilberto, at least in the first phase of bossa nova; but it should not be forgotten that his career had started before the innovations that took place in the late '50s. In a 1968 interview, Jobim himself observed that bossa nova was only a phase in his career; 80 percent of his compositions—including "chamber songs, movie soundtracks, symphonic music, lots of *sambas-canções* and *choros*"—could not be considered bossa nova at all.[10]

Indeed, Jobim's musical education began when he was thirteen, and it was a classical education. His first teacher was Hans Joachim Koellreuter, a German musician who came to Brazil fleeing Nazism and who introduced the twelve-tone system in the country. Koellreuter claims he taught Jobim the elements of classical harmony and counterpoint and "basic piano playing," his intention being to give his student a "well-rounded" musical education.[11] Later Jobim studied classical piano under Lúcia Branco, Tomás Gutierrez de Terán (a friend of Villa-Lobos), and Paulo Silva. But soon he felt discouraged by the sort of "scholastic" training given at the Escola Nacional de Música, and began to resort to private tutoring. From an early age he was interested in orchestration; he went to classical concerts at the Teatro Municipal and bought sheet music and recordings of whatever captured his attention at the time: Stravinsky, Schoenberg, and Prokofiev. In order to make a living, in the early '50s he began to work in Copacabana nightclubs playing the piano; then he landed a job at the Continental recording company, writing scores for musically illiterate songwriters and making arrangements for orchestra. At Continental he made the acquaintance of such arrangers as Radamés Gnattali, Gaya, Léo Peracchi, and Lyrio Panicalli.[12]

But what seems most conspicuous in Tom Jobim's career is the affinity between his work as a popular musician and a tradition in classical music in which the figure of Villa-Lobos looms large, if not as its founder at least as its major representative. This tradition relies heavily on *excess*, both in instrumental and in choral music, as a way to present the exuberance and vigor of the Brazilian land and Brazilian culture.[13] There is then an intersection of classical music with popular music marked by an aesthetics of grandiosity, in which musicians such as Tomás Terán and Radamés Gnatalli may be seen as mediators between Villa-Lobos and Tom Jobim. Terán, a Spanish pianist, came to Brazil at the age of twenty-seven because of his fascination with the work of Villa-Lobos, in particular the suite *A prole do bebê*, which he had heard played by Arthur Rubinstein in Buenos Aires. He became a specialist in Villa-Lobos, whom he met in Paris in 1924. He returned to Europe and played Villa-Lobos's works in Paris. In the early '30s the Brazilian composer invited him to teach at the Conservatório de Música and the Sociedade de Cultura Artística do Rio de Janeiro, and he accepted the invitation.[14]

Terán became Jobim's teacher, and he called his student's attention to the importance of Gnattali in his musical training. Jobim began to have closer contacts with Gnattali in 1954, during the recording of the *Sinfonia do Rio de Janeiro* (coauthored by Jobim and Billy Blanco), for which Gnattali wrote the arrangements; and working with him at Continental during the following year Jobim learned to orchestrate popular songs.[15] But quite aside from the technical aspects of instrumentation, it is clear that Jobim and Gnattali shared two attitudes: whether as musicians, composers, or arrangers, they were active in classical music and popular music with equal ease; and they felt free to experiment with all kinds of styles, adopting either the register of *excess* or that of *simplicity*. This procedure, which was a characteristic of Gnattali's, allowed him to bring about a veritable revolution in popular-music arrangements beginning in the early '30s. Until then popular singers were usually accompanied by so-called *regionais*, small groups of instrumentalists with limited skills. Gnattali's experiments with orchestration—together with those of Pixinguinha at the Victor recording company from 1932 on—drew on his classical training as a pianist and violist, and included elements from symphonic music and jazz. Gnattali's career as arranger spanned several decades, first at Columbia and later at Rádio Nacional, through the '40s and into the '50s.[16]

An analysis of Gnattali's musical career is of the greatest importance to my purposes, to the extent that it highlights a *modernist* stance. Like the modernist musicians of the preceding generation, Gnattali was concerned with the creation of a "national idiom" through music. His compositions, like those by Villa-Lobos and others, fed on the popular repertoire. But his modernist predecessors tended to concentrate exclusively on classical music and to incorporate basically folk material, rejecting on ideological grounds the popular music produced for mass consumption—what Mário de Andrade[17] had dubbed "*o popularesco*" ("the popularesque"). Pressed, perhaps, by the difficulty of supporting himself as a classical musician in Rio de Janeiro, Gnattali became increasingly involved with popular music, working as pianist in theaters and movie theaters, and later, as we have seen, as violist and arranger. In these nightspots he made the acquaintance of such pop musicians as Luciano Perrone, Pixinguinha and other *choro* players, as well as the "*pianeiros*" (pianists) employed at Casa Vieira Machado, on Rua do Ouvidor, "whose music he wrote down and from whom he learned to play the piano in the Brazilian style—in fact, a style that at the time existed only in Rio de Janeiro."[18] In addition to composing popular music, not only *choros* but other genres as well, Gnattali had an impact on the way this music was played, by introducing sophisticated orchestral arrangements. Carlos Didier observes that Gnattali's activities also included the opposite of this procedure—namely, the introduction of elements from *choro*, popular piano music, and American jazz into classical music. According to Didier, it was at Rádio Nacional that Gnattali achieved maturity as orchestrator and composer; there he was able to give free rain to his creativity and indulge in musical experimentation. Working with such fine musicians as Léo Peracchi, Romeu Ghipsman, and Lyrio Panicalli, he "wrote and arranged music for trios, quartets, quintets, and explored new timbres."[19]

Particularly since the early '40s, Gnattali also acted as a kind of mediator between more sophisticated musical styles and Brazilian music, developing a stylized form of samba with string orchestras and a kind of harmony based on classical music and jazz. The product of Gnattali's experiments apparently became a parameter for the musicians who created bossa nova in the late '50s.[20] It was in 1954, for example, that Gnattali began to work with Jobim, on the *Sinfonia do Rio de Janeiro*, released that same year by Continental. The music was written by Jobim and Billy Blanco; the arrangement was the responsibility of Gnattali, while Jobim conducted the orchestra. The *Sinfonia* is divided into several movements, each focusing on one particular aspect of the natural or cultural environment of Rio de Janeiro. A number of singers took part in the recording, among them Dick Farney, Gilberto Milfont, Elisete Cardoso, and Emilinha Borba. Structured like a musical, the *Sinfonia* was compared by Jaime Negreiros, a major music critic of the period, to Gershwin's *An American in Paris*.[21] Gnattali emphasizes those aspects of the music that celebrate Rio—"the mountain, the sun, the sea," "the *favela*," "the streets, samba and other features of the city"—combining symphonic instruments and others used in popular music: "strings, brasses, woodwinds, bells, accordion, quartet and piano, bass, acoustic and electric guitar and wire-brush drums."[22]

In 1955 Jobim began to work as an arranger at Continental, and the convergence between his career and Gnattali's became even more marked. It was only natural that Gnattali should invite Jobim to appear on *Quando os maestros se encontram*, a Rádio Nacional program, conducting the symphonic piece *Lenda*, written by Jobim himself in memory to his father, Jorge Jobim.[23]

But the young composer was doing other things besides writing symphonic pieces. In 1953 a Jobim song was recorded for the first time, by Maurici Moura, as a 78-rpm record on the Sinter label: "Incerteza," a *samba-canção* coauthored by Newton Mendonça. Sérgio Cabral observes that this song is very much in the vein of the '50s; the lyrics express a lover's sufferings.[24] But in addition to melodramatic *sambas-canções* Jobim, who was quite versatile even this early in his career, was composing songs of an entirely different character, such as "Teresa da praia," written (with Billy Blanco) in 1954 at the request of Dick Farney, who wanted to sing it in a duo with Lúcio Alves. Tune and lyrics tell the story of a friendly conflict between two young men in love with the same girl who frequents Leblon Beach. In contrast with the nocturnal atmosphere of "Incerteza," which mentions "a moonless night," "Teresa da praia" is a sun-drenched tune, full of high spirits. Toward the end, the two friends give up arguing over the girl and decide to "leave Teresa on the beach / to the sun's kisses / and the sea's embraces." The melody, a *samba-canção* with a bluesy tang—a "*sambablue*," according to Cabral,[25] contributes much to the song's light-heartedness.

From the very beginning of his career, therefore, Jobim made it clear that he was not limited to a single kind of musical sensibility. He could produce an exuberant piece for symphony orchestra just as he could toss off a casual, intimist song like "Teresa da praia." But it is just as clear that he had a taste for the *excessive* from the start: his early musical interests in the '40s included Gershwin, Ravel, Debussy, and Villa-Lobos, and he was also fascinated when he "discovered" the work of the Russian masters Rachmaninoff, Prokofiev, and Stravinsky.[26]

To return to our starting point, it is certainly true that Jobim adopted the bossa nova style, of which "Desafinado" and "Samba de uma nota só" (coauthored by Newton Mendonça) are archetypal representatives, very much in the intimist spirit João Gilberto sought to impart to the new movement. But there was a certain amount of tension in the Jobim-Gilberto collaboration, as Ruy Castro shows in his account of the production of the LP *Canção do amor demais* in 1958, a milestone in the history of bossa nova. From the very beginning, disagreements arose between the artists involved in the project—Gilberto, Jobim, Vinícius de Moraes, and Elisete Cardoso, in addition to the other instrumentalists—over the conception and the actual recording of the album. Whereas Gilberto searched for a new language, all the others had a more conventional orientation (or so at least it seemed to Gilberto). Gilberto disapproved of Elisete's overly "solemn" singing, and he found Moraes's lyrics for "Serenata do adeus" frankly kitschy. By this time Jobim's career had been indelibly marked by the contact with Moraes; they had begun working together in 1956, when the poet invited him to write the music for his verse play *Orfeu do Carnaval*, eventually shown at the Teatro Municipal. Then Moraes asked him for additional music to be used in the movie version, *Black Orpheus*, which received a number of prizes abroad and made Jobim famous.[27]

But once the initial phase of bossa nova was over, Jobim's taste for excess came to the fore again, and he went back to portraying Brazil along modernist lines, as a vital horn of plenty of natural and cultural resources. In fact, in the early '60s bossa nova aesthetics itself was gradually forced to coexist with the return of excess as representation of cultural vigor. First came the Centro de Cultura Popular, an organization associated with the leftist União Nacional dos Estudantes (National Student Union), which encouraged the merging of the bossa nova rhythm with other musical styles, particularly northeastern forms. Then came the Afro sounds of Jorge Ben and Baden Powell; and immediately after, in the mid-'60s, there was the new generation represented by such songwriters and instrumentalists as Chico Buarque de Hollanda, Edu Lobo, Caetano Veloso, and Gilberto Gil.

Chico Buarque is a good example of a musician of the post–bossa nova generation who incorporated into his work Gilberto's new guitar beat but also added to it various other elements from the Brazilian musical repertoire.[28] Buarque readily acknowledges that, when he was about fifteen, he heard for the first time Gilberto's recording of "Chega de saudade" and was immediately converted to bossa nova: "It was then that I began to play the guitar. I started making music just then." But Buarque also says that, although bossa nova's break with tradition is inherent to the style, this did not keep him from resorting to other sources for his own compositions, particularly those associated with so-called traditional samba. According to Buarque, the "complete break" lasted for only three or four years, after which some of the major names in bossa nova returned to Noel Rosa, Cartola, and Nelson Cavaquinho, and set about writing songs that no longer fit into the bossa nova mold.[29] In fact, one of Buarque's very first songs, "A Rita," is a samba that recreates the tongue-in-cheek torch-song mode associated with Rosa, who is explicitly mentioned in the lyrics.

But if we consider other elements besides songwriting, we find that Buarque was influenced by such aspects of bossa nova as, for instance, the intimate stance he adopted in his public performances, when, like Gilberto, he used "bench and guitar" as his only props on an otherwise bare stage. Buarque agrees that this performance aesthetics was congenial to his view of his own role as an artist, since he never saw himself as a "stage performer . . . with costumes, masks and a lot of moving around," but solely as a "performing songwriter." By stepping onstage with his usual workaday clothes and singing as he would at home, Buarque steadfastly refuses to create an artistic persona. This attitude, he says, is "a head-on reaction against the radio show aesthetics, the glitter thing, Cauby Peixoto and the other big stars." By rejecting this sort of extroversion, bossa nova created a different sphere, with "performers who weren't performers and singers who weren't singers."[30]

Edu Lobo adopts a similar position, rejecting not only the mask but also the stage itself; his artistic identity is built basically on his work as a songwriter. All his other activities, as instrumentalist, orchestrator, and singer, are no more than "outgrowths" of his songwriting. To him, the stage is simply a requirement of his profession—or, put differently, a necessity imposed by the fact that, since it is impossible to survive in Brazil solely on royalties, songwriters are forced to perform.[31] On purely musical terms, Lobo is perhaps the best representative in the '60s generation of the tradition started by Gnattali in popular music. In addition to writing songs he is also active in orchestration, which he studied in the United States for two years. And although he calls himself a popular musician, Lobo has a technical background in music that is equaled by few of his peers, which accounts for the sophistication of his harmonies and his arrangements. Like Gnattali, he favors a more exuberant, less restrained kind of modernist aesthetic; his favorite composers are Ravel, Stravinsky, Bartók, Copland, Prokofiev—and, of course, Villa-Lobos. Indeed, Lobo questions what he sees as an excessive emphasis on jazz as a formative element of bossa nova; he believes the influence of older musicians—particularly Villa-Lobos—was just as important. According to him, the more lyrical songs of bossa nova, written by Jobim, Carlinhos Lyra, and Baden Powell, among others, show the impact of "Villa's spirit." Lobo admits that his own music was influenced by Gilberto's guitar beat, though he sees his own work as an offshoot of bossa nova, for he, like other musicians of his generation, tends to combine various elements from a wide musical repertoire rather than remain within the limits of a clearly defined style. This is where he sees Villa-Lobos's influence on his own musical formation; the flexibility that characterizes the master's work served him as a paradigm for blending the northeastern music he heard in Recife—where he spent the summer holidays every year until the age of eighteen, hearing "popular stuff, *frevos*, all kinds of street sounds"— with the harmonic sophistication of bossa nova. Thus Lobo, like Buarque, stresses the uniqueness of the generation he belongs to, the post–bossa nova generation. While the more orthodox among the older musicians devised what virtually amounted to a bossa nova formula, according to Lobo, others soon began to adopt a freer style—for instance, Sérgio Ricardo, Carlos Lyra, and Baden Powell. These musicians, he says, came "to realize that Brazil is not just Rio de Janeiro."[32]

Admittedly, there is more to the post–bossa nova generation than the individual contributions of Chico Buarque and Edu Lobo. But these two songwriters can be seen as emblematic of their generation not only because of their importance in shaping musical taste in their time but also because they have something in common: it is surely no accident that they have cowritten so many songs. Although Buarque is an all-around songwriter while Lobo is more specifically a composer—most of the time he works in partnership with a lyricist—both are characterized by a sensibility that privileges a specific reading of tradition. Both like to revive musical texts of the past—or confined to particular geographical areas—that they find valuable. And rather than quote from such material they prefer to base their own work on information gleaned from it after a long period of attentive listening. The two songwriters, then, may be said to favor a strategy of "re-creation," which is typical of certain modernist tendencies of German origin. For instance, Edward Sapir, associated with the U.S. culture and personality school, deals with the issue of cultural heritage in a very special way. Strongly indebted to Nietzsche, he questions the passive acceptance of the legacy of the past for the creation of a "healthy" national identity. To Sapir, the creative process does not imply "a manufacture of form *ex nihilo*," in which case the individual would be powerless if he did not resort to his cultural heritage. On the other hand, however, form, handed down by tradition, must be submitted to one's "will," for "the passive perpetuator of a cultural tradition gives us merely a manner, the shell of a life that once was."[33] It is in this spirit that Buarque and Lobo value the Brazilian musical tradition, but they operate so as to create something *unique* on the basis of the various options available to them. When Buarque, for instance, turns to the urban samba of the '30s, he tends to favor Noel Rosa's songs that center on the figure of the musician as *malandro*, a subversive character that is congenial with the rebellious stance he himself adopted toward the military regime in the latter half of the '60s.

Even such a sketchy overview of some of the dominant trends in Brazilian pop music of the '60s is enough to indicate that all of them—except for bossa nova—have one characteristic in common: they privilege *inclusion* as their major procedure, which places them on the side of Lévi-Strauss's *bricoleur*. Buarque and Lobo, as we have seen, resort to re-creation, as is typical of a certain modernist tradition associated with German Neo-Romanticism that left strong marks in Mário de Andrade. In his 1928 *Ensaio sobre a música brasileira*,[34] Mário asserts that a vital cultural configuration by means of music—that is, the development of "art music"—is possible only with the use of what he calls the "*populário*," folk music with deep roots in the national tradition. But the full actualization of "art music" also requires formal elaboration, the transformation of traditional musical material into "classical" music. In other words, what he advocates is *re-creation*.

The Tropicalistas, to the extent that they also operate with the idea of inclusion, exemplify a modernist sensibility as well. But in their case there is rather a convergence with Oswald de Andrade, who tended to collect—or, to use his own term, "devour"—material from all quarters of the cultural repertoire in order to reorganize it in accordance with a consistent synthesis, but with no totalizing intent; it was more in the manner of a collage. Like Oswald de Andrade, the Tropicalistas adopt an "anthropophagic" attitude, devouring elements both archaic (associated with tradition) and modern (related to technical innovations). In the same way, cultural imports are incorporated with no concern over the possibility of contaminating an imagined national purity, for Brazilian culture is seen as rich and powerful enough to devour anything that might come from abroad: "We were never catechized. Instead, we celebrated carnival."[35]

In the Tropicalista movement the musical tradition is valued, but the cultural elements to be used are assembled differently. The Tropicalista notion of "cultural wealth" encompasses everything from rock, that ubiquitous cultural import, to established regional rhythms, and is flexible enough to accommodate kitsch as one more component of the nation's treasure. This amounts to an amplification of the concept of "cultural wealth": it is not just the more "sophisticated" popular music that is precious, but also what is aesthetically "poor." The sophistication is evident in the elaborateness of the songs, in the meticulous arrangements, the performances, the album covers—elements that show the influence of the progressive rock of the period. By incorporating the Beatles' impact into their aesthetics, the Tropicalistas were updating the attitude of the preceding generation, which ten years later had integrated into bossa nova the most progressive jazz of their own time. In addition, the Tropicalistas accepted their role as performers with a vengeance, adopting all sorts of masks and choreographic elements, embodying in their own personae the sort of syncretism they effected by combining various musical genres. Just as there is a relation between the Tropicalistas' aesthetics and their artistic personae, so there is isomorphic correspondence between tune and lyrics from the outset. The arrangements are just as important. Rock-derived electric guitars coexist with kitschy violins and the regional twang of the *berimbau*. The guitar in particular, taken from the sphere of rock and incorporated into the Tropicalista scene, became the symbol of a cultural movement, in association with the use of brightly colored costumes, Afro hairstyles, and flashy, parodistic stage business.[36]

But rock is only one element in a variety of disparate ingredients; the Tropicalistas resorted to texts of all kinds, and—more importantly—developed them by means of such metalinguistic processes as *parody* and *pastiche*. Even, however, when relying on parody, which is necessarily critical, the Tropicalista attitude was never corrosive; tradition tended to be handled with a blend of "love" and "humor," to quote from Oswald de Andrade's two-word poem.

For example, Tropicália's attitude toward bossa nova is purely loving, utterly devoid of parodistic elements, particularly in relation to João Gilberto. In his 1969 musical manifesto, "Saudosismo," Caetano Veloso reaffirms Gilberto's decision to "sing out of key":

> No more nostalgia: the fact is
> we've all learned with João to sing
> now and forever out of key

But whereas bossa nova follows a model of restraint, Tropicália relies on excess, to the point of reviving traditions that, as we have seen, had been rejected by bossa nova musicians: the grandiose orchestral arrangements, bristling with strings and brasses, that had been introduced by Gnattali and Pixinguinha; the operatic vocal style of Francisco Alves; the sort of praise of Brazilian cultural wealth best exemplified by Ary Barroso's "Aquarela do Brasil" ("Brazil"); and the torch-song mawkishness that dates back to the '20s and culminated with the *sambas-canções* of the '40s and '50s.[37] In the same vein, the Tropicalistas dusted off the singer-songwriter Vicente Celestino, who at the time was derided as the epitome of bad taste, and the clownish television emcee Chacrinha, famous for his outrageous costumes and grotesque stage routines, was adopted by the movement to the point of becoming one of its symbols—he was explicitly mentioned and saluted in "Aquele abraço," Gilberto Gil's famous good-bye song, released at the time he and Veloso went into exile in 1969. In this way, two antagonistic traditions were incorporated into the same movement: the *unadornedness* associated with bossa nova and the *histrionism* of the traditional popular repertoire. By doing so, Tropicália proposed a new approach to *differ-*

ence, an affirmative, undifferentiated stance toward every facet of the Brazilian universe: kitschy and cool, homespun and imported, classical and popular, rural and urban, and so on.

The Tropicalista attitude has no use for the notion of a closed form: there is no formula for a Tropicalista song, as there is for a bossa nova number or a Carnival *samba-enredo*; elements of the most varied closed forms may be used, sometimes in a single song. In particular, there is a clear attempt to deconstruct of the opposition most vehemently insisted upon in the period: that between the "authentically Brazilian" and the "corrupting foreign" elements. To this opposition the Tropicalistas respond with portmanteau words made up of a term evocative of Brazilian culture and another referring to Anglo-American mass culture, such as *"batmacumba"* ("Batman" + *"macumba,"* common term for Afro-Brazilian cults) and *"bumba-iê-iê-boi"* (*"bumba-meu-boi,"* a Brazilian folk dance + *"iê-iê-iê,"* term used in the mid-'60s to refer to the rock of the early Beatles and similar groups, as well as their Brazilian imitators). On the musical plane, the fusion is achieved by a creative use of the rhythmic similarities between rock and *baião*—a style of popular music from the northeast—both with a fast, strongly stressed binary beat and relatively little syncopation. Another dichotomy that Tropicália attempts to deconstruct is that between the accessible language of pop music and the learned metalanguage of criticism (and literature). The songs written by Veloso, Gil, and the other Tropicalistas, both on the plane of music and on that of words, resort to "high" and "low" elements: the harmonic, melodic, and poetic sophistication of "Clara" coexists with the ironic simplicity of "Baby"; the elaborate lyrics of "Alegria, alegria" are set to an unpretentious, catchy *iê-iê-iê* tune.

To repeat the argument sketched out in the conclusion of my *O violão azul*, the exclusive attitude of the engineer was dominant in Brazilian culture for only a short, relatively atypical period. At a time of assertion of industrial modernity, the ideals of functionality and objectivity became the standard not only in architecture, art, and "classical" music (dodecaphonism) but also in poetry and popular music. But as soon as this moment of optimistic faith in the modernization of Brazil was over, with the rising tensions and uncertainties that marked the late '60s, the strategy of the bricoleur—inclusive, flexible, unabashedly subjectivistic and whimsical—once again assumed the central position it had occupied since the turn of the century.

NOTES

1. Interview with researchers of the CESAP (Centro de Estudos Sociais Aplicados), Universidade Candido Mendes, on June 25, 1998.

2. Interview with CESAP researchers, Oct. 9, 1999.

3. José Miguel Wisnik, *O coro dos contrários: a música em torno da Semana de 22*, 2nd ed. (São Paulo: Duas Cidades, 1983).

4. Jacques Derrida, *A escritura e a diferença* (São Paulo: Perspectiva, 1971).

5. Oswald de Andrade, "Manifesto antropófago," in *Obras completas* (Rio de Janeiro: Civilização Brasileira, 1972).

6. Claude Lévi-Strauss, *O pensamento selvagem* (Campinas: Papirus), 1989, 33.

7. Lévi-Strauss, *O pensamento selvagem*, 52.

8. Ruy Castro, *Chega de saudade: a história e as histórias da bossa nova* (São Paulo: Companhia das Letras, 1991).

9. To use a phrase coined by Augusto de Campos, *Balanço da bossa* (São Paulo: Perspectiva, 1968).

10. Interview with José Eduardo Homem de Mello on Oct. 17, 1968: José Eduardo Homem de Mello, "Antônio Carlos Jobim," in *Música popular brasileira* (São Paulo: Edições Melhoramentos; EDUSPE, 1976), 15–18.

11. Hans Koellreuter, quoted in Sérgio Cabral, *Antônio Carlos Jobim: uma biografia* (Rio de Janeiro: Lumiar, 1997), 45.

12. Interview with José Eduardo Homem de Mello (1976).

13. Santuza Cambraia Naves, *O violão azul: modernismo e música popular* (Rio de Janeiro: Editora FGV, 1998).

14. Cabral, *Antônio Carlos Jobim*.

15. Cabral, *Antônio Carlos Jobim*.

16. Carlos Didier, *Radamés Gnattali* (Rio de Janeiro: Brasiliana Produções, 1996).

17. Mário de Andrade, *Ensaio sobre a música brasileira* (São Paulo: Livraria Martins Editora, 1962).

18. Didier, *Radamés Gnattali*, 16.

19. Didier, *Radamés Gnattali*, 23–24.

20. Didier, *Radamés Gnattali*.

21. Cabral, *Antônio Carlos Jobim*.

22. Didier, *Radamés Gnattali*, 27–28.

23. Cabral, *Antônio Carlos Jobim*.

24. Cabral, *Antônio Carlos Jobim*.

25. Cabral, *Antônio Carlos Jobim*.

26. Cabral, *Antônio Carlos Jobim*.

27. Cabral, *Antônio Carlos Jobim*.

28. Maria Micaela Bissio Neiva Moreira, "'Do samba eu não abro mão': Chico Buarque nos anos 60." (Monograph presented at the Department of Sociology and Political Science, PUC/Rio, July 1999).

29. Interview with CESAP researchers, April 5, 1999.

30. Interview with CESAP researchers, April 5, 1999.

31. Interview with CESAP researchers, March 18, 1999.

32. Interview with CESAP researchers, March 18, 1999.

33. Edward Sapir, "Culture, genuine and spurious" in *Selected Writings in Language, Culture, and Personality* ed. David G. Mandelbaum (Berkeley, Los Angeles, and London: University of California Press, 1985).

34. Andrade, *Ensaio sobre a música brasileira*.
35. Andrade, "Manifesto antropófago," 16.
36. Santuza Cambraia Naves Ribeiro. "Objeto não identificado: a trajetória de Caetano Veloso." (Master's thesis presented at the Graduate Program in Social Anthropology, Museu Nacional, Universidade Federal do Rio de Janeiro, 1988).
37. Castro, *Chega de saudade*.

BIBLIOGRAPHY

Andrade, Mário de. *Ensaio sobre a música brasileira*. São Paulo: Livraria Martins Editora, 1962.

Andrade, Oswald de. "Manifesto antropófago." In *Obras completas*. Rio de Janeiro: Civilização Brasileira, 1972.

Cabral, Sérgio. *Antônio Carlos Jobim: uma biografia*. Rio de Janeiro: Lumiar, 1997.

Campos, Augusto de. *Balanço da bossa*. São Paulo: Perspectiva, 1968.

Castro, Ruy. *Chega de saudade: a história e as histórias da bossa nova*. São Paulo: Companhia das Letras, 1991.

Derrida, Jacques. *A escritura e a diferença*. São Paulo: Perspectiva, 1971.

Didier, Carlos. *Radamés Gnattali*. Rio de Janeiro: Brasiliana Produções, 1996.

Lévi-Strauss, Claude. *O pensamento selvagem*. Campinas: Papirus Editora, 1989.

Mello, José Eduardo Homem de. "Antônio Carlos Jobim." In *Música popular brasileira*, 15–18. São Paulo: Edições Melhoramentos; EDUSP: 1976.

Moreira, Maria Micaela Bissio Neiva. "'Do samba eu não abro mão': Chico Buarque nos anos 60." Monograph presented at the Department of Sociology and Political Science, PUC/Rio, July 1999.

Naves, Santuza Cambraia. *O violão azul: modernismo e música popular*. Rio de Janeiro: Editora da Fundação Getúlio Vargas, 1998.

Ribeiro, Santuza Cambraia Naves. "Objeto não identificado: a trajetória de Caetano Veloso." Master's thesis presented at the Graduate Program in Social Anthropology, Museu Nacional, Universidade Federal do Rio de Janeiro, 1988.

Sapir, Edward. "Culture, Genuine and Spurious." In *Selected Writings in Language, Culture, and Personality*, edited by David G. Mandelbaum. Berkeley: University of California Press, 1985.

Wisnik, José Miguel. *O coro dos contrários: a música em torno da Semana de 22*. 2nd ed. São Paulo: Duas Cidades, 1983.

13

Elective Infidelities: Intellectuals and Politics

Helena Bomeny

Irrespective of my friendship for you and of the liberties I take with you, it is always certain that in front of you I never forget the minister, which frightens me, makes me smaller and inferior. This, by the way, drives me mad and is the reason why I always shy away from highly placed personalities. From a distance, by letter, I can explain myself better, and tend to agree less.

— Mário de Andrade, February 23, 1939

It is true that I have always collaborated with the friend (and only a friend, by the way, could forgive the impertinence that usually surrounds my collaboration) and not with the minister, or the government, but it would be impossible to dissociate these entities and, were I able to do so, this might serve as an excuse for me, but would not benefit the minister.

— Carlos Drummond de Andrade, March 25, 1936

If it is no longer possible to address education and culture in Republican Brazil without mentioning the Gustavo Capanema ministry (1934–1945), it is not possible either to think of the relationship between intellectuals and power without reference to Julien Benda's (1867–1956) *La Trahison des Clercs,* a book that has already become a classic on this issue. "Until today," confirms Michel Winock, "*La Trahison des Clercs [Treason of the clerks]* continues to be an emblematic book, debatable and debated, sometimes vehemently, but a mandatory reference for all reflection and history concerning the role of intellectuals in the State."[1]

Julien Benda's book addresses a key problem of contemporary culture: the relationship between politics and spiritual life. To think of this issue is to think of the meaning of the word *clerc* (clerk) for the author. Making no distinction between lay people and people of the frock, Benda takes the term in its broader sense: *clercs* are all those who do not aim at a practical, short-term result, all those who maintain the cult of Art and pure Thought, who take joy from spiritual pleasure: "In a way they say: My Kingdom is not of this world. And in fact, for more than two thousand years, until recent days, I perceive throughout history, an uninterrupted chain of philosophers, religious people, literati, artists, sages . . . whose movement is a formal opposition to the realism of the crowd."[2] The *clerc* is a kind of loner, free from the passions that drive ordinary people such as love of family, race, country, and the passion of class: he or she is the eternal champion of universal truth and in his or her quest no compromise is ever entertained. They are Witnesses of the Spirit, and could not care less whether their individual testimony is up to date or not, effective or not. Throughout history, the noble theory of the *clercs* worthy of the name has advanced: Plato, Saint Thomas Aquinas, Leonardo da Vinci, Malebranche, Spinoza and, above all, Socrates, "the perfect model of a *clerc*."

Indeed, by his presence alone, the *clerc* is a factor of disturbance to the State: his or her mission is to protest against all spiritual lessening, even if demanded in the name of the Homeland. Loyal to their essence, the *clercs* affront the realism of States, which, thus confronted, are less faithful to their own essence and make them drink hemlock. For Benda, the treason of intellectuals starts at the precise moment they enter the shifting arena of history, a moment when they surrender the universal values of the spirit—truth, justice and freedom—to the irrational powers of instinct, to the spirit of the people, of the institution, etc. The *clercs*, whether intellectuals, philosophers, or literati, defined as secular clerics must, according to Benda, maintain those universal values against the intrusion of the political spirit of their time. Who else could so do, since lay people are necessarily involved in action and mundane passions? Here we have a strict humanist rationalism resisting the sirensong romantic spirit of the people. Today, however, it is no longer so. Moved by the desire for money, power or by a romantic sensuality, modern *clercs* fail to place disinterested values at the top of spiritual hierarchies. They became agents of the temporal. Although he does not ignore, throughout history, the infidelities of *clercs* to their mission, Benda is concerned rather in stressing the overall trend of contemporary intelligence to join the lines of the infidels. Intellectuals no longer renounce the temptation of placing themselves at the service of their political passions. The *clercs'* is a spiritual treason: it consists less of committing themselves to a political action than in pretending that it is fair to direct intelligence toward immediate, worldly triumphs. And in this turnabout of the purity of intelligence of the spirit, Benda blames Germany for being, in Europe, the country that introduced the religion of the rational soul, of race, the cult of force, the apology for war, the nationalist philosophies of history. The treason of the *clercs* is, in fact, linked to the crisis of sensitivity that pervaded Europe in the last two hundred years: it is a romantic malady, a consequence of the preference of sensitivity over reason, of the visible over the invisible, the carnal over the spiritual.

Taken to the limit, Julien Benda's thesis could result in a radical separation between the realms of life and thought and denial of any possible influence of the latter over the former. But this is not so. Benda himself sustained the links with the world of life and the influence over day-to-day processes, provided the ideals of justice were preserved. Whenever they kept themselves as "officiants of abstract justice," removing their exercise of intelligence from the passion for some terrestrial object, intellectuals did not betray. The publication of the book, in 1927, had a very clear direction. It challenged many contemporary intellectuals and writers, bringing to the surface the problem of the entire nineteenth-century intelligentsia and the generalized influence of a philosophical doctrine such as pragmatism.

Criticized as extemporaneous, Julien Benda's book would end up being an elegy to the old Greek and classic intellectualism. The *La Trahison* thus joined a rather widespread current of the spirit after World War I, illustrated by Gide's theory of unselfishness and Jacques Rivière's "demobilization of literature." And the most recurring criticism of the book is that the author does not take into account the profound transformations of modern society, the pressures of political and economic demands on the personality, a pressure never known before. Michel Winock mentions the scathing criticism of Albert Thibaudet, in June 1928, published in the *NRF,* a French magazine acknowledged as belonging to the literary right, in which he says: "What transpires in Benda is Israel's prophetism. The wise man is a man of the desert, taking his nourishment from locusts and wild honey and announcing: Shame! Shame on the cities and States. Actually, the story of the wise man unfaithful to his mission is in the Bible. It is the story of Jonah."[3] Winock himself advances his comment on Benda's thesis to soften the author's intention. Benda does not wish the wise to rule the world. The kingdom of philosophers could only exist if human things were no longer human and became divine. "All he wishes is that the religion of wise man is understood so that no one can surrender to human passions without a bad conscience." And "it is precisely there that the new spiritual wise men of the West fail, where they betray their mission telling men: *be loyal to the land.*"[4]

Anyway, whether criticized or more accepted, partisan to an idealism that is meaningless in the urbanized and industrialized world, not only did Benda's book become an almost mandatory starting point for those who follow his concern with unraveling the representations of the intellectuals—as

Edward Said in his *Representations of the Intellectual*—but also a reference among intellectuals themselves, in the reflections, answers, or justifications for their form of political participation. One might say that the impact of Benda's thesis corresponds to uneasiness typical of the intellectual world: independence and distancing of thought from the forms of its appropriation by politics. This is the key whereby I can understand Drummond, the poet,[5] when he says that, since they are "contemplative," intellectuals are harmless (i.e., there would be no correspondence between the questions and inquiries of the mind, typical of the spirit, and intervention in the world of actions).

In Brazil of the Vargas era, the dilemma of participation by intellectuals in politics had one of its memorable moments in the Capanema ministry, which concentrated a good portion of the examples that are always recalled to address the never-peaceful relationship between intellectuals and politics. How can we understand the assent of some, and the reclusion imposed on others?

INTELLECTUALS IN THE CABINET

The consequences of what he [Capanema] did are incalculable. Follow my reasoning. Without the Ministry of Education building (which at the time was received as the work of a madman) we would not see Lucio Costa, Niemeyer, Carlos Leão and Cândido Portinari stand out as they did. They were understood by Capanema and his close assistants (Drummond, Rodrigo, Mário de Andrade and others). Without this understanding, we would not have Pampulha, whose architectural and landscape conception was valued by the immense Kubitschek. Without Pampulha we would not have had Brasília, of the same Juscelino Kubitschek, which turned the course of our history—leading Brazil to its western frontiers. The roots of all this, the generating seed, the nourishing fertilizer, are in the intelligence of Capanema and his assistants.[6]

Playing with the opening words of this text, I reiterate: If it is no longer possible to speak of education and culture in Brazil without mentioning Gustavo Capanema—Minister of Education from 1934 to 1945—it is also impossible to remember that ministry without reference to the intellectuals that composed the so-called Capanema constellation. The memory of their participation in government has been recovered with an uneasy feeling because we must consider this period as part of the Estado Novo (New State—1937–1945), a milestone of authoritarian rule in Brazil. How much did these intellectuals consent in the setting up of authoritarianism? How much of the political restrictions and curtailment of freedom did they accept? A wide range of associations and responsibilities has been considered. Sérgio Miceli's *Intelectuais e classe dirigente no Brasil* (Intellectuals and the Ruling

Class in Brazil) *(1920–1945)*, published in 1979, became an icon of this type of questioning.[7] Actually, the relationship between intellectuals and power has been a life-long program of work for Sérgio Miceli. His latest book *Intelectuais à Brasileira* (Intellectuals Brazilian Style), reviews old studies, confirming them in the methodological perspective to which he has committed himself throughout twenty or so years of research.[8] In a different tone, *Tempos de Capanema* (Times of Capanema) also addressed the tension between the action of the intellectuals and government decisions in that ministry.[9] My own book, *Guardiães da Razão* (Guardians of Reason), centers on the action of the modernist intellectuals from Minas Gerais in national politics, which forced me to address the difficulties imposed on this particular group by the workings of the processes of institutionalizing the State and the day-to-day tension in these relations.[10] More recently, the book organized by Ângela Castro Gomes, *O ministro e seu ministério* (The Minister and his Ministry), returns to the same theme, a theme that ended up as a permanent reference in the studies reviewing this particular context.[11]

At the core of this period of unquestioning patronage of Brazilian politics was a group of intellectuals from the most varied fields and social backgrounds. It is true that hindsight benefits these later studies, but it also involves a risk: a distant viewpoint may lead to oversimplifying since subsequent developments are already known. Or, as Bolivar Lamounier so appropriately put it: "Basically, what one projects on the past is an aspiration, a desire that occurs at a later time. Therefore, one could perhaps say that the interpreter positions himself or herself as a creditor of the past, not a debtor as befits the historian."[12] The resulting associations prevent the analysis from considering elements that could add new shades of meaning and compose the dynamics of tensions—as well as conflict—that this type of adherence implies. What became known later guides the interpretation of what happened before. The past is then viewed in the colors of a future that is already present at the time its recovery is attempted.

This remark should be understood as neither an excuse nor an indication of total unawareness or detachment of the players regarding the processes they were involved in. Simon Schwartzman is absolutely right when, commenting the participation of Carlos Drummond de Andrade in the Estado Novo cabinet, he says: "To justify Drummond's uncomfortable presence in this ministry simply by his friendship [with the Minister], or to say that his was merely a bureaucratic and administrative activity is to belittle his intelligence and values."[13] His caution forces us to broaden the horizons of the field, expanding our interpretation to other dimensions, one of which places the invitation from the higher echelons of government and its acceptance by the intellectuals in the context of what has been widely acknowledged in the specialized literature as the construction of the Welfare State. In Brazil this is associated with the Vargas Era. This is a point that drew the attention of other researchers delving into the 1930s. As an example, I would like to quote from Lucia Lippi Oliveira's "As raízes da ordem: os intelectuais, a cultura e o Estado" (Roots of order: intellectuals, culture and the State):

> In its complex web of "tradition" and "modernization," the Estado Novo had a substantial appeal to the Brazilian intelligentsia. Many who left modernism—both among those who joined the radical movements of the '30s and those who remained linked to traditional parties—ended up in a common stream involved in the project of construction of the national State. Modernist literati, integralist[14] politicians, positivists, Catholics, socialists can be seen working side by side."[15]

This movement, however, was not restricted to Brazil. On the contrary, it pervaded all of Latin America. The erection of a national State aimed at establishing policies to protect important spheres of social life—education, health, culture, the arts and architecture, national heritage, administration, and so on—justified the demand for experts, thus involving intellectuals from various fields and giving opportunities to enlightened and outspoken individuals or, as Guerreiro Ramos puts it, *pragmatic critics,* capable of suggesting and designing initiatives for all the above-mentioned fields. The admission and the activity of those intellectuals and enlightened individuals differ in more than style, as they inform on the diverse fields of policy conception and adherence to values. Guerreiro Ramos's categorization, which I quote in a note, reveals the complexity of the relationship between intellectuals and politics in the 1930s.[16] This small exercise will help us to understand the substantial number of intellectuals who accepted the call of government at that time.

If we go back to the 1920s, we will understand the prompt response of so many intellectuals to the calls from the post-1930 state bureaucracy. In the field of education for instance, we will see hordes of reformers in almost all states of the federation. Pioneers in the defense of a national education system, they viewed mass illiteracy as a sign of Brazil's backwardness, and claimed a federal policy in favor of education. Their criticisms are well known: Brazil was hostage to the voluptuousness and voluntarism of local elites; Brazilian education held hostage by elitism, the unpredictability of investment, the carelessness of its rulers. The country needed a State policy that would ensure access and the basic right to lay and free public education. And above all, projects in this sector lacked planning, organization, reliability, and regularity.

Turning to culture, all we need to do is follow Mário de Andrade's journeys through the country, collecting, cataloguing, classifying, and valuing both symbolic and material heritage for the purpose of highlighting Brazilian originality—evidence of which could be found in all regional corners—in a Herculean effort to ascribe a meaning to them and to defend the development of a national policy to preserve our cultural heritage: only the State could have sufficient resources to implement such a national policy of memory and historic heritage preservation.

If we shift our gaze to science, our companions on this journey into the past will now be the physicians and sanitarians, who—since the 1910s—had been diagnosing the increasing, yawning gap in Brazil between disease, ignorance, and the benefits that society could reap from the incorporation of scientific progress in favor of health.[17] Education, culture, and science of a nation waiting for a State that would release them for the benefit of all, which could ensure they would become a social heritage. Hence, the construction of society was pending the construction of a State that would incorporate it and sustain its flight into key areas and spaces of social interaction.

In the United States, the experience of patronage had always been associated with various sponsors of the arts, hence to sectors and players of civil society. Historically, State intervention in such endeavors had not been welcome. In Latin America, on the contrary, patronage found in the State its strongest, most reliable and legitimate sponsor. Here, the rhetoric of a greater involvement of civil society, or the so-called third sector, in the promotion of social activities is rather recent and embryonic. It still seeks support in a process derived from the reform of the State toward lower protectionism, from the rupture of the Welfare State—a phenomenon attributed to what is being diffusely called neoliberalism. The widespread critical reaction among Latin American intellectuals to this new format of relations validates the thesis that we are undergoing the rupture of a tradition that held the State as the largest sponsor, the first guarantor of social development. Contrasting with the United States, where "it is natural for society to criticize the State, since this has traditionally been considered an evil, albeit necessary,"[18] our intelligentsia have greater distrust in the capacity, willingness, intention of regular investments originating from the world of interests, the private sphere.

This distrust in the private world is justified. Local bossism (*mandonismo*), *coronelismo*,[19] greed, and personalism that pervaded the traditional oligarchic politics controlled by voluntaristic and voluptuous bosses lacking in public spirit, and a weak State are the results of this type of negotiation—which were definitely classified by Vitor Nunes Leal in his classic *Coronelismo, enxada e voto* (Coronelismo, hoe and vote), left indelible scars in the Brazilian intellectual tradition. In this key, the outcry for national policies can be understood as a way out of the particularism, of predatory privatism. The belief in the efficiency of a model casting the State as the promoter of social policies also resounds in the criticism to the traditional model. The construction of the National State implied criticism of the First Republic (1889–1930). Reviewing the discourse of intellectuals in the publications of the Estado Novo, particularly the *Cultura Política* magazine, Angela Gomes addresses the frame of mind in which that generation tried to build the "other tradition," and as she appropriately synthesized, the modernist generation was the "mediator of the transition that had begun in the 1920s and was being concluded in the '40s. The modernists rose magnificently to the task both because they reinstated the theme of Brazilianism with militant characteristics and because they were the intellectuals available to occupy the public offices of the Estado Novo."[20]

At the turn of the nineteenth century, Brazilian intellectuals considered the modernization of the country, betting heavily on State intervention in the articulation and/or moderation of social forces. Perhaps this explains why even liberals like Anísio Teixeira, inspired by the United States and with a strong tradition of distrust of the role of the interventive State, conditioned Brazilian renewal to state action.

Early in the twentieth century, order and progress overcame democratic aspirations. They were seen as necessary prior steps in a discussion of democracy based on more reliable terms. The notions of progress and democracy did not necessarily advance hand in hand. Science could provide the key to more predictable and well-supported notions of rationality of procedures, creation of national systems in the areas of social policies—health, education, culture, heritage, labor relations, social security. Hence, belief in State intervention and faith in the progress of science sedimented the intellectual project of a significant portion of the post-1930 generation in Brazil. In a letter addressed to Monteiro Lobato, Anísio Teixeira, an intellectual unquestionably linked to democracy and freedom, stressed:

> We are immersed in an atmosphere such as the one that must have dominated Europe in 1848: we are still seeking political and civil freedom! When will we see that the problem of organization, not the political problem, is what really matters? Let men [and women] be prepared. Let technicians be formed. They shall organize. From organization, wealth will come. And all else, healthy politics, freedom, etc., etc.—will be added.[21]

And Anísio himself—a prime target of the authoritarianism that prevailed during the Vargas administration—joyfully received both the creation of the Ministry of Education and Health, in 1930, and the invitation from the then Minister Francisco Campos[22] to cooperate with the government in the reform of secondary education. The long-awaited action of the State could finally be felt, says Anísio in various letters kept in his personal archives. Therefore, it is not surprising that representatives from all segments of intelligent life participated in a government that assumed a model of intervention designed with arguments of rationality, planning, and opposition to regionalisms, the oligarchies, local bossism (*mandonismo*)—a modern State, at last. This is the major reason why it was so widely accepted among the most important groups of intellectuals of that generation.

To speak of intellectuals and power at a time in Brazil's history when culture and politics overlapped to the point of conferring on politics an entirely different dimension[23] is an exercise that requires some exceptions. If it is true—as specialized literature consistently points out—that there was an extensive participation by intellectuals in the design of political actions in several fields (education, culture, heritage), in the formulation of a doctrinal system to legitimize the Estado Novo, in the definition of a broad propaganda project using the various media of the time (printed press, radio, cinema, and theater), it is also true that some of those intellectuals were preferentially targeted in the calling to account that inevitably ensued. Risking perhaps an overstatement, I would say that few caused so much indignation and calling to account as the poet Carlos Drummond de Andrade, to the point that no mention can be made of the most well-known ministry of the Vargas administration without recalling the loyal and permanent head of Capanema's office, the minister's private secretary during the eleven years he remained in office.

The history of the close ties between intellectuals and power in the Capanema ministry is a history whose roots can be traced to before he took over as a minister. In a specific moment in time and in a particular geographic space, a group of friends gathered all that was required to define the course of a generation. Here, generation is understood in the classical meaning ascribed by Karl Mannheim: a particular form of local identity that encompasses age groups inserted in a same sociohistorical process. What is important in this definition is the fact that they are groups conceived as people of similar ages sharing common experiences that distinguish them from their contemporaries in other age groups. It is the dimension of socially shared experiences that bestows a special meaning on Mannheim's formulation.[24] The moment we refer to is the decade of 1920, and the space is the city of Belo Horizonte, capital city of the first modernist generation of Minas Gerais.

INTELLECTUALS OF A PARTICULAR CITY

"In the month of August, we started reading through the night, during the day, at any free moment we had. No movies, Bar do Ponto, black girls, no time wasted." Thus Pedro Nava leads us back to 1921, to his days as a medical student, to the romping of a generation of young intellectuals and to the youth of a city, Belo Horizonte, then twenty-four years old. In *Beira-Mar* he makes this journey through time and takes us to visit his friends at Rua da Bahia (Bahia Street). Not only does he impart his first experience as a public servant but makes a detailed description of his daily walks from office to home, invariably following new routes, taking pleasure in getting lost in the streets of this city. "Rua da Bahia and all the building facades," he says, "are imprinted in my memory as the faces of old friends." Nava, the urban drifter, started there, in the Belo Horizonte of the 1920's, a habit that he would follow to exhaustion in the city of Rio de Janeiro decades later. His obsession in mapping both human types and the lines of the city was one of the strongest characteristics of this citizen of both Juiz de Fora, Minas Gerais, and Rio de Janeiro. One can say that in the memoirs of Pedro Nava both human and urban geographies are intertwined.

Little by little, the young men perceived the gap between their intellectual expectations and the limits imposed by this parochial city, this new capital still with an atmosphere like a hamlet. Their effort in presenting themselves as participants of an ideal of unity, moderation, prudence, and balance—values expressed in the ideas of *mineiridade*—the quality of being *mineiro* (i.e., from Minas Gerais)—corresponded to their efforts to create the image of a capital, center of culture and political *locus* capable of influencing the destiny of the character of their home state. The trajectories of Pedro Nava and Drummond symbolize the trajectory of an entire generation, which is perhaps emblematic of the failure to transform Belo Horizonte of the 1920s into the cultural capital, cosmopolitan and universal, intended in the Cartesian design of Aarão Reis. And yet they tried. They produced environments in which they could be as modern as they dreamed despite the hamlet-like city they lived in. Even the resistance of the former Curral del Rey to being subjected to an urban mold was sung by the poets and writers. The "ghosts" of Belo Horizonte that inspired their chronicles and poems, which reappear in the delicious narrative of Heloísa Starling, can be understood as the victory of the hamlet, of tradition over the modernizing pressure and mold announced by the new capital of reason. The ghosts resisted time and stubbornly remained there.[25]

The group of young people introduced by Nava was rather large for the then parochial environment of Belo Horizonte in the 1920s: Abgar Renault, Alberto Campos, Carlos Drummond de Andrade, Emílio Moura, Francisco Martins de Almeida, Gabriel de Rezende Passos, Gustavo Capanema Filho, Hamilton de Paula, Heitor Augusto de Souza, João Alphonsus de Guimaraens, João Guimarães Alves, João Pinheiro Filho, Mario Álvares da Silva Campos, Mario Casassanta, and Milton Campos. They formed the *Grupo do Estrela*, taking the name of the coffeehouse where they met.[26]

Among the members of this group, Carlos Drummond was the one who was exposed to the vexation of having to justify his permanence in the Estado Novo cabinet and his loyalty to the minister. Arriving in the capital of the state in 1920, he soon joined the "boys of Belo Horizonte," none of whom was from Belo Horizonte, and the reason was soon revealed: they were as old as—sometimes older than—the city inaugurated in 1897. They came from various places, villages of Minas Gerais: Itabira, Dores de Indaiá, Pitangui, Mariana, and Juiz de Fora are the birthplaces of Drummond, Francisco Campos, Capanema, João Alphonsus, and Pedro Nava respectively. This small group of intellectuals stands for the exodus that took place in populating the new capital of the state. It is this small group of literati that introduced Belo Horizonte into the literary chronicles. In this urban environment, a fraternity was formed, comprising "young lawyers, physicians, poets, journalists, some fifteen or twenty in all, not subjected to, but influenced by common trends and habits—which, at the time, best reflected the "mineiro" taste for freedom, irony and reflection."[27] After all, they were intellectuals, hence, in the words of Drummond, harmless, since they were "contemplative."

Belo Horizonte lacked a concrete structural frame to fully realize this individualistic ideal. The way to compensate for this was to move beyond the local boundaries via intellectual exercise, by formalization and abstraction. The insatiable hunger for books, the eagerness for French literary novelties, fresh from the hub of western culture, the conversation around literary creation, the freedom their dialogue consented, all working as fuel for the joy and pleasure of that special group of young men that the country would soon get acquainted with in national politics. Due perhaps to youthful naiveté, they wagered on the supremacy of literature over context, on the revolutionary transformation of conventions by intellect. As Francisco Iglesias, a professional journalist since youth, said, it was difficult for Drummond to abstain from politics. "In addition, in Minas intellectuals had always been connected to government through bureaucracy: rare was the writer that did not work in some department, usually as private secretary to the state president [title of the state governor at the time] or a member of his cabinet."[28] Drummond worked at the *Minas Gerais*—the official journal of the administration, which opened space to literature printing critiques, poems, chronicles, and philosophical essays.

Invited by Capanema to join him as private secretary at the ministry, Carlos Drummond de Andrade moved to Rio de Janeiro, then capital of the country, in 1934. There he would live until his death on August 17, 1987. During his days in the ministry he perfected his talent as a "scribe," a talent first revealed and refined in the days of journalism at the *Minas Gerais*, and in his participation in Cristiano Machado's term at the Inland Secretariat, in 1930, having remained in the position when Machado was succeeded by Gustavo Capanema himself. "Under aliases or the signature of PRM bosses or no signature at all I wrote letters, speeches, interviews, newspaper articles, editorials, loose papers."[29] Therefore, the invitation to the federal government was not fortuitous: in addition to his close friendship with Capanema, the poet had wide experience at the state level and had cooperated with the future minister during his term at the Inland Secretariat, which was responsible for the security of the state. In those days, the Minister of Education was Capanema's mentor Francisco Campos, later Minister of Justice, who orchestrated the agreement between the Catholic Church, the state political forces, and the central government that would lead Capanema to the office of minister.[30]

The generation of the '20s had rather cultivated meetings at the fraternity. Short stories, chronicles, letters, and memoirs confirm the pleasure and the intellectual benefits they obtained from those regular assemblies consecrated as quasi-religious moments. The fraternity continued to meet in the next decades and, despite the dwindling number of intellectuals who entered politics, admitted other young people who would soon become a reference in the country. In the 1950s, Belo Horizonte was still remembered as the place where the elders met the newly arrived. In the words of Silviano Santiago, "JK [Juscelino Kubitschek] was the governor of Minas Gerais at that time. The elders were professors who taught around a table in a confectioner's shop. . . . By transgressing the classical rules of petit bourgeois teaching, they led the young to transgress the conventional notions of the *mineira* society."[31] Throughout the following decades, conversation in bars, bookstores, and confectioners' shops turned from a habit into almost a ritual in the cultivation of intellectuals in this city of the modernist intellectuals of Minas Gerais.

BETWEEN POLITICS AND FREEDOM OF SPIRIT

The participation of intellectuals in the Capanema ministry amalgamated two kinds of movements. On one side, an answer to the call of the State for the development of policies addressing the various areas of social life—a positive reaction that can be understood in the context of the construction of the Welfare State that I mentioned earlier—and on the other, a movement of adherence and distancing, enthusiasm and refusal caused by the tension that has in Julien Benda's thesis a good point of reference. The three examples used in this chapter—Pedro Nava, Mário de Andrade, and Carlos Drummond—are typical and help us in outlining the alternating manifestations of praise and criticism, a stop-and-go, often conflicting activity, indicating the partial loyalty of the intellectuals to politics. Outside the government, watching from afar, Nava distinguishes himself from the other two, but still reveals some similarities.

The first of such similarities is the underlying sincere friendship I already mentioned. They praise the modern dimension of that particular ministry, which in their view—and especially regarding architectural projects—would have opened the doors to civilization for Brazil. Other equally illustrious contemporaries follow Pedro Nava in this assessment. In a famous letter to Capanema, Lúcio Costa, who later would attain worldwide acknowledgement as author of Brasilia's urban plan, comments the inauguration of the Ministry building saying: "Were the minister another man, this building would not exist. Your qualities, and possibly some of your defects made this work feasible. No other public man, here or elsewhere, would have had the courage to carry out such a radically innovative work under such unfavorable conditions."[32]

It is a perfect statement. The "some of your defects" Lúcio Costa mentions is a reference to the minister's decision to charge Lúcio Costa himself with the construction of the Ministry of Education building, later acknowledged as a milestone of modern architecture in Brazil. Capanema waived the result of a public contest and appointed Lúcio Costa, who immediately gathered a group of architects—all of whom had failed to classify in the contest—to develop the project. The group recommended that Le Corbusier—French-born Swiss architect and most powerful advocate of the modernist school—should be invited to Brazil to consult on both the ministry building and the university campus. Henrique Mindlin, an architect of the subsequent generation, tells us how the result of the event overcame the condemnation of the procedure:

In an atmosphere of generalized artistic indecision, the prizes were awarded to purely academic projects, while other works of great value and within a modern concept presented by a group of young artists were dismissed. It was then that one of those unexpected events that change the course of history took place: the Minister of Education, Gustavo Capanema, inspired by the combination of vision, daring and common sense that characterized him, took the personal decision that has been considered the greatest individual contribution to the development of modern architecture in Brazil. Relying on the opinion of several acknowledged critics, particularly Mário de Andrade, Carlos Drummond de Andrade, Rodrigo Mello Franco de Andrade and Manuel Bandeira, and also on M. Piacentini, Italian architect who participated in the design of the campus, Capanema, after awarding the prizes to the winners, asked Lúcio Costa, one of those who had failed to classify, to present a new project. Upon Lúcio Costa's request, this invitation was extended to other architects that had also failed to classify. Thus the new group was formed, composed of Carlos

Leão, Jorge Moreira and Affonso Eduardo Reidy, soon joined by Oscar Niemeyer and Ernani Vasconcellos.[33]

The testimonies of Nava and the architects Lúcio Costa and Henrique Mindlin's reveal a consensus in the circle of Brazilian architecture around a project acknowledged as the opening moment of a modern movement in the country. Therefore, in this case both the intellectuals and those in power are perfectly synchronized, i.e. power not only imposed restraints on intellectuals but also created the conditions that enabled intellectual activity to flourish, materializing in the project of modern architecture in Brazil. The references signed by Carlos Drummond and Mário de Andrade reveal another face of the same relationship with power: the uneasiness regarding the procedures to which they were subject as intellectuals immersed in the dynamics of central government bureaucracy.

Reactions, as I mentioned earlier, were varied. The letters addressed to the minister are an invaluable source of information that helps us perceive the ambiguity of the marriage between men of the spirit and the routines of power. Mário de Andrade's letters exemplify the impact of bureaucratic impersonality on the sensitivity of the modernist intellectual:

> My desire to serve well breaks under the memory of what education bureaucracy is like in this country of ours. I have had such a difficult experience in the reform of the Instituto Nacional de Música [National Institute of Music], in which I took part, invited by then minister Francisco Campos. . . . We put up a heroic fight, Luciano Gallet, Sá Pereira and me. And what for? For our extremely naive idealism to be completely destroyed by an unbending bureaucratic organism.[34]

They did put up a great fight because, contrary to Drummond, Mário de Andrade was positively provoked by any call to design projects, to create an organ capable of preserving culture and of valuing Brazilian cultural heritage. His correspondence with Capanema mirrors this seesaw between the drive to action and the unavoidable battle with the stubborn bureaucracy that conspired against any idea, project, or cause.

When he writes to Capanema, Mário de Andrade is tired, faced with insurmountable financial problems and impatient with bureaucratic procedures. In one of his letters he expressed his disagreement with the government's decision to close the Universidade do Distrito Federal (UDF), in 1939. He addresses the minister in a harsh tone:

> the least of which was not the destruction of UDF. I could not submit to the reasons you gave for this; I painfully regret the effacing of the only place of the freest, most modern and most inquisitive education we had left in Brazil after what you had

done to the Faculdade de Filosofia e Letras de São Paulo [The São Paulo School of Letters and Philosophy] This spirit, even if present teachers were to be preserved, will not survive in the Universidade do Brasil, since freedom is frail, shuns pomp, the pompous and unwieldy bureaucracy.[35]

Mário de Andrade's letters were posted from Rio de Janeiro, the seat of federal power, where he lived in a kind of exile. Correspondence was always an effective medium for this compulsive letter-writer, this frail and sensitive modernist from São Paulo. The letter in which he bids farewell, asking the minister permission to return to São Paulo after an "exile" in Rio, reveals the full dimension of his loyalty to the life of the spirit.[36] He had left everything in São Paulo: a ten-thousand-book library, a personal collection of works of art that was already important at the time, his urban environment, his pianos, all that identified and nourished him, not to mention the most important:

> For three years I have been living like this, only half of me here, neither continuing my studies nor finishing my books for lack of what remained there. Indeed, I have done nothing useful in these three years, at least nothing that can give me the illusion of possible usefulness, and I ended up with the firm conscience that I am being demoralized. . . . And I can no longer bear this conscience of personal demoralization that has been nagging me for months now.[37]

Drummond is more silent, but not more detached. He is a quiet, shy presence in his rare and always oblique public appearances, and silent in the absence of letters—"which I am incurably incapable of writing."[38] However, the way some of those who did write letters to the minister refer to the private secretary–poet reveal his intimacy, his at-ease stance in the routine procedures of political management. Intellectuals, architects, writers who wrote to Capanema include "Carlos" as an extension of the minister. "I only ask you to let me know by a word of yours or Carlos" (Mário de Andrade); "ask Carlos to explain what you want from me" (Mário de Andrade); "my dear Capanema: a big hug to you and another to Carlos" (Gilberto Freyre).[39] With great adroitness and spontaneity Drummond followed the trajectory of the generation of private secretaries.

The first modernist generation of Minas Gerais was a generation of public employees, of private secretaries of high authorities. Drummond classified himself as "poet-employee," the "unconvinced official scribe" and many followed him, both in the government of Minas and in his move to the federal capital invited by the minister Capanema. The *mineiro* intellectuals led the development of a policy on the national historic and artistic heritage and an educational reform that remained unchanged until 1961, in addition to occupying innumerous positions in institutes and public administration offices in the federal capital.

Minas and Belo Horizonte in particular were invaluable sources of young talent for the public services during the '30s. Typically, they were intellectuals, writers, and poets. The combination of country youth and the *ethos* of the public employee pulls the pendulum of traditionalism toward the intellectuals themselves. In opposition to the irreverence of their mid-twenties, the stability of official routine checked their impulse to flee convention, keeping the beat of regularity. However, this combination of literature and public office characterizes more than the *mineiro* intellectuals.

> One should observe that almost the entire Brazilian literature, both in the past and the present, is a literature of public employees. . . . One must count on them to keep among us a certain reflexive and ironic tradition, a certain mien between disenchantment and pious outlook in interpreting and telling men, their actions, their love pains and their deepest aspirations—which perhaps only a writer who is a public employee could offer us, building his edifice of clouds under the protection of the Bureaucratic Order, as an inoffensive, subsidized madman.[40]

During his entire stay in the ministry, throughout Capanema's term, Drummond's activity was marked by a diligent and always discreet participation in doing what both office and talent allowed him—as direct assistant to the minister and scribe. At an event that motivated the title of this work, he tasted the conflict between loyalty to the spirit, to his own values and commitment to politics. Refusing to attend a conference on "anticommunism" his friend Alceu Amoroso Lima was going to present, the poet-employee wrote to the minister asking him to release him from the position as his private secretary because he did not consider it appropriate for a person in such a position to refuse to participate in an event promoted by the ministry where he serves. Capanema certainly did not take his request into consideration, and they both came to some form of agreement as Drummond's permanence attests.

Mário de Andrade's activities in the ministry were prolonged, in memory as well as institutionally, thanks to his policy for the preservation of our heritage. Both Mário de Andrade and Rodrigo Melo Franco de Andrade became forever linked to the project of preservation of the historic and artistic heritage. In a sense, it is possible to see a certain proximity between the assessment of the intellectuals and architecture in Capanema's Brazil and the assessment that finally prevailed in the development of a special agency to care for our heritage: both projects are linked to what was later acknowledged as initiatives of the State in favor of the modernization of Brazil and valuation of our national culture. Drummond's work involved all policy areas of the ministry, but he became more closely associated with this group of intellectuals mobilized around these two areas. Actually, after being relieved from his service at the ministry, Drummond would remain, until retirement, at the Serviço de

Patrimônio Histórico e Artístico Nacional (SPHAN—the National Historic and Artistic Heritage Protection Service). These are the arguments, I believe, that led Regina da Luz Moreira to conclude that "both in literature and plastic arts, Capanema tried to position himself above the political and ideological differences that divided the country. Assisted by his private secretary, the poet Carlos Drummond de Andrade, he gathered a diversified team composed, among others, by Mário de Andrade, Cândido Portinari, Manuel Bandeira, Heitor Villa-Lobos, Cecília Meireles, Lúcio Costa, Vinícius de Morais, Afonso Arinos de Melo Franco and Rodrigo Melo Franco de Andrade."[41]

The area of education makes us confront an entirely different reality. Perhaps this distinction can be better understood if we consider that education is an area that defines the orientation of minds, and interferes in the election of values. At that particular time in Brazilian political history, education was expected to inspire what should become the "new man" for a "new State," as Capanema used to say, echoing the words of President Vargas. The dispute between projects and the clash of ideas find in education the space where the battle is more publicly relevant. And, in education, we can track the most radical movement of adherence and expulsion, incorporation or reclusion that intellectuals like Anísio Teixeira exemplified by their own public life.

The architectural aestheticism and culturalism involved in the preservation of national memory and heritage contrast with a sociology of education characterized by forward and backward movements, interventions of the various players, and the most diverse ideologies. This is the last point I would like to examine in more detail.

Works of art rather absolve iniquitous fidelities to public politics. They defy the functionalist perspective in thinking through the relationship between intellectuals and power. Works of art disorganize this scheme. The talent of Villa-Lobos overlaps the images produced under the Estado Novo, which reveal his intimacy with power. Fernando Pessoa's poems are stronger (and more independent) than the memory of his alleged sympathy with fascism. Wagner's music eventually becomes autonomous and overcomes his always remembered and profoundly disquieting association with Hitler. In its permanence, transcendence, timelessness, in its insurmountable capacity to move, Art seems larger than politics, never subject to contingencies and contexts. In distinguishing between Art and science, Max Weber said that Art is not made to be overcome, a distinction that in this case can be extended to Art and politics. Perhaps this is why the adherence of artists, poets, writers, and composers to politics is denounced and the discomfort heightened, but, at the same time, the accused are defended in a reaction from those that value the work of Art above its creator. The defense of Art minimizes the uncomfortable links of its creators with questionable programs, projects, ideologies, and policies. It is immortal and transcendent Art—not the mortal creators—that is being absolved, as if, in absolving, each of us who keeps loving Art despite the treasons—or infidelities, as Julien Benda wanted—of its creators.

The intellectuals involved in education do not have the same chance of absolution. Here, intellectuals, creators, and policies are mixed because their ideas and formulations imply implementation, imply the test of the real world and, above all, imply direct interferences with the routine of people's lives when they materialize. They reorient conducts and procedures, lead actions or intercept projects, whether ongoing or still being conceived. The formulation itself is confronted by other concurring perspectives, other conceptions, other ways of implementation, other ideologies. In a paper where she analyzes the educational debate of the '30s, Clarice Nunes defines the question rather well:

> Professional educators were not alone in the real space they occupied in trying to build their identity and organize culture, education, the State and society. They had competitors, and those others were also formulating projects and proposals, opening spaces, making alliances or not with those in power. The professional educators and their opponents and allies, even temporary ones, occupied positions in a field of possibilities and it would be useless to define their fight and what it represented without defining the fight of their competitors and the meaning it has for themselves in the same field.[42]

Who competes with Drummond's poems? Or Cecília Meireles's? Or Manuel Bandeira's? With Heitor Villa-Lobos's compositions? The lines of Lúcio Costa and Oscar Niemeyer? The drawings of Portinari? Why choose between one and the other? Which manual of human interaction states that adherence to one form of artistic manifestation supposes the exclusion or redefinition of another? Thus, the world or Art is, both by definition and nature, essentially plural and free. And, most intriguing and disquieting of all: art is independent and autonomous regarding any surrender to, and contingent copulation with, power. In hindsight, the intellectuals and the Estado Novo, sensitivity and authoritarianism—delicate reconstructions in their many stumbles—took me back to the feeling that Gilberto Freyre unforgettably translated in his journey through colonial life in *Casa Grande e Senzala (The Masters and the Slaves)*: "It is a past that when we study it, we touch raw nerves, a past that intertwines with each of our own lives."

NOTES

1. Michel Winock, *O século dos intelectuais* [*Le Siècle des Intellectuels*] (Paris, Seuil, 1997). Portuguese translation by Eloá Jacobina (Rio de Janeiro: Bertrand Brasil, 2000), 248.

2. Julien Benda, from Winock, *O século dos intelectuais*, 248–57. (Brasil: 2000, Second part, chapter 21, "A traição dos intelectuais," 248–57).

3. From Winock, *O século dos intelectuais,* 256.

4. Winock, *O século dos intelectuais,* 256.

5. Reputedly the greatest contemporary Brazilian poet, Carlos Drummond de Andrade was born in Itabira do Mato Dentro, Minas Gerais, in 1902. Since 1930, when his first book was published, Drummond's fame as one of the greatest lyric Brazilian poets of all time never stopped growing. Some of his most important books are *Alguma Poesia* (1930); *Brejo das Almas* (1934); *Sentimento do Mundo* (1940); and *Rosa do Povo* (1945). His lengthy correspondence with Mário de Andrade, the paramount figure among Brazilian modernists, has been published in *Lições de Amigo*, a work where the reader can follow, in a wealth of details, the courses and the tensions that marked the modernist movement in Brazil.

6. Pedro Nava, letter to Helena Bomeny dated January 21, 1983.

7. Sergio Miceli, *Intelectuais e classe dirigente no Brasil (1920–1945).* (São Paulo: Difel, 1979).

8. Sergio Miceli, *Intelectuais à brasileira* (São Paulo: Companhia das Letras, 2001).

9. Simon Schwartzman, Helena Maria Bousquet Bomeny, and Vanda Maria Ribeiro Costa, *Tempos de Capanema*, 1st ed. (Rio de Janeiro: Editora Paz e Terra, 1984). There was a second issue in 2000, coedited by Editora Paz e Terra and Editora da Fundação Getulio Vargas, Rio de Janeiro.

10. Helena Bomeny, *Guardiães da Razão: Modernistas Mineiros* (Rio de Janeiro; São Paulo: Ed. UFRJ; Tempo Brasileiro, 1994).

11. Angela Maria de Castro Gomes, ed., *O ministro e seu ministério* (Rio de Janeiro; Bragança Paulista: Ed. FGV; EDUSF, 2000).

12. Bolívar Lamounier, comments at the panel on post-1930 intellectuals and culture of the September 1980 seminar organized the CPDOC—Centro de Pesquisa e Documentação Histórica da Fundação Getúlio Vargas, in "A Revolução de 30. Seminário Internacional" (The Revolution of 1930. International Seminar) in *Coleção Temas Brasileiros* 54 (Brasília: Ed.UnB, sponsored by Fundação Roberto Marinho, 1982), 551.

13. Simon Schwartzman, "A transição mineira," (the "mineira"—from Minas Gerais—transition). Reviewing Francisco Iglesias' *História, Política e Mineiridade em Drummond* [History, Politics and mineiridade—the quality of "mineiro"—in Drummond]—Some Poesy" Rio de Janeiro: Fundação Cultural Banco do Brasil, April 24 1990, mimeo), 2.

14. *Integralismo* was a political movement inspired by Fascism.

15. Lucia Lippi Oliveira, "As raízes da ordem: os intelectuais, a cultura e o Estado," in *A Revolução de 30. Seminário Internacional*, 508.

16. "Among the *core* names of the intellectual scene in the 1930s, representative of the critic pragmatism, some individuals stand out, such as Francisco Campos, ideologue of the Estado Novo legality; Gustavo Capanema, who, as minister of education, not only presided over the institutional reform of education, but also acted as mediator between the Estado Novo and writers that resisted longer the appeals from

the establishment; Lindolfo Collor and Agamenon Magalhães, who markedly influenced the new labor and union organization laws. As theoreticians, rather than as politicians properly, Oliveira Viana and Azevedo Amaral are also included in the *core* gallery, each one having authored studies on peculiar Brazilian conditions that reveal a critical position vis-à-vis imported science and culture. Gilberto Amado, Martins de Almeida, Virgínio Santa Rosa, Caio Prado Júnior, and Nestor Duarte were *independent* intellectuals in this period. The books they wrote, respectively *Eleição e representação* (1931) (Election and Representation), *Brasil errado* (1932) (The wrong Brazil), *O sentido do tenentismo* (1933) (The meaning the Lieutenant movement), *Evolução política do Brasil* (1933) (Political Evolution of Brazil), *A ordem privada e a organização política nacional* (1939) (Private order and the national political organization) were attempts at diagnosing the country's political regimes that largely averted the typical sins of the hypercorrect positioning. Among the *combative* intellectuals in my categorization I certainly include Luís Carlos Prestes, Otávio Mangabeira, Aparício Toreli (the Baron of Itararé), and others." Alberto Guerreiro Ramos, "A inteligência brasileira na década de 1930, à luz da perspectiva de 1980," (The Brazilian intelligentsia in the 1930s viewed in a 1980 perspective," in *A revolução de 30*, 537.

17. Luis Antonio Castro Santos, "O pensamento sanitarista na Primeira República: uma ideologia de construção da nacionalidade" (Sanitarian thought in the First Republic: an ideology of nationality construction) *Dados* 28, no. 2 (1985): 193–210; Gilberto Hochman, *A era do saneamento: as bases da política de saúde pública no Brasil* (The era of sanitation—the foundation of public health in Brazil) (São Paulo, Anpocs; HUCITEC, 1998); Nisia Trindade de Lima, *Um sertão chamado Brasil: Intelectuais e representações da identidade nacional* (A hinterland named Brazil—intellectuals and representations of national identity) (Rio de Janeiro: IUPERJ; Revan, 1999).

18. Mauricio Tenório Trillo, *De cómo ignorar* (México, CIDE/FCE: 2000).

19. *Coronelismo* refers to the rule of local landed leaders in distant, typically rural communities. Originally the emperor Pedro II had granted such leaders the title "Colonel of the National Guard" to ensure both their loyalty to the Brazilian Crown and his control over the vast countryside.

20. Angela Castro Gomes, *História e Historiadores* (History and Historians) (Rio de Janeiro: Ed FGV, 1996), 139.

21. Letter from Anísio Teixeira to Monteiro Lobato in *Conversa entre amigos: correspondência escolhida entre Anísio Teixeira e Monteiro Lobato* (Conversation between friends: selected correspondence) (Salvador; Rio de Janeiro: Fundação Cultural Estado da Bahia/CPDOC/FGV, 1986), 56.

22. Francisco Luís da Silva Campos was born in Dores do Indaiá, Minas Gerais, on November 18, 1891. A jurist of acknowledged erudition, Campos participated in the country's political life since the 1920s, as Member of the Federal Congress. He played an important role in the 1930 Revolution and was the first incumbent of the new Ministry of Education. His name is associated with at least two uniquely important facts: the Education Reform of 1931, considered one of the most important in Brazil, and the writing of the "Polaka" (the 1937 Constitution) that inaugu-

rated the authoritarian Estado Novo regime. He died in Belo Horizonte on November 1, 1968.

23. Lucia Lippi Oliveira, Mônica Pimenta Velloso, and Angela Maria Castro Gomes's researches published in *Estado Novo. Ideologia e Poder* (Estado Novo. Ideology and Power) (1982) are, even today, seminal references to anyone interested in the involvement of intellectuals in the formulation of a policy for a State that was intended to be new.

24. An excellent synthesis of the concept of generation can be seen in Alan B. Spitzer, "The Historical Problem of Generations," *American Historical Review* 78 no. 5 (December 1973): 1353–85.

25. Heloisa Starling, *Fantasmas necessários: a cidade como emblema da modernidade tardia* (Required ghosts: the city as an emblem of late modernity) (Belo Horizonte: 2000, mimeo).

26. Pedro Nava, "Recado de uma geração" (Message from a generation). Preface to *A Revista*, founded in Belo Horizonte in 1925–1926 by Carlos Drummond de Andrade, Emílio Moura, Francisco Martins de Almeida, and Gregoriano Canêdo.

27. Carlos Drummond de Andrade, "Recordações de Província," in *Passeios na ilha: divagações sobre a vida literária e outras matérias* (Rio de Janeiro: Livraria José Olympio Editora, 1975).

28. Iglesias, *História, Política e Mineiridade em Drummond*, 6.

29. Iglesias, *História, Política e Mineiridade em Drummond*, 7.

30. Helena Maria Bousquet Bomeny, "A estratégia da conciliação: Minas Gerais e a abertura política dos anos 30," (Strategy of Conciliation. Minas Gerais and the Political Opening of the 1930's) in *Regionalismo e centralização política: Partidos e constituinte nos anos 30*, ed. Ângela Maria de Castro Gomes (Rio de Janeiro: Editora Nova Fronteira, 1980).

31. Silviano Santiago, "De passarinhos e formiguinhas," *Jornal do Brasil* (sábado, 20 de março de 1999. *Caderno Idéias/Livros)*, 5.

32. Lúcio Costa, letter to the Minister Capanema, dated October 3, 1945. Gustavo Capanema Archives, CPDOC, Fundação Getulio Vargas.

33. Henrique Mindlin, *Arquitetura Moderna no Brasil*, (Modern Architecture in Brazil) (Rio de Janeiro: Aeroplano Editora, 1999), 27.

34. Letter from Mário de Andrade to Capanema on April 30, 1935. Gustavo Capanema Archive, CPDOC, Fundação Getulio Vargas, Rio de Janeiro.

35. Carta de Mário de Andrade a Capanema em 23 de fevereiro de 1939. Arquivo Gustavo Capanema, CPDOC, Fundação Getulio Vargas, Rio de Janeiro.

36. Mário de Andrade's letters during his "exile" in Rio were collected by Moacyr Werneck de Castro and published as a book: *Mario de Andrade. Exílio no Rio* (Rio de Janeiro: Rocco, 1989).

37. Letter from Mário de Andrade to Minister Capanema on May 4, 1942. Gustavo Capanema Archive, CPDOC, Fundação Getulio Vargas, Rio de Janeiro.

38. Letter from Drummond to Capanema, Gustavo Capanema Archive, CPDOC, Fundação Getulio Vargas, Rio de Janeiro.

39. From letters to the minister at the Capanema Archive, CPDOC, Rio de Janeiro.

40. Carlos Drummond de Andrade, "Passeios na ilha," in Iglesias, *História, Política e Mineiridade em Drummond*," 8.
41. Regina da Luz Moreira, "Introduction to the Capanema Inventory," in *Arquivo Gustavo Capanema: Inventário Analítico* (Gustavo Capanema Archives: Analytical Inventory). (Sponsored by the Ministério da Cultura and the Fundação Vitae) ed. Regina da Luz Moreira (Rio de Janeiro, CPDOC, 2000), 14.
42. Clarice Nunes, "O Estado Novo e o debate educacional," in *Memória intelectual da educação brasileira* ed. Marcos Cezar de Freitas (Bragança Paulista: EDUSF, 1999), 34.

BIBLIOGRAPHY

Andrade, Carlos Drummond de. "Recordações de província." In *Passeios na ilha: divagações sobre a vida literária e outras matéria*. Rio de Janeiro: José Olympio, 1975.

Benda, Julien. *The Treason of the Intellectuals (1928)*. Trans. Richard Aldington. New York: Norton, 1969.

Bomeny, Helena. "A estratégia da conciliação: Minas Gerais e a abertura política dos anos 30." In *Regionalismo e centralização política: Partidos e Constituinte nos anos 30*, edited by Angela Maria de Castro Gomes. Rio de Janeiro: Nova Fronteira, 1980.

———. *Guardiães da razão: Modernistas mineiros*. Rio de Janeiro; São Paulo: EdUFRJ; Tempo Brasileiro, 1994.

Castro, Moacyr Werneck de, ed. *Mario de Andrade: Exílio no Rio*. Rio de Janeiro, Rocco, 1989.

Conversa entre amigos: correspondência escolhida entre Anísio Teixeira e Monteiro Lobato. Salvador; Rio de Janeiro: Fundação Cultural Estado da Bahia; CPDOC-FGV, 1986.

Freyre, Gilberto. *Casa Grande e Senzala*. São Paulo: Record, 1996.

Gomes, Angela Castro. *História e historiadores*. Rio de Janeiro, FGV, 1996.

———, ed. *O ministro e seu ministério*. Rio de Janeiro; Bragança Paulista: FGV, EdUSF, 2000.

Hochman, Gilberto. *A era do saneamento: as bases da política de saúde pública no Brasil*. São Paulo: Anpocs; Hucitec, 1998.

Iglesias, Francisco. *História, política e mineiridade em Drummond*. Rio de Janeiro: Fundação Cultural Banco do Brasil, 1990. mimeo.

Lima, Nisia Trindade de. *Um sertão chamado Brasil. Intelectuais e representações da identidade nacional*. Rio de Janeiro: IUPERJ; Revan, 1999.

Miceli, Sergio. *Intelectuais e classe dirigente no Brasil (1920–1945)*. São Paulo: Difel, 1979.

———. *Intelectuais à brasileira*. São Paulo: Companhia das Letras, 2001.

Mindlin, Henrique. *Arquitetura moderna no Brasil*. Rio de Janeiro: Aeroplano, 1999.

Moreira, Regina da Luz, ed. *Arquivo Gustavo Capanema: Inventário analítico*. Rio de Janeiro: CPDOC, 2000.

Nava, Pedro. "Recado de uma geração." Prefacio de *A Revista* Texto escrito para reedição em fac-simile de *A Revista* (Belo Horizonte, 1925–1926). Edição patrocinada pela Metal Leve. São Paulo, 1978.

———. *Beira-Mar: Memorias/4.* 2nd ed. Rio de Janeiro: Livraria Jose Olympio Editora, 1979.

Nunes, Clarice. "O Estado Novo e o debate educacional." In *Memória intelectual da educação brasileira,* edited by Marcos Cezar de Freitas. Bragança Paulista, EdUSF, 1999.

Oliveira, Lucia Lippi. "As raízes da ordem: os intelectuais, a cultura e o Estado." In *A Revolução de 30. Seminário internacional.* Brasília: UnB, 1982. (Coleção Temas Brasileiros 54.)

Oliveira, Lucia Lippi, Mônica Pimenta Velloso, and Angela Maria Castro Gomes. *Estado Novo. Ideologia e Poder.* Rio de Janeiro: Editora Zahar, 1982.

Ramos, Alberto Guerreiro. "A inteligência brasileira na década de 1930, à luz da perspectiva de 1980." In *A Revolução de 30. Seminário internacional.* Brasília: UnB, 1982. (Coleção Temas Brasileiros 54.)

Said, Edward W. *Representations of the Intellectual.* New York: Vintage Books, 1996.

Santiago, Silviano. "De passarinhos e formiguinhas." *Jornal do Brasil,* March 20, 1999, Caderno Idéias/Livros, 5.

Santos, Luis Antonio Castro. "O pensamento sanitarista na Primeira República: uma ideologia de construção da nacionalidade." *Dados,* 28, no. 2 (1985): 193–210.

Schwartzman, Simon. "'A transição mineira': Reviewing Francisco Iglesias' 'História, Política e Mineiridade em Drummond' [History, Politics and mineiridade—the quality of "mineiro"—in Drummond]—Some Poesy." Rio de Janeiro: Fundação Cultural Banco do Brasil, April 24, 1990, mimeo, 2.

Schwartzman, Simon, Helena Maria Bousquet Bomeny, and Vanda Maria Ribeiro Costa. *Tempos de Capanema.* 2nd ed. Rio de Janeiro: Editora Paz and Terra e Ed. FGV, 2000.

Spitzer, Alan B. "The Historical Problem of Generations." *American Historical Review* 78, no. 5 (December 1973): 1353–85.

Starling, Heloisa. *Fantasmas necessários: a cidade como emblema da modernidade tardia.* Belo Horizonte, 2000, mimeo.

Trillo, Mauricio Tenório. *De cómo ignorar.* México: CIDE/FCE, 2000.

Winock, Michel. *O século dos intelectuais.* Rio de Janeiro: Bertrand Brasil, 2000.

14

An Amphibious Literature

Silviano Santiago

Amphibious, adj. [Gr. *amphibios*, living a double life; *amphi-*, on both sides + *bios*, life]. . . . 3. having two natures or qualities; of a mixed nature.

—*Webster's Dictionary*

I come from a country in which a considerable segment of the population yet remains illiterate, a fact that has consequences for the literature and arts produced there. To wit, we—we writers—always have believed that the publication in book form of the literary texts that we have invented is just as important as any persuasive effect that such a book is able to have in the political arena, whether it be read solely by the narrow and elite social group of literary consumers or discussed and commented upon by the mass media. Lacking any better descriptive means of explanation, I shall avail myself here of a metaphor: our literary system is like a subterranean river, a river that runs from its source to its mouth without ever touching its own banks, which nevertheless give the river its shape.

Another consequence of the illiteracy that runs rampant among the underprivileged, and one related to the extraordinary rise of the electronic media, transcends the field of literature proper. Overnight, the writer becomes a public intellectual. He reaches a public that his books cannot. The most dramatic element of illiteracy in Brazil is that it has served as fertile ground for the growth of the electronic media, with the resultant withering of the print media. Every Brazilian knows how to listen to the radio and to watch television; few know how or want to read. This disconcerting fact pertains not only to the underprivileged but has been the national consensus since the beginning of the military dictatorship in 1964.

If, in a country of more than 150 million inhabitants, the per capita rate of book consumption is exceedingly low, the *spoken words* of one who plies the literary trade may nevertheless be made accessible to the electronic media without serious hindrances—especially, though not exclusively, in the cases of educational and cable TV. When granted to him by his colleagues in the television media, interviews often serve the writer as a springboard for a public discussion of ideas that are *implicit* in the literary text. The book itself, as something that one reads, is only rarely considered. The image of oneself as an intellectual takes over; one's ideas, no matter how complex they may be, are assimilated. These phenomena give rise to a revolutionary engine, one that impels the common television viewer to confront the nation's problems rather than to rely merely on his life's daily galls as the basis for revolt. There is also, however, the dangerous cult of personality that hovers over the writer's apprenticeship. Many young writers find themselves so content with the image of the public intellectual that they begin to neglect their practice of the literary art, or abandon it once and for all.

If the banks of the metaphorical river to which I referred above pass far from the book, they do manage to approach it indirectly through the oblique trajectory of the television interview. The interview is the mode that the writer has found that enables him to communicate with a larger public without sacrificing the exclusive privileges of the career that he has embraced. As opposed to what happens in societies in which there is a higher rate of literacy and education, in Brazil the publication of a high-quality book may serve as the *motive* for an interview, but never as its *end*. In other words, the marketing of quality books in Brazil does not include, or rarely includes, the electronic media. In compensation, ideas of a revolutionary tenor circulate with more frequency among Brazilian television viewers than they do among "First World" viewers.

Book and interview, paper and screen, writing and speech—we find ourselves faced with real irreconcilables, which serve the writer as accomplices in his doubling as an intellectual but which for the public at large remain mutually exclusive.

With the passing of the decades, the practice of literature in Brazil has been cloaking itself in new garb, that is, with a dual ideological purpose. In its exploration of the tangled knots born of the direct observation of both everyday and historic events, and in its spurring one to reflect on the status of privileged observers, our literature presents figuratively the socioeconomic and educational poverty of the majority of the nation's population. It also defines, through its irreverent, merciless practice of self-criticism, the unique and exclusive group that in one way or another has exercised the classic forms of power and governance in the nations of Latin America.

On the one hand, the literary work seeks to demonstrate in an objective manner the need to remedy the misery of the poor and to raise their condition to that of human beings (no longer do I call for their condition to be that of citizens); on the other hand, however, it also attempts to put forth—through its decision to draw its characters from the authors' own social circle—an analysis of the persistent blunders and injustices of the bourgeoisie. From this dual and antipodal ideological base—from which it is impossible for writers to extricate themselves because of the role that they, as we have seen, continue to play in the public sphere of Brazilian society—comes the *amphibious* nature of our artistic production.

In the twentieth century, our best books, in their application of the liberating, rigorous, and individualistic principles of Europe's aesthetic avant-garde, focused on Art and, at the same time, on Politics, in their wish to expose and denounce by means of literature not only the ills to which Brazil's colonial, slavocratic past gave birth but also the dictatorial regimes that have undermined the life of the republic. A writer's activity as an artist cannot be separated from its political influence, nor can the influence of politics on a citizen be separated from his or her artistic activity. The whole is completed in such a way that it appears incomplete, though only in appearance. In dramatizing the serious problems of Brazilian society in its global context and the impasses that Brazil has faced as a nation, literature seeks, in an evident paradox, to speak in particular to the responsible Brazilian citizen. There are not many, unfortunately.

As a consequence of its dual and antipodal ideological base there arises in our literature a thematic vacuum that, in my opinion, ends up being filled by the large quantity of translations of foreign literature consumed in Brazil. We possess both an agile and up-to-date editorial industry and a cosmopolitan book market hungry for novelties. In the uniqueness of our editorial industry and book market lie two reasons that justify the importance yet given to literary craftsmanship by writers who, without the fierce competition of foreign literature, would have abandoned long ago all attempts at making art. This thematic vacuum relates to our literature's meager portrayal of the dominant problems of the middle class, which gets squeezed between society's two extremes. Brazilian literature has caricatured and passed over the social, economic, and existential complexity of the petite bourgeoisie, honing the edge of its critique on an antiquated socioeconomic portrait of the country, one similar to that bequeathed to us by the late nineteenth century. If Brazil as a nation has succeeded in attaining material progress, it remains very far from social progress. Brazil's writers and intellectuals are more than sensitive to this disequilibrium.

It is no coincidence that in our literature the middle class only becomes aware of its situation through a kind of social declassification. Nor is it a coincidence that the theme of the decadence and fall of the large rural families runs through the whole of our twentieth-century literature, leading some critics to take the Faulknerian title of a novel of Lúcio Cardoso—*Chronicle of a Murdered House* (1959)—as a metaphor and emblem for the formation of the country's urban middle class. They are the rich oligarchs dispossessed of their economic power by industrialization and transformed into public functionaries and liberal professionals by the nation-state's quest for modernization. In the streets of the metropolis they meet the ambitious immigrant families responsible for the creation and growth of industrial Brazil. Ex-oligarchs and newly rich immigrants, all linked in some way to foreign capital, constitute the heterogeneous middle of large urban populations, a middle unfortunately rarely encountered in our best literature.

Traveling beyond its own national borders by means of its translation into multiple and diverse foreign idioms, the Brazilian book goes in search of new readers, ones different from those formed by decades of both legitimate and illegitimate literary practice. The amphibious character of our artistic production can appear—and many times does appear—less than attractive to the demanding eyes of foreign readers. Their metropolitan gaze has become acquainted with books through the lens of the remarkable Western literary tradition, rather than through that of the politics of national reality into which the Brazilian is thrown and of the politics of global reality into which all of us finally find ourselves thrown.

The foreign public (and by such terms as "foreign public" and "foreign reader" I am attempting to characterize, perhaps clumsily, those readers who live in countries generally considered as belonging to the "First World") is accustomed to being radical in its artistic taste. It is accustomed to being radical in its choice of which literary text to purchase. Because of this it has little propensity to tolerate, on the one hand, political discussion in its aesthetics and, on the other, aesthetic flourishes in its politics. The cosmopolitan foreign reader, let me say again, is accustomed to being radical in his definitions of disciplinary fields.

In his generous radicalism, the foreign reader has been doubly disappointed in his judgment of Brazilian literary production. He rejects *a priori* those works that are defined by an amphibious nature. They serve for him neither as examples of art nor as examples of politics. He opts to dissect and dismember those ambivalent elements which, when combined, constitute the thematic and ideological duplicity found in Brazilian literature, and isolates them as autonomous entities, each with a life of its own. Either Art or Politics defines his choice as a consumer. Never both at the same time and in the same place. Art *and* Politics. Such a hybrid appears to him to be a phantasm. It is a phantasm that without a doubt catches him off guard in his quotidian existence as an inhabitant of the "First World"—even if he may happen to be someone less respectful of national borders and disciplinary conventions. As in *Hamlet*, the phantasm of hybridity may whisper in his ear: "the time is out of joint: Oh cursed spite, / That ever I was borne to set it right."

The foreign reader does not wish to understand the reasons why, in Brazilian literature, the legitimate wants to be illegitimate in order that the illegitimate can be legitimate in its turn. His desire as a reader is not founded on the desire of the literary text. He requires distance. He needs to distinguish between the aesthetics of Art and the politics of the Political. He needs what the text needs not. He has no need for the text that does not need him. And never the twain shall meet, as the saying goes. He does not understand that the double movement of contamination found in the best Brazilian literature is no cause for him to lament the loss of the aesthetic, much less for pragmatic criticism. Such contamination precedes literary *form*, by means of which the text's lucidity asserts itself as double: an amphibian literary form demands the lucidity of the writer as well as that of the reader, both permeated by their precarious status as citizens in a nation dominated by injustice.

The foreign reader tends to seek out, and tries to read, those books that denounce nakedly and stridently the miserable conditions in which the majority of the Brazilian population lives. These are in general books that concern themselves little with satisfying the basic requirements needed to transform brute socioeconomic facts into a work of art. They are closer to journalistic writing (not to be confused with journalistic language, which can be a notable stylistic resource) than to literature. The sheer brutality of the representations moves the reader to sentimental concern for Brazil (that country of human disgraces and civic catastrophes), to admiration for the writer (the courage and fearlessness of his denunciation), and to the praise that he heaps on the book.

Let us have no illusions: crass and cruel brutality can also move the foreign reader to commiseration.

Before anything else, the foreign reader is filled with Christian sentiments. This is good. Yet it becomes bad when he confuses his good sentiments and intentions with a mixture of abstract altruism and removed philanthropy, or when he allows himself to be confused by his very goodness, becoming less attentive to the world's cries, and, in his own eyes, less deplorable in his comforts. He finds himself so immersed in the heady rush of the book's denunciations that he forgets—in the course of his reading—to reflect upon his role, minimal as it may be, in the story that, had it been dramatized with less lamentable artistry, might have nailed hypocrisy to the wall. The reader filled with good intentions takes nourishment from the brutality thus fed to him, but loses his bearings under its crushing blows. This brutality is the space where the reader's good intentions exorcise the spell cast by the subaltern other. He plays no part in the latter's hard, unending reality. And, if he should, he prefers that it be as though viewed through binoculars: over there, far away, between the covers of a book, in a marginal country. Once the book is closed, his good intentions breathe their last.

However, we, for our own part, have among us writers that are indifferent to the dual ideological substratum of which I spoke earlier. Curiously, it is through their indifference to the problems of our country's misery that they have managed to find a captive audience in others. It is difficult to criticize literary companions who have chosen the path of artistic purity in a country where, for whatever reasons, their books would never be bought by their fellow citizens. They present themselves as hermits or ascetics. They feel tested by the cruel reality that surprises them around every corner and seek out, nevertheless, artistic purity. They desire the reincarnation, in a work of literature that they struggle to complete and which struggles to make money, of a Platonic ethics (Virtue, the Good, Light . . .).

The foreign reader, in his disciplined and disciplinary radicalism, seeks to buy and to read—along with the exclusively political, at times demagogic, book—the pure work of literature. This work presents the grand little dramas of humanity with stylistic rigor and psychological delicacy. In its confessed universalism and aristocratism the work is stripped of any original connection that it had to the culture out of which it arose. It transcends geographical boundaries in order to install itself in the eternity of the artistic work. A complicity of sensibility and caste unite the book's Brazilian author and its cosmopolitan foreign reader by means of the repeated performance of a reading that is totally committed to the strong, traditional values of Western literature.

In the work of pure Brazilian literature, there is represented, in the form of a mirror, the portrait of Dorian Gray. The work's literary stylization does not render the problems of *representation* more acute, but rather elides them with a pass of the artist's magic wand. The bargain struck with Time, with a capital "T," emasculates the untimely ravages of time, with a small "t." Eternity is made writing, and literary writing is made atemporal.

By disregarding its own other—the politics of the nation—the space specifically literary is ample and vast, without stylistic borders or ideological barricades. Brazilian and foreign writers, Brazilian and foreign readers—together inhabit a community of the elect, where the purity of artistic principles and values dominates. The work of art is an object of stirring emotions and delight for its initiates. This is not bad for Brazilian literature, a literature that one wishes to be just as contemporary and sophisticated as the other literatures from the part of the world to which we belong. And this is not bad for those writers who, having opted for the hybrid, never ignore the unending lessons of literary craft.

Have we reached an impasse? A parting of the ways for the book of high quality Brazilian literature and the foreign reader? Ought we all perhaps to stay in our own corners, since one group's idiosyncrasies clash with the idiosyncrasies of another? I do not believe so. Before anything else, this is the reason for such cultural encounters as this one, in which each nation's territory and flag are laid aside, though not abandoned, in order that we might proceed together on the road to mutual understanding. One seeks to acquaint oneself better with a particular sort of knowledge—literary knowledge of the Brazilian sort—in order that it may serve at the same time as a sign that each one of us seeks that universal experience in which one loses oneself in order to find oneself again in language and in the experience of the Other.

This does not entail allocating to the participants of this meeting—who are here to discuss the unique characteristics of those literatures written in Portuguese—this does not entail allocating to the participants, I repeat, that optimism which dominant groups, as unquestioned and unquestioning masters, reserve for themselves. Rather it entails embracing a tenacious and unyielding optimism. An optimism that is exhausting and sweat-drenched, trudging and fearless, a polemical optimism, to be constructed by each of us, by all of us. The precarious process of constructing utopia is important. The hastily built building, passable as a dwelling place, only exists on earth for the rich and powerful and, as it always has been and ever shall be, in the Kingdom of the Heavens for all humans.

Were one to analyze this precarious process of constructing utopia of which I am speaking, one would see that it is not so different from the process of constructing the literary work that I have been classifying as amphibious, or hybrid.

There is no way not to classify oneself as a visionary if you are a writer in a country like Brazil. "Visionary" means that you have visions—whether literary or political—which means that the educational and socioeconomic situation of your country need not always remain the same. It can and will improve.

The Brazilian writer has a vision of Art as a form of knowledge, one that is just as legitimate as those forms of knowledge that the exact and the human and social sciences believe that they alone possess. He also has a vision of Politics as the practice of an art that seeks the people's good and just government, dissociating it from the demagoguery of rulers, the populism of charismatic leaders, and the military force of those who seek order by any means necessary.

Art and Politics have given their voices to Brazilian literature in order to affirm that education, as Anísio Teixeira told us way back in 1957 (the year in which I entered the Federal University of Minas Gerais), is not a privilege of the few. It is worthwhile to repeat his words on this occasion: "When, at the French Convention, the ideal of public school education for all citizens was formulated, they were not thinking so much of making the existent schools universal, but of a new conception of society in which the privileges of class, wealth and heredity would not exist, and [in which] the individual would be able to seek out at school his position in social life."

Were it not that education, since colonial times, has been the privilege of the few, we might have been able perhaps to describe the panorama of contemporary Brazilian literature differently. Perhaps the legitimate might not have had to seek out the illegitimate in order that this, the illegitimate, spawned by the hybrid mixing of Art and Politics, might in turn become legitimate. Perhaps we might have limited ourselves simply to the two principles of aesthetics: the work of literature exists *ut delectet* and *ut moveat* ("to delight" and "to move"). We might have been able to limit ourselves to these two principles, and leave to the side a third: *ut doceat* ("to teach").

This, and not any other, is the manner in which it has occurred to me to narrate for you on this spring day the panorama of contemporary Brazilian literature.

Index

abolition, 69, 98, 126, 130, 150, 156, 157, 228, 236, 240, 241, 242, 243, 244, 247
Abreu, Capistrano de, 215
administrative law, 64, 104
affirmative action, 161
Africa, 124, 128, 132, 144, 146, 243, 248
african americans, 120, 135, 138
african cults, 130, 148, 154
AI-5, 175
Alencar, José de, 239
Allopoiesis, 73
Almeida, Francisco Martins de, 276, 287
Alves, João Guimarães, 276
Alves, Lúcio, 257
Amado, Jorge, 125, 126, 136, 138
Amazon river, 96
American bebop, 252
Andrade, Mário de, 256, 261, 264, 267, 271, 272, 278-283, 287, 288
Andrade, Oswald de, 253, 261, 262, 264
Andrade, Rodrigo Melo Franco, 279, 282, 283
Angell, Roger (Robert), 153, 167n58, 167n74
anglo-saxon cânon, 217
Antonil, 215

Araújo, Ricardo Benzaquén de, 179, 186n11, 186n12, 186n13, 188
Arendt, Hanna, 77n7, 87, 206n14, 207n31, 208n44, 208-210, 227-229, 232n6, 232n8, 233n14, 233
Argentina, 42, 57n45, 59, 92, 96
Art, 177, 178, 181, 182, 187n20, 251, 261, 263, 268, 281, 283, 284, 292-298
Assis, Machado de, 175, 185n2, 206n17, 206n18 206n19, 209, 235, 237-239, 241, 243, 244, 246n1, 246n2, 246n3, 247n6, 247n8, 247n10, 247n14, 247n15, 248n17, 248n18, 248n19, 248n20, 248n25, 248n28, 249n30, 249n32, 249n33
authoritarian period, 46, 73, 74
authoritarian regime, 46, 50, 175, 177, 178, 184
autonomy of law, 66, 69, 79, 80n33
Autopoiesis, 66, 71, 72, 73, 79, 80, 86, 89, 90
Azevedo, Célia Marinha de, 120
Azevedo, Thales de, 142, 148, 152, 167n72

Bahia, 122, 123, 133, 134n3, 135n22, 135n23, 168n72, 169-171, 199, 276, 286n21, 288

About the Contributors

Leonardo Avritzer is associate professor in the Department of Political Science at the Federal University of Minas Gerais. He is the author of *A Moralidade da Democracy*, which received the Anpocs Award for best book of the year in social sciences in 1997. He is the author of *Democracy and the Public Space in Latin America* (2002).

Helena Bomeny is sociologist and researcher at the CPDOC (Center of Historic Research and Documentation) of the Getúlio Vargas Foundation and professor of sociology at the University of the State of Rio de Janeiro. She is the author of *Darcy Ribeiro: Sociologia de um indisciplinado* (Belo Horizonte: Ed. UFMG) and *Os Intelectuais da Educação* (Rio de Janeiro: Jorge Zahar, Ed. UFRJ).

Dain Borges is associate professor of history at the University of Chicago. He edited the new Library of Latin America translation of Machado de Assis, *Esau and Jacob* (2000). He is the author of *The Family in Bahia, Brazil, 1870–1945* (1992) and of articles on ideas in Brazil, including "Intellectuals and the Forgetting of Slavery in Brazil," *Annals of Scholarship* (1996). His work in progress, "Races, Crowds and Souls in Brazilian Social Thought, 1880–1922," examines debates about religious innovation among thinkers such as Euclides da Cunha, Nina Rodrigues, Manoel Querino, João do Rio, and Lima Barreto, as well as Machado de Assis.

Antonio Sérgio Alfredo Guimarães is professor in the department of sociology, Universidade de São Paulo (USP). He graduated with a degree in sociology from the University of Wisconsin, Madison (1988). He is the

309

author of *Preconceito e Discriminação* (1998); *Racismo e Anti-Racismo no Brasil* (1999); *Tirando a Máscara: Ensaios sobre o Racismo no Brasil* (2000); *Beyond Racism: Race and Inequality in Brazil, South Africa, and the United States* (2001); and *Classes, Raças e Democracia* (2002).

Marcos Chor Maio is a senior researcher at the Casa de Oswaldo Cruz in Rio de Janeiro. He earned a PhD in political science from the Instituto Universitário de Pesquisas do Rio de Janeiro (IUPERJ). He is also professor in the graduate program of History of Science of Health at Oswaldo Cruz Foundation. He is the author of *Nem Rotschild Nem Trotsky: o pensamento anti-semita de Gustavo Barroso* and has published many articles on race, ethnicity, Brazilian social thought, and the history of Brazilian social sciences. He coedited *Raça, Ciência e Sociedade* with Ricardo Ventura Santos, *Ideais de Modernidade e Sociologia no Brasil* with Glaucia Villas Boas and edited *Ciência, Politica e Relacões Internacionais: Ensaios Sobre Paulo Carneiro*.

Santuza Cambraia Naves is an anthropologist and researcher at the CE-SAP/UCAM (Center of Applied Social Studies) and professor of anthropology at the Pontifical Catholic University, Rio de Janeiro. She is the author of *O Violão Azul: modernismo e música popular*.

Marcelo Neves is visiting professor at the Institute of Sociology of the University of Flensburg, Germany. From 1983 until 2002, he was professor of general theory of state at the law school of the Federal University of Pernambuco, Recife, Brazil. He was a visiting research fellow at Johann Wolfgang Goethe University (Frankfurt am Main, Germany), at the Institute of Federalism of the University of Fribourg (Switzerland), and at the London School of Economics and Political Sciences. He was visiting professor in the department of social sciences of Johann Wolfgang Goethe University (Frankfurt am Main, Germany) and at the law school of the University of Fribourg (Switzerland).

Paulo Jorge da Silva Ribeiro is a sociologist and professor of sociology at the Pontifical Catholic University of Rio de Janeiro. Author of *A perda da inocência: etnografia e literatura como discursividades da crise do Rio de Janeiro contemporâneo* (forthcoming).

Silviano Santiago is professor of literature and researcher at the CIEC/UFRJ (Center of Interdisciplinary Studies of Culture) of the Federal University of Rio de Janeiro. He is the author of many books on literary critique, including the recent *Nas malhas da letra*. He has also written many novels, such as *Em liberdade*, *Stella Manhattam*, and *Viagem ao México*.

João Trajano Sento-Sé is a political scientist and coordinator of the post-graduation course in social sciences of the University of the State of Rio de Janeiro. He is the author of *Brizolismo: Estetização da Política e Carisma*.

Valter Sinder is an anthropologist and coordinator of the course of social sciences of the Pontifical Catholic University, Rio de Janeiro, and professor of anthropology at the University of the State of Rio de Janeiro. He is the author of *Configurações da Narrativa: Literatura, Verdade e Etnografia*.

Thomas E. Skidmore is the Carlos Manuel de Cespedes Professor of History Emeritus, Brown University. He has an MA from Oxford University and a PhD from Harvard University. He is the author of *Brazil: Five Centuries of Change* (2000) and, with Peter H. Smith, *Modern Latin America* (5th ed., 2001).

Jessé Souza is professor in the department of sociology, Universidade Estadual do Norte Fluminense (UENF), Rio de Janeiro. He has a PhD in sociology from the University of Heidelberg and is the author of many books on social theory and peripheral modernization. His latest book is *A construção Social da Subcidadania* (2003). His work in progress, "Brazil Beyond the Myth," examines the political and social consequences, such as the naturalization of inequality, of Brazilian peripherical modernization.

Heloisa Maria Murgel Starling is professor at the history department, Universidade Federal de Minas Gerais (UFMG), Belo Horizonte, and author of many books on the sociology of literature and history. She is editor of *Pensar a República* (2000).

Luiz Werneck Vianna is professor in the department of sociology, Instituto Universitário de Pesquisas do Rio de Janeiro (IUPERJ). He has a PhD in political science from the University of São Paulo and is the author of many books on political sociology and Brazilian social thinking, among them *Liberalismo e Sindicato no Brazil* (1999). He is currently the president of the Brazilian Association of Social Sciences (ANPOCS).